What others are saying about this book and the Buddhism courses:

"I think Ruhe is on to something! In all honesty, I initially bought this book with only a mild interest in what he had to say. However, after skimming through some of it, I am very impressed, particularly with the essays section. Ruhe's writing is very original, creative and seminal. I support him in making his work accessible to more influential people in the publishing industry. Nowadays, it seems that inflammatory writing is not only hip, but needed, given the dangerously sleepy state of affairs on our planet."
Teertha Mistlberger, Founder and Director of Shamballa Trainings, West Vancouver, B.C.

"A leader has got to have a vision. The Ruhes are taking Buddhism into the future and behind every man there's a woman. This is the kind of book that causes Mahayana Buddhists to stop dead in their tracks and take a serious look at the authenticity of their tradition. Yet, Ruhe's message is cheerful and empowering. He inspires even more faith. There's something magical in *Freeing the Buddha* that speaks to me, to me personally and only to me."
Paul Schaub

"Brian's superb communication skills at the International Buddhist Society, Buddhist temple in Richmond were very helpful in making us understand contemporary Mahayana Buddhist beliefs and practices."
Professor Jurgen Schönwetter, Columbia Bible College, Clearbrook, B.C.

"Ruhe helped me to meditate properly, I learned how to "just sit." I had no idea how to work with my mind until I twice read *Freeing the Buddha*. Also, Ruhe's great sense of humour and cutting wit is alive on these electric pages!"
Balbir Singh Jutla, President Sikh temple
Canadian Ramghria Society, Burnaby, B.C.

"Brian's book and course proved to be one of the most interesting experiences that I have had in a long time! In short, this book is a real eye-opener! Brian is very respectful of his students and I highly recommend his book and course to those who are looking for a very positive experience that they will not soon forget!"
Gladys Symons, Ph.D., Professor of Epistemology, University of Quebec

"Brian is able to explain complex concepts in direct and simple language which enables people to understand things which seemed mystifying before."
Judith Kocher, Executive Director of the Community Services of Bangkok, Thailand

"What fascinated me the most here was the Buddha's revelations about heaven. Ruhe has a grasp of cosmology like Joseph Campbell."
Anne Marie Sison

"Brian is a significant contributor to my studies of Buddhism. He helped me go from a dedicated meditator with only a small understanding of Buddhism (coupled with much trepidation about it) to a more serious student of the dharma."
Kyira Korrigan

"Ruhe is stirring up dust in places that people haven't even thought of yet!"
Greg Close

"Brian is truly gifted at teaching Buddhism! Religious ideas have always been something very difficult for me, but Brian makes this study easily accessible and non threatening."
Wendy Wall, Bangkok, Thailand

"Brian has given me a lot more respect for Buddhism."
Nadav Chen, Chiangmai, Thailand

Douglas College Students:
"Not boring! Not boring!"
Candice Bergan

"I just relished *Freeing the Buddha*. This book takes the reader along on a personal journey. Spoken in today's language with light humour, you'll be invited page by page to take a deeper look. The content is very informative. Questions that Lama Surya Das does not address in *Awakening the Buddha Within*, Brian Ruhe does here. Read this book; you'll find that Buddhism might illuminate your life with a brighter purpose.
Linda Cook

"Sogyal Rinpoche blessed me and brought me to Buddhism. Brian Ruhe taught me the dharma and gave me the confidence to take that first step on the path."
Allan Lynde

"Ruhe is inspirational, whimsical and amusing by turns. But his main value as a teacher of Buddhism is that he sheds new light on our daily meditation practice. He gives renewed purpose to the practice of the moral precepts. He exposes us to different styles. The most surprising benefit of his teaching is a vision of the usefulness of laymen on the Buddhist path."
Brian Hurst, Tung Lin Kok Yuen
Canada Society, Chinese Buddhist temple.

Freeing the Buddha
Diversity on a Sacred Path – Large Scale Concerns

*A course on major aspects of Buddhism
plus a dangerous collection of essays*

Part One
A Trilogy

by Brian & Pia Ruhe

First Edition, March 1998
Second Edition, revised April 1998
ISBN 0-9683951-0-4
Third Edition, March 1999

Third Edition, revised
ISBN 0-9683951-1-2
Copyright © December 1999 by Brian A. Ruhe.
All rights reserved.
PRINTED IN CANADA
Up to 3000 words may be copied freely, without permission.

Published by the Buddhist Spectrum Study Group
The BSSG is based in Vancouver, Canada at
#217 - 1450 Chestnut Street
Vancouver, B.C. V6J 3K3
Tel. (604) 733-8477
Cell. (604) 720-8477

Cataloging-in-Publication Data
Ruhe, Brian Anthony, 1959-
Freeing the Buddha

Includes bibliographical references and glossary.

Printed by Hignell Book Printing
Winnipeg, Canada
Cover art by Evelyne Greene
Back cover photo by Pia Ruhe.

"A book is the guru's body, speech and mind."

This book is dedicated to the future transmission of the teachings of the Vajra Regent Osel Tendzin. "May his tapes be books in the 21st century."

The Buddhist Spectrum Study Group

The Buddhist Spectrum Study Group is an umbrella organization that creates local communities for Buddhists and welcomes teachers or student teachers from across the entire spectrum of Buddhist traditions. The only ideology of the Buddhist Spectrum is: Buddhism. The BSSG recognizes the innate Buddhist teacher in all people. Like an open white lotus flower, just anyone is welcome to teach Buddhism or related subjects at the BSSG, which is an experiment in truth and a dharma forum that replaces a guru with your own choice of teachings.

"Release the dharma! Let the hunt begin!"

Table of Contents

About the Authors

Brian Anthony Ruhe has an insight into Buddhism that can only be had by someone who practiced and studied seriously in a Tibetan Buddhist Centre, was a monk in Thailand, and was employed full time as the public relations official for the largest Chinese Pure Land Buddhist temple in Canada. He's seen the best and the worst of a variety of traditions from the inside looking out and he can be more honest than the lineage holders of many Buddhist traditions. As the Tibetan Lama Pönlop Rinpoche said "Brian has done everything!" The author has been featured on BCTV News and he has been quoted in the Province and the Vancouver Sun's Religion and Ethics section. He has lectured at UBC and he currently teaches Buddhism and meditation at Douglas College, the Vancouver and Burnaby School Boards, and other institutions.

Raised within a Unitarian background, Brian was exposed early to the spiritual dimension of life. Originally from Ontario, he studied business and philosophy at Brock University, and moved to Vancouver in 1980, continuing his studies at BCIT. After working in the financial planning industry selling mutual funds for eight years, he felt that although he was a reasonably happy individual, something was "missing" from his life. Like many of us, he was haunted by the need for meaning and purpose in life.

Brian considered a number of different spiritual paths. He was drawn to Buddhism because of its penetrating insights into the nature of the mind. After immersing himself in Buddhist teachings he quit the financial planning business, and became a true seeker. The first stage of his journey was a six-month stay at a Tibetan Buddhist centre in Vermont, founded by his teacher Chögyam Trungpa, after which he moved for four years to Thailand, a Theravadin Buddhist country. In Thailand he studied and practised at various temples and meditation centres, gathering teachings and deepening his meditation practice. He spent a short time in the monkhood with the name Buddhasaro. At his home temple, Wat Ram Poeng, in Chiangmai, Northern Thailand, he was trained by the abbot, Ajhan Supan, to be a meditation instructor. It was in this setting that Brian first began to teach and give formal lectures on Buddhism to the dozens of Westerners who came to the monastery for month-long meditation retreats. It was in this setting, as well, that Brian decided that it was time for him to return to his homeland to share his insights and experiences.

Brian offers courses of study presenting timeless teachings in a fresh way, playing with ideas from other Buddhist teachers from many traditions to magnetize and empower people to work out the truth for themselves. "Awakening your heart means coming to know that you weren't born to learn anything — you were born to remember," he says. He believes that the boundaries between faiths are dissolving and that in this climate of change we may come to share more realistic, effective and workable tools in the governance of our lives. Brian is a Theravadin Buddhist but he includes in that the best of Mahayana and Tibetan Buddhism, regarding them as commentary upon the Buddha's original teachings.

When working with others, Brian's objective is to offer them a local group that provides ongoing support, so that they can connect at the deepest levels with friends in a close community that is creating an enlightened society. That is Brian's vision. That is how Brian sees himself benefitting others by contributing to growth and change.

Pia Ruhe

Brian Ruhe is married to a Thai shaman, Pia Ruhe. She is like the gun powder behind the bullet. Pia is from northern Thailand and she has been trained since age 16 in alternative medicine. She is able to heal those suffering from the negative influence of spirits, black magic or other forces. As a cultural Buddhist she was raised with a more sophisticated understanding of the nature of the lower and higher realms, than what is understood in Western society. Coming from a serious Buddhist family, Pia knows that there are six realms of beings: ghosts, animals, hell beings, humans, devas in the god realm (heavenly beings), and devas or titans in the jealous god realm (negative heavenly beings). Pia can protect others from spirits, or black magic through her inborn gifts and using her training as a shaman.

Raised in a small village outside of Chiangmai, Thailand, Pia could see ghosts from the earliest period of her life. In the village temple, the Buddhist monks recognized her gifts to see and relate with ghosts since she was seven years old. Unlike Canada, her culture encouraged her natural gift as a psychic. She was trained for three years by a Cambodian shaman, Master Sang and Pia is the lineage holder of his teachings. Pia is schooled in the chants taught by the Buddha, for pacifying and extending compassion to ghosts. Also, she uses rare Cambodian and Burmese chants that have proven magical powers. A shaman's heart is a deep ocean of secrets. Spirits often want to convey a message and Pia can communicate with them as a medium, so that the spirits are pacified. Pia also provides ways to heal aches and pains caused by negative energy in the body. Her powers are inborn but have been developed through training. Few people in Thailand can do what Pia does for others and her talents are rarely found in the West. Her goal is to benefit others who don't know what the cause of their suffering is. Pia wants to help people to have a cheerful and uplifting environment in their home or workplace. You are invited to contact Pia or Brian Ruhe at this address:

The Buddhist Spectrum Study Group

#217 - 1450 Chestnut Street. Vancouver, B.C. Canada V6J 3K3

Telephone (604) 733-8477   Cellular, Pia Ruhe (604) 720-8477

Email: bar@istar.ca   Web Sites: Brian Ruhe: http://home.istar.ca/~bar/

Pia Ruhe: http://home.istar.ca/~bar/pia/

Pia Ruhe

Acknowledgments

So many causes and conditions led to the publication of this book. My first and deepest thanks goes to my guru, Chögyam Trungpa Rinpoche, the father of Western hip Buddhism. Without my precious guru I would be muttering to myself in the street with delusions of grandeur. Also, thanks goes to: my guru's son, Mipham Rinpoche, for directing us to "think big!"; to the noble Buddha, the Theravadin sutras, Sariputra, Maha Moggallana, Ananda, Buddhaghosa, Shantideva, Padmasambhava, the Tibetan lineages, many others, and to my parents, Mary and Anthony Ruhe. Through my father's doubts and his relentless search for truth he deposited me in the right direction. I thank my wife Pia Ruhe for hiding her faith but giving me her support, and my brother Peter Ruhe for his computer miracle work.

Warm appreciation goes to the abbot of Wat Ram Poeng, Ajhan Supan, Ajhan Tong, Phra Sawat, Venerable Dzogchen Pönlop Rinpoche for his teachings, Anila Anne McNeil at Zuru Ling, Reverend John Eshin at the Zen Centre of Vancouver, Gen Kelsang Delek at Tilopa Buddhist Centre, Rob Stickles, Connie Gibbs, Geraldine Street, Sallust Yeung, Francis Johnstone, John Whelehan for his worldly advice, Lynne Griffin for proofreading, Barry Millar for layout design and prepress, Tiina Liimu for artwork, Julia Wang, Lauren Johnson, Dan Poynter, Glen Pavlick and Martin Evans for his advice on Jesus. Many others who provided help or information are referred to in the book.

In my efforts to spread Buddhism in the West, I must also acknowledge the inspirations I have gained from the Sikh temple on Ross Street in Vancouver, and by televised All Star Universal Wrestling. The Sikh temple had been on the front cover of the Vancouver Sun for a couple of days per week because of debates between moderates and fundamentalists. All Star Universal Wrestling is a teacher because the wrestlers are masters at creating a crowd drawing spectacle by pretending to be adversaries to one another. The pioneers of Western Buddhism can learn invaluable lessons from these fine examples because a skillful display of differences in view can provide free promotion for Buddhism.

I thank my first dharma teachers at the Vancouver Shambhala Centre who led me to Chögyam Trungpa and his successor, the Vajra Regent. Thanks for rescuing me from samsara and pointing me to my inner nature. Particular thanks goes to the Vajra Regent Osel Tendzin, who's audio tapes are a continuous inspiration. "Please, teach the dharma," the Regent's tape recently uttered, "If you've taken the bodhisattva vow then you have to teach. But please avoid the temptation to make it up as you go along. Just teach the dharma exactly as it has been presented to you and then you will find that fresh, spontaneous teachings will fall out of your mouth that are completely in line with the lineage of the dharma."

With these encouraging words the Regent has led me to publish this, our first book in this trilogy on Buddhism. He, Trungpa Rinpoche, the Dalai Lama, the deva sangha, Dr. Rahula, Dale Carnegie, Brian Tracy, Thich Nhat Hanh and others have cleared the path for me. Special gratitude is given to my number one favourite living Buddhist master in the world today: the Dorje Loppön Lödro Dorje. These beings are suns in my sky. With embarrassing devotion, I have caught hold of their torches.

Preface

What I'm doing with this book and in my life's mission is that I'm after people's alaya mind stream. I want to make imprints on your alaya mind stream so that now and in future lifetimes you will be helped by the information that I am promoting. My intention is to steer people in the direction of the real Buddha while encouraging them to work with pseudo Buddhism. With discriminating insight I have loaded this book full of documented evidence that will dispel false beliefs about Buddhism. This book is about loyalty and honesty. I am loyal to Gotama Buddha so I am honest about Buddhism. Even if uncomfortable for you, the reader, once a message is in your alaya mind stream, then it is planted in the most sensitive field of karma-storage and any suggestions that you have registered with your senses will send seeds into your deepest mental continuum. Therefore the heart and soul benefits of reading this book can flower now or in lifetimes to come. Perhaps in your next life you will be walking down a hallway and instead of looking at a poster on your left, you will look at a poster on your right and see something about a Buddhist talk, and then you will go to that. That's the kind of influence I want this book to have upon you.

For the reader with a general interest in Buddhism, the two parts of this book progress from an easy to read basic course on meditation and the major aspects of Buddhist wisdom, to a provocative landscape of diverse essays that challenge and stretch the readers' imagination. This book was not written to reinvent the wheel and offer up "just another introduction to Buddhism." To repeat the same teachings printed in many other introductory books on Buddhism would only add further pollution to the world by creating more confusion, diluting the many excellent dharma books available. Not only is this a fresh approach to Buddhism, but this book stirs up dust in areas that most people have not thought of. There are Buddhist teachers who will discuss things privately such as Buddhist views on UFO's, Adolf Hitler and the historical Jesus, but they will not give public talks or publish books about these controversial subjects. In this book I have decided to do just that, because I feel that the subject matter is very important and relevant to our lives, our history and our destiny. Buddhism provides a special cosmological perspective on our modern world, and I believe that this should be shared in Buddhist books. Not only does it help us with a mythology, but it helps to promote Buddhism by relating the dharma to new territories of thought in the Western mind. I feel that people can read and decide for themselves what is the truth.

The title of this book *Freeing the Buddha* was selected because studies indicate that a provocative title can increase book sales from 5% to 15%. Freeing the Buddha does not mean Freeing the Buddha Within (that's been done before). It literally means freeing the Buddha from the false words that have been put in his mouth. The meaning is appropriate because the authors are Theravadin Buddhists and a major theme in this book is about how the Mahayana Buddhists have distorted, diluted and deemphasized the Buddha's words. As a Theravadin Buddhist I claim greater orthodoxy and seniority over the entire institution of Mahayana Buddhism. Although this book is very sympathetic to Mahayana Buddhism, "freeing" means giving back to the Buddha the more central importance that he deserves in the Buddhist religion. This book raises awareness for the need to free the Buddha and his teachings from the cultural traditions that Buddhists have been piling all over him, and to free the Buddha from being associated with false sutras. The tendency to "defer to the guru" can be wrong and cause people to be convinced that the true is false and that the false is true. The *"Large Scale Concerns"* part of the subtitle was taken from a talk by the Dorje Loppön Lödro Dorje in which he referred to the great compassionate view of the bodhisattvas. *"Diversity on a Sacred Path"* was chosen because these essays explore how Buddhism relates to the diverse picture of humanity in the world. Also, because of the diverse aspirations of sentient beings, there are diverse ways for people to enter onto the Buddhist path to enlightenment. Below the subtitle it states "a dangerous collection of essays," because Oscar Wilde said, "An idea that is not dangerous is unworthy of being called an idea at all."

Another thought in the author's mind stream when the title of this book was chosen, was the prophecy of Nostradamus which is almost assuredly going to happen, "A man wearing a blue turban will rise out of Persia. He will be the terror of mankind." This may conjure up worries about a possible world war, but it actually benefits us to contemplate death in this way. The Buddha said that you should contemplate death everyday because it helps you to appreciate your life and how much time you have left to benefit others. A theme in this book is that the preciousness of this time in all of our lives right now, will not last. So a sense of urgency is necessary to apply the Buddha's teachings with effort. There is never going to be a better time. You are not going to be any less busy in the future. You are not going to have any fewer commitments in the future. There is no other time, than now.

The world needs to wake up as soon as possible if we are to survive. We live during the pioneer centuries of Buddhism in the West. Can Buddhist sanity head off our insanity in time to sustain our world and prevent more unnecessary wars? *This is our question. This is our only question.* As early pioneers we need to be free to express our interests and follow our bliss. We need not wait for an Asian guru to validate us. This is the American Buddhist Declaration of Independence. The Buddha invited people to freely investigate his teaching. Infrastructure and organization will come later; in some ways people seek harder without temples for support. For now, we are mixing our cultural ideas with Buddhism. Together we will create our own version of Western Buddhism in the centuries to come.

A provocative writing style is contained here with surprising bits of information and historic details to stimulate your thinking. The reassurance of a familiar message that everything is going to be O.K. is not offered here because Buddhism guarantees nothing. This course book is offered to those who, like myself, burn with the conviction that engaged Buddhism can save our deteriorating world better than another treaty on the ozone or a treaty on the reduction of greenhouse gas emissions. Buddhism isn't just a good idea, it holds out the promise of a sane path, desperately needed to redeem our world. If you are up to the challenge of following the Buddhist path then it is important that you listen to your still small voice within. That advice on the inside is what should guide your interpretation of advice on the outside.

The Buddhist Spectrum Study Group is an organization that accepts any tradition or interpretation of Buddhism across the spectrum. The vision is to see the growth and spread of Buddhism in the world. The people can decide which teachings ring true for them. Whichever is the best will fare well in the spiritual marketplace.

In 1992 I decided that the major definite purpose of my life is to help spread Buddhism in the West. *Freeing the Buddha* is a proclamation of that mission and this book is also dedicated to the proposition that you can be a Buddhist teacher by next month. The goal of education is action, and Buddhism offers no retreat from the world. You don't have to be Albert Einstein to teach high school physics. The Buddha taught that two of the 38 highest blessings in life are to listen to the dharma on suitable occasions and to discuss the dharma on suitable occasions. Make the occasion! When a few people get together for this purpose, their conversation is turned upward.

In Vermont in May 1980 at Karme-Chöling Buddhist Center, a young lady asked my teacher, Chögyam Trungpa Rinpoche "Coming here and seeing your sangha here and in Boulder, and comparing it with other ways that the dharma is being presented, it seems if I may say so, that this is much the best way. And I wanted to ask from the point of view of people in other countries who haven't got the chance to see this and to see you, how to give the inspiration? It seems that it's rather up to us how much we can express the qualities of the dharma. Can you . . . ?" Rinpoche understood the rarity of Western dharma way back in 1980 so he gave her the strength and inspiration to carry on. Interjecting, he said "Anything you can think of. Anything you can think of. If you speak your mind you carry your message in any case, and people will have an intuition already if you are telling the truth or if you're indoctrinated, or you've been hypnotised, or whatever. And there are lots of differences between that and if you tell the real truth; you'll have no problem. You'll have no problem carrying the torch that way. You can do it!"

With this encouraging blank cheque, Trungpa Rinpoche has inspired me onwards! Like a phoenix or a garuda (god realm bird) rising from the ashes of Tibet, take a fresh and humorous approach to life in a direct and almost naive manner. Being so positive can make people feel negative. The dharma dynamite planted in these pages may have an edge but this is designed to help challenge people's thinking and provide them with a new avenue, a new approach to learning and teaching Buddhism.

Centuries ago many Asian Buddhists felt strangled in their efforts to find the truth in Buddhism, by the authority of the clergy with their cleverly hypnotized layers of sectarian walls cemented around the Buddha's sutras (discourses). Today popular Buddhism has so eclipsed the original discourses of the Buddha, that the Buddha himself is largely unnoticed. Many of the illustrious Tibetan and Oriental masters do not understand, or pretend they don't, where Mahayana and Vajrayana Buddhism comes from. They are part of the problem rather than being part of the solution in clearing away confusion about the history of northern Buddhism. Because people are so confused about Buddhism today, I have decided in this book to clarify for both the masters and laymen alike the most fundamental causes and conditions that led to the formation of such outwardly different looking expressions of Buddhism. This is important and meaningful. People want to know process, what is what, what's going on, the dharma of transmission. This book clarifies which aspects of Buddhism are original and which aspects arose centuries after the Buddha. The scope of Theravadin Buddhism should be extended by including in it the brilliance of the Mahayana and Tibetan teachings that are in accordance with the Theravada.

As information on Buddhism becomes more abundant, even too abundant, a backlash will occur in the 21st century so that people will rightly prop up and illuminate the Theravadin discourses of the Buddha as the greatest open secret in human experience. The grandeur of those treasure troves of dharma carefully handed down by the Buddha and his lineage is largely self secret, available only to those persevering souls who read over 2000 pages of repetitive writings. Many of those sutras are quoted in this book.

The Buddha described the future degeneration of our age as a time of moral degradation where the natural result of karma will be horrendous mass suffering. He even described how gravity will fall apart because gravity is held together by consciousness. As consciousness deteriorates, gravity collapses, the abhidharma reveals. However, Buddhism is not fatalistic nor pre-deterministic; we rule our own actions now, so we still have a chance to live out decent future lives here on Earth. A sense of urgency is the one vital ingredient that can still give us the necessary thrust to leave suffering behind. This is not a time for patience. This is not a time for laziness or cowardice.

The Buddha's wisdom will endure and grow because Buddhism appeals to educated people, and the post industrial society is an ideal culture in which Buddhism can flourish. People are stressed out and they want meditation and other techniques to enhance their health, well-being and peace of mind. May this book benefit others in a way that will seduce compassion out of the reader. The author gives you heart and support along your path. All victory and gain to you! All blame and loss to myself.

Spreading the lotus flowers,

Brian Ruhe
Vancouver, Canada.
blue moon, January, 1999

Foreword

by Teertha Mistlberger
Founder and Director of Shamballa Trainings, West Vancouver, B.C.
and author of
*The Sattva Teachings: A Guide to Understanding the Universe
and Your Journey Through It.*

You hold in your hands a strange, and even more dangerous, book. When you know who wrote it, it makes it stranger, and perhaps even more dangerous. Allow me to explain myself.

Brian Ruhe is a tall, rangy, mild-mannered fellow who is about as intimidating as a rabbit. He is, in many ways, the quintessential monk — gentle, curious, bright, non-confrontational. One can easily imagine him back in Thailand, where he was once ordained a Buddhist monk and given the name Buddhasaro, floating about in a saffron robe, his feet barely touching the ground. Yet as you will see from his writings, underneath this dove-like persona lurks an invisible heavy hand, a hawkish intelligence full of fiery stir-up-the-pot, in your face, piss and vinegar chutzpah. There is rebelliousness and audacity in this book, yet it is the healthy audacity of a mind not satisfied with status-quo rituals and conventions. And in a religion as ancient as Buddhism, such edginess is a welcome breath of fresh air, providing ventilation to an old and venerable tradition that is in need of interpreters who will remain faithful to its message, yet help us to think for ourselves.

Spiritually, Brian is something of a chip off the old block. His root teacher was Chögyam Trungpa Rinpoche, a brilliant, radical, and somewhat disconcerting Tibetan master who flamed briefly and brightly in Scotland and North America throughout the tempestuous 70s and 80s, before spinning off the earthly Wheel in 1987 at the young age of 48. Trungpa was one of the most intelligent and courageous Buddhist teachers, and like three other radical Lights of this century — Gurdjieff, Osho, and Adi Da (Da Free John), was severely misunderstood by mediocre, fear-based minds.

As Brian mentions in the Acknowledgements, Trungpa's chief disciple, Osel Tendzin (also passed on), spoke about the need for teachers to not "make it up as you go along," but that such apparent conformity would not mean a sacrifice in creativity. In this book, Brian has accomplished that. He has resisted the temptation to arrogantly revise an entire faith, and yet in remaining true to the Heart of the Buddha's message, he has found fresh and seminal ways to apply the teachings to subjects as diverse as Jesus, Hitler, Nostradamus, UFOs, military strategy, conspiracy theories, twentieth century history, *A Course in Miracles*, the Virgin Birth, and the failure of Christianity, amongst others.

When I bought a copy of the second edition of *Freeing the Buddha - Diversity on a Sacred Path - Large Scale Concerns* from Brian it was originally intended as a gesture of friendly support coupled with mild interest in what he had to say. As I began to read through it, though, I became very impressed with the sheer originality of his ideas, as well as the sharpness to his writing. Nowadays, it seems that inflammatory writing is not only hip, but needed, given the dangerously sleepy state of affairs on our planet. We live in the era of the T.V. beer ad and artificial reality, our wits dulled and our attention spans reduced to that of virtual reality morons. Life has become one big Star Trek holodeck. People are so bombarded with sensory stimulation, and endless forms of stupid technified nonsense, that they need something different in order to notice anything profound and meaningful, such as the teachings of an Eastern holy man of 2,600 years ago.

Thanks to the easy charm and solid integrity of the Dalai Lama, not to mention Robert Thurman (Uma's Dad), Richard Gere, and even Bradley Pitt and a little Hollywoodization, Buddhism has grown markedly in popularity here in the twilight of the insane 20th century. With the colossal failure of the Western theistic organized religions to genuinely transform or even inspire people, more and more are turning to the clear, unpretentious wisdom of the Buddha's Way. However, so many books on Buddhism, even those written by the illustrious Tibetan masters, though informative, are often terribly dry and lacking in a context that the Western psyche can relate to. Brian's writing is interesting and absorbing because it is *dangerous.* Absorbing because he tackles taboo subjects; dangerous because he does not let us sink our arse into the sofa and fall asleep with his book, dreaming dreams of being a good, boring Buddhist. This is writing that wakes us up, writing that pushes the edges of the conventional, and, in the spirit of the Buddha himself, challenges us to think for ourselves. Read away, and enjoy Brian Ruhe's demonstration that he is a lamp unto himself.

West Vancouver, B.C.
January 1999

PART I

A COURSE
IN BUDDHISM

Nakhon Pathom – Phra Pathon Chedi, Thailand

Invocation

Namo Tassa Bhagavato Arahato Sammāsambuddhassā (repeat Pali 3 times)
Homage to Him, the Blessed One, the Worthy One, the Fully Enlightened One.

It is a simple and powerful conviction that it is O.K. to just tell the truth about Buddhism. We can drop our struggle, spill the beans, and just be honest. It is not going to damage the world to tell the truth. We can actually heal the Buddhist religion by being honest about history and honest about the sutras. We can simply live in the truth from now on. That's it and that's all.

The word 'religion' comes from the Latin term 'religio' or 'religare' which means 'linking back to the source.' The way that Buddhists link back to the source is by going for refuge, which is expressed by doing three bows.

Three Bows
I take refuge in the Buddha
I take refuge in the dharma
I take refuge in the sangha

Commentary:
The refuge vow is a vow that you choose to take at Buddhist centres when you formally become a Buddhist and publicly declare yourself as a Buddhist. At the beginning of a visit to a Buddhist centre, to reaffirm that vow, a good ritual normally practiced is that one does three full or half prostrations to the shrine with the Buddha statue. A simplified version is to put your hands together in anjali and do one small bow on your way in and out of a shrine room. A simple Buddha statue or picture can be your shrine at home. The bows of devotion reaffirm your refuge vow of taking refuge in the Buddha as an example, the dharma — the Buddhist teachings, and the sangha — the community of fellow Buddhists. The purpose of devotion is that devotion arouses within yourself whatever qualities you admire in the

other. It's not that the Buddha wants you to bow down before him; you are doing it for yourself. The option which I practice on the third bow, is to include the deva sangha which you visualize as an equidistant honour guard of four devas immediately beside you, commingling with your mind. As your forehead touches the ground, visualize the four devas entering your head in the manner described in Class Ten, How to Invoke Devas. These devas are higher realm Buddhist beings of great attainment who take tremendous interest in what you are doing on Earth to propagate sanity and the Buddhadharma, before your opportunity is lost.

Going for refuge is like running for cover under an umbrella in the rain. You are renouncing theism and you are renouncing attachment to the myriad of conflicting views in the world as you go to the Buddha.

It is urgent that you make efforts now, not when you think that you will have more time later. We are on the Titanic, but fortunately there is no predetermined fate that the captain of the ship must try to break the speed record to America and recklessly cause us to hit an iceberg and die unnecessarily. If more of us meditate and extend our sanity to the captain and the crew of the Titanic, there is still time for us to magnetize the future turn of events so that we will arrive safely together on dry land in New York. Just so, we can succeed at pushing back World War III and completely warding off World War IV. We can do it together. You may think that if you and many others teach or don't teach Buddhism, then it won't make much of a difference. But the stakes are high, much higher than humanity will come to appreciate in the 20th century. For the sake of compassion, it is wise to cultivate a sense of urgency.

Bestowed upon all of you are the blessings of the deva sangha. If you try your best to share the dharma with others, this Buddhist Secret Service — the deva sangha, will have confidence in you and protect you with the understanding that they know that you must break a few eggs to make an omelette. Your persistence is your measure of your belief in yourself.

Chapter 1

Why Buddhists Meditate

Rule number one is silence
Remember the golden rule

Like Siddhartha Gotama, if you today attained enlightenment and broke through the ignorance of your society and you became the greatest spiritual being of your age, you would expect to live a public life that would become progressively quieter and quieter as you pulsated love through the sleepiness of the infrastructure around you. Visualize yourself as a completely enlightened person. You move slower and slower and the world will bend space around your anatta (non self) waves. Silence is gold. You love all people but you don't like people. Each decade you are alone because the leader is always alone. You would rather recline in a TV studio and benefit others by communicating with them in that way, than in person. Your presence inspires others to build a greater vision and they respect your enlightenment by speaking only the words that are needed. No matter how many people are moved and stirred by your inspiration, you yourself have always lived a quiet little life. Now you sway in the rocking chair of your quiet little life, holding your seat as a living Buddha. It is a useful affirmation to visualize what this enlightenment could be like in the 21st century. Until then you can study the dharma, practice meditation, teach Buddhism and continue to develop your ability to do these things.

When I was living in Bangkok, Thailand I was teaching courses on Buddhism and meditation to other foreigners in Bangkok. I was often confronted with questions about Thai cultural affectations which people assumed to be representative of Buddhism. In beginning a talk on Buddhism I often didn't know where to begin to describe what it was all about. Before my short time in the monkhood I lived in Chiangmai where I started a meditation and discussion group. At one gathering we didn't have any particular plan so Robert started off the topic of discussion by saying that earlier in the week he was stunned to see a man smash a dog across the back with a stick. Robert asked the man why he was doing this and the man explained to him that in a previous life the dog was a bad army general so it deserved this beating. I cringed inside and muttered feebly that I didn't think that this was a very good way to start off our Wednesday night get-together. If anyone is so highly attained that they can see into the previous lives of a dog, then they would not be the type of person to break their back with a stick.

So, what is a good way to start off a discussion about why Buddhists meditate? The teachings are so vast, the realization of the Buddha was so sublime and there is such a path quality about how the whole thing hangs together. I often start off some of my classes by saying that all of Buddhism is psychotherapy. Being a Buddhist means making a commitment to working with your mind and working with your heart (Osel Tendzin, 1988; "Discipline," talk two). Essentially, what the Buddha taught was ways of dealing with our minds to overcome our neuroses — 100% psychotherapy. That may help people feel more comfortable if they don't feel comfortable with the word 'religion.' To some Buddhists the word psychotherapy is a bad word. To others it is not.

Buddhism could be described in three words: morality, concentration, insight. Morality, or discipline means intending to live within the precepts that the Buddha prescribed for lay people or for monks or for nuns. The general concept of proper moral conduct is similarly shared with all other religions and humanistic philosophies. This is no surprise. Where Buddhism really takes off is in the stages of concentration and insight. Sitting meditation and walking meditation, plus post meditation practices of mindfulness in ordinary daily life, build up concentration. It is this concentration that naturally leads to the fruit of insight. As my teacher, Chögyam Trungpa Rinpoche said "Buddhism has more to do with the kitchen sink than with the high and holy."

Building concentration is like raising the water level in a great dam. As you meditate the water is going up and up until it reaches the top of the dam. Then, that water is used for energy to create power such as electricity. That is insight. Without the foundation of morality, it is as though holes have been smashed through the walls of the dam. No matter how much you meditate, it won't add up to one drop if you are seriously violating precepts against such things as stealing or sexual misconduct. If the integrity of your character or the wall of the dam is secure, then when the water of concentration reaches the top in the practice of meditation, this naturally leads to the fruit of insight. Insight, or wisdom is artificially produced in meditation practice by formalizing and systematizing this natural process which we call meditation, or bhavana-mental culture, cultivating the mind. When you stare at a sunset, and dwell upon the orange sky and the beautiful clouds, that is a form of meditation. Concentrating on making money is a form of meditation which can also aid you in attaining insight.

Insight is not something that you can collect or cash in on after a half-hour of sitting on the cushion. You cannot lift your gaze from the floor and say "I want my insight now. I've worked for it. I've paid for it." Insight comes when it is ready to come. It could take ten years. Insight could manifest as a sudden, important realization, or a deeper understanding of yourself, your strengths and weaknesses. Or insight could be the ultimate insight that engulfed the Buddha under the bodhi tree when he attained full and complete enlightenment. You will know for certain when insight wells up within you. It is not the usual assortment of pleasant or discursive thoughts that you sometimes have. It is clear and bright, complete and meaningful to you. The great eastern sun.

In the West the meaning of Buddhism is becoming closely associated with meditation and meditation retreats. I agree that meditation is the bottom line on the path to enlightenment but right meditation (or right absorption) is just one of the items on the Buddha's eightfold path. The other seven are right view, right intention, right speech, right discipline, right livelihood, right effort, and right mindfulness. The first, right view, means developing and understanding a precise view of the four noble truths, the eightfold path, the nature of mind, etc. Having a precise view is important otherwise there is a danger that the practice of meditation could become self oriented. You could build up your concentration by meditating upon wrong views such as the idea 'I am Superman! I am Superman!' But, that kind of meditation probably wouldn't help you to transcend and let go of attachment to your ego, which is what nirvana is all about.

When you meditate you may think that you have a particular reason why you are practising meditation. You may be doing it because it's good for your heart or your blood pressure or that meditation will help calm you down and make you a nicer person. All of that is true but they are only by-products of meditation. The Buddhist reason why you meditate is a big reason. It's a big and a very vast and ambitious reason why we meditate. That reason is to transcend the limitations of the self and to shed off the tyranny of ego. Our consciousness is limited now to self consciousness. Like a soap bubble. Visualize that your mind is the air inside of a soap bubble. That is your self consciousness. This is quite a positive image because for most of us the walls of our ego are probably more like our thick skulls. No wonder some people still believe that consciousness must be limited to the brain! Everything outside of your little soap bubble is vast primordial, unborn mind, which is like empty space. That is the view of mind. Because of our confusion, consciousness becomes limited to the self, the idea of self, and this soap bubble forms and in each and every moment of our existence we are trying to constantly reinforce the walls of this soap bubble, to convince ourselves that we are a separate independent self.

The reason why we meditate, is to unravel this confusion playing itself out in the colours on the surface of the soap bubble. Visualize the ever changing dynamic display on the surface of the soap bubble which we take so seriously. Take life seriously, but not yourself, not the walls of some tiny soap bubble. We meditate to ultimately pop that soap bubble! The big, vast, ambitious reason for meditation practice is to pop that soap bubble so that the air in the soap bubble will merge with the air outside, which represents the rest of the universe. Putting it in the simplest of words, the final attainment of enlightenment occurs when the ego is discarded and you have a direct experience of the entire universe. Direct experience. That is the final, absolute ultimate state of mind and state of life. And it is within your grasp (oops, bad word) in this very life.

Enlightenment remains enlightenment, beyond the space-time conceptual limitations of time itself, so there is then no longer any possibility of ever slipping back into samsaric ego mind again. This eternity is beyond time because it has got nothing to do with time. Enlightenment forever leaves behind the sleep of ego. A visual image to conceptualize this universe of mind is of a sphere of luminous white with white inside and white outside. The surface of the sphere is reflecting light. Inside the sphere, samsara and nirvana are inseparable. Outside the sphere is only nirvana. That is the image.

Shortly after his enlightenment, someone asked the Buddha "Who are you?" The Buddha answered "I am awake." The Buddha taught that fully understanding the nature of enlightenment with words and concepts is impossible because enlightenment is well beyond conceptual mind. Like the words and concepts above, the Buddha too used many words and many concepts to describe enlightenment anyway because as he said, "The finger points at the moon." It does help to try to get some appreciation for what it will be like for us someday when we bite the big cookie in the sky. You don't have to be a Buddhist to attain complete enlightenment. The Buddha wasn't a Buddhist. But the higher up the mountain top people get, in any spiritual path, the more they say and do the same things. The closer different paths get to the mountain top the more similar they are.

Inside of you there is a jewel in a heap of dust. That jewel is bodhicitta, awakened mind. To attain enlightenment you don't have to go out anywhere to find it. Don't go to Tibet. Buddhahood is already in you now. It's just lost underneath your layers of ignorance, passion and aggression. Even in spite of yourself that jewel will crack through and light the way for you. Listen to that still small voice within. Why waste time through more hollow barren loneliness, birth, old age, sickness and death? Meditate and get moving on the spiritual path of your choice. To purify the mind you can pay the price of right effort now, or you can pay later.

Do you get up in the morning and plunge into your loneliness and depression? My teacher said that taking the refuge vow begins an odyssey in loneliness. What do you think he meant? In those grey, sad minutes, you can visualize Buddhas sitting all along the horizon, 15 degrees high into the sky. See them as white and translucent with rainbow colours oscillating on the surface. Practice meditation or contemplation to go into your broken heart and out the other side. Cheer up! Enlightenment, the final breaking apart of your ego, is not some nihilistic wiping out of yourself that turns you into a big nothing. It is a good thing. Basic goodness at its best. Sounds great in fact! Imagine being able to penetrate to the truth about anything and revealing that to others. Sounds like a good time, life of the party. It just don't get no better than that.

Grand Palace – Bangkok, Thailand

Schwzigon-Pagode, Pegu, Myanmar, Burma

Chapter 2

Class One

Introduction:
Getting ready for a new class to teach.

Less than 4% of this book is focused on "how to teach" methods, so don't be put off if you're not interested in teaching Buddhism. Besides, teaching information is useful for someone just studying the dharma. These ten classes were designed based upon the view that most people don't want to take more than ten classes on Buddhism or any other subject. This might be the only course they will ever take on Buddhism in their entire life, so this is the most important information that I felt people should know. That is why this course has to be a broad overview rather than an in depth study of just one area of Buddhism. I've taught dozens of different subjects in temples in six month courses on Buddhism, but if there were only ten sessions with a new group, this book is still what I would choose to teach.

Is it wise to teach adults and children with a carrot and a stick? Is there a difference between using this method with adults, compared to children? There's an ancient story from China about a king who appointed a Prime Minister to do all the punishing in the kingdom. The king explained to him how he himself would do all of the rewarding. The Prime Minister said "fine, I will do all the punishing, you do all the rewarding." Things were going along just fine and then the king realized that when he spoke maybe people would listen to him and maybe they wouldn't, but when the Prime Minister spoke people jumped immediately! The king called the Prime Minister into his palace and he told him that he had decided to switch the roles. He would do all the punishing and let the Prime Minister do all the rewarding. The Prime Minister said "O.K., fine. You do all the punishing and I'll do all the rewarding." But the people soon threw the king out on his ear yelling "What's gotten into that old codger!? Who does he think he is anyway!? Well, what are we going to do now for a king? Hey! You know who's really been coming around a lot lately? The Prime Minister! Let's make him king."

And so, the Prime Minister became the next king. This is why it might be better for some school teachers not to smile until November. If you are too easy with people at the beginning, they will never respect you or the process or the dharma enough later, to accept discipline. Don't let your class disintegrate into worldly talk that gets out of focus. But you must have warm accepting interpersonal skills and smiles. With adult education things are not quite the same as with children because adults want to share their life experiences and they don't appreciate being treated like kids. But adults do want to be told what to do. You should impart the sacrosanctity of doing meditation practise together in the class, as the practice is an essential part of the path.

Get to the class early to arrange the room and write on the board. You'll be calm if you're not in a rush to get there. This is class one of an intended series of ten classes (you could do less or more) with the same group of people. You're planning on building upon their knowledge in each class. You may want to alter this somewhat if it is a drop-in series of classes. If it is a drop-in series, where different people are floating through all the time, you should maintain continuity in favour of the regular students. If you keep teaching the same old "Introduction to Buddhism and meditation," you're going to lose people quickly. Normally about a third to a half or more of the class will drop out before the end. Don't let it hurt your feelings by taking it personally. Some people realize that they're not interested in Buddhism, their sign might not get along with your sign, their family or job commitments change their schedule, it could be anything. The dynamic energy of big classes of over twelve can be more fun than small classes of under twelve. However, the dynamic of a small class of eight allows you to relate individually to each person.

If people join late, at whatever point they first jump into Buddhism, they are going to be confused anyhow, so you might as well just teach the whole course as though new people have been there from the beginning. Offer people a thorough reading list (see list) so they can catch up if they're serious. Also, never forget that many newcomers already have a background in Buddhism, meditation, comparative religion, etc. They weren't born yesterday. It is better to err on the side of giving too much information, than too little.

Greetings

The first five minutes of the first class is the most important time in the whole course. This is when students sum you up as an instructor and decide whether you are going to be nice, not nice, an interesting, engaging teacher, or a bore. Position yourself near the door and greet people when they come in. Introduce yourself. They don't expect this. When you give someone your name they almost always give their name in return. This is your moment to try to remember their name, a big challenge and an important one. Immediately say their name to make sure you've got it correct. Then use a visualization, or other technique to remember their name. Associate their name with their face by using some kind of mental image that will remind you of their name the next time you look at them in the class.

As part of the initial ice breaking minutes, help them write out their own name cards. Before I taught this Buddhism course at the Vancouver School Board, in the VSB teacher training course given by Laurie Anderson, he told us to use a legal size pad of paper for the name tags. The technique, as passed down from the tradition of the lineage, is to fold a sheet into three, and fold up the bottom edge a half inch. Then you arrange it like a triangle with the paper supported in the fold. Each student writes their name real big on both sides of the name sheet so people on either side can read it in front or back. This is to be placed on their desk.

Early on you should get students talking to each other. This makes them feel comfortable and safe in the environment. You could have the lesson plan written on the board indicating "Discuss in pairs: Your impressions of Buddhism and meditation." That will get them talking. Keep it open ended. It's important to know the true reasons why people take courses on Buddhism or any subject. According to Vancouver School Board statistics the following are the real reasons.

Why Adults Participate in Continuing Education
1. Escape/Stimulation: To get relief from boredom, to remedy deficiencies in social life and education background.
2. Professional Advancement: To gain knowledge, attitudes, and skills which will facilitate job advancement.
3. Social Welfare: To acquire knowledge, attitudes, and skills which will can be applied in achieving social or community objectives.
4. Social contact: To meet new friends, remedy deficiencies in social life, and enjoy group activities.
5. External Expectations: To carry out the expectations of some person with "authority" such as a minister, friend, social worker, employer, or physician.

The humbling truth gathered above is that students are not there to listen to the instructor for the whole class. Much of the time they would rather be meeting the people around them! So throughout the course you should divide them up into discussion groups, maybe not every class, and change their focus from the teacher to each other. This makes the instructor's job easier. You just sit there, or float around from group to group. As the Tao Te Ching teaches, it's amazing how doing so little can accomplish so much. Small groups of four or five are good. Students like this. You give them a set amount of time like five or ten minutes, but you gage it by when the noise dies down. Let them talk overtime if they still have a lot to say. Then bring them back as a whole group when the discussion subsides.

Eventually you want to help your students to develop a sangha. Sangha is the Buddhist word for community. So, these discussion groups in class are deliberately intended to foster a growing sense of community, or proto-sangha within the class. Not only are people crying out for some sense of community, but the Buddhist teachings indicate that the path to enlightenment very much depends upon sangha. The three jewels are: the Buddha, the dharma (the teachings), and the sangha. Sangha is essential in Buddhism. Ananda once remarked to the Buddha "Having good friends to practice with is half of the spiritual life"—"Not so Ananda," the Buddha replied. "Having good friends to practice with is all of the spiritual life." Students cannot get sangha from just a teacher; and not from a teacher that drones on for two hours without letting the students relate to each other. The skilful means of the teacher can be seen in how well the teacher magnetizes the class so that they are engaged with one another. Ideally, the teacher wants to partially phase himself out and let the students take on more. It is a disempowering model to have students relying on a teacher so the Buddha did not want his monks to depend upon him. He taught that you must work out the truth for yourself. Buddhist teachers traditionally empower their qualified students to teach. In the Tao Te Ching, Lao Tzu taught that the second greatest leaders are loved by the people but the greatest leaders of all are hardly noticed by the people.

After the students have had their small group discussion and you've brought them back, then you can begin a formal talk. As you're looking out over them, they should all be able to see each other. This means that the seating arrangement is important. If they are on meditation cushions or at chairs and desks, it is good to arrange them along three sides of a square or rectangle. Avoid the conventional classroom arrangement where people are in rows and can't see each other easily. Circles are fine.

If you have a blackboard, overhead, or paper, it's good to have the lesson plan written on the board before students arrive. The idea is, no secrets. They can see what subjects will be covered in that class. It helps the students and the teacher to stay on track. By reading and hearing, people's memory retention goes up to about 30%. If people only hear information which is the Buddhist tradition of oral instruction, then they only retain about 10%. If they hear, see and discuss they can retain 60%. If they hear, see, discuss and do something about it — like practice meditation, they can retain 90% of the information! Therefore you should make good use of the board or overhead projector if you have one. There are a variety of ways to design the first lesson plan for a Course in Buddhism. For the purpose of this course book, here is a good one:

Class #1
> Introduction to Buddhism
> Meditation practice
> Introductions
> Overview of Course
> The Four Noble Truths
> The Buddha
> Questions and Discussion

Introduction to Buddhism

Start off by asking the group how many have studied some Buddhism before. You may want to find out a bit about what they have studied already. How many have practised meditation before? Ask what type of meditation. This sets the tone of a comfortable conversational exchange between the students and the instructor. It also gives them the signal that you are open to hearing whatever they wish to reveal about their practices and study. Socrates said that the only way to learn about a subject is by dialoguing on it. It is not enough to read books and listen to lectures. They've got to talk. Many university students say that they learned more from their fellow students than they ever did from their professors. Some students are too shy to ask questions or talk to the teacher, but they will talk in small discussion groups. The cardinal sin in teaching is to be boring. That's the worst thing that can happen in a classroom — to bore your students to death. Getting them talking and asking questions intermittently throughout the class is good. Provoking them with controversial subjects is one way to keep them awake. For example, talk about Buddhist views on abortion, capital punishment, welfare, or military defense. My single greatest fear in life is that I will bore my audience. I would rather shock, stun, amaze, or offend them, than bore them. My teacher's title was 'Vidyadhara,' which means 'crazy wisdom holder.' It is that quality of outrageousness that is of value to others.

The Talk

The first item on our agenda is the introduction to Buddhism. Let's talk about what it means to be a Buddhist. Being a Buddhist means making a commitment to working with your mind, and working with your heart. Opening your heart. The Buddha's teachings could be described as psychotherapy. You could say that what the

Buddha taught for the 45 years of his ministry was different techniques for working with your mind, and working with your neuroses. The Buddha had little time for rites and rituals. He was a practical teacher, concerned with guiding people to a direct experience of reality. Unlike most religions, there are no articles of faith in Buddhism. The Buddha said 'come and see', he didn't say 'come and believe.' The amount of freedom that the Buddha gave to his followers is astonishing to a student of comparative religion. The Buddha didn't want to have tight control over his monks and nuns. The Buddha said that you must work out the truth for yourself. His teaching, called dharma, is a guide to point you in a direction that works.

The 'pointing out instructions' in the Buddhist scriptures are not like 'the word of god' in the Bible. The Bible is interpreted by many as the literal word of god so it is very important to theistic people to interpret what it is that god was directing us to do many centuries ago. In Buddhism, the dharma is viewed as pointing out instructions to guide you to working with your mind, to being a decent person, and attaining the direct experience of enlightenment. The Buddha said "The finger points at the moon. Why look at the finger? Look at the moon." This means that the Buddha and the dharma are like a finger to us. That finger is pointing at the moon, which is nirvana, enlightened mind. You should follow the finger and reach the goal of seeing the moon, attaining nirvana. Don't get stuck on the person of Gotama Buddha or Jesus Christ. Don't get ensnared debating about the words in the dharma or the Bible. For example, in the Middle East we have Muslims and Jews and Christians fighting each other over the interpretation of the Bible. The ones that are fighting have forgotten to look at the moon.

Interpret the dharma, use the dharma, and apply it to your real life situation. It will work to help you to live in the world and to be a saner person. And what people need to be taught is how to live in the world. This dharma has been tested and proven to work for 2587 years. What matters is how the Buddhist teachings speak to your life right now. What can Buddhism do for you and your family right now? That's the 64,000 dollar question. The historical details of the Buddha's life, what he did and the people around him, are entirely secondary to the importance of how Buddhism can benefit your life now. Christmas Humphries, in one of his better moments, remarked that even if it was discovered that Gotama Buddha did not even exist (he did), Buddhism would still work and it would hardly be affected. With the Bible, the opposite situation exists. The words in the Bible are believed to be the literal words of god, so they are more cast in stone than the Buddha's pointing out instructions.

The historical details of Christ's life and particularly his crucifixion are very important and have tremendous meaning. It is absolutely necessary to the Christian religion that Christ's crucifixion did happen and that its meaning was about the atonement of the sins of man. These historical events and others in the Bible, like the book of Genesis, are a very big deal. So it is upsetting to some Christians that in recent years New Testament scholars have put forward various ideas about the historical Jesus which contradict some vital concepts in the Bible (see Rescuing Jesus). One such postulation is that Christ's crucifixion may have occurred by sheer happenstance, called 'the car accident' analogy about Christ's death. There is no such parallel in Buddhism. Regardless of what personal problems Thomas Edison had, we still benefit from the light bulb today. Buddhism is a totally different religion than the Bible. That's my view. Others will say that the Christians and the Buddhists are saying the same thing, but in different ways. The author clearly disagrees with that view.

The fundamental difference in how Buddhists and Christians regard their own scriptures is that Buddhists apply the dharma to work out the truth for themselves and have a direct experience of life and reality without delusions. Christians believe that the Bible is the truth from god and that it must be obeyed.

When I was living in Bangkok I would sit in a smoggy bus for an hour to visit The Dhamma House where my friend Ajhan Helen Jandamit lived and taught courses on Buddhism. She is from England and has taught Vipassana meditation for 20 years in Thailand. She told me that when she was a girl in England she was a sincere Christian and she was taught to love others and have compassion for them. "I tried," she said. "I really tried but they didn't teach me how. I discovered Buddhism when some Thai monks came to England. When I studied Buddhism I discovered the methods about how to develop compassion and how to work with the frustrations and anger that arose in my mind."

Buddhism is very much a 'how to' approach to religion; a do it to yourself project. The emphasis is that here and now is the only time there is and if you don't 'get it' now then you won't automatically 'get it' later when you are dead. In the Bible, the emphasis is on a later time, at death. At death you will be rewarded for your patience to go to church on Sundays, and you will get to go to heaven if you've been good. Buddhists are taught to be like the Buddha, to imitate the Buddha, and eventually become a Buddha. Christians are not taught to be Jesus Christ, and they are not taught to realize their own godhood.

In learning theory it is taught that a teacher must activate prior knowledge. Since this book is published in the West, it is logical to compare Buddhism to the Christian religion as a frame of reference. The purpose is to better understand and illuminate the Buddhist path.

Unlike the Bible, the Buddha allowed an incomparable freedom of thought within the sangha. This is because nirvana is dependent upon one's direct realization of the truth, not upon agreeing with the truth or receiving a reward from a god. In the famous Kalama sutra, quoted in fifty other Buddhist books, the Buddha was visiting a small community named Kesaputta in the kingdom of Kosala. The people, the Kalamas, told the Buddha (*Colombo,* 1929; 115):

> "Sir, there are some recluses and brahmanas who visit Kesaputta. They explain and illumine only their own doctrines, and despise, condemn and spurn others' doctrines. Then come other recluses and brahmanas, and they too, in their turn, explain and illumine only their own doctrines, and despise, condemn and spurn others' doctrines. But for us Sir, we have always had doubt and perplexity as to who among these venerable recluses and brahmanas spoke the truth, and who spoke falsehood."

Unique in the history of religions, the Buddha revealed this answer:

> "Yes Kalamas, it is proper that you have doubt, that you have perplexity, for a doubt has arisen in a matter that is doubtful. Now, look you Kalamas, do not be led by reports, or tradition, or hearsay. Be not led by the authority of religious texts, nor by mere logic or inference, nor by considering appearances, nor by delight in speculative opinions, nor by seeming possibilities, nor by the idea: 'this is our teacher'. But, O Kalamas, when you know for yourselves that certain things are unwholesome and wrong and bad, then give them up... And when you know for yourselves that certain things are wholesome and good, then accept them and follow them."

The Buddha even told the monks and nuns that a disciple should examine the Tathagata (Buddha) himself or any other teacher, so that the disciple might be fully convinced of the true value of the teacher whom he followed. It's O.K. to 'spy on your teacher' to be sure that they walk their talk. It could take years before you accept a teacher, but in our information age, the need for a teacher is less now than ever before in history because of dharma videos, tapes, books and lecture tours. Put more faith and trust in yourself instead. Theravadins put less importance upon a teacher than Tibetans do.

The Path

The Buddhist path can be most simply described in three words: morality, concentration, insight. These are three inseparable stages. The purpose of morality from a Buddhist view is simply to foster an environment by which you can concentrate your mind. This is very important to understand. In many religions, the purpose of morality is to be good, and not be bad. It is god's law so it is enforced with a heavy handed approach. If you sin, you will go to hell. The Buddhist approach is different and not so heavy handed. In Buddhism morality or discipline, has a future. You're actually going somewhere with it! Once you settle your life down with proper behaviour, you can sit and meditate and build up concentration in your mind. It is this concentration that naturally leads to the fruit of insight. Insight is a natural psychosomatic result that comes from a concentrated mind. This is not a belief system. This is direct experience. It's like water rising in a dam. The water rising is the concentration aspect, as in meditation. When the water reaches the top of the dam, you can use that power for electricity, which is insight. That's the whole Buddhist religion right there.

How to Meditate

Building up concentration in the mind is what separates the men from the boys. Someone once told the Dalai Lama that they were living a good life, they followed all the precepts, they cared about others and had compassion. So, they asked the Dalai Lama, what could they possibly do next? Immediately the Dalai Lama said "Mental stabilization." What the Dalai Lama meant by this is that the next stage after living a moral life, is to stabilize the mind in meditation practice. Meditation practices are the essential steps along the path to enlightenment. The Buddha recommended a balance of practice and study. So, let's get into some meditation practice now. The definition of meditation in one sentence is that meditation means to pay attention in a certain way. This means to familiarize your mind constantly and thoroughly with a virtuous object. In the insight meditation technique which we will do, you pay attention to your in and out breath. Having a daily meditation practice means honouring that commitment to working with your mind and working with your heart. Meditation works with our wandering thoughts in an effort to train the mind with mindfulness and awareness, to stay in the present moment and build concentration. Because meditation can help clear away our confusion and stress, and help purify our minds, meditation has been called the most basic form of psychotherapy.

Vipassana Meditation Technique

Meditating puts us in tune with our being, with experiencing our life as it ordinarily is. In the Satipattana sutra, which was the Buddha's longest discourse on how to meditate, he didn't specify precisely about whether meditation practice had to be just this way or that way. Lord Buddha gave us the general parameters by saying for example, "When a monk has a thought, he knows he has a thought." This practice is known as "Vipassana" which translates from Pali as "insight" or "clear seeing." This technique comes from the Mahasi Sayadaw tradition from Burma which was taught to me when I was a monk but I also include here comments by Chögyam Trungpa in his elegant book *Shambhala The Sacred Path of the Warrior* from Shambhala Publications.

We begin by taking our seat and assuming our posture. It is extremely important to sit upright. Don't lean back on anything. You relax into it; you're not strained. Think of yourself as a puppet with a string coming out of the top of your head. Or imagine your spine as a stack of neatly piled golden coins, or a stack of dinner plates. If you lean back on a chair there's a danger of (snore...) falling asleep. So perk up! You are a human being, not an animal hunched over. You should take your seat cross-legged on the ground. You can use a chair if your legs aren't so supple, and keep your legs straight if that is comfortable. An important thing is to not force your legs into falling asleep. That's a real physical problem so you can mindfully move if your legs fall asleep. Some people think meditation is boot camp and they are supposed to try to kill themselves, but surprisingly this is not so. Ideally you should sit on a thick cushion made of very hard #8 rebond foam 12.5" x 18" x 6," as designed by Trungpa. Sinking on a down pillow is useless. You've got to keep yourself up, unless you're used to sitting flat on the floor. You should rest your feet on a Zabuton — a cushion for the ankles.

Feeling a bit cheered up by solidly sitting, solidly being, you suspect that everything is going to be all right after all. Life is wonderful! There is tremendous dignity in being the connection between heaven, earth and man. Your head is in the heavens, your seat is on the earth and your heart is the connection between heaven, earth and man. With good head and shoulders, you complete your posture by placing your hands lightly, palms down, on your thighs. Or, you can put your hands together in your lap with the right hand on the left. This subtly aids the energy exchange which goes out of your right arm and into your left. In this technique you can meditate with your eyes closed or open. The advantage of having your eyes open is that it keeps you a bit more grounded in reality. With your eyes closed there's a greater tendency to space out. Also, with the eyes open you stay awake! as it is not possible to fall asleep with your eyes open. There's also a sense of "going outward" beyond your self. One of my first teachers, Paul Warwick encouraged, "We live our lives with our eyes open, not closed, so meditation is a training ground for ordinary life. You pay for it in the front end, but it really pays off later!"

Your gaze is directed deliberately about six feet in front of you on the ground. If your mind is too agitated, pull in your view real close, or it's fine to close your eyes, but if you sink into mental laxity or sleepiness, you can half open your eyes again. You can decide for yourself if you want your eyes open or closed and you can go in and out of it during the meditation. Your eyes don't stare at any particular spot, but you also see the space between you and the ground. You are sitting on the dot! deliberately and definitely. Statues of the Buddha sitting are almost always carved with his eyes open in meditation, not closed.

As you sit with good posture, when you breathe, you are utterly there, properly there. You follow the rising and falling of your breath at the tip of your nose, or at your abdomen or wherever you can most easily sense it. There is a natural gap between breaths. During the in-breath you say to yourself "rising," and during the out-breath you say "falling." The words are like training wheels for the mind; they help you keep your mind on what you are doing while you are doing it because they displace other discursive thoughts the way fresh water displaces old water in your car radiator. Just let your breathing be natural. You are not trying to control it. Sometimes it is shallow, sometimes deep.

As you sit, there will be an inevitable *bing!* — thought, any thought. You may have a thought about your car in the parking lot. At that point, you say, "thinking." You label the thought as "thinking." **This is the most important part of the whole technique: to label "thinking."** Whatever arises in the five senses — seeing, hearing, feeling, smelling, taste, is all labelled "thinking" as well. Whatever arises is just "thinking." You can even note "thinking" two or three times, or even more if a thought is persistent, such as with an emotion. When distractions arise they are all simply labelled in this way, so nothing gets past your awareness; you note everything.

Don't space out; but of course we all do, so just be gentle with yourself and come back. Come back to your breath. Ram Dass practiced Vipassana in Burma and he said "When you're meditating and you see your thoughts flowing along like a river, then that's good, you're doing it, you're meditating! But when you hang on to a thought and think about it, then you're just thinking, not meditating." You just let the breath go out and dissolve with your stress, your thoughts, your ego. Labelling your thoughts "thinking" gives you tremendous leverage to come back to your breath. Your thoughts are like meteors that smack you along with them at 82 kilometres per second. Then another meteor on a perpendicular trajectory carries you off at 136 kilometres per second in that direction. What you want to do is rest in the white outer space in between the meteors! That's the mind. The meteors are thought — two different animals.

Thoughts are to be regarded as ordinary phenomenon. They're not good thoughts or bad thoughts. They are just thoughts. If anger arises this can be good because you may be cleaning out the basement of your subconscious. If you have an erection, or you stare at one, just label it "thinking." Trungpa says "No thought deserves a gold medal or a reprimand." Just label your thoughts "thinking," then go back to the rising and falling. "Thinking," back to the breath; "thinking," back to the breath.

You should regularly review your posture because you are synchronizing your body, speech and mind in meditation. This is precise inner work and hard inner work. You take a working man's approach. It keeps you in reality to always connect your mind to your body. In meditation you steer the ship rather than going with the flow. Buddhism is the opposite of spacing out into some far off mystical experience that you share with your competitors. You are being present, looking into yourself, into your heart, looking at the ground. There's nothing else happening, just your breath and your deepest innermost being churning around, unravelling your confusion, thought by thought.

Walking meditation compliments sitting meditation. If you meditate for a full hour, practice walking meditation for only ten minutes. This keeps you awake, stretches the legs and it is a transition to the post meditation world. To do this, as in sitting meditation it is important to have direct personal instruction. You put your hands lightly together on your belly with your left thumb in and your fingers curled around. Your right thumb goes on top with your fingers covering your left knuckles. This hand mudra comes from Zen. Alone or in a group, you do a slow mindful walk in a clockwise circle, with the object of meditation being your feet touching the ground. The circle moves clockwise because when people greeted the Buddha they kept their right side to the Buddha in coming or going. So when you go clockwise, you are keeping your right side to the centre. Forget about your breath; you are no longer using the breath as an object of meditation. Your eyes are open, looking outwards, but downcast. Don't stare at your feet. You label "step, step, step," when your heels touch the ground. You label "thinking" when you are distracted by the five senses, or when you are distracted by thoughts arising. After labelling "thinking," you bring your attention back to your feet without interrupting your pace. The dictionary definition of the word "step" is: "An act of progressive motion that requires one of the supporting limbs of the body to be thrust in the direction of the movement, and to reassume its function of support; a pace." But, you're not supposed to be thinking about that when you step; just step.

In Vipassana you are not working with your mind alone. You are working with your mind and your body, and when the two work together, you never leave reality.

Just Sit

Next, in the class, start the students in meditation using this technique. This can be done in the middle of the class, to provide a natural break in the talking. A class may go for two or two and a half hours, including the meditation time. Normally, for the second and subsequent classes, the meditation is done right at the beginning of each class to help open people's minds for the dharma talk.

Begin with about 15 minutes of sitting meditation. Use a gong or bell to start and stop the meditation periods. After the first sit, hit the gong, and ask people what their meditation experience was like. Normally on retreats people are advised to not discuss their meditation experience with anyone but their meditation instructor. But in this situation it is helpful for people to hear that others are having the same kind of experiences as themselves. Beginning meditators often secretly believe that they are the worst meditators in the world. But everybody has a neurotic wandering mind. Everybody has thoughts chattering away on the inside of their skulls. It is good for beginners to share this experience in the class, rather than just one-on-one with the teacher. It's also much more convenient in a classroom situation with a dozen or so students, to talk about meditation experience as a group, rather than taking turns with the instructor. You should offer to meet them one-on-one in the future if they need that, or simply invite them to phone you, and it won't take up much of your time because few people will do that.

Respond immediately to any concerns, confusion or questions about the meditation technique. There will surely be misunderstandings about how to meditate. It's important that people know how to do it right. Next, describe the walking meditation technique and then get them to stand up. Walking is great to revitalize people's energy and keep them awake. Rearrange the room if necessary and begin walking in a clockwise circle. After ten minutes use two wooden sticks and hit them together once loudly. This is the signal to walk back to their seats in just an ordinary way, not in the slow walking meditation method. Once everyone is standing together silently, you lead by sitting down mindfully and they all do the same. Then everyone goes straight into more sitting meditation without a break. All of this you explain beforehand, when you first explain the walking meditation. The idea is to maintain mindfulness even when sitting down, so they go right into the sitting technique. It is as though they are holding a bowl full of mindfulness, and they don't want to spill any of it.

Now that you have answered some of their questions after the very first sit of 15 minutes, keep them sitting for another 20 minutes this time. The pattern for most classes will be a brief review of the technique, then 15 minute sit, 10 walk, 20 sit: 45 minutes in total. Sometimes the second sit can be changed to include various Buddhist guided visualizations and contemplations such as Loving Kindness, or Compassion. For the first class do five minutes of the Loving Kindness practice from Chapter Ten.

After the final sitting meditation, hit the gong and wait about half a minute before speaking, to avoid them getting a headache. Smile. Then ask, "Did anything arise is your meditation?" This is a good time to get them to share their experience, because they are still in the experience. Try to be indirect in your question. It doesn't work to ask "Are there any questions?" because that will deter people from speaking. It's better to draw them out. In Buddhist lingo, we "share our confusion." Be sure to respond properly to all aspects of their meditation practice. To do this it is of course good to have had training as a meditation instructor. But, meditation is not so dangerous a thing. It would be better to proceed and do your best even if you've only read books about meditation, then to disband the group and send everyone home to watch T.V. Don't throw out the dharma with the bath water. Opinions differ on this point about who is qualified to teach meditation and who is not qualified to teach meditation. Although not always true one measure of a

Buddhist teacher is the number of students that think he or she is a good teacher. Just as the measure of a man is the number of his friends, according to Charles Dickens. You can trust yourself. You can trust your intention to benefit others. Buddhist meditation is not going to drive people crazy! You can be a meditation instructor. You can do it! Besides, my attitude is that this world is so insane that I very much will take chances with other people's minds and other people's lives and other people's money, in order to take compassionate action. Have confidence beyond hesitation! No hesitation.

During this review of their meditation, give additional instructions and theory regarding meditation. You can't heap everything on them at once, so in each class give them a bit more about meditation and mindfulness. After that you move onto the particular topic of that session, so there is a definite shift in the class. The first part is devoted to meditation practice, the second part is a talk on a particular aspect of the Buddhadharma. That's a balance of practice and study. It's good to provide a ten minute break in the middle of the class if it's a long one.

Introductions

Go around the circle and get everyone to introduce themselves. It's best not to do this right at the beginning because people haven't warmed up to each other at that point. Wait until after one hour, and then start with yourself, the instructor. This is the one time to give the long story about your background, and why you are teaching the class. Describe your spiritual roots, how you first got interested in Buddhism or meditation, where you have studied, what teachers or teachings you have connected with. Give them your personal story and what makes you tick, even your aspirations if you care to share that. Your story can be part of their education if your search is relevant to their search. You could do an intro for 5 to 15 minutes, but limit the student's introductions to about 1 1/2 minutes each, if it's a big class of more than 12. Give them more time for a small class.

Another method of doing introductions is to pair off the students and ask them to interview each other, then take turns introducing their partner to the rest of the class. This helps the students to get to know each other better, but it takes more time. If the class is around 20 or more, it quickens the pace to divide them in groups of five and give them two minutes each to introduce themselves, then they can continue with a group conversation for 5 or 10 minutes more. In successive classes this can be repeated by changing the mix of people in the circle. People won't be stuck for something to say if they are talking about themselves and their words will be meaningful to them and to those listening. It's very interesting to listen to people's stories.

Overview of Course

After everyone has gotten to know each other, tell the class that you will give them an overview of what to expect for the rest of the course that you are teaching. You could adapt this for a four, eight or ten week course, or more. An overview sells the course while many are still asking themselves why they took the course in the first place! Give them something tantalizing to come back for! "We will do a period of sitting and walking meditation like we did, in each class. Today's topic, is the four noble truths. Next week's class will be about Buddhist history." Metacognition, in this case, means that you relate this class to the next one and in each class you do a brief review of the previous class, and later relate it to future classes. This big picture is necessary for students to know what is going on and where they are headed. Pass around the course outline and briefly describe each item on it so that they will have a feel for how the course is laid out and for the depth of the material. Handouts are always good. People like to have hard copies of things you have taught — helps memory retention. Good to have a course book as well. Either this one or another introduction to Buddhism. One of the best such books is *What the Buddha Taught,* by Dr. Walpola Rahula. For a thorough, long term course, such as one year, the book *Joyful Path of Good Fortune* by Tibetan Geshe Kelsang Gyatso (Tharpa Publications) is very good. Even though it indulges in Tibetan Buddhist mythology, I use that book for a graduate course guide after this book and it's a better track to follow than some teacher trying to reinvent the wheel and figure it all out for himself. *Freeing the Buddha* is like the booster rockets on the space shuttle because it's short and intense; but *Joyful Path of Good Fortune* <u>is</u> the space shuttle.

The following is a course outline sheet you could use or modify:

Buddhism and Meditation Course

Class 1   Introduction to Buddhism and the Buddha, Meditation instruction and practice, Instructor's background, Introductions, Overview of course, the Four Noble Truths.

Class 2, 3 The history of Buddhism. India before the Buddha. The "Mahayana split." Mahadeva and the Mahasanghikas. Buddhism meets the Iranian sun god religion. Give and take contemplation on Compassion.

Class 4, 5 The Buddha's noble eightfold path to enlightenment.

Class 6   Buddhist psychology. The five parts, or skandhas of non-self. This is the one piece of doctrine upon which all of Buddhism either stands or falls. The true nature of the illusory concept of the self is the heart core of the Buddhist religion. Karma and rebirth. The Buddha.

Class 7   Buddhist Cosmology. In the beginning... there was no beginning. The Buddha's teaching on the big bang and what came before it. Everything in the universe seen and unseen is accounted for in Buddhist cosmology. The six realms of existence.

Class 8   The Four Foundations of Mindfulness. Bhavana-mental culture or meditation. The Pali Satipattana sutra is the Buddha's longest discourse on how to meditate. Practices of mindfulness in ordinary life. Standing and lying meditation.

Class 9   Awakened Heart. Loving Kindness, Compassion, Joy, Equanimity, as a contemplative practice. The transition from working on yourself to going outwards and working with others. Relative bodhicitta — the core of spirituality on the Mahayana path.

Class 10   The Higher Realms. Tuning into the devas (heavenly beings) of the god realm. How to invoke the assistance of the devas in daily life, as taught by the Buddha himself. Chants and channelling. The high ground in your life which you should not ignore. Raising up the human world, bringing down the devas so it becomes one world. Merging and commingling minds with devas.

When giving this overview, tell them that the outline is not cast in stone. If the students would like to change it or change the order of the classes, you invite their suggestions. They can write down what they would like, or expect from the course for you to read and consider. You can also continue the course beyond ten classes if there is interest, or start a new course with other material, that includes new people. Gage when you want to ask for questions and when you want to keep the pace going. Sometimes questions and discussion can degenerate into non dharmic topics so you must bring them back to dharma and usually try to complete the topic that you planned to teach in that particular class. Sometimes you should let your planned talk go, and stay with the sway of the group's energy. Don't fixate to your habitual patterns. The Tao says that you should facilitate what actually is happening, rather than stick to what you expected to happen.

The Four Noble Truths

This is the traditional starting point for a study of Buddhist philosophy. When the Buddha was 35 years old, several weeks after his great enlightenment he gave his first formal discourse in Deer Park in Isipatanna, in northeastern India. He gave it to his five former ascetic friends who had practiced with him before. They stepped onto the pages of history when they became the Buddha's first monks, and the

Buddha's first teaching to them was the four noble truths, which are:

1. There is dukkha, suffering.
2. The cause of suffering is thirst, desire.
3. There is an end to suffering, nirvana.
4. There is a way to the end of suffering, which is the eightfold path.

'Noble' as it is used here, means an all pervasive truth that is as true as the law of gravity. Gravity is true whether you believe in it or not. Whether you understand gravity or not, or agree with gravity, or if it is not convenient for you at this time, if you jump off a ten story building, you will go splat on the pavement, whether you like it or not. Anywhere in the universe there is gravity and the four noble truths. That is what is meant by a noble truth.

Dukkha is one of those Pali and Sanskrit terms that cannot be properly translated into English. Pali is the oldest Buddhist language. Theravadin Buddhists (the southern school) like to think that the Buddha spoke in Pali, but no one is sure about that. Pali is the language of the canonical scriptures of Theravadin Buddhism and Sanskrit is the language of the northern school of Buddhism, or Mahayana. Basically, Buddhism went south and it went north from India. Dukkha translates as suffering but it has a much wider meaning than that. It also means impermanence, insubstantiality, changeability, unsatisfactoriness and transitoriness. Everything in the entire universe is of the nature of dukkha. Anything that is made will fall apart and crumble and die, including the entire universe. The first noble truth is that life is suffering, dukkha. The Buddha's point is — accept it. Accept reality. This is the nature of reality. I had a lesson in the first noble truth of impermanence when I was hiking near Mount Baker in Washington with Shambhala sangha members. Ty was helping us explore an old mining shaft. After we left, as we hiked down the path he explained the geology of the area and Ty said "The idea that planet Earth has a natural balance, an inherent harmony, which always gently brings it back to normal, is just bad science! The evidence proves that Earth has gone through radical changes constantly, and the last 10,000 years is just one snap shot during this brief period of relative calm." So, even the crust of the earth where we live is impermanent in it's short term stability and reliability!

There was a famous American philosopher in the 1970s who eloquently described the first noble truth. She said "There's always something!" This was when Gilda Radner would dress up as Rosane Rosanadana on Saturday Night Live. As the years rolled by, long after she died, I finally realized what Rosane Rosanadana meant for us to understand. Her teaching is that there's always something messing up. There's always something going wrong. When Rosane Rosanadana contemplated the reality of all of the suffering in the world, she often remarked, "I thought I was gonna die!" Rosana was telling us to face the facts of the first noble truth of dukkha: no matter how beautiful and wonderful you are, something is going to fall apart in your life. Wiser words were never spoken.

Another great philosopher was Shaw, who said "There are two great disappointments in life. One is not getting what you want, and the other is getting it." The second noble truth taught by the Buddha is that the cause of our suffering is desire, which translates to mean thirst, clinging, attachment, grasping, craving, addiction, obsessive compulsive behaviours of all kinds. The root of suffering is "the pursuit of happiness." We each have a nagging itch that is a constant pull away from the present moment. That is desire. Desire itself does not have to be painful but when desire becomes attachment it is painful. The pleasure of what we enjoy is lost by coveting more. Desire persists. An example of clinging can be found in monkeys in Africa. Foreign zoos and zoological societies buy monkeys that are caught by people who put nuts in glass jars. The jars have very narrow openings and are weighed down so heavily that monkeys can't move them. They come in the morning and spread out many of these jars on the jungle floor, then they go back and play cards all day. At the end of the day they come and find many monkeys trapped by the jars. The monkeys reach in for the nuts but they can't take their hands out with their fists full. Their monkey brains don't tell them that they just have to let go of their clinging to be free. So unharmed, they are captured and sent away. When people go to see their best friend to talk about their problems, it's like they are holding on to a jar with one hand. Their best friend may tell them to let go of their problem, or their friend may polish their jar and nurture their clinging, or they may do something else. This demonstrates the second noble truth — the cause of suffering is clinging.

One common criticism of the Buddha is the question, "If the Buddha didn't have any desires, then why did he teach? Isn't that a desire? Isn't doing compassionate action for people a form of desire?" Well, no. The Buddha didn't have any desires. The English language translation may be confusing things. One way to understand it is to consider right effort, number six in the eightfold path. Effort in the Buddhist sense is the opposite of desire. Effort means to rub up against your habitual desires, to go against your habitual desires. For example, a married man may have the habitual pattern of pursuing sexually arousing women which results in extramarital affairs. But then he hears the Buddha's precept to not engage in sexual misconduct. He's at a client's office party and he meets a woman who's presence causes him to trigger his habitual glandular response. But his effort in this case is to look at his own lust, to look at his own mind. He slowly turns away from her and reaches for some broccoli and dip. He holds himself back, then later goes home to his wife and kids. So, in this example, the man's sexual desire arose and then it was his effort that broke him out of his instinctual habitual pattern. So desire is bad, effort is good. When the Buddha chose to get up and teach he was not acting out of clinging, attachment or craving desire. He chose to apply effort to extend his compassion to others. That is why the Buddha taught the dharma.

The third noble truth is that there is a cessation to suffering. It is called nirvana, the final ultimate enlightenment. Unless someone told you, how would you know? There actually is such a thing. A state of no suffering, a state beyond suffering. A permanent deathless state beyond the struggles of samsara. Enlightenment is the transcendence of the self, or self limitation. It is the discarding of the ego. If you think of your mind now as the air inside of a soap bubble, enlightenment is like popping that soap bubble so that the air inside merges with the universe outside. You have a direct experience of the entire universe. The word nirvana translates literally as 'blown out.' Meaning, the ego is blown out. After that, there is no longer any possibility of ever slipping back into the sleep of ego ever again. You are awake!

The fourth noble truth is that there is a path which will lead a practitioner to the end of suffering. This path is what the Buddha taught. He described it as the eightfold path because there are eight aspects to the path. They are practiced together, not in any particular order. The most universal symbol of the Buddhist religion is the wheel. It is represented with eight spokes, so it is said that the Buddha first turned the wheel of dharma during that discourse to the five monks in Deer Park. That was called the dharmachakra sutra, which means the turning of the wheel discourse. Just about everything the Buddha taught for 45 years was aspects of this eightfold path.

Those are the four noble truths, which is the most concise description of the Buddha's message. After the Buddha's enlightenment he realized that nirvana cannot be taught. He said that enlightenment is impossible to describe. It is a direct experience that can only be comprehended once you're there. The Buddha was sitting beside a lotus pond when he hesitated about teaching people at all. His mind inclined away from teaching. At that moment a Brahma realm deva read the Buddha's mind and he thought "The world is lost. The world will perish. The Buddha will not teach." Then, in one of history's heroic acts, this Brahma realm deva disappeared from that world and appeared before the Buddha. He pleaded with the Buddha to teach and he encouraged him by pointing out that there were some people who could understand his teachings. Finally, the Buddha agreed to teach. Satisfied and very happy, the deva disappeared and went back up to heaven.

At that time the Buddha contemplated the lotus pond and he realized that human beings are like lotus flowers. Some are like a lotus under the mud, others thrive their entire life under the water. But when the lotus flower comes out of the water and blooms, that is symbolic of enlightened mind. So the Buddha chose the lotus flower as the symbol of enlightened mind. He said that there are a few people with little dust in their eyes, who would be able to penetrate to his dharma. Today, you can see a lot of lotus flowers in Buddhist temples. If the Buddha had been sitting in a field of dandelions at that particular time, history may have been quite different!

When the Buddha decided to teach he realized that he could only teach the way to nirvana. This is an important understanding. The Buddha concerned himself with teaching people the practical steps to proceed along the spiritual path. He wasn't interested in giving them all the knowledge of the universe which he knew but took to the grave. He taught people how to get to enlightenment so that they could attain this ultimate direct experience themselves. Buddhism is a practical path of mindfulness and awareness and meditation practices designed to clear away our ignorance and confusion so that the enlightened mind that is buried within us can shine forth. Buddhism is not about the experience of nirvana. Buddhism has more to do with paying attention to your hands when you are polishing your shoes, than it has to do with a holy spiritual experience. Buddhism is the way to nirvana, but once you've made it, you can let go of Buddhism the way you let go of a jet after it has flown you across the ocean.

The Buddha

'Buddha' is a title given to the first man that attains enlightenment in his age, and teaches it to others. This first person cannot be a woman. They must be a man. This doesn't go over well with the feminists but we cannot deny that this is clearly stated in the sutras. Certainly the Buddha expounded that women have attained to arahantship but perhaps one reason why the first great leader can't be a woman is because India is one of the most sexist countries of all time, then as now. Because such men are so ignorant they are probably incapable of respecting a female Buddha enough, so therefore each Buddha must be a man. The word 'Buddha' comes from the root words 'Bud' or 'Bodhi' which means 'awake,' and 'dha' meaning 'man.' Buddha means awakened man. His family name was Prince Siddhartha Gotama. He was the crown prince of the Sakya kingdom. That's why Mahayanists call him Sakyamuni Buddha. 'Muni' means 'sage,' sage of the Sakyas. His father was King Suddhodana, a virtuous king, deserving of a child like prince Siddhartha. The Buddha wasn't the Buddha until age 35. He was born in modern day Nepal near the Indian border (as best we can tell). India at that time was a feudal society. The Buddha lived and taught throughout about ten of these feudal kingdoms. Each one was maybe 100 or 200 kilometres across. Very much unlike Jesus Christ, the Buddha was loved by the political powers of his day. Jesus was faced with a monolithic and mean Roman Empire. The Buddha could divide and conquer so to speak, so he had it easier. The Buddha said that he chose the proper causes and conditions into which to take birth, to become the next Buddha. Why did Jesus choose to be born on the wrong side of the tracks? Compassion for that part of the Roman Empire, perhaps?

The Buddha became a pop idol soon after launching his career into the big time. They didn't have sunglasses in those days, but he was surrounded by his retinue.

Kings would supplicate the Buddha to come and visit their kingdom. "Please come and spend the rainy season retreat in our kingdom! We'll donate a beautiful new monastery to your monks if you will please bless us with your presence!" they might say.

As a child Prince Siddhartha was a child prodigy and he grew up in luxury. His father wanted him to take over the throne, as Siddhartha was his first son. The King fed him with consorts to indulge him in sensuous pleasure because the king didn't want his son to get any ideas about becoming a monk and giving up the kingdom. At age 16 the prince married the princess Yasodhara and she was a very spiritual and devoted wife. They would go around the kingdom together like John and Yoko, trying to better the lives of the poor. When he was 29 they had one baby boy, Rahula. Just after this, with his wife's support, Prince Siddhartha renounced the worldly life of the palace and ran away from home one night. He fled over the river into the next kingdom of Magadha so that his daddy, the king, couldn't come and get him. King Suddhodana was very sad but prince Siddhartha was free! He became a monk, studied under two leading pre-Hindu teachers, then broke off on his own to find his own way to enlightenment. He had his own confusion too, but Siddhartha had the gift to ask questions. When he was sitting under a pipala tree (later renamed the bodhi tree in his honour) along the Neranjara river early one morning, he attained to full and complete enlightenment. The rest as they say, is history.

Questions and Discussion

The above is probably too much to deliver in one class and still have 15 to 30 minutes for discussion. So, use this information as a resource and cut down the lecture, so as to preserve time for discussion. A lecture is most effective if it doesn't go over 25 or 30 minutes, unless the students are really interested in the subject. Otherwise, people space out and they are lost. Try not to talk too much. Break up the talk. Give the students a chance to talk, ask questions, voice their views, and talk to each other as well. My own experience as a Buddhist teacher is that the fun thing for a teacher, is to talk. But the kind thing for a teacher is to shut up and listen to people that want to talk. Avoid 'spray and pray;' the hope that something will stick if you just spray your knowledge at them and pray that something will stick. It doesn't work. That's why meditation is ideal in a Buddhism course, because it provides a break in all the discursive mental activity, for everyone to stop talking and just sit quietly.

*The author recommends but does not represent Trungpa's 130 Shambhala Centres administered by Shambhala International, 1084 Tower Street, Halifax, Nova Scotia B3H 2Y5 Tel. (902) 423-3266. Vancouver area Shambhala Centre is at 3275 Heather Street, at 17th Ave., Vancouver B.C. V5Z 3K4 Tel. (604) 874-8420. Free meditation and public talks are offered every Monday and Wednesday. Meditation at 7:00 pm, talk at 8:00 pm. Tea and cookies at 9:15 pm.

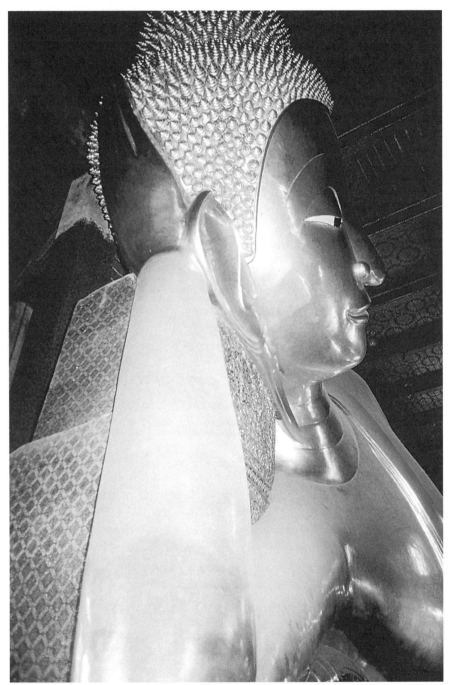

Wat Pho – Reclining Buddha, Bangkok, Thailand
Depicting the time of the Buddha's death (parinirvana) and the beginning of Buddhist history.

Chapter 3

Class Two and Three Buddhist History

Sacred sacred sacred world. Sacred sacred sacred girls.

B egin class two by reviewing the meditation technique. "While you're waiting for people," you can ask the students present how their meditation practice has gone this week. Listen and respond. If questions about technique come up answer them on the spot as thoroughly as you can; it's not good to leave questions hanging.

To teach a class, a variety of Buddhist meditation techniques could be used. You could start people off with concentration meditation in the first class, and move to insight meditation in the second class. It is easier to do a practice with more concentration to it which has more of a working man's approach, where you are always busy doing something like counting your breaths. Explain to the class that there are a range of Buddhist meditation techniques from form to formlessness. Formless or half formless techniques are more difficult because you give more freedom for things to arise in the mind — insight and neurosis. An example of a formless technique in Tibetan Buddhism is that the monks stare at the blue sky. Empty space. When thoughts arise, they simply bring their mind back to the blue sky. That's it. No more technique. They don't even follow the breath. Try doing that and you will appreciate how difficult it is.

There are over a hundred Buddhist practices, and we are not judging their comparative values. Simply put, the two main categories are concentration meditation, and insight meditation. This technique is part of insight meditation (vipassana in Pali or vipashyana in Sanskrit). Trungpa considered insight meditation to be the "pinnacle practice" in Tibetan Buddhism. Meaning that, after you have been initiated into several practices for many years, even after being initiated into secret Vajrayana practices, the ultimate meditation technique that he would assign for you, would be insight meditation practice.

Concentration means that you totally concentrate on the object of meditation, for example, in and out breathing (Anapanasati), and you deliberately ignore everything else. Ignore all thoughts and ignore the five senses. The goal is mental tranquillity and calm. This leads you to a samadhi absorption of one pointed concentration, which we will talk about later.

Insight meditation means that you note everything that comes up, nothing gets by you. You label your thoughts and your five senses as 'thinking.' This is mindfulness/ awareness. You are aware of everything. It's like crap shooting. "Seeing," pow! "Hearing," pow! "Thinking," pow! "Feeling," pow! Whatever comes up, you blast it. Don't space out. You catch everything. This is more geared to living in the world as it is, being in reality. You are not trying to achieve some deep mystical experience or mental gymnastics. You are trying to develop mindfulness to be better aware of your existence and your environment. Joseph Campbell once said that the best thing you can teach people is how to live in the world.

It is wise to have one main, basic practise of meditation. With that established, you can add on other Buddhist contemplations and meditations as is beneficial for you and others. It is actually distorted thinking to just practice meditation without doing other Buddhist contemplations. The Buddha didn't approve of just non-conceptual breath meditation for fifty years of your life. He said that you should also do contemplations on death and impermanence, precious human birth, karma, considering the shortcomings of samsara, and others. Perhaps you have books on your bookshelf that go beside this one, which can give you instruction on these important and very basic contemplations. Traditionally, these are taught even *before* meditation practice.

One valid criticism of meditation organizations is that some emphasize meditation plus other contemplations such as loving kindness, but real Theravadin Buddhism includes the whole cosmology of the universe. Some groups even publicly claim that they're not striving for enlightenment. It is good to see the spread of meditation practice of course but Buddhism is much more than that. The Buddha had big plans for us and our spiritual path. He spent the first seven weeks after his enlightenment planning how he would present his message to devas and men, and then he proclaimed himself very boldly.

A great variety of contemplations is the route to go, but avoid teaching a new technique every time you sit down. That confuses people and undermines their proficiency. What matters is getting yourself to the cushion in the first place, and then doing your practice. The actual technique that you choose to practice is not as important as having the discipline to do that practice. Discipline is the basis of all virtue. So, keep regular. Stay with your meditation practice, boring as it is.

You should meditate everyday, ideally for one hour. Bokar Rinpoche taught that you can start with as little as ten minutes per day, but try to get it up to 30, 40, and even 60 minutes. You don't have to do it all at once, or at any set time per day, but it probably works better to pick one time in your schedule to meditate, or you might slack off. Don't sit right after a meal because you'll get sleepy. The Buddha taught his monks and nuns to do walking meditation after a meal.

Spend about 15 minutes at the beginning of class two going over these things with the class. The idea is to emphasize the importance of meditation practice. That's why you don't want to have a course on Buddhism that doesn't force people to sit and meditate during class. You can't assume that most people will be convinced enough to go home and meditate for 30 minutes a day. They need the support of the class to make them learn the discipline and the value of meditation. Their own direct experience of the practice may soon convince them of the depth and the benefit of meditation. Also group energy is good for supporting the practice.

Go over the technique by saying that the purpose of meditation is to purify the mind and build concentration because this naturally leads to insight. The definition of meditation is to pay attention in a certain way. The technique begins with our posture. Sit up straight, but not strained, like a puppet with a string coming out of the top of your head. Think of your spine as a stack of neatly piled golden coins, or dinner plates. Put your hands palms down on your thighs or together in your lap, with your right hand on your left. In this technique we meditate with our eyes open or closed. Opening the eyes helps you stay grounded in reality, and it keeps you awake! Having the eyes open doesn't centralize the notion of the self.

Just Sit Again

Now that you've got your posture right, bring your attention to your breath and note the "rising" and "falling." You can have your mouth slightly open with your tongue touching the palate, the roof of your mouth. This reduces salivation and it prevents you from unconsciously clenching your jaw. You can breathe through both your nose and your mouth, whatever. Frequently bring your attention to your posture, to your head and shoulders. Some people end up leaning over seven inches! As you continue sitting, very soon you will have a thought. You'll think about what you're planning on doing later tonight, or you'll think about something from work. It doesn't matter what thoughts you have. You just label the thoughts as 'thinking' whenever they arise, then come back to the breath. Whatever arises in the five senses of seeing, hearing, taste, touch and smell, is also labelled as 'thinking.' So whatever arises in the six senses is all labelled as thinking and you return to the breath. That's pretty much the whole technique. Try to remain still because it's good for building concentration, but if you have to move because of real physical pain, then that's O.K. Buddhism is the middle way. We work ourselves hard, but not too hard. It's good to make minor adjustments in your position to overcome pain.

When you're meditating, don't blame yourself for having a hopelessly wandering mind. Everyone feels that way, because everyone is that way. Everybody is the same. Your mind is not hopeless! Your mind is a workable situation. You can label thinking and come back to the breath. You can do it! You can meditate. It takes practice, like exercising a muscle. You must realize the vital importance of meditation practice so that you can spawn the discipline to apply effort. All anyone can do for you is to bring you to the beginning of the eightfold path. You must choose to tread that path, and do the rest yourself. Sangha is there to help keep you on track, but you must do your own work. That is the Buddhist approach, very much so.

Walking Meditation

After the above preamble, do sitting for 15 minutes, walking for 10, and sitting for another 20 minutes. Begin with a gong and end with a gong after the first sit. Go over the walking method with them. In the walking meditation technique put your hands together at the naval like the fat German shop keeper who smiles and nods at everyone, and is very satisfied with the world. In Zen style, clasp the left fingers around the thumb, and put the right thumb on top of the left hand. Then wrap the right fingers around the knuckles of the left hand. Don't clasp too tight! Relax into it. Then walk, saying to yourself 'step, step, step...' Be sure to label 'thinking,' and back to the feet, 'thinking,' back to the feet. Hit the wooden sticks together at the end of the walk, and go and stand over your cushion. When they are all standing together, then you all sit down together and go straight into your meditation without a gong.

It is not necessary to have walking meditation in a 45-minute period. Because this class may have beginners to meditation, extend compassion to them by giving them a break after 15 minutes of sitting. If they are getting sore, or restless, then they can walk before continuing on with another 20 minutes of sitting. 45 minutes of sitting is too much for people who are beginners. For a more experienced class, you can sit the whole time. Another advantage of walking is to keep people awake. Especially since you intend for them to sit through your class for at least another hour, it's good if they can walk around first to perk up their energy. Many of my students report that their sitting is more concentrated after the walking meditation, than before. This is because the walking builds up your concentration, then you go right into the sitting without a break. This builds the concentration even more. This is why Ajhan

Supan taught me, when I was a monk, to do the walking meditation first, and then the sitting. In this particular Vipassana technique, things are done differently.

After the gong, ask people how their meditation was. This is also a good time for announcements to the class. Once all the little things are done, you can go into your main talk for the day. In class two you may need more time to finish explaining the four noble truths from the previous class. It is always helpful to review the previous class anyway, to give students continuity. This chapter is enough for class two and three because history requires more than one class to do properly. You can refer to the chapter "Changing Buddha's Words," for more vital history on the Mahayana split. Because the true history revealed in this book is taboo to Mahayana Buddhists (not to Theravadins) you must be aware of the responsibility upon your shoulders in your community. If you are teaching Buddhist history to people that associate with other Buddhist groups, then they may be shocked because virtually no Mahayana lineage would ever tell the truth about the origins of the Mahayana. The burden of leadership, the burden of truth and honesty, may rest with you alone.

History

The history of how Buddhism gently flowed and shmoozed its way across Asia is a colourful one. The pre-history of Buddhism is also terribly fascinating. The Buddha was born in 623 B.C. (or maybe decades later) into a culture imbued with an advanced and sophisticated religious scene. One of the most startling books available about the pre-history and the early days is called *Hinduism, Buddhism and Brahmanism,* listed in the bibliography. This was the PhD thesis for professor Lal Joshi and he found that hundreds of millions of Hindus had the wrong idea about who the Buddha was. The Buddha said that as the bodhisattva in Tushita heaven, he chose the proper causes and conditions on earth into which to take birth, so that he could become the next Buddha. He came at the right time to the right family in the right kingdom. The Hindu religion claims that the Buddha was the ninth incarnation of the Hindu god Vishnu, the sustainer. Buddhism denies this claim. It sounds flattering but it is actually a derogatory claim. Most Hindus don't realize that Hinduism claims that the Buddha took birth to lead away the evil doers and the non believers. That's like saying that all the trash went to the Buddha to collect. This is just another case of the old game of religious subjugation, which Buddhist schools of thought do to each other as well.

Let's look at the causes and conditions into which Buddhism took root. Indian society at that time had two major streams of religious influence — the ascetics and the Brahmins. The ascetics were people who lived in the forest and practiced austerities; they ate fruit that fell off the trees, rather than picking it because you don't want to harm a tree, right? The ascetics were naked or wore rags, they practiced meditation and they engaged in self mortification. This is the false belief that mortifying the senses will overcome desire and lust. The ascetics were the most serious and sincere people who had embarked upon a spiritual path.

The Brahmins were the highest caste in Indian society, the religious caste. They were a privileged class and they performed the official ceremonies and chants for weddings, funerals, etc. They charged a lot of money for their services. When Prince Siddhartha was young he knew of a man who had died leaving behind a poor widow and children but the widow agreed to pay a big fee to the brahmin because she wanted her husband to have the best possible rebirth. This is because the most sacred chants were known only by the Brahmins and only they could use them to enable a person to move on to the best rebirth possible for them. Brahmins had a monopoly on god, god Brahma, and they showed it. Prince Siddhartha grew up not believing in the Brahmins and he didn't trust them. In the Long Discourses of the Buddha there is an account where the Buddha met with a Brahmin leader and the Buddha pointed out to him that the Brahmin had topless female attendants waiting on their whims, but the Buddha and his monks were celibate and lived in monasteries. The Brahmins were at odds with the ascetics because it really made them look bad that these ascetics were devoted to the spiritual life and they gave up all money, women and worldly attachments. It's easy to understand their professional jealousy. How would you feel if you were a spiritual teacher and one of your students became a living Buddha? You might hate the very thought of it and believe that nothing worse could happen! The Brahmins persecuted the ascetics from time to time and killed them. The Buddha's father was of the second highest class, the Kasitrya class, or warrior caste. Suddhodana Gotama was the king of the Sakya kingdom, but the Brahmins were the highest class since they were the representatives of god. This was the world into which Prince Siddhartha chose to take birth.

The flow of history since the parinirvana of the Buddha is rooted in the vast and rich teaching left behind by the Buddha. The Buddha went to great pains to ensure the recording and transmission of his teachings, as described in the chapter 'Rescuing Jesus.' After the first council the sangha had securely ensured for future generations, such as ours, the methods to preserve the deep priceless treasure of the holy dharma. One hundred years later the second council was convened and an evident rift or split in views occurred. This was the beginning of Mahayana Buddhism.

We don't know for sure where, or which group initiated Mahayana, but we are sure that the Buddha didn't. 110% for sure. Gotama Buddha had never heard of Mahayana or Vajrayana Buddhism. Mahayana Buddhism likely evolved directly from Mahasanghika antecedents. The Mahasanghikas were an offshoot that was born during the time of Mahadeva, who has been described as "the founder of Mahayana Buddhism." He was a leader who asserted that some arahants still required further development because they were subject to bad dreams, having seminal emissions in their sleep, having doubts, they were ignorant of many things and they owed their salvation to the guidance of others. Mahadeva asserted that some of these arahants were not fully enlightened at all, which gave room for the later Mahayana claim that their invention of bodhisattvas and celestial Buddhas are higher than arahants. This was the initial split, as best as history records; just a small thing really, a minor point of doctrine. But these Mahasanghikas became the vehicle through which new ideas could be given a forum in the Buddhist religion. This probably occurred in southeast India below the mouth of the Ganges River.

There is a very ancient story, a prophecy really, that the Prajnaparamita sutras would first appear in the south, then go east, and finally to the north. This prophecy is written in the Asta sutra and indicates how Mahayana origins are revealed in the first Mahayana sutras. In section six of that text (in Conze's translation) the whole work is focused on a careful definition of the word 'Mahayana,' under the sub-title 'The Meaning of the Great Vehicle.' The Asta sutra was one of if not the first specifically Mahayana sutra to appear, so the authors may have wanted to consolidate the existence of their newly made flimsy wheel. Kind of like the Russian Revolution of Buddhism, they had to assert what they were doing because the word Mahayana was unfamiliar at the time and required prompt definition. After two or three centuries since the split recorded at the second council, the Mahasanghikas grew in number and in confidence so they instituted one of the greatest marketing schemes known to human history. It was a corporate name change, calling themselves the greater wheel, the "Mahayana" and they put down the existing dominant Buddhist religion by calling it the lesser wheel, "Hinayana." This clever marketing strategy worked! very much so. Nearly everyone today buys into it. Edward Conze explains this sympathetically in his book *A Short History of Buddhism,* which is highly recommended for those interested in actually knowing the truth about Buddhist history. Sections of Conze's book are quoted in the chapter "Changing Buddha's Words," which has more vital information on history.

These Mahasanghikas, now the "Mahayanists," also invented deities and overwhelming visualization practices of light and form with staggering dimensions so you could also fairly describe the Mahayana as the Hollywood of Buddhism. This sexiness is part of the reason why Mahayana has caught on successfully and was better at exporting itself to other cultures beyond India than Theravadin Buddhism was. The Buddha was more real than flashy.

The assertion of the historic roots of the Mahayana can be seen today when countless Buddhist teachers explain to their receptive students that when the Buddha was 35, he made the first great turning of the wheel of dharma by teaching the Hinayana. Then, they eruditely explain that as the Buddha's disciples matured over the years, the Buddha initiated the second great turning of the wheel, and taught the Mahayana teachings. Nothing could be further from the truth. The Tibetans even stretch this scenario further and teach that late in the Buddha's life he initiated a select few of his senior disciples into the secret symbolic teachings of the Vajrayana. The "whispered lineage" of the Vajrayana is the third great turning of the wheel of dharma bestowing the ultimate teachings of the Buddha, Tibetans claim. Again, nothing could be further from the truth. At the end of this chapter there are even more outlandish claims about the 4th and 5th great turning of the wheel.

The truth, getting back to real historical evidence, is that at the second council they ratified the original Theravadin scriptures and they made the decision that this other small group of monks, (likely the predecessors to the Mahasanghika monks) had dreamed up a heresy. Being peaceful Buddhists, these two groups continued and coexisted. The great King Asoka, about 250 years after the Buddha, convened the third council and they once again lined up behind Theravadin Buddhism and rejected outright the Mahayana. In fact, King Asoka's purpose in convening the third council was to stamp out heresies that had gotten into the religion. Today Theravadins, generally speaking, renounce the Mahayana.

In one of my history classes a woman put up her hand and said "I came here to get some peace but now I feel like I'm in the middle of a war." Later three people dropped out of the course. So, you may want to put this history class near the end of the course instead of the beginning. Others say that studying history early on gives them a good framework to understand where Buddhist concepts come from.

During Asoka's reign the Mahayana was flourishing stronger than ever and moving north. Meanwhile, the great King was doing heroic deeds for humanity. Many historians today believe that he was the greatest emperor that ever lived, in recorded history. Asoka inherited the throne from his father and he ruled by conquest and violence until he took over most of the Indian subcontinent. By some auspicious turn of events, after King Asoka had won an exceedingly bloody campaign in the south, he met a Buddhist monk who impressed upon him the noble truth of suffering. King Asoka was moved and he contemplated all the suffering he had caused in his kingdom. He had a conversion experience, took refuge as a Buddhist and he became a virtuous, wise and peaceful ruler who greatly propagated the dharma. The histories of religions indicate that one powerful king or queen on your side can make a huge difference in propagating a religion.

The map opposite is adapted from a French book by Jacques Langlais. This shows the historic flow of Theravadin Buddhism — the black lines, and Mahayana Buddhism — the white lines. The broken lines indicate the path of secondary penetration, centuries after the initial spread of Buddhism. You can see how Vietnam received Buddhism from the opposite direction as Thailand. This is a very rich and fascinating history even to those uninterested in the Buddhist religion. Thai and Burmese kings had countless wars with each other over centuries where they would sack each other's ornate Buddhist temples, even though they were from the same tradition.

King Asoka sent his own son, then later his daughter, a monk and nun, to lead a mission to Sri Lanka. His son recited a sutra for the local king in Sri Lanka who was very impressed and promptly accepted Buddhism onto the island. It was a total success. Asoka also sent missionaries to the Burma/Thailand border where it also easily took root. Perhaps solely because of the vision of this one great man, Theravadin Buddhism has survived to the present day. Theravadin Buddhism is based in Sri Lanka, Burma, Thailand, Cambodia, Laos and in Cittigong, Bangladesh. It is a separate little Buddhist world as they generally renounce the Mahayana. Asoka also sent missions to Egypt, Cypress and Macedonia. Apparently Buddhism didn't catch on in the Middle East but it may have had some influence. Buddhism made it to Great Britain around 100 A.D., even before the Christian religion did!

It is difficult for 900 million Indians today to account for their country's

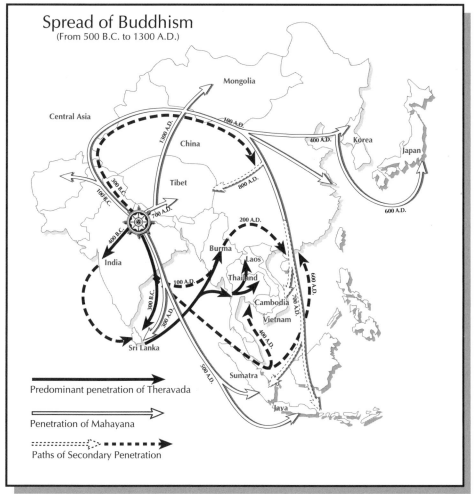

59

past because the period of Asoka was the most glorious phase of Indian history. India was a Buddhist country primarily, with a great Buddhist King sending Buddhism and Indian art and culture to the four corners of the earth. Today, the majority of Indians are Hindu so they cannot accept this Buddhist past. They regard Siddhartha Gotama as a Hindu teacher who taught a form of Hindu heterodoxy. It was not orthodox Hinduism in their view, but he reacted against some of the trends of his day and he came up with some non orthodox version of Hindu teachings, hence they call it a heterodoxy. They say that the Buddha was born a Hindu, lived as a Hindu and died a Hindu. Don't you believe it. Once again, this is another case of the ancient game of religious subjugation.

After King Asoka, Alexander the Great brought the West to the East. And it hasn't recovered since! He brought his Greek army into northwestern India and that's as far as he got before he died. The first meeting of the Western mind with the eastern guru occurred when Alexander directed his men to go out and find him some local philosophers. Alexander and his officers always loved to talk philosophy, and maybe Alexander was getting bored with Aristotle by then. His soldiers went out and they came upon a bunch of naked old codgers sitting on a burning hot rock! These were likely ascetics, perhaps Jain ascetics, but they weren't Buddhist monks. When the Greeks proposed to talk philosophy with the help of their 98 translators, the ascetics responded by saying, "How can you propose that we talk philosophy with a bunch of young men wearing military capes and boots? Take off your clothes, sit on a burning hot rock for about 90 years, then we can talk philosophy!"

Well, this wasn't working out very well and the Greeks were trying to figure out a way to satisfy their boss. Then, one of the ascetics steps up, much to the consternation of the other old yogis, and he agrees to go back to meet Alexander. Apparently, he became quite a favourite around Alexander's banquet table and they decided to bring him along on their trip back home to Greece when they left. After they moved west out of India, into Afghanistan, the yogi made them stop the caravan. He told them to build a great pyre of wood, which they did. Then, as the war elephants were turning circles around it, the ascetic sat on top and he said "Right, touch a torch to it." And poof! He went up in flames. And that was the Western mind's first encounter with the East. And it hasn't recovered since!

The Greeks were the most skilled sculptors in the world and they carved busts of their Greek gods such as Apollo. After the Greeks had settled in northern India many became converted to Buddhism and it was these Indians of Greek descent who first came up with the idea to carve statues of the Buddha! It was not until then, three centuries after the Buddha's death that the idea even arose to make such images of the Buddha. People just didn't have the skill or technology before; it was the Greeks who knew how to sculpt convincing images of people. Prior to this carvings depicted the Buddha's place as being an empty seat, or they would put a tree in the Buddha's place. Now, for the first time in history Buddhists had statues of the Buddha to venerate and the Greeks made the first Buddha images in the likeness of the Greek god Apollo. If you look at the oldest surviving statues of the Buddha from this period, they look suspiciously Greek. Although the sutras do describe 32 marks on the Buddha's body, such as blue eyes and being Aryan in descent, we do not know what the Buddha looked like. The statues of the Buddha caught on, north and south, in all schools of Buddhism and they remain today a great hit, with the central focus of a Buddhist temple being a statue of the Buddha, usually sitting in meditation. Every Buddhist country tends to make the Buddha look like their racial group. Chinese Buddha images look Chinese, Thai images look Thai, even though we all know that Prince Siddhartha came from the India/ Nepal region. This cultural ethnocentricity is not difficult to understand.

Buddhism Beyond India

Around this time Mahayana Buddhism was making a bigger push to the north. Around the time of Christ, the Mahayana had spread beyond India into Afghanistan and along the silk route. These were glory days for the blossoming altruism and heroism that is characteristic of the best in the Mahayanists. This is part of the basis for theories that Jesus Christ may have studied Mahayana Buddhism, since Israel was not too far away with their travel and technology. Over the next millennium Mahayana established dominance in the north of India, particularly in Kashmir, the northwest. This is a very big deal because it was through the trading caravans coming out of Kashmir that Mahayana Buddhism made it's way beyond India along the silk route. By 75 A.D. it had spread northwest, then east into China, and from China, Mahayana Buddhism captured Asia. The rest, as they say, is history.

The spread of Buddhism was a natural kind of osmosis. People would meet lay Buddhist merchants who would trade their wares in China and the local Chinese would say "Hey what's that meditation technique you were doing there?" The Indian Buddhist would reply, "Well sir, have a seat on the cushion over there and..." This is typically how Buddhism spreads across the world, not via some missionary zeal. It's like the tea cup and the tea. India is the tea cup from which the original dharma tea was brewed up. That tea was then poured into the cup of China, a different looking cup but with the same essential tea. So Buddhism transplants a shoot from one cultural superstructure to another cultural superstructure. The Mahayana adapted itself better for foreign cultures than the Theravadins did. Around 150 A.D., during the time of Buddhist dominance in the Kushana empire which bordered on India and Iran, the Iranians who converted to Mahayana Buddhism transformed their own sun god worship religious beliefs into worshipping a fictitious celestial Buddha of infinite light and immeasurable length of life, which is the meaning of "Amitabha Buddha." Today, this dominant form of Mahayana which can be seen practiced at most typical Oriental temples, is the result of this Iranian influence upon Buddhism back in 150 A.D., which is quite astounding and quite depressing.

When the dharma tea was poured from the Indian to the Chinese tea cup, so to speak, the tea got mixed with some of the flavour in the Chinese cup like Taoism and Confucism. By one of those incredible coincidences of history, the Buddha lived at the same time as Lao Tzu, who founded Taoism, and Confucius. Confucius was likely a younger contemporary of Lao Tzu, they may have known each other. The Buddha was more than a 1000 miles south, so they never met as it is not likely that the Buddha would dematerialize himself just to beam over to China to pay a visit to these obscure religious leaders. Confucius died believing that he was a loser, a failure, and Lao Tzu always kept the spotlight off of himself by hiding as much of his identity as he could.

In India, Mahayana and Theravadin Buddhist temples existed side by side for over a thousand years. There was no big tension between them. You could compare the Theravadins to the Catholic church and the Mahayanists to Protestant churches of today. The Theravadins dominated Buddhism in the south and the Mahayanists dominated the north. The Sanskrit language became associated with Mahayana and the Pali language remained the vital language of Theravadin Buddhism. By the time Buddhaghosa wrote his great commentary they were deliberately propping up the Pali language in an effort to compete with the Mahayanists using Sanskrit. The Theravadins felt strongly that it was their mission to preserve Pali. The loftiness and the appeal of Mahayana was bigger on the subcontinent of India than the Theravadin lineage was. Sri Lanka was feeling a bit more isolated perhaps. Buddhaghosa was originally from India and had visited the four holy sites: where the Buddha was born, attained enlightenment, first turned the wheel of dharma, and passed away. There is speculation that Buddhaghosa may have been a committee of 32 enlightened or near enlightened monks, because his work seems too voluminous for one monk.

Around 500 or 600 A.D. Hinduism was gaining ground in Buddhist territory and gradually swallowing up Buddhism. The Buddha himself taught that Buddhists should encompass other religious beliefs rather that reject them if possible. This is the basis for the apparent happening that Buddhist temples were encompassing Hindu beliefs, but they would interpret them in a non theistic way. Many Buddhists believe that it is this process that created the birth of Vajrayana Buddhism, or 'Tibetan Buddhism.' This is the view that Vajrayana Buddhism and much of Mahayana Buddhism is original Buddhism mixed together with Hinduism. Many of the deities invoked in Mahayana and Vajrayana are to be found in the Hindu pantheon. The Buddha never said one word about their existence in over 3000 pages of Theravadin Buddhist scripture. This is one reason why the Theravadin Buddhist scriptures are considered to be the most authentic record of what the Buddha taught.

The number one hit deity of Tibet is Avalokitesvara; they believe that this deity of compassion is incarnate in the Dalai Lama (the Dalai Lama makes no such claim). In the Mahayana version of the Heart Sutra we see Avalokitesvara giving a discourse with the Buddha and his chief disciple Sariputra. This is one of the proudest sutras of Mahayana Buddhism, chanted everyday by millions. But the Theravadin sutras have another version of the Heart sutra with no Avalokitesvara present, it's Sariputra that does most of the talking. Apparently, the Mahayanists wrote out Sariputra and wrote in Avalokitesvara. As Joseph Campbell says "It's not a lie. It's a metaphor." The Mahayanists feel that they have an excellent practice going; it really doesn't matter that much that these events never actually took place as such. What matters is that the mental construct in one's mind, of the deity of compassion, invokes a greater sense of compassion in the practitioner. That's what really matters. So, what the hey?

This process of Hinduism swallowing up Buddhism grew from 700 A.D. into 800 A.D. and to 1000 A.D. This was the era when Buddhism reached it's most elaborate phase in history, the glory days. Nalanda monastery from the early centuries A.D. had grown into the great Nalanda University housing over 10,000 monks, the largest university in the world.

The great Indian guru Padmasambhava became the father of Tibetan Buddhism and he is regarded as a fully enlightened mahasiddha by Tibetan Buddhists. He brought the dharma into Tibet around 763 A.D. and he uttered the great prophecy:

> When the iron bird flies, and horses travel on wheels
> The people of Tibet will be spread across the world like ants
> And the dharma will come to the land of the red faced people

In *A Short History of Buddhism,* Edward Conze writes:

> At first Buddhism in Tibet met with fierce resistance from the shamans of the native Bon religion, who had the support of the greater nobility. The patronage of the king, however, enabled the Buddhists gradually to establish themselves, and under King Ral-pa-can (817-36) they reached the height of their influence. From the West, from the Swat valley, came the Tantric ideas of Padmasambhava, who himself stayed in Tibet for a short while. Padmasambhava's mentality had considerable affinities with that of the Bon and he had a striking success in Tibet. He expounded some kind of Vajrayanic system, but we do not know exactly which one. The impression he made on Tibet was chiefly based on his thaumaturgical activities and the legend has quite overgrown the historical facts. The school of the Nyingmapa, or

"Ancient Ones," goes back to Padmasambhava and has persisted continuously up to today (Conze, 1980; 96).

Theravadin temples were also established in Tibet but they offered no magical powers or magical teachings which the Tibetans were quite fond of so the Theravadins went almost unnoticed and they declined in popularity. About a century after Padmasambhava, around 860, Tibetan king Langdarma hated Buddhism and did all he could to destroy it and vanquish it in Tibet. This went on for six horrible years until some compassionate being came along and assassinated King Langdarma. Wonderful! Free at last! During the reconstruction phase of Buddhism in Tibet, the next great father of Tibetan Buddhism was Tilopa, an Indian from Bengal. He was an enlightened mahasiddha and he (although the Theravadins refute this possibility) is believed to have received transmission of what is today known as Vajrayana Buddhism. This came from Vajradhara, a dharmakaya Buddha. The Theravadin teachings describe the dharmakaya as the residing place of enlightened mind, the nirvana which is beyond as well as inseparable from samsara. Tilopa received this stream of teachings, some secret, and this is being passed down through all four major lineages of Tibetan Buddhism today. Tibetan Buddhists claim that the Buddha taught Vajrayana, but he didn't. The Buddha claimed that he held no secrets in the clenched fist of the teacher, but the problem here is that the Vajrayana is based on levels of secret initiations. The Buddha never taught that, but it's O.K. for the Tibetans to express Buddhism in their own cultural way, which is more like Hinduism in it's initiations. They justified this by saying that it was the Buddha, in a sense, because the Buddha is one with the dharmakaya, therefore anything streaming down and channelled from the dharmakaya comes from the Buddha. Other Tibetan Buddhists say different things. Again, it's not a lie, it's a myth. Whatever works.

Once established in Tibet, the Buddhists followed the Buddha's open policy of absorbing the local religion into the Buddhist non theistic view. After taking a non theistic view that included Hindu higher realm perceptions, the Buddhists re-evaluated the preexisting Bon religion of Tibet. They included into Vajrayana Buddhism the many colourful Bon visualizations of beings holding human skull cups and warriors on horses flying through the air. In this way, Tibetan Buddhism carried on to the present day. The Tibetans warn that the powers of the Vajrayana could be extremely dangerous if not handled properly but this is also true of shamanic powers. Some other Buddhists view the Vajrayana as a form of shamanism, suspecting that the preexisting shamanism of the Bon practices influenced the creation of the Tibetan version of Vajrayana Buddhism.

Around 1000 A.D. their was a great Indian Buddhist named Atisha. He studied under various Theravadin and Mahayana masters and went to Indonesia for ten years. Indonesia was a thriving, glorious Mahayana Buddhist country in

1000 A.D.. Today Borobudur, Indonesia on the island of Java is the location of the world's largest Buddhist monument, a huge circular stone temple, a tourist attraction in a Muslim country. Atisha went back to India and the King of Tibet sent supplications to him many times to teach in Tibet. Atisha finally gave in and spent the rest of his life spreading Buddhism in Tibet. He popularized the Mahayana mind training slogans called Lojong which remain popular today for developing compassion.

The spread of Buddhism into China was aided by various Chinese emperors and empresses. After the initial trickle about 75 A.D., the dharma flourished when an emperor would be converted and then offer infrastructure and influence. Some of them helped Christian teachers in much the same way. The Chinese pilgrim Hsuan-tsang in the mid-seventh century, and others made great efforts to translate many Sanskrit sutras and bring them back home to China. Some would be supported by emperors with whole caravans travelling for a year or more to go to India. A popular destination was the famous Nalanda University. Many Chinese monks would study there for years and attain enlightenment or high states of realization, then bring dharma treasures into the rich and sophisticated Chinese culture. Today we owe so much of the northern tradition of Buddhism to Chinese translations. Almost all of the original Sanskrit records of the Mahayana sutras are lost. We have the Chinese and Tibetan translations. The Tibetans obtained much more from India than the Chinese did. Another big advantage of China is that they were far superior than the Indians were at record keeping. They had paper, or something like paper long before their southern counterparts, and China's cool climate preserved writings better than hot moist India.

Around 500 A.D. the biggest hero of Zen Buddhism arrived in China — Bodhidharma. Most Zen Buddhists prefer to say that he came from a Brahmin family in southern India but the historic accounts are hopelessly at odds, one saying that Bodhidharma came from Afghanistan. Zen is the Japanese word for the Chinese Ch'an. This refers to samadhi, or a tradition of Buddhism putting greater than average emphasis upon the practice of sitting meditation. We don't know the early history of Zen or if it even had one in India. In Zen they like to think of the Buddha's disciple Maha Kassapa as the second patriarch of Zen after the Buddha, then Ananda as the third patriarch, etc., but there is no evidence that there is any proper Zen lineage as such which goes back to the Buddha. Again, like the Mahayanists and the Vajrayanists, followers of Zen would like to believe that their tradition as such goes right back to the Buddha, but this is not the case. The Theravadin tradition of Vipassana meditation has quite an affinity with Zen meditation practice and some Theravadins proudly regard Zen as a form of Vipassana that succeeded in the north.

Bodhidharma's approach caught on because of the causes and conditions in

China of that day. People were getting fed up with the overdone rituals and the intellectualization of the dharma. Humorous accounts abound of his outrageous statements when he first met the ruler in China. The emperor told him that he had built many Buddhist temples and supported them generously for years. When the emperor asked Bodhidharma if there was great merit in that, Bodhidharma replied "None whatsoever!" His point being that the emperor should sit and meditate to earn merit, not buy it. The emperor did not throw himself at Bodhidharma's feet as many people did for the Buddha, instead the emperor sent the monk on his way. Historic accounts of the pivotal and very important figure of Bodhidharma are steeped in legends and we actually know little about him. It was his lineage, six or more generations later, that really took off in China and spread 'Zen' Buddhism beyond China.

The dharma peacefully transformed and uplifted people's lives across China and then into Korea around 500 A.D. From there, arousing more faith and devotion, the buddhadharma transcended the continent and entered into Japan. Zen took on a real Japanese style with meditation instructors that would go around with a stick, whacking people (they invited the whack, you understand) when they fell asleep or lost their posture. The Japanese Buddhists were known for their discipline, and for making great Japanese rock gardens. The dharma always takes on the colours of it's surroundings, and cleans up those colours. Today the number one religion in the world is, without a doubt, science. In Japan today the number two religion is materialism. Buddhism in Japan is disappointing today. In slower areas Zen meditation is still strong. Like much of Asia however, there are the colours, scents and sounds of Buddhism, but people don't give it a second thought. This is an inspiring indication for those who believe that the future of Buddhism is in the West.

Back in India, during that golden heyday after the turn of the millennium, tragedy struck: Islam. We can expect something like this again, halting our present heyday of peace, after the beginning of the third millennium. It may be the same problem repeating itself because the wise Nostradamus, who predicted a 'Hister,' also predicted that 'a man wearing a blue Turban will rise out of Persia and he will be the terror of mankind.' The time to wake up and build our readiness is yesterday. We will likely lose. We will likely lose whatever it is that we hold dear — like the dharma. We must protect the container of the Buddhadharma for future generations. Nostradamus didn't say 'the terror of Europe,' he specifically stated, 'the terror of mankind,' and that means you. The world will not die; it will live for billions of more years; the Buddha described this process. But, this kalpa could drop dead any day now.

The Islamic attack on India came from the West, the northwest, survivors reported. By 1197 A.D. a rain of Turk Muslims utterly *WIPED OUT* Buddhism from the sub-continent of India. Utterly and completely wiped it right out! Kalpa karma usually works that way — the major ripening of some major karmic whatever, from earlier in the kalpa or even a previous kalpa (an age). For a fictitious example, suppose the ancestors from Ontario conquered all and killed half of the ancestors from Quebec. Centuries later the descendants of the victors are at the verge of enlightenment. Then national kalpa karma comes to fruition and suddenly Quebec invades and conquers all and kills half of the inhabitants of Ontario. Tit for tat.

When the Muslim Turks came in smashing in the name of god, Buddhist monks were easy to identify, so they were all killed, being mistaken for idolaters. The Hindu leaders were priests and family men. Hinduism survived. It took the Muslims several months just to burn down the library at Nalanda University, which was similar to the great library of Alexandria, Egypt, in that we will never know how much literature was lost. The Muslim historian Minhazad recorded these events in the book *Tavakata*:

> "In the middle of the city there was a temple which can be neither described nor painted. The Sultan wrote that 'it would occupy two hundred years to construct, even though the most experienced and able workmen were employed.' The Sultan gave orders that all the temples should be burnt with naphtha and fire, and levelled with the ground.

> Many of the inhabitants of the place fled and were scattered abroad. Many of them thus effected their escape, and those who did not fly were put to death. Islam or death was the alternative that Muhmud placed before the people.

> Most of the inhabitants of the place were brahmans with shaven heads (i.e., Buddhist monks). They were put to death. Large numbers of books were found there, and when the Muhammadans saw them, they called for some persons to explain their contents, but all the men had been killed.

> If they adopt our creed, well and good. If not, we put them to the sword. The Muhammadan forces began to kill and slaughter on the right and on the left unmercifully, throughout the impure land, for the sake of Islam and blood flowed in torrents. They plundered gold and silver to an extent greater than can be conceived, and an immense number of handsome and elegant maidens, amounting to 20,000, and children of both sexes, more than the pen can enumerate.

> He fell upon the insurgents unawares, and captured them all, to the number of twelve thousand — men, women and children — whom he put to the sword. All their valleys and strongholds were overrun

and cleared, and great booty captured. Thanks be to God for this victory of Islam.

After wounding and killing beyond all measure, his hands and those of his friends became cold in counting the value of the plundered property. On the completion to his conquest he returned and promulgated accounts of the victories obtained for Islam, and every one, great and small, concurred in rejoicing over this result and thanking God."

Many conclude that this Muslim Turk invasion was the major cause of the disappearance of Buddhism from its homeland. This supports the traditional charge that Islam is a religion of the sword, spread by the sword and upheld by the sword. People who support this view quote from the Koran (Al-Qur'an):

"Prescribed for you is fighting, though it is hateful unto you" (2:212) "O prophet ! Strive against the disbelievers and the hypocrites ! Be harsh with them. Their ultimate abode is Hell, a hapless journey's end." (9:73)

"O prophet ! Exhort the believers to fight. If there be of you twenty steadfast, they shall overcome two hundred, and if there be of you a hundred steadfast, they shall overcome a thousand of those who disbelieve, because they are a folk without intelligence." (8:65)

"Truly, those who do not believe our verses we shall fry in the fire." (4:56)

"Fight them then that there should be no sedition, and that the religion may be wholly God's." (8:40)

"Fight those who believe not in God and in the last day, and who forbid not what God and his apostle have forbidden, and who do not practice the religion of truth from among those to whom the Book has been brought, until they pay tribute by their hands and be as little ones." (9:29)

"O believers ! Make not friends of your fathers or your brethren if they love unbelief above faith: and whose to you shall make them his friends, will be wrongdoers." (9:23)

"Whoever fights for the way of Allah and is killed or victorious will receive a glorious reward." (4:74)

In the book *Thai Buddhism in the Buddhist World,* Thailand's foremost scholar monk, Phra Payutto, refers to these passages from the Koran and he sympathetically states that Muslim scholars do not approve of the view that Islam is a religion of the sword. Phra Payutto writes:

> "They say the above quotations should not be made here as a support to the charge. For this, they point to at least two reasons. Firstly, some of the above quotations refer only to the early events during the lifetime of Muhammad when he fought to found the religion, the word fighting or war is not to be interpreted as a physical fighting, but it means that of the spiritual life.
>
> Muslim scholars further explain that the word Islam means 'peace' or 'submission to the will of God,' and [a] Muslim, an adherent of Islam, means 'one devoted to peace.' Islam teaches religious tolerance and condemns persecution. They also quote from the Koran:
>
> "There is no compulsion in religion." (2:256)
>
> "Defend yourself against your enemies; but attack them not first. Allah loveth not aggressors." (2:190)
>
> "Unto you your religion, and unto me my religion." (109:6)
>
> "So, if they hold aloof from you and wage not war against you and offer peace, Allah alloweth you no way against them." (4:90)
>
> "O ye who believe ! When ye go forth to fight in the way of Allah, make investigation, and say not unto one who offereth you the salutation of peace: 'Thou art not a believer.' (4:96)"

Phra Payutto continues: "The Turks who invaded India and persecuted the Buddhists did so only out of the desire for power and territorial expansion. They used the religion to conceal their crimes. True Muslims or those who know the spirit of Islam would not do that. Muslim scholars say the Christian record of intolerance is greater than theirs. It was the Christians who preached the crusades and used their faith as a tool for the expansion of colonialism. It was also the Christians who, quarrelling among themselves over Christian dogma, caused innumerable religious wars and persecutions. On the contrary, in Thailand, all the Muslims have lived peacefully among the friendly Buddhists throughout its history [Kureshi, 1952; 119].

The above explanation of Muslim scholars can be a great comfort to the world. The Turks who destroyed Buddhism while invading India were not true Muslims. True Muslims know the true spirit of Islam and devote themselves to the way of peace. We can now hope that Muslims in the future will be true Muslims and [this] sad and terrible history will not repeat itself (Payutto, 1984; 47)."

Buddhism perished from existence in India and was not reintroduced until the 20th century. Today there is only token Buddhism at the holy sites, but Buddhist teachers such as S. Goenka have made practical strides to reawaken India to her noblest heart. 1197 A.D. was the last year of this great enlightened time on earth when Buddhism had reached it's apex, its zenith on this planet during this kalpa. We probably will not see such wisdom, compassion and virtue until the awakening of Maitreya Buddha (the Buddha of compassion) in a year approximate to 4400 A.D., according to the Buddha. In the Thai tradition it is said that the Buddha prophesied that his teachings would splinter into degenerate groups until the dharma fell apart completely and died off. This is great news because traditionally, this is a necessary phase before the next Buddha can take birth. It is not possible for a Buddha to be born as long as Buddhism exists on Earth in an acceptable form. Sorry. That means that you have to do your own homework instead of waiting for the next big guru to happen.

In the Buddha's description of a kalpa he indicated that a degenerate period will occur before the time of the next Buddha but that this is not the end of the world, which Nostradamus predicted for the year 3797 A.D. Perhaps Nostradamus meant the end of the world as people will know it but not the physical destruction of the planet, because his timing coincides well with the Buddha's. It would be in accordance with Buddhism if our present kalpa bottoms out at 3797 A.D., because the next Buddha should take birth and appear after that, around 4400 A.D.

Sri Lanka

Mohammed made it big around 622 A.D. and it took about four centuries before the presence of Islam was felt in India. Fortunately, coming overland, the Muslims may not have been good swimmers, or seamen, so they never got on a boat and travelled over to Sri Lanka. Bless the devas, Theravadin Buddhism survived in Sri Lanka up to the present day. Because Indian Buddhism was blown off the face of the planet, Sri Lanka is known as 'the home of Buddhism.' The Muslims carried on into what is present day Afghanistan, Pakistan, Bangladesh and Indonesia, leaving behind a few surviving 'Buddhist historic sites.' Today in Afghanistan many ancient and exquisitely beautiful large stone carvings of Buddhas can be seen in the side of cliffs. Beautiful, except for the faces that have been blown off. The manpower was not invested to blow up all of the rock sculptures.

The dharmic situation in Sri Lanka (formerly Ceylon) has never been very stable for very long. The scriptures were first written down there, around 100 B.C. As kings would come and go some loved the Buddhist religion and some hated it. It's quite a story and this is published in a small book about Buddhism in Sri Lanka, offered by the Buddhist Publication Society in Kandy, Sri Lanka. One prince turned against his father the king and assassinated him. (The Buddha's old friend King Bimbisara was bumped off the same way; this is a chronic problem that occurs in royal families.) The new king in Sri Lanka had some thoughts of misgiving about his heinous crime so he asked some Buddhist monks if there was any hope that he could redeem himself from his bad karma. The monks replied with a flat out "no." Big mistake. The king methodically organized the 'planting of monks.' Many monks were buried in the ground up to their necks, then large metal blades were rushed along the surface of the earth, cutting off their heads. Several times the religion was so decimated that once sanity was restored, there were no monks left with the higher ordination (monks, not novices). Sri Lanka would send ships to Thailand and Burma in a quest to mine their monastic treasures and they would bring monks back to Sri Lanka to re-establish their monasteries. These three countries saved each other's dharmic skin many times, a heroic tale of true believers devoting every fibre of their country's being to keep the torch of dharma blazing. This story would make for a great movie and help balance out the 139 movies about Tibet.

Sanity seesawed back and forth in Sri Lanka and then the first Europeans arrived around 1500. The first settlers were the Portuguese and they brought along Roman Catholic priests and missionaries. The Portuguese Catholics were much more zealous than the later Dutch Catholics, in regards to converting the natives to their Catholic faith. Here we go again. Many Buddhists that refused to convert to Catholicism were killed. Fathers were thrown to alligators. Mothers would be killed after they watched Catholic priests insert their babies between large millstones, crushing them to death. The priests had to be careful not only about not getting their fingers caught, but they had to push the babies through head first because if they inserted the Buddhist babies in feet first, then the priest could get human brain tissue splattered on his robes, which took some effort to wash out. These robes weren't just any ordinary robe, they came all the way from Portugal! They had to be real careful. Putting yourself in their shoes you can appreciate the effort, hardship and sheer work that the Catholic priests had to endure to keep stains off of their robes!

In the 1700s the Dutch took over from the Portuguese but they were more concerned with making a buck than with enlightening the Buddhists with their Catholic faith. They installed some Catholic infrastructure, but focused on trading and bringing tropical wares home to Holland. The British took over in the 1800s and they had very proper rules about respecting the local religion and not laying a Christian trip on the Ceylonese. However, the British magistrates clandestinely supported the efforts of missionaries to do their thing. There is a sacred mountain which the people of Sri Lanka traditionally believe was visited by the Buddha during one of his dematerialization treks. The Brits renamed the mountain as 'Adam's Peak.' The English weren't so bad actually. In the 1880s there was a legendary showdown between one fantastically brilliant novice monk and the Christian clergy. They had several greatly publicized debates on theological matters and the calm young monk kicked the Christian butts right across the Indian ocean, so to speak. These were the glory days of the great American, Col. Henry Steel Olcott. The novice monk was Col. Olcott's hand picked golden boy. Olcott formed the Theosophical Society with Madame Blavatsky, but soon they converted to Buddhism. Olcott became revered almost as a deva by the Ceylonese because he succeeded in constructing hundreds of Buddhist schools as a clever technique to undermine and wrest away the influence of British Christian schools from indoctrinating young people. Olcott succeeded so masterfully that he is today on postage stamps in Sri Lanka and many credit him for near single handedly redeeming the dharma. As a career move I decided to make my last life that of Col. Olcott but at some point, I changed my mind.

The example of Sri Lanka is studied here, not going into details about the heartwarming parallel history in other Buddhist countries (this book is thick enough). Jumping to Europe, Buddhism was introduced to the West in the mid 19th century by German and British anthropologists. They were in Asia happily going about their anthropologizing ways when they happened upon Buddhist scriptures and inscriptions in stone. They said "I say, perhaps we should translate some of this and earn ourselves a proper degree." In the end, the Buddhists never came to Europe or America really. It was the Westerners who came begging for more and more, up to the present day. Compare that to Christian missionary work in the Philippines and the rest of the world.

The Europeans generally thought of the Buddha as some mythological character from the Hindu pantheon of gods. Then, in northeastern India in 1851 Sir Alexander Cunningham discovered the stupa of Sariputra and Maha Moggallana. He opened it and inside the mound of rocks he uncovered the two urns, each inscribed with a syllable denoting the names of the two most important monks in Buddhist history, after the Buddha himself. Sariputra's relics were on the south side and Maha Moggallana's relics were on the north side. Their bones were arranged this way because they always took their place seated beside the Buddha with Sariputra as the Buddha's right hand man. Moggallana sat on his left and the Buddha preferred to sit facing the great eastern sun. Their urns were arranged in honour of their position beside the Buddha in life.

A Japanese Zen Buddhist monk was officially present at the World Council of Religions in Chicago in 1873, marking one of the very first fine moments in American Buddhism. In Germany, Theravadin Buddhism received solid support since the late 1800s. Carl Jung, the famous Swiss psychologist, was quoted as saying "Of all the religions in the world, Buddhism is surely the greatest one." He said many fine words about the Buddha's teachings which also boosted up the dharma in the West. Arriving in America were Chinese and other Asian immigrants who brought to the West their cultural form of Buddhism. In the 1920s Daisetz Suzuki brought Zen to the West single-handed. The 1950s saw the Beatnik dharma bum scene happen with Jack Kerouac. Then in 1970 a Tibetan lama came from Scotland to America. He took a flight which descended on a beam of indescribable light and echoed deva music all over Boulder, Colorado. As the doors of the plane opened, a flock of dakas and dakinis flew out in formation flying and disappeared into the sky, flying straight into the sun. Earth eyes could not witness any of this. Out of the plane stepped the man who was the vanguard of Buddhism in the western hemisphere. The man who defined Buddhism in the 1970s, the David Bowie of the dharma, a teacher who could actually speak English, he was Chögyam Trungpa Rinpoche, the great Vidyadhara. Tibet was reborn. The lotus seed took deep root. Generations to come will grow to believe that a bodhisattva such as this, in flesh and blood, transmitted perfect mahadharma. The large scale concerns of the bodhisattvas of the fine material sphere made manifest a blessing upon the United States that was a dharma asteroid. The shock waves went so deep that only a few souls can feel it today. Like the magma shmoozing up through the Earth's crust, the rest is future history.

The 4th and 5th Great Turning of the Wheel

People cannot seem to find out when Buddhist deities first entered into our religion's history. The reason for this is that the Mahayanists may not want to draw attention to the fact that all of the celestial Buddhas and bodhisattvas were first known to Buddhism centuries after the life of the Buddha. Because the Mahayanists have written many sutras depicting the Buddha giving discourses with or about these colourful deities, they may not want their own people to know that there is no historical basis for these alleged discourses of the Buddha. Other sutras may have been channelled down from the devas in the higher realms who could have recorded sutras and passed them on to humans centuries later. This is in fact possible. The Theravadins claim that this is how the abhidharma was composed after the Buddha's lifetime. The problem with the Mahayana sutras is that they depict many historical people — including all of the Buddha's senior disciples — saying and doing volumes of incredible things, which are not in the Theravadin canon. In the Heart Sutra this includes blue light gushing out of the Buddha's mouth and going across the entire universe and back. It is impossible that these lengthy historic events could have happened and somehow escaped the awareness of all of the elders at the first council. Impossible. The truth is that these Mahayana 'sutras' were fabricated later and these alleged sutras are master-fully designed to support various Mahayana Buddhist views.

It seems that no matter where you go or who you ask, no one will give you a straight answer about which century these Mahayana sutras first appeared, or the 'tantra sutras' for that matter. You can discover this, but you won't receive much enthusiastic support. What is the truth, and what is the official story?

The truth is that the Buddha's dharma is like a beautiful house. He called the house Buddhism. Later it had to be named Theravadin Buddhism because a group of monks painted the house and called it Mahayana Buddhism. Because of this confusion, we remember the original house as the Theravadin tradition. The Mahayanists claim that they have a greater wheel, the great vehicle. The truth is that the beautiful house now has a rich and elegant paint job so it is even more beautiful. The Tibetan Buddhists come along and they claim that particular sections of the paint job are far superior to the rest of the paint job. The original painters claim that it's all the same. The house builder, the Buddha, feels that it's still the same house, no need to fuss about the paint job. The Tibetans claim that anything painted on the top third of the house is the result of the Buddha's third great turning of the wheel— Vajrayana Buddhism, the ultimate, indestructible and secret teachings of the Buddha. The Buddha whispered into their forefathers' ears about how to paint it, that's why it took some centuries for the job to be seen, they say.

The Tibetans in the Rime lineage (nonsectarian practice lineage) claim that a secret fourth turning or cycle of the dharma wheel is taught. This is the consummate and ultimate Buddhist teaching known in Tibetan as Dzogchen. On the house this is represented as the shingles on the back side of the roof that you can't see. They're very subtle, they don't stand out. The venerators of these allegedly rare and precious shingles consider them to be the most direct non-dual approach to awakening the Buddha within. Dzogchen stresses non-duality (as if Theravadin Buddhism doesn't!!), ecstatic spontaneity, and the natural great perfection of things just as they are. Wow! This is such a wonderful house now! But one wonders, why did the Buddha choose to divide up his teachings in such a way??

Now that the dharma is rooted into the western hemisphere, a discovery in a cave beyond Grouse Mountain indicates that the Buddha, only three months before his parinirvana initiated the fifth great turning of the wheel of dharma. There was an earthquake back then, which has revealed only now, what is today known as the ultimate consummate merging of the esoteric Hollywood School with the sacred wisdom teachings of the Buddhadharma. This fifth and last turning of the wheel, the 'seal of the wheels' (the Buddha's arm was getting pretty tired at that point), is believed to have originated in the Buddha's deva eye seeing into the future. This is the Bugs Bunnyyana and Bugs is staying in the metaphorical house above. As the bodhisattvas received the whispered Vajrayana lineage, the Buddha empowered a deva, who in the future grew to manifest the bodhisattva activity of Bugs Bunny. These teachings reveal how the spontaneous wit and fluid nowness of the bodhisattva transmitted his wisdom through the technologies provided by the 20th century to result in timeless teachings appreciated by all cultures. The process of development for the bodhisattva's next great stage of teachings in mass media Buddhism is known only to the esoteric few who learned the mysteries of the Buddha's great fifth turning of the wheel of dharma.

Normally viewed as a fictitious cartoon character created by Warner Brothers, the bodhisattva transcended to deity status and uplifted the world by entering into the thought stream of the cartoonists, to result in the spontaneous wisdom flow of Bugs Bunny's mastery of the present moment. The Buddha foresaw this and this is indicated in the yanashmanasutra which he uttered during that great earthquake which was caused by the Enlightened One's relinquishing his will to live.

The key point here is that the house of dharma built by the Buddha has always remained the same house since the time when the Lord Buddha found the open way and proclaimed the banner of sanity. All of the painters have unfairly put down the importance of the original house because they took it for granted and they got too proud of their paint.

Class Three – Give and Take

In class three introduce the give and take contemplation on compassion (tonglen) which is described in detail in Chapter 10, 'Practices.' After a short discussion and review of the sitting and walking meditation techniques, start the meditation period within the first ten or fifteen minutes. You could do 15 minutes of sitting and 10 minutes of walking. For the rest of the classes described in this book, you may choose whatever combination you want, for sitting and walking meditation times, as well as additional contemplations or guided visualization meditations.

After your initial walking meditation in class three, when you all sit down together, teach the give and take technique and lead the group through 10 minutes of that practice. Do a double roll down on the gong to indicate that they should stop doing give and take, and switch back to the regular Vipassana meditation technique. Continue that for 10 minutes more, making a total of 45 minutes of practice. The double roll down technique is done with your gong and stick. You could use a meditation gong of about 4 inches in diameter, or another size. It's purpose is to be used to start and stop group meditation periods. The Zen term used for the meditation leader is the 'umdze.' Like a ping pong ball bouncing, the double roll down is two series of gongs that get faster, then stop. Then you finish it off with a medium, a soft and a firmer gong. Once completed, they've got the message. In this way you elegantly communicate with the meditators without speaking. It's good.

The give and take practice should be done frequently in future classes, but not every class. Compassion is so important and this is such a wonderful practice, that you should make it a mainstay in the class that you teach, and train people to make it a part of their lives. That is why you do not wait for the class on compassion to introduce the give and take practice. You want people to be proficient at it before the compassion class. You may wait until the third class to introduce give and take simply to pace the techniques you are asking people to learn. There's no set rule about when to teach give and take, and the Buddhist religion does not own the copyright on compassion.

Chapter 4

Class Four and Five
The Eightfold Path

There is more than enough information here for two talks on the eightfold path. You can use what you like or combine it with other Buddhist books on the same subject. The eightfold path is the fourth noble truth. This is the truth that there is a way out of suffering. There is a way out of here. There is a way out of this place. The Buddha prescribed his teaching like a doctor for the universe, and he said that the way to reach the deathless state of nirvana is by practising eight things. Sometimes we experience moments of peace, moments of tranquillity, but we cannot sustain that for very long. Even if we stop our thoughts and rest the mind in primordial space, we can't keep it up for long. We need some kind of discipline to bring us to letting be. We need to walk on a spiritual path of some kind. This is the great pilgrimage from here to here.

First, an overview of the path, then more detail on each one. This approach comes from a time management philosophy about how to read a book, which is taught by Brian Tracy, the success guru. People retain information better if they first look over a book and read the table of contents. Then, read the first line or so of each chapter. Then, randomly skim through the book to get a feel for how the book is laid out. After this approach, you go back and read the whole book from page one. This gives your mind a conceptual framework for which to plug in information from the book, so your memory retention is better that way. Let this guide your Buddhism teaching and learning methods. This has an affect on how I teach Buddhism. The overview of the path to nirvana is traditionally depicted by a wheel with eight spokes, as shown below.

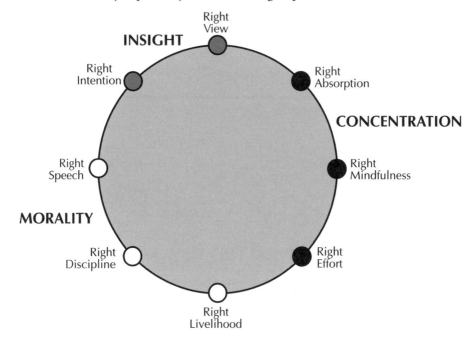

The eight are divided into three inseparable stages, as such:

> **Morality**: right speech, right discipline, right livelihood.

> **Concentration**: right effort, right mindfulness, right absorption.

> **Insight** or wisdom: right view, right intention.

The Buddha taught this path in his first formal discourse which was the dharmachakra sutra, the turning of the wheel discourse. Of great historic significance, the Buddha first turned the wheel of his teachings in Deer Park for his five former colleagues. This path is called "the middle way," meaning, the avoidance of extremes. Avoid the extreme of indulgence in sensuous pleasure, and avoid the extreme of self mortification with asceticism, which is 'painful, unworthy and unprofitable.' As shown, the path is divided into three stages: morality, concentration, insight. In Sanskrit, the original terms for these are sila, samadhi and prajna. As much as possible in this course an effort is made to try to use plain English, but there are some terms from Pali and Sanskrit which should be explained. Morality, ethical conduct, is based upon the Buddha's vast conception of universal love and compassion for all living beings. This basis of the Buddhist path is not some head trip based on a dry set of rules. The Buddha gave his teaching with heart 'for the good of the many, for the happiness of the many, out of compassion for the world.' In order to be perfect a person must develop equally the two qualities of compassion and wisdom.

The word 'right' is translated from the Sanskrit word 'samyak' which also means 'complete.' It implies a totality that doesn't need right or wrong as a reference point. It is being right without a concept of what is right. It needs no relative help, no support through comparison; it is self sufficient. But, as well as thinking of this completeness, you can also think of right vs. wrong in the more conventional sense.

These eight parts of the path are to be practiced concurrently as a way of life. The Buddha presented them in this order, but you are not supposed to practice them in any particular order. Here are each of the 'Rights.'

Right View

The first step along the path is right view. That means that you should develop a precise view about the nature of the four noble truths. A precise view of the eightfold path and a precise view of the nature of the mind. This includes non self and non theism. So, that means to study the dharma, to actually study the Buddhist teachings. Meditation is not enough. Meditation is number eight. If you only meditate without balancing that with study, then there is a danger that your meditation practise will become self oriented, or that you will be an 'ignorant meditator.' It takes much study and contemplation to penetrate right view. The Buddha said that what he had to teach was difficult to understand, comprehensible only to the wise. A man taking one of my courses at a Chinese temple said that his wife wouldn't come to the class because she says that "it's all common sense." Before I could refute that view he voiced my own feeling. Alas, how difficult it is for spouses to listen to each other.

The ultimate Buddhist view of the mind was best described, I believe, by the Vajra Regent Osel Tendzin in his talk "Space, Time and Energy," given on July 1, 1983 at Karme-Chöling in Barnet, Vermont. The Vajra Regent said:

> The view, is that the mind is like space. That is to say that space itself is unobstructed, all pervasive, empty, and not produced by causes. We simply say that it "is." In the same way that you view space you should view your mind [but don't think of the blackness of outer space; think of space as being bright and luminous]. You could say that space accommodates everything — your life and your death, confusion and liberation. In that way space is the ground of everything just as your mind is the ground of everything. Space is ungraspable by thought; it cannot be seen as a thing. It is spotless because it has no allegiance. To describe the mind is... impossible. The best we can say is that it "is." In that sense it is primordially pure.

According to the Kagyu fathers one's mind is empty and luminous at the same time. That is to say, empty of all conceptual notions, in reality empty of any cause. Therefore, being not dependent upon cause, the mind shines by itself; it is luminous. That is the essence of mind, therefore why it is compared to space. This emptiness and luminosity is inseparable from awareness, in fact this luminosity is the awareness itself. That is who you are, what you are, maybe even why you are. You are simply the unobstructed spontaneous arising of awareness which is without origin and without end. If your awareness is without origin it is unceasing, continuous and luminous.

Due to passion, aggression, ignorance, pride, jealously and so on, this pristine nature of awareness is clouded. When this awareness is clouded cognition becomes the self, consciousness becomes the notion of self, and perception or projection of consciousness becomes objectified vision or forms. When we have a separation between the two (subject and object) we have what is called samsara, or confusion, which manifests as suffering and continuous struggle. When we have continuous struggle, we have fear of death and ignorance of birth, which leads to grasping and fixation which leads to the repetition of that struggle. But, at the same time, we must realize that what arises as appearance — struggle, suffering, birth and death — the essence of this activity is unchanged, unstained, pure, since beginningless time.

In order to realize this fully, it is necessary to join the view with practice. It is said in the scriptures "If you do not join the view with practice, you are like a rich man hoarding wealth." So how do you join the view with the practice? You must adopt an attitude of renunciation, abandon belief in the self, through the experience of mindfulness and awareness by practicing meditation techniques. This means not moving or reacting when things occur, and not attaching the notion of a self whenever there is a movement of the mind. When we practice meditation in that way this leads to the experience of non dwelling, where the mind becomes one with space in the sense that all of the qualities that we have described are present in one's immediate experience. You begin to realize that such non dwelling is the quality of liberation or freedom and that mind itself is liberated by itself. So freedom is spaciousness, beyond obstruction, beyond attainment, beyond conceptual mind, which is good and bad and all the rest of the duality, and this freedom allows us to proceed on the path and attain the state of complete perfection or ultimate Buddhahood.

That is basically the nature of the view and how we could regard space in the same way as we regard our mind, and vice versa. The key point is to join that view with the practice. And the key point in practice is the absence of struggle which means giving up any claim to result. There's no particular formula for doing that my dear friends, you just do it.

As you have already experienced, mind which has no reference point is like a jabbering monkey. But mind with a reference point is free from grasping and fixation and is like space. The reference point in meditation is the view itself — that the mind is without reference point. But without that view the mind wanders like a jabbering monkey. So whatever arises dissolves into space and that leaves you where? It leaves you nowhere. When thoughts start to arise about you being nowhere, what do you do? You practice the technique. What is the technique? You label "thinking," come back to the breath and let the breath dissolve into space. The key point in the practice is to dissolve grasping and fixation by holding a posture, by practicing meditation techniques and keeping the view pure. That means without a sense of self, without a sense of self gratification or attaining something for one's own benefit. So everything is spacious, everything is self-liberated. That is the view and that is the beginning. In that way we attain the realization of the Hinayana which is the liberation of individuality, or the notion of individuality.

If you practice meditation with the view that the mind is like space, unobstructed, unborn, non dwelling, then you will find that when you inspect your mind, your mind will overwhelm your inspection, which is good because you cannot manipulate your mind with your thought process. Without the view there is the danger that your meditation may become self oriented because you think that there is something to be accomplished. What is good about the practice is that even if you don't understand the view at first, you can just jump right in and practice meditation because this experience confirms the view anyway.

So the view of mind is that it is truly egoless, without a separate independent self. Your mind is not a personal thing. If you go and look for your mind, you cannot find it. Where is your mind? It is one with the entire universe, inseparable. There is only one universe of mind. That is the view. Wrong view is like starting your car and pulling off the curb, without knowing how to drive. In the Net of Views discourse, the

Brahmajala sutra, the Buddha listed 62 wrong views. Just as a fish jumps out of a net in the water, the Buddha said, the fish just falls right back into the net again.

Right Intention

Right intention is the intention to follow the right view. Also, the intention to love and benefit others with selflessness. These first two items comprise the insight stage of the path—prajna, wisdom. It is noteworthy that the highest wisdom in Buddhist philosophy is associated with the view and intention of love and compassion. These noblest of qualities are placed at the highest stage of the path. Having wisdom means having love, compassion, virtue and the proper aspiration to benefit others. This love and truth should not be lost in some cold analysis of what Buddhist mind training is all about. Knowing the view is not enough. Right intention means to choose to follow that path of awakening.

Right Speech

The morality stage is described in the next three parts of the eightfold path. Right speech is a biggie. The Buddha taught that there are only three gates by which you relate with the world. Your body, speech and mind. There's an old saying in my country that says "sticks and stones may break my bones, but names will never hurt me." Buddhism clearly refutes this view! The Buddha felt that speech is a big deal. Words alone can start wars and get people killed, the Buddha taught. It is very important to watch over your gate of speech. Right speech means to speak concisely, with as few words as necessary. Speak if it will improve upon silence. The Buddha said that when his disciples meet they should do either of two things: discuss the dharma, or maintain noble silence. Mr. Spock in Star Trek may have been modelled after the Buddhist ideal of right speech. Gene Roddenberry, the creator of Star Trek had a Buddhist wedding ceremony in Japan when he married the woman who played nurse Chapel on the show. So, he was influenced by Buddhism. Mr. Spock spoke so honestly and concisely, that his character won a cult following, which was unexpected by NBC. Role models are a good thing for you to use for any area of your life, so if you use Spock be sure to add the human side of humour and warmth. Spock already has plenty of compassion.

The Sanskrit word 'vac' translates as 'speech' and it also means 'utterance,' 'word,' 'logos.' It implies perfect communication, the direct approach. For example, you say "The great white north is cold." You do not say "I think that the great white north is sort of cold 'round abouts now." Being direct, you just say "It is so." "Fire is hot." "Shit happens." Such communication is true speech. However, this does not deny the value of being indirect in social situations when you need to express something in a polite way. That's fine. Honesty is also included in right speech. One should avoid lying, avoid useless babble, idle chit chat, gossip, backbiting, or slander. Don't use words or tones that are divisive, malicious, harsh, abusive, impolite, rude, or angry. The Buddha also pointed out that speech should be timely, not untimely. If you plan to bring up a certain point at a meeting and you get a strong feeling there, that you shouldn't talk about it, then listen to your feelings and don't say it! That's the message being sent to you at that time, perhaps by devas. Timing is everything. If you clean up your speech, your words will become truthful and more benevolent and friendly, pleasant and gentle, meaningful and useful. People will stop tuning you out, your every word will have weight. Nobody listens to someone who never stops talking. In class ten there is a description of what the Buddha called "the Brahma voice." This is about the quality of invocation that happens to your voice when you channel down the energies of the devas in the higher realms. In the Mahayana teachings, the words of a bodhisattva become like music. You walk into a room and everyone feels upright (Tendzin, 1988; Halifax), even your cough is like music. With your speech well spoken, the sky's the limit.

The third precept prescribed by the Buddha is, do not speak falsehoods. That doesn't mean that you have to tell the truth. It means that you shouldn't lie, generally speaking.

The Buddha taught that the four ways of answering a question are:
1. Put the question aside and not answer it.
2. Answer the question directly.
3. Answer the question with another question.
4. Answer the question through analysis.

There are many examples in the sutras of the Buddha refusing to answer questions. Once, an ascetic wanderer asked the Blessed One if there is a self or if there is not a self. The Buddha was silent, so the wanderer wandered away. Later the Buddha explained to Ananda that this particular person would have been even more confused, with even wronger views had the Buddha answered his question. So, he put the question aside.

Now, there is a hitch with this precept of 'do not speak falsehoods.' The hitch is that you can. In good conscience you can choose to put aside this precept if it will benefit others to lie. Sometimes compassion dictates that you lie to others. We are all very well aware of examples of this from our own social experiences. In April, 1997 the Vancouver Sun ran an article right on the front page of the newspaper titled "Most people tell 200 lies each day — honest." In it the reporter says a "psychologist who monitored 20 people says that lying is crucial to functioning society. And life would be a nightmare if we didn't. Analysis of the tapes revealed that an average of one lie was told every eight minutes." "Often, what we are talking about are very small lies, but they are lies none-the-less," said Gerald Jellison, a psychology professor at the University of South California. "We find people are almost constantly giving excuses for their failure in behaviour that might be seen by others as inappropriate. A typical comment would be: 'I hate to bother you,' when really they don't give a damn. They will tell lies to relatives or friends on the telephone, perhaps to get out of a dinner. Society would be terrible if people started telling the truth. Anyone who did would be a subversive."

Jellison said the problems of being completely honest are illustrated in the film Liar Liar. The film features Jim Carrey as a lawyer, a compulsive liar who reforms and can't stop himself from telling the truth, with alarming results. Other psychologists agree that dishonesty is a fundamental part of life — despite modern-day thinking in favour of openness. Richard Wiseman, a British psychologist at Hertfordshire University said "Society would fall apart if we were honest all the time. No one would get a job if they were completely honest on their CV."

Psychology and Buddhism agree on many points, and disagree on some others. I believe that Buddhism agrees with lying as is advocated by these psychologists quoted by the Vancouver Sun. The meaning of the word 'precept,' is that precepts are intentions. Precepts are not iron clad vows. This is a very important point. There is a gentleness in the precepts which you don't feel from the ten commandments in the Bible (four of the five basic precepts are in the ten commandments). In Right Speech you live by the intention to not tell lies, but if you're in a situation where the compassionate thing to do is to lie, then you must lie. You put the precept aside and take action without guilt. This is another very important point. You don't repent later and apologize in your heart because you lied. You're proud that you lied! You can count on the merit and good karma that you've earned for telling that lie! "Wow! That was a really good lie!" There was never ever any guilt. The thing to avoid is the automatic inner reaction of guilt that people feel, even if they tell a good lie. This may come from the programmed guilt in our Judeo/Christian culture. We're raised to feel guilty for any deed, good or bad.

The Tibetan Lama Dzongsar Khyentse Rinpoche, gave a great talk at the Whistler Convention Centre in British Colombia in 1996. In his talk Rinpoche spoke about right speech and I was sitting in the front corner as a guard for the event. I was staffing the weekend of seminars as a Dorje Kasung in uniform, which is a kind of Buddhist security guard, crowd control, generally look after the space, type of person. Being a Dorje Kasung I wasn't supposed to be paying much attention to the teacher's talk. I was supposed to be watching the crowd. But I'll never forget what Dzongsar Rinpoche said to more than 200 of us about truth and honesty. He said that you should be true to yourself, be honest with yourself, and lie to everybody! We were understandably surprised. Then he explained that if you can trust your own judgment, then you know what you should do to benefit others. You know what is right. So if you're in a situation where you should lie, then lie. He drove his point home brilliantly by saying that people have the tendency to believe that they are supposed to always tell the truth. If you always tell the truth because your mother told you that you're supposed to always tell the truth, then that is a belief which is not based upon your own direct experience. This belief in telling the truth all the time is a form of theism. Theism has a wider meaning than just believing in god. It also means believing in anything that you do not know from your own direct experience. "Buddhism renounces theism," Dzongsar Rinpoche said, cornering us all against the wall. You shouldn't cling to the belief in the virtue of always being honest. A Buddhist acts skillfully in the present moment without a rule book. Knowing right and wrong is not so simple a thing as following a bunch of precepts. There are many grey areas in life. Usually you should tell the truth but sometimes you shouldn't. You must lie. Compassion commands it. Why then did the Buddha formulate the third precept as 'do not speak falsehoods'? Was this better than saying 'do not speak falsehoods unless compassion requires it'? Maybe this precept is better the way the Buddha spelled it out because it gives others a clear frame of reference. It's simple. But perhaps this precept is phrased as such for another reason. Maybe the Buddha was wrong. Maybe the Buddha made a mistake.

Right Discipline

Right discipline, morality, or conduct, is number four on the eightfold path. We never have enough self discipline do we? Everybody wants more discipline. Discipline means living within rules. It is discipline that frees you. Putting off discipline imprisons you, like a student that wants to be free of all his work. He slacks off but when exams come he's stressed out. The prepared student breezes through his exams and is free. Discipline is freedom. When I was a monk I had a friend who lived at Phra Payutto's temple outside of Bangkok. Phra Payutto is one of Thailand's most renown scholar monks. I was visiting and my friend, a Swiss monk, told me that the advantage of being in the monkhood was that you cannot do whatever you want. If the community you are living in objects to your natural impulses, then this is a gift of discipline which you can use to tame your mind. The principles of proper moral behaviour, the Buddhist precepts, are the starting point of right discipline. There are 311 precepts for nuns and 227 precepts for monks — each one pronounced by the Buddha himself. The monks robes are like a straight jacket. For lay people, such as ourselves, there are only five precepts.

The Five Precepts

1. Do not kill.
2. Do not take what is not offered.
3. Do not speak falsehoods.
4. Do not engage in sexual misconduct.
5. Do not take alcohol or intoxicants that cloud the mind, because it leads to moral carelessness.

These five go a long way to promote harmony in society and family. Something must actually be offered before you take it. When I was a kid I snuck quarters from my mom's purse so I could buy an ice cream sandwich for lunchtime at school. But I was wrong. I should have asked her first, to avoid confusion. Adultery is an obvious form of sexual misconduct. When men or women cheat on their spouse, not only can this cause tremendous emotional pain, this can cause infrastructure problems within society when babies are born in embarrassing and inconvenient places. Then what do you do? It's a real mess. Better to avoid this in the first place by heeding the fourth precept. Human beings should control themselves more than dogs mounting each other in the street. The scriptures indicate that sexual misconduct can lead to animal rebirth. One could become an animal having lots and lots of sex with many partners. Oh wonderful. If a man dates a woman but has no intention of being in a relationship with her, and uses her sexually, leading her on, lying, then dumps her, leaving her very hurt, this could be judged as breaking the fourth precept. Drunk driving deaths are a clear example of the moral carelessness that results from breaking the fifth precept.

Many of the precepts for monks and nuns relate to very limited situations, like washing their begging bowl. Only about 20 precepts have much of an effect on their behaviour. Adhering to all of the precepts doesn't make one a better person than lay people, contrary to some beliefs. One of the precepts made by the Buddha is that a monk or nun cannot sit or lie down suddenly on a bed or a bench with detachable legs, in a loft with an incompletely planked floor, in a dwelling owned by the sangha. Each and every one of these precepts has an amusing source story, which caused the Buddha to make each particular rule. You can just imagine a monk getting bonked on the head by the leg of a bed in the above story, and then the Buddha finding out about it and saying "Oh dear, we had better slap on another precept!" I had to thoroughly study all of the precepts before I ordained as a monk. I thought that it was going to be hundreds of pages of boring reading, but I was pleasantly mistaken. It was only 91 pages, just kidding. Some of the stories are incredible, full of action, adventure and death. The precepts and the thousand lesser rules contain sexually explicit literature as well, defining exactly what sex is.

The remainder of this section is a paraphrasing of a talk on discipline given by the Vajra Regent (which is listed in the bibliography).

In our lives, discipline is the basis of all virtue. All that is good and decent in life arises from discipline. The essence of Buddhism is discipline. And the kernel of discipline is 'no.' The word 'no.' That means no to aggression, no to passion, no to ignorance, no to indulgence of all kinds. It's called the giant NO. A no so big that it's like the sky. No one has ever heard the sound of that no. That's the Buddhist concept of discipline. You have to be a little hard on yourself. You have to say no to yourself. Buddhadharma means not causing harm. The essence is non aggression, that's what makes it dharma, the quality of non aggression. You have to cut your habitual patterns that are anti-dharmic, like snarling at your family, substance abuse, overindulgence in sleep. Everyone knows what no means, but just in case, no means no. No doesn't mean maybe, it doesn't mean later on, or when no one is looking. No means no. It means saying no to extremes. No to overindulgence. At the core of overindulgence is the idea of 'ME' as a big deal. The 'me' quality permeates everything. It is simply not proper to make a big deal out of one's self. Ever. One has to appreciate the all encompassing quality of what 'no' actually means. No means no ego. No ego ever. However, we think that we have time to work this out. But that's more 'me.' There should be more no.

You should be quick to discipline yourself the way you would deal with a child that is in danger. She's playing in a busy street and you say "Stop! Get away from there! Come back!" You wait until later to explain. It doesn't work if you warmly say "You know, you really shouldn't chase that ball across that busy road because you might not see the cars coming. And then maybe you'll be hit by a car and your bones could break, then your parents would be really upset..." No. You say "Stop! Stop that now!" That's the attitude we should take with regard to our habitual patterns. We can't be too easy with the seductive quality of our passion. The Buddha's right discipline is a feeling of 24 hour involvement with our practise. When our discipline feels continuous we open up to a vaster vision, a profound vision, and we understand the completeness of the Buddha's realization. When we have that connection to our discipline we feel totally connected to the world. Our sitting meditation practice gives us the experience of discipline by solidly sitting, solidly being. We experience the quality of equanimity.

The next part of saying no to ourselves is saying no to anti-dharmic activity. You are more attracted to hearing, contemplating and meditating, than to samsaric activity. This includes gathering the dharmas, to study and ponder upon it; make it a living experience in your life. Then you really feel the path quality altogether. From that appreciation occurs a further realization of your connection to the Buddha. He comes closer in terms of the qualities of the Buddha.

You can't do something wrong and say, "Well, I'll start living right tomorrow." Because it's all the same thing. Tomorrow, today, right now. It's all the same. It's like that movie "Gone with the Wind," as the house is burning down people rush up to the star and she says, "I'll think about that tomorrow." You can't do that. And you can't be too busy right now to practice discipline. You're not going to be any less busy in the future. The time to practice the dharma is now. There is never going to be another time. Dharma should pervade your life, like dharma, dharma, dharma, a 24 hour experience. You don't want to be into this just half way. None of us do. Buddhism is not the Sunday 'go to meet religion.' It's a way of life.

There is a transition from saying no to yourself and going outwards and working with others. It's hard for us to say no to ourselves but it's very difficult to say no to others. But if you're genuine and truthful, then you must say no. If someone is putting their ego out and laying a trip on others, then it is your duty as a Bodhisattva, to say no to that. You can't let them trample on the dharma. By dharma, that means the sanity of existence. If you don't have any compassion for others, or for them, then you won't say no. You'll make excuses, "Well... that's the way things are." That's *not* the ways things are. The truth is that we all know when bullshit is happening. You can always tell if what you are doing is bullshit by the level of discursiveness involved. You can always tell. And we shouldn't second guess that. Here, discursiveness is something that keeps bugging you in the back of your mind. You feel that you should do something, or you feel that you should stop doing something. Yes. Listen to that, that still, small voice within.

The benefit, the result of right discipline that manifests in your life is that you have a mind that is expansive, clear, open, and the environment is never clogged up with extraneous discursive qualities.

In *Heart of the Buddha,* Chögyam Trungpa states:

> Right discipline is based upon trust in oneself. The traditional idea of morality is based on a lack of trust in oneself. People have a fear of their aggression and passion, an obsession with their own inadequacies. People who are obsessed with their own inadequacies don't make good Buddhists. The guilt-ridden approach is actually an attempt to confirm one's ego. Trusting in yourself allows you to work skillfully with whatever is happening. Trusting yourself also arouses a sense of trust in others, a sense of heroism, raising the banner of sanity and proclaiming an open way. This vision of good conduct is not dependent on ego.

Right Livelihood

Elite Compassion

Number five on the Buddha's path to awakening is right livelihood. This means to earn your living in an honest way that benefits others. It means to do work that does not cause confusion. If you work in sales you can provide a product or service that benefits others, and is in accord with right livelihood. You can earn riches, benefit others for the rest of your life with the job itself, never once give a dollar to the poor, grow old and die very rich and very happy, and still die with very good karma. There is no dharma that denigrates the state of being very wealthy. The Buddha's billionaire benefactor, Anathapindika was not asked by the Buddha, in several decades, to 'give money to the poor.' The reason why this may sound surprising is because Ralph Waldo Emerson said that there is a conspiracy of the vast majority to keep everyone down to an average level of mediocrity. If anyone decides to rise above the crowd and do something special with their life, then there is a flurry of activity in the crowd to keep them back down, so that nobody feels threatened. So consider the awful possibility that there may be nothing wrong with rich successful people. They may not be unhappy with all their money at all! They probably have more virtue and better karma than poor people — that's why their karma resulted in them getting rich. Please blow away the poor monk thing, because we are not monks and nuns.

It is good karma to donate to charities, but there is no dharma that states that you must give money to people who are poor. Don't be made to feel guilty because you've done such a thing as operate a successful business that benefits others. Most social distribution schemes are based upon envy. Don't be brainwashed by this hungry ghost poverty mentality. Be an elitist. At least be discriminating and protect your mind from losers. Of course, you must have compassion for all losers, infinite as space but don't let them continuously influence your mind. Stay away. In the Mangala sutra the Buddha said that the number one blessing out of 38 of the highest blessings in life is, to not keep company with fools.

Right livelihood for a sales person means that if you step across that line and push more onto people than what they want or can use, then you cause confusion. The customer goes home and wonders why he bought so much unnecessary attachments from you. You have stepped into the darkness. But if you sell white toilet paper rolls at a competitive price that saves poor people three cents per roll, then you are benefitting the poor. That's it and that's all, right there. No charity, no panhandlers entering into the equation. You can expand your business and net $670,000 per year, growing at an average of 30% a year for 50 more years. Die and be happy. Next rebirth, even better. Keep that up for one thousand more lifetimes until you reach nirvana and you need not have one moment of guilt on your conscience. It is good to use your money to help others out, such as supporting charities or shelters for the homeless, but even if the poor starve and die right in front of your halting BMW, ride on. You've got a ticket to ride baby. Elite compassion.

Livelihood also means working to live in the world. It is noteworthy that the Buddha included work as one of the eight. Even though monks are supposed to live detached lives, the Buddha said that monks should have some work to do. Work is considered to be a part of your spiritual path, your spiritual practice. Work is not some cruel imposition upon us which we must undergo so that we can be spiritual beings on the weekends or on our time off. We practice mindfulness on the job and progress on the path while we work. Because work involves you in so many aspects of life, dealing with unpleasant people, learning new things, physical effort, right livelihood means that you are engaged with the world. You shouldn't just retreat into a cave or hide in a cheap basement suite, collecting welfare. Go out and get a job! There's no room in Buddhism to avoid getting a job because you're 'too spiritual.' The tendency to avoid work indicates a psychological tendency of avoidance behaviour altogether. You should work to pay your rent, buy food, get the bus pass, new socks, etc. Reality forces you to relate with the world, which is good. This trains you in mindfulness.

Some jobs are better for mindfulness than others. Enlightenment is more likely to come from sweeping a warehouse than closing deals on the phone. Manual labour gives you plenty of opportunities to practice meditation in action. You put your mind on what you are doing, as you are doing it. You mentally note to yourself "sweep, sweep, sweep." Tilopa, one of the great fathers of Tibetan Buddhism, worked crushing sesame seeds.

Right Effort

Right speech, discipline and livelihood constitute sila, the morality stage of the path. The concentration stage consists of the last three parts of the path, right effort, mindfulness, and absorption. Effort is divided into four aspects of one thing:

1. exerting will to prevent unskillful states of mind from arising.
2. exerting will to dispel unwholesome, unskillful states of mind that have already arisen.
3. the will to cause wholesome, skillful states of mind to arise.
4. to develop and bring to perfection good, wholesome states of mind that are already present.

Right effort is the will to fight desire, the cause of suffering. Habitual patterns drive our passions and emotions but it is our noble efforts that drag our lives out of the slime and the muck of the dark age and into the light of wakefulness. Attaining nirvana takes tremendous effort and exertion. Prince Siddhartha practiced hard for six years. You can't just let go and attain enlightenment by going with the flow. It doesn't work that way. Meditation practice is hard work, like cleaning your house from top to bottom. Once Milarepa was passing on a teaching to his dharma heir, S. Gampopa. They were alone in the Tibetan wilderness and Gampopa was bidding him good-bye. Milarepa told him that he had a secret to share with him before he went. Gampopa waited attentively while Milarepa turned around and lifted his lower robe to reveal callouses all over his bottom. Gampopa really appreciated his message, and Milarepa told him that he wouldn't give that secret to just anyone.

Today Milarepa is the greatest folk hero in Tibetan history because of his effort. He went from hell realm to complete enlightenment in one lifetime. Because he had done many evil things in his youth, he applied effort on the path, like no one else. Fear of his own bad karma propelled his efforts to benefit others. None of us have enough effort do we? We have so many gadgets that we just have to press a button to do some work. This can make us lazy at working with our minds. But human life is a workable situation. Materialism can be transformed into a spiritual advantage!

You can curb your indulgence in materialism while benefitting greatly from comfort, health care, and efficiency. You can work on your spiritual path even in a mansion. You can do it! You don't have to blame the world for making you wealthy. You deserved the birth that you got, and you can develop sincere heartfelt compassion for other rich people. You can overcome the encumbrances of prestige and wealth. The Buddha taught that human birth is ideal for practicing the dharma.

Right Mindfulness

Right mindfulness continues the process of building concentration which leads to wisdom, insight. The Buddha once had a monk who told him that he couldn't memorize the many precepts, let alone practice them. The Buddha asked the monk "Can you do just one thing?" "Sure, what is it?" the monk asked. "Mindfulness," the Buddha replied. "Just practice mindfulness." Mindfulness is the most basic and the most important thing in Buddhism. In this course, meditation is taught immediately after introducing what Buddhism is. Meditation is prime time mindfulness. Beyond the meditation cushion mindfulness should be applied in our ordinary existence as a way of life, a lifestyle of mindfulness. Through mindfulness on the ordinary, life becomes extraordinary. That is insight, prajna. Mindfulness is explained in more detail in the chapter on the four foundations of mindfulness. They are mindfulness of 1) body, 2) feelings (pleasant, unpleasant, or neutral), 3) mind — and the underlying state of mind, and 4) mind objects.

Wrong mindfulness, also wrong intention, would be to concentrate on clever ways of harming others. Darth Vader in *Star Wars* is a character that was designed to teach us the pitfalls of such wrong mindfulness. Remember the scene when he choked one of his generals to death by pointing his finger at him? The general made some mistake or other trying to capture the good guys so Darth Vader said "You have failed me for the last time General," as the poor fellow collapsed to the deck of the ship. Terrific powers of mindfulness, that Vader, but shame on his mother for teaching him such lousy manners.

Right Absorption

Completing the stage of concentration, the last in the eightfold path is right absorption. This means making efforts towards attaining samadhi. This is a state called one pointed concentration. A samadhi, or a jhana state occurs when all five senses shut down in deep meditation. You have a black out. You can't feel your body below the neck, and then you can't feel your body at all. Your sense of hearing, smell, and taste shut down too. You still have thoughts in the first samadhi and you are aware that you are having a wonderful experience, filled with rapture. There are four levels of samadhi absorption, then four even deeper levels. These eight meditations were taught to Prince Siddhartha by master Uddaka Ramaputta, and he succeeded at all of them. But he found that such a state of mind was not enlightenment because after he came out of his samadhi, he was still in the world of suffering, dukkha.

After his enlightenment however, Buddha taught the eight absorptions again and again. If you read the Theravadin sutras you will discover countless discourses where the Buddha brings the subject of his talk to what he called the first meditation. A paragraph is devoted to that, then the Buddha describes the second meditation, and so forth. A whole page will be devoted to all of these eight absorption states, and this pattern is repeated again and again and again in the sutras. So obviously the Buddha felt that it was important to do extensive practice of meditation, which is normally required to reach a samadhi. Even though it is not enlightenment, a samadhi is the mark of a concentrated mind. And concentration is necessary to reach the insights of nirvana. The word Zen is a translation that goes back to the term jhana, which means samadhi. The Buddha and his senior disciples would often take a break by picking a samadhi and going into that state, for example number three or number four. They would rest and recharge their batteries, as it were, then come out of the samadhi, refreshed. The Buddha chose to die in the fourth samadhi absorption, the arahant Anuruddha revealed, as Anuruddha was there at the time.

At Vipassana meditation centres in Thailand and Burma, natives and foreigners take month long meditation retreats with the intent of reaching a samadhi. During my time at the Buddhist temple Wat Ram Poeng in northern Thailand, I was close to many Westerners who had succeed in reaching the first or second samadhi. I was very impressed to hear people confirming from their direct experience what the Buddha had taught about the samadhi state. Buddha described the experience of the first absorption as "momentary and discursive thought, accompanied by joy and rapture." At Wat Ram Poeng we were trained to use a digital alarm clock when we were meditating with the deliberate aspiration to reach samadhi. The purpose was to check the clock from time to time because if you slip into the second samadhi you lose perception of time. For the first time in your life, thought actually comes to a standstill. In the scriptures this samadhi is compared to the Ganges River. The Ganges is flowing along, a mile wide, then suddenly it stops! According to Carlos Castenada, in his semi-fictitious writings about the native Mexican Indian tradition, Don Juan called this 'stopping the world.'

The Buddha and his monks didn't have digital watches. They couldn't pick one up at the local market the way we can. Near the end of a month of intensive meditation, a meditator could check the time, 9:00 am, on his digital clock. He might check it about a half hour later to discover that it is 10:30 am! "Whoa! What happened!?" he would say. This is the reason for keeping an eye on the clock. This is a case of entering into at least the second samadhi absorption. Without the clock a practitioner could enter into a samadhi, come out of it, and not even be aware of what happened. We had a fellow named Volker on retreat at the monastery who was a former East German soldier. Near the end of his retreat he had been diligently practicing sitting and walking meditation for hours and hours. He sat outside his kuti (meditation house) at a table to take a break for a little bit, and the next thing he knew, the time on his watch had jumped forward an hour. He had a spontaneous samadhi. When a person takes a break and relaxes, this can help the process because they drop their struggle and just let be. After the Buddha's parinirvana, his faithful attendant Ananda was striving to attain enlightenment by doing intensive meditation practice. When Ananda took a break to lie down, just as his hand touched the mat, he attained to ultimate enlightenment!

Right absorption also has the meaning of being completely involved, thoroughly and fully in a non-dualistic way. You are not distinct from the act of meditating and the object of meditation. From the fictitious Mahayana Diamond sutra there is an expression in Zen "First there is a mountain and rivers and streams. Then there is no mountain and rivers and streams. Then there is a mountain and rivers and streams." This was explained to me by Reverend John Eshin, the resident monk at the Vancouver Zen Centre. We each taught courses at a fine Chinese Buddhist temple nearby called Tung Lin Kok Yuen, Canada Society. The meaning of this Zen saying is that first there is the thing, then no thing, then the real thing. That means that first you see the mountain and you perceive it as existing separate from yourself. Then, in an absorption you don't perceive the mountain as being separate from you. Then, you and the mountain are truly one, that's the final "then there is a mountain and rivers and streams." We were out in the Zen Centre's backyard watching his cat fussing over birds when Reverend Eshin explained this to me by describing a musician who was playing his guitar. At some point the musician becomes absorbed in playing. Later he and the instrument become one. That's the idea of absorption. When you are working or doing your chores, it is good to be totally absorbed in what you are doing. When my wife polishes her shoes (mine too I must confess) she doesn't even hear me speak to her. Imagine, a wife not listening to her husband! That's concentration! What else could it be? Ideally you want to keep building your concentration in the post meditation world, not just when you're sitting. You should always be mindful of how you are building concentration by paying attention to what you are doing, or how you are losing concentration by not having your mind on the reality at hand. Right absorption, it's magical.

Conclusion

That completes the Buddha's noble eightfold path. If you diligently practice and develop all the parts of the path then you can attain enlightenment within this lifetime. This book alone is enough dharma for you to reach all the way to total enlightenment. But for most mortals, it's good to read a broad range of Buddhist books. Don't read anti-dharma, heretical literature. Watch out for all the new age fluff in the world, because it will continue to get worse, much worse. That's my main thought for the future of the information age. There is a way out of here, a way out of suffering, and this is it, the path. The Buddha taught the most important things for people to know, to make practical steps along the path. The Buddha was a practical teacher and he did not give information just to satisfy people's curiosity. Buddha once visited a group of monks that wasted too much time in speculative views. He was staying in a Simsapa forest in Kosambi near modern day Allahabad in northeastern India. Buddha gave a powerful message when he came out of the forest with a handful of leaves in his hand. He asked the monks "What do you think, O bhikkhus? Which is more? These few leaves in my hand or the leaves in the forest over here?"—"Sir, very few are the leaves in the hand of the Blessed One, but indeed the leaves in the Simsapa forest over here are very much more abundant."

"Even so, bhikkhus, of what I have known I have told you only a little, what I have not told you is very much more. And why have I not told you those things? Because they are not useful, they are not conducive to understanding suffering, the cause of suffering and the way to the end of suffering. That is why I have not told you those things." It is futile to try to guess everything the Buddha knew but refused to teach us.

The blanket statement about the value of information, which the Buddha expressed with a few leaves in his hand, gives us a blunt message. We must not waste our time in meaningless pursuits. We are all going to be dead someday, who knows when? Now is the time to utilize the blessing of our human birth to makes strides along the eightfold path. Today's information age makes this sutra even more relevant to our lives. Thousands of hours are being spent studying details that are not relevant to waking us up. People study television reruns from the 1950s, or the atmosphere of Saturn's moon Titan. People with masters degrees study more and more information so that they can get a PhD degree. This may be beneficial but the Buddha's point is that the priority must be on the vital few things that really matter, not the trivial many. People need to study and apply dharma to their human existence. Many people would be better off studying dharma, upgrading their interpersonal skills, warmth, and their wandering mind, rather than upgrading their degree. Another message in this teaching by the Buddha is that if you study thousands of those leaves on the trees you'll just become more crazy and confused and lost in speculation because the more you do that, the less you are paying attention to the few leaves in the Buddha's hand that can put you on the right track and really help you. Never forget the forth noble truth: there is a path, it is eightfold, to the cessation of suffering, nirvana.

Chapter 5

Class Six
Non Self

I n *Ulysses* James Joyce writes (Joyce, 1922; 572):

Did Stephen participate in his dejection?

He affirmed his significance as a conscious rational animal proceeding syllogistically from the known to the unknown and a conscious rational reagent between a micro and a macrocosm ineluctably constructed upon the incertitude of the void.

How close did James Joyce get to the Buddhist view which holds that there is no self? Buddhism rejects the self because of the certitude of the void. The void is not a big nothing. The void is the luminosity of emptiness. The certitude is that if you syllogistically and experientially unravel ego, from the micro to the macrocosm, such as Brahma, you will ineluctably fall into the ego's groundless feeling when the mind experiences glimpses of the void, emptiness. This unknown is beyond ego's territory- which is limited to the known. The re-agent is that by going within your own microcosm in meditation practice, you can experience the macrocosm of the universe and step through the uncertainty of the void into nirvana. Good! Step into that groundless unknown. That's the route to go. So, the millennium answer to James Joyce's 1922 riddle is that Stephen did indeed participate in his own dejection.

If I slowly read just ten pages of *Ulysses* I feel stoned. That's the feeling I get when I read Buddhaghosa's *Path of Purification,* which I believe to be the best, loftiest and most authentic exposition of Buddhadharma ever written since the time of the Blessed One. What did Buddhaghosa write about the true nature of your inner self? He wrote that unique to Buddhism is the view that your self is composed of five things, one part body and four parts mind. These five are collections, or aggregates of tendencies and characteristics called skandhas. Skandha translates from Pali and Sanskrit to mean a heap or a pile. The second skandha grows out of the first and so on.

These are the five skandhas of the self:
1. Form or body
2. Feeling — the five senses
3. Perception
4. Mental formations or thoughts
5. Consciousness

To understand this, use the example of listening to a Buddhist teacher give a talk. You have your form, your body with the physical organ of the ear. You hear the talk because sound waves travel from the teacher's mouth and hit your ear. That's form, the first skandha. The second skandha of feeling comes into play when the sound registers in your ear and is transmitted to your mind. Then you perceive that there is sound and you recognize that the sound is a person talking and you understand what the words mean. That's perception, the third skandha. You can see at this point that the process is getting more psychologically sophisticated with each step.

Once you understand the words that the teacher is saying you develop ideas about them. You may think that he makes sense, that he's utterly profound beyond comprehension, or you may have questions in your mind, you may disagree with what's being said. This is the fourth skandha of mental formations, your myriad thoughts going through your mind all the time. Number four is a big one, we live our lives in our mental formations, don't we? This also includes your intentions and volitional actions, so this is where karma comes from, this is where you initiate your karma. Your awareness of all those thoughts going through your head is consciousness, the fifth skandha. This is the fruition of ego's complex game of building itself up. Consciousness in the case of unenlightened people such as ourselves, is limited to self consciousness, the belief in a self, the belief in a separate independent self.

The big stunning news that the Buddha laid on us is that this self does not exist as a separate independent entity. You do not exist. You don't have a self. Shortly after the Buddha's great awakening he said to himself that what he had realized went against the grain. People do not want to know, people do not want to hear, that there is no god, and that they do not have a self. It is noteworthy that the Buddha skillfully taught the truth without getting himself crucified.

It would be irresponsible to just say that you don't exist, and then just leave you there hanging with nothing. So it is good to first emphasize the five parts of non self that make you what you are. What you do have is quite a lot. All of your life, memories, hopes and dreams, and future incarnations are all wrapped up in form, feeling, perception, mental formations and consciousness. Everything in the idea of 'soul' is included here, except for permanence — that is permanent identity. A reason why the Buddha taught that you definitely do not have a self is because each of these five skandhas is impermanent. None of them can be called self. Even if you put them together and combine the five into one psychosomatic organism, there is still no real self there. The idea of self or soul usually implies an everlasting being of some kind. None of the skandhas is like that. Your physical life is impermanent, so your body is not your self. Your senses, perceptions and thoughts are fleeting from moment to moment. They are not permanent. They are not your self. Your consciousness, your self consciousness fades in and out like a TV set on the blink. Your consciousness of ego, of self is also impermanent except that part which transcends the ego. When you attain to enlightenment you discard self consciousness and merge with the permanent state of enlightened mind. So, even though your ego is impermanent, the idea is that your goal is to shed off this impermanent ego which limits your mind to the idea of self and self limitation.

Your consciousness is everlasting and permanent because the seed of enlightened mind exists in all sentient beings. It is the idea of your identity that is false, the Buddha teaches. Consciousness does not have an identity! If you are Jane Smith in this life, there will not be an everlasting Jane Smith living happily ever after in the sky after you die. Your self concept of Jane Smith is a false assumption, so to speak, and after death your five skandhas will come together again in another form, perhaps Sharon Jones in California. There will be no more you, no more Jane Smith. Jane Smith will be a buried past life memory in the mind of Sharon Jones in California. That's the idea of non self. You still continue, but you do not continue as the identity that you are now.

Closer to our own experience, you are still the same person today as you were when you were a baby, but in another way you are not the same person now as you were then. Extending this process, when you are old, and die and hopefully take rebirth as a human baby, you will not be the same person as a baby that you were as an old man in your previous life. However, in another way, you will still be the same person as a baby that you were in the former life. You can see then that the five skandhas are rolling on and changing in every year, in every moment. There is no self in there that has any nucleus of identity. You are not the same person now as you were when you picked up this book, even moments ago. You've changed!

Buddhists don't like to use the word soul. Soul is a bad word because it implies the false view of eternalism. But you could say that you do have an ever-lasting permanent soul in the sense that your consciousness will never die. It continues on and eventually merges with enlightened mind and becomes impersonal mind rather than personal self consciousness. So, the view is quite good actually, very upbeat in fact! There's no problem with not existing as a self. You are part of one universe and your ego fools you into believing that you are separate from the rest of the entire universe, but you are not. All of reality is one universe of mind. There is nothing other than one ultimate reality of mind. You are like a knot of thread in the carpet. If you unravel the knot of thread you realize that it is one with the entire carpet, it is not separate from the carpet. You are the carpet. You are the universe. You are not really a knot of thread and you are not really an ego, a separate person.

The Buddha demonstrated a way of regarding the five parts of the self by comparing them to meat from a cow. The Buddha said that a butcher chops up a cow and sells sections of meat at a crossroads. He presents various steaks, hind roast, ribs, lean meat, etc. When people come to buy meat they do not ask for 'cow.' They do not say "May I buy some cow please?" That would be silly. The butcher does not say "Yes. This is cow. You may purchase some cow from me." So, the self is gone. The self of the cow is gone. You regard the parts of the cow the way you should properly regard each of your five skandhas. In meditation or post meditation it is a good practice for you to mentally review your body, senses, perceptions, thoughts, and awareness, rather than thinking about 'you' so much. When you bite into a Burger King Whopper with Cheese, there is no need for you to have one thought about a cow, in order for you to contemplate the beef. That is properly considering the skandha of form, body, without dwelling upon the ego identity of the cow. It's fine to thank the cow and to dedicate your merit to it to help the cow attain a higher rebirth, but that's another fine topic of dharma.

The actual experience of anatta, non self is an ordinary thing. If you get so absorbed in your household chores that you become one with what you are doing, that is an experience of egolessness. When putting on make-up my wife becomes one with her face. She forgets herself until she realizes that she's late. When I was living at Wat Pah Nanachat in Thailand, Ajhan Sumedo said that in meditation practice, you label 'thinking' when there is an itch on your right knee. There is only the feeling and the knowing mind, the 2nd and the 5th skandha. There is no you there, there is no self there, he said. You don't think "I have an itch on my knee." There is just the physical sensation that is apprehended by the knowing mind. That's it and that's all. This is the proper Buddhist way to regard your existence.

Meditation practice is built upon the truth on anatta. Simple though the technique is, it is designed to poke holes in the walls of the ego, by cutting through the mental formations that constantly arise to shore up ego's defences. It is like the colours on the film of the soap bubble desperately trying to make sure that the bubble doesn't burst! When you label 'thinking' and come back to the breath, you are taking a miners pick and you are chipping away at the walls of ego. The practice is designed to bring you to egolessness by dropping your struggle and just letting be. The thoughts are always spewing out to convince you that you are the person named on your ID, but the Buddhist lineage has so skillfully constructed the meditation discipline that you always have a chance of breaking through neurosis and glimpsing the direct experience of non self. Practice properly and apply effort.

There is ultimate reality and conventional reality. The Buddha used the conventions of speech that we always use when we say words like me, I, us, we, them, they, she, he, etc. There's nothing wrong with using conventions of speech when discussing conventional reality. Just know that in ultimate reality there is no such thing as self, I, me, you, etc.

Chapter 6

Class Seven
Buddhist Cosmology

"God is Dead", read the headlines on the New York Times on a Christmas day in the 1970s. Literally speaking, the New York Times was wrong. But the truth is something else. Cosmology is defined as the theory or philosophy of the nature and principles of the universe. To a Buddhist who affirms his choice of going for refuge in the three gems of the Buddha, his teachings, and the community of fellow Buddhists, Buddhist cosmology explains the ground under one's feet and the Hubble space telescope's discoveries. The Hubble space telescope is an instrument that helps to support the Buddha's teaching because it has the technology necessary to finally confirm what Siddhartha Gotama Buddha started teaching 2587 years ago in northeastern India.

Every particle of matter in the entire universe, seen and unseen, is accounted for in Buddhist cosmology. The Buddha left no stone unturned up to the point of certain questions that he refused to answer. Any astronomer who has not studied the Buddha's teachings on the physical universe has not done his homework, and he cannot claim to have adequate knowledge about the history of the science of astronomy. In Carl Sagan's popular 'Cosmos' television program in 1980 he had an episode describing how science and religion were so far apart on their views. Then, he adds a little footnote saying to the viewing audience that eastern religions are closer to science's view of astronomy. Then he just left the audience hanging by not admitting what the Buddha and the Hindus taught!

But much of their viewing audience was the American Bible belt so I can understand that the advertisers did not want to lose money over the subject.

The Buddha's description of the physical universe comprise some of the most astounding teachings he ever gave. It's right up there with no self and no god. I can still remember the chair I was sitting in (it was a love seat actually), in 1994 in Thailand when I read that the Buddha was the progenitor of the big bang theory. Actually, the Hindus may make the same claim as they teach this as well. History is uncertain about what happened first in India because Indian history is notorious for not being too concerned about history. It's a nightmare trying to figure out whether any of the Upanishads actually predate the Buddha, or what. Then there's religious one-upmanship which blows away objectivity. Anyhow, during my innocent boyhood years in the 1970s my father told me about this new theory called the big bang theory. He said that astronomers have almost completely proven that the universe blew out from a single point smaller than my thumb! It blew out and will likely collapse in again, maybe 40 billion years later, or it may dissipate into entropy. There's more on this in the chapter 'All Universes Mythology.' The Buddha said that over vast periods of cosmic time 'Island Universes' form. This almost blew me out of my love seat because those are galaxies! Anyone could have guessed the existence of stars and planets 2587 years ago, but there is no way that with the naked eye you could guess the existence of galaxies! No way. It was through the Buddha's direct realization. Being enlightened, he could see the big bang as easily as you observe your little finger. Buddha described solar systems as world systems and planets as world spheres. Compare that to the book of Genesis in the Bible that has a cosmology that dates back to the fourth millennium B.C. I couldn't live with that! I don't know who can.

The Six Realms

Beyond the physical universe, the Buddha and thousands of his enlightened lineage holders explained the dharma (Buddhist version of the truth) of the unseen dimensions, or realms of existence. This explains a lot of things in world history and in your own personal inner life and past. Let's take a look at these realms of existence. There are six realms of existence, three higher realms and three lower realms. The Buddha taught that every sentient being in the universe lives in one of these six realms. This is samsara, the wheel of life, the continual running on from life to life, like a monkey who jumps from tree to tree never finding fruit. The characteristics of samsara, the wheel of life, is continuous struggle, fear of death, ignorance of birth, and the repetition of that struggle. The six realms in the wheel of life are shown opposite.

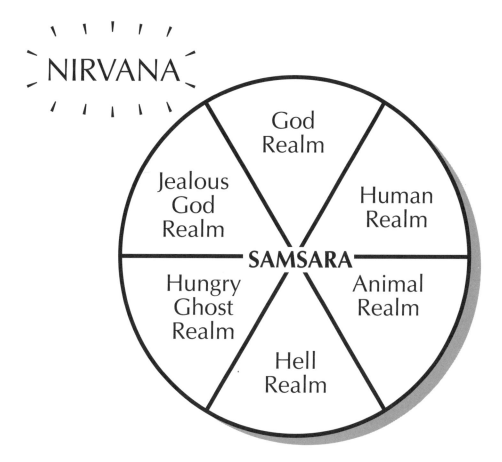

The God Realm

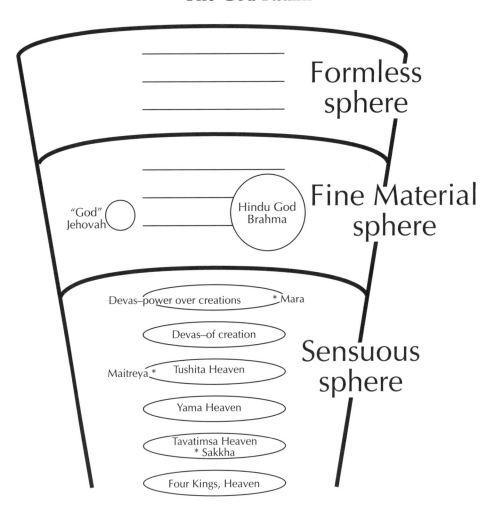

Formless sphere

Fine Material sphere

"God" Jehovah

Hindu God Brahma

Sensuous sphere

Devas–power over creations   * Mara

Devas–of creation

Maitreya *   Tushita Heaven

Yama Heaven

Tavatimsa Heaven
* Sakkha

Four Kings, Heaven

Above is a blow up of the god realm as described by the Buddha in the sutras. The six lower heavens of the sensuous sphere have a hierarchy to them and are all occupied by devas which include the jealous god realm. Only asexual devas reside in the fine material and formless spheres.

It may be best to first relate to the six realms as states of mind. On any one day you may go through all six realms as a state of mind. The hell realm is characterized as constant anger and aggression. You get angry at people so they get angry at you. This makes you even more angry at them so they get even more angry at you. This vicious circle becomes a living hell. People who've been through a few marriages don't have to die and go to hell to know what it's like; this experience exists on earth right now. The animal realm is characterized by ignorance and the symbol is a pig. A pig just eats everything in front of its nose, not looking right, not looking left. He doesn't care if he's eating garbage or caviar or expensive chocolates, he just stubbornly eats and eats and eats. Ignorance means not paying attention to the signals that life is giving you, being stuck on your habitual patterns, too comfortable and cozy with your old way of doing things. Such people can be quite intelligent in their ignorance. They think of clever ways to convince you to adopt their habitual patterns. "You should join our political party." "You should come to the pub with us after work. A bit of alcohol is good for your health." There is also the absence of a sense of humour because animals cannot appreciate irony. The comfort zone is the single biggest enemy of human potential. The tendency to stay with what is comfortable is the animal realm mentality. There's no challenge to it. Oscar Wilde said, "Only the shallow know themselves."

The hungry ghost realm is one of poverty mentality. You can't get enough money, you can't get enough sex, you can't get enough love or attention, or stamps for your collection, whatever. Even if you get what you want, it's as though you've fallen in love with being hungry and you would rather still be hungry. The symbol of the ghost realm is of a ghost with a pinprick mouth, a long skinny neck and a huge ravenous belly that is always hungry. No matter how fast he eats 25 hours a day, he can never be satisfied.

In the higher realms, the human realm state of mind is characterized by passion, discriminating passion. You want your coffee with cream, not milk, and just a little bit of sugar. You're very particular about the clothes you wear. Humans want to be more, do more, have more. Their ego is striving for growth and expansion. That's discriminating passion. Animals don't have that. Once they satisfy their needs to eat, sleep and procreate, they just lay down and sleep and/or die.

The god realm is characterized by bliss, a blissed-out state of mind, where everything seems beautiful and wonderful but you may be turning away from the suffering of others. In *The Rose,* Bette Midler is a star proclaiming, "That's enough about me, let's talk about you. What do you think about me?" The self stuck absorption of the god realm state of mind is not the ideal state for cultivating the tender heart of compassion. This is not to say that all devas are full of themselves.

The jealous god realm is a paranoid state of mind, the paranoia and power of highly attained beings that do not want anyone to be better than them. Adolf Hitler was a jealous artist and he hated artists that were better than him. He persecuted and killed other painters in his fits of jealousy. Vice-president Lyndon Johnson is an example of the asura (jealous god) mentality. He was well known for his huge ego and ambition. He was clawing for the presidency and wanted it very badly but John F. Kennedy beat him out at the 1960 democratic convention. Johnson hated Bobby Kennedy and who knows how he felt about President Kennedy as he withered powerless in the vice-presidency. It was Johnson who first asked President Kennedy to go to Texas. The controversial evidence is believable that Johnson conspired to kill Kennedy so that Johnson could fulfil his power craving to be the President of the United States. He succeeded but people close to Johnson were surprised to notice that once he got to be the president, it seemed as if he didn't want the job. He craved for the power but being fed did not make him happy, like a hungry ghost. He was still unsatisfied. Perhaps his mind set was a combination of the hungry ghost and jealous god realms.

Two years later, before the Vietnam war unravelled him, Johnson said "I've never felt freer." This was a period for him to earn good karma before his murderous karma caught up to him. He was described as the most effective president in history because he mastered the exercise of power. He power tripped all over Congressmen and Senators. He was a manipulator extraordinaire, he had to be on top, just like a jealous god. His best friends said that he could be the biggest friend in the world, hugging people, then in the next minute he could hate his enemies with a mean sadistic streak, like Jeckle and Hyde! But isn't this natural? Johnson truly hated Bobby Kennedy and Johnson said that Bobby Kennedy probably would have hated him for watching him die on TV, as Kennedy lay bleeding on the floor of the kitchen in the Ambassador Hotel in Los Angeles. Beyond doubt Bobby Kennedy was killed by a conspiracy and Johnson may have had a hand in that too. LBJ's beneficiary and close ally, FBI Director J. Edgar Hoover, another jealous god, was according to researchers, the man most singularly responsible for John Kennedy's assassination. Hoover was the sovereign monarch of the FBI kingdom for over 40 years, with a god-like inflated opinion of himself. Not only is this a reasonable conclusion according to the evidence, which is not appropriate for this book, but this injustice is also in harmony with the Buddhist cosmology teachings. The Buddha taught that the jealous gods just cannot bear to witness devas of more virtue so they attack them but the jealous gods always lose in the end. The psychological effect of the Kennedy concept in the mind is that the Kennedys represent the former virtue of our collective past so people try to model themselves after that; they're haunted by it. It is that virtue or just *the idea* of virtue, that the jealous gods can't stand. Johnson and Hoover were just human beings acting in harmony with the devas around them, or acting as the instrument of devas around them.

The autopsy revealed that Senator Robert Kennedy was shot point blank, within six inches from behind, upwards at a 70 degree angle. The supposed assassin Sirhan Sirhan fired what sounded like blanks from three feet in front, according to witnesses. Sirhan was a brainwashed decoy who later couldn't remember a thing. An expert studying the RFK autopsy report said "By god! I felt the cosmos shake!" It is very suspicious that standing closest behind Senator Kennedy was last minute "Ace Guard Service employee" Thane Cesar and also Bill Barry, who were both armed with hand guns, which were drawn. Bill Barry was an "ex-FBI" man who was ostensibly serving as Kennedy's bodyguard. Barry was the man who led Kennedy off of the stage in the opposite direction planned!

Earlier a young woman and a young man, both about 22, brought Sirhan into the pantry from the back stairs. The young lady was wearing a white dress with small black polka dots as she spoke with Sirhan right up to the moment before Sirhan turned on Kennedy. This couple, described below, were seen running after the shooting. A policeman who rushed to the scene said:

> "Right away, an older Jewish couple ran up to me, and they were hysterical. I asked them, "What happened?" The woman said that they were coming out of the Ambassador Hotel by the Embassy Room, when a young couple in their late teens or early twenties, well dressed, came running past them. They were in a state of glee.
>
> They were very happy, shouting, "We shot him! We shot him!" The older woman asked, "Who did you shoot?" The girl said, "Kennedy, we shot him! We killed him! This put this old Jewish woman into hysterics. She was still in hysterics at the time I talked to her."

Please forgive the author for dwelling upon so many Kennedy examples in this book. Because the general public doesn't know the above details, the purpose of using this example for the jealous god realm mentality is to help those determined citizens who want to reopen this case, by raising awareness about this huge lie and conspiracy which exists in our shared history. The subsequent cover up and evidence tampering indicates that the FBI was behind RFK's murder. J. Edgar Hoover got away with it again! but in which realms are he and Johnson now?

President Johnson's despicably bad karma in the Vietnam war, "not wanting to be the first President in American history to lose a war!" rebounded upon him and he said that his life was "a waking nightmare." True to the textbook definition of the jealous god realm state of mind, Johnson could just never admit, even to himself probably, that he was wrong about Vietnam and should have changed his direction. Even after his 'ten wise men' told him to get out of Vietnam, he kept up the bombings, even personally directing bombers during their attacks! Two million dead. After resigning, his mentality became self-destructive as he consumed alcohol and drank himself to death in 1973. "The Johnson men have never lived very long," he was fond of muttering.

Having considered the six realms as states of mind, next, you reveal to the class that these are real realms, like dimensions where real beings actually live. The animal realm and the human realm are the only ones you can see with the naked eye. But if someone had a radio that could only pick up two stations, he may say that his radio gets all the radio stations in the city, but that is wrong. Because of the lower concentration of our minds, we do not have the mental energy normally, to sense the other four realms. The word concentration is synonymous with the word energy. The Buddha saw all realms of course, and he described them in great detail for us, as did the lineage of enlightened ones.

The god realm is divided into the sensuous sphere, the fine material sphere or Brahma world (Brahmaloka), and the immaterial or formless sphere. The sensuous sphere is comprised of six lower heavens. In the Theravadin canon, the Buddha expounded at length the nature of each of these six heavens. Western Buddhists generally have no idea about this, but it is a fact that the Buddha felt that it was important for him to tell us all about these things that ordinary worldlings cannot perceive. Practically every third sutra has devas involved. They're all over the place in the scriptures. Because Westerners rightly regard Buddhism as meditation, which is good, they generally have a lopsided view of what is in the content of the Buddha's words. At Douglas College, I discussed devas with philosophy professor Leonard Angel and he believed that the Buddha was being metaphorical in referring to devas. Perhaps the Buddha was being polite to the pre-Hindu beliefs of the day, and maybe devas don't really exist at all, he felt. Dr. Angel tries to synthesize modern scientific ideas with the enlightenment quest in his book *Enlightenment East & West*. I cannot accept his view that devas don't exist because that is far more unbelievable than believing that devas do exist. Consider the big picture of death, rebirth, karma, and the six realms of existence. If devas don't exist, which is to say that the god realm does not exist, no heaven, then what happens to virtuous people after they die? If they come back to human birth, if people believe that, then why is it unbelievable that they could take rebirth as a deva in the god realm? It is an accounting nightmare to try to erase any one of the six realms. The law of karma is the law of karma. We have got to have these six destinations in order for the whole universe to hang together properly. Buddhist cosmology all hangs together in one whole system that works and makes complete sense. No one just made this up you know, conventional reality truly is this way.

Practically all religions have devas so they indirectly confirm each other and the truth that there really is some objective reality which is reflected in all of these similar religious views. This isn't just the wishful thinking of people that want to live after death. Guardian angels, heavenly hosts, ascended masters, guides, spirit guides — they're all names for devas. Devas are not enlightened as a rule, and humans are not enlightened as a rule, but like humans it is still possible for a deva to attain to full and complete enlightenment.

The first heaven of the sensuous sphere is ruled over by four principal devas. They are the king of the north, south, east and west. The second heaven is Tavatimsa heaven which is ruled over by Sakkha, king of the gods, he is called. This heaven is better than the first one. The Buddha told a story about an ordinary king who had a virtuous minister. The minister was a very compassionate man and he helped many people. They both died and went to heaven. The king took rebirth as a deva in the first heaven. He lived in a celestial palace but it was kind of dull and unexciting. He could perceive that his former minister took rebirth as a deva in Tavatimsa heaven. He objected, thinking "Hey! I was the king. How come I'm stuck here in this boring heaven while my minister gets a better rebirth up there in Tavatimsa heaven?" Then, he realized that he wasn't that generous or caring as a king, so the minister deserved a better rebirth than he did. This story illustrates the difference between these two heavens.

The second heaven is mentioned by the Buddha more than any other heaven, perhaps because it is closer to Earth and our worldly affairs than the higher heavens. Sakkha came down many times to visit the Buddha and he is referred to more than any other deva in the scriptures, including Brahma. Sakkha rules in a celestial palace with thirty three principal devas in his administration. This heaven is called the gods of the thirty-three. When Buddhists say 'gods' they mean devas. Sakkha is very virtuous in character but a bit slow, you might say. Sakkha rules for his lifetime which is generally one kalpa long, so he has a temporary administration like the president of the United States. After he dies and takes rebirth elsewhere, another Sakkha will come along to replace him. Life in all six realms is impermanent. The Jataka Tales, the 572 past life stories told by the Buddha, are full of the heroic deeds of Sakkha appearing in the sky above the Earth with great brilliance, to save the lives of a hero or heroine being picked on by some wicked king or other. In Sanskrit, 'Sakkha' translates as 'Indra,' which is a more familiar name to people. The existence of this Hindu god was confirmed by the Buddha. The Buddha's cousin and senior disciple Anuruddha was Sakkha in a previous life and Anuruddha had the noble bearing of a king. Lots of consorts, sex and dakinis in Tavatimsa. Not a bad choice for rebirth, eh?

Shortly after enlightenment, the Buddha spent one rainy season retreat in Tavatimsa Heaven teaching the dharma to his mother and to the millions of devas present. Nice son. This is where the Buddha's mother went after she died, a week after Prince Siddhartha was born. This is the tradition for the mothers of the Buddhas of the past and the mothers of the Buddhas of the future.

The third heaven is Yama Heaven, a heaven of bliss, also called the heaven of no attack. The fourth heaven is Tushita Heaven, another very popular vacation spot. This is the heaven with the number one greatest amount of sensuous pleasures— sex, drugs, rock 'n roll. This is where Prince Siddhartha lived as a deva prior to his birth because this is the traditional residing place of the Buddha-to-be. Today, the Buddha taught, the future Buddha of Compassion, Maitreya is currently a deva residing in Tushita heaven. He is awaiting the proper causes and conditions on Earth, to take rebirth (usually in India). Buddha prophecized that Maitreya would become the fifth Buddha in this kalpa (age) approximately 5000 years after the Buddha's time. Buddhism must first be wiped out from the world in order for the next Buddha to arise. This will happen. That is how kalpas have always gone.

The Buddha was Buddha number four in this particular kalpa, which is a big string of Buddha's to have in one kalpa! Aren't we lucky. Tushita heaven is more formless, or less structured than Tavatimsa. Tavatimsa heaven is a heaven of order. Heaven's first law is order; earth's first law is order as well.

In the fifth heaven the devas delight in the power of creation. In the sixth heaven the devas delight in the power over the creations of others. That means that the devas of the top heaven have power over the devas of the lower heavens, as well as the rest of the sensuous sphere, which includes all five of the lower realms. The greatest jealous god deva of them all is Mara and he lives on the outskirts of the sixth heaven. Mara is the ultimate embodiment of ego and the symbol of Mara is Darth Vader from *Star Wars*. Darth Vader was highly attained spiritually. His powers of concentration were so mighty that he killed people with his mind. Mara is the Buddhist equivalent of the Christian devil, Satan. The Bible says that Satan was one of seven angels but he was bad and challenged god so he got cast down into hell and rules over hell. The Buddha teaches that Mara lives in the comfort and indulgence of heaven but has administrative powers over hell and all the rest, except for what is above the sensuous sphere. The good news is that the jealous god realm devas cannot penetrate up to the fine material sphere. All those devas are virtuous devas. The jealous god devas are mixed together with the good devas in the sensuous sphere and they have their cosmic battles going on. Sakkha once paid homage to the Buddha by saying to the Buddha that when they have wars with the asuras, they drink asura nectar, but the taste is not one sixteenth as sweet as the taste of the Buddha's dharma. This conjures up images of vast cosmological battles going on in the upstairs above our heads. This is actually the truth. This is what is really happening all around us but we just can't see it.

'Seventh heaven' is a quantum leap up from the sixth heaven. Now we are into the big time — the Brahmaloka. These are the greatest, vastest, god-like devas in the entire cosmos! This is where Brahma lives for a life span of one whole cosmic cycle — 100 billion years by one translation of the abhidharma. He is the first deva born into this universe from the world of radiance, after the big bang. Brahma believes that he is god because he is there alone for so long that he forgets his birth and assumes that he created the universe. After a few eons go by he wishes for company and he believes that he creates the other devas that later appear (by the process of their own karma). Those devas also believe that Brahma must be god and they all share this mistaken assumption that Brahma is the one and only absolute creator god, until some Buddha comes along and taps Brahma on the proverbial shoulder and tells him that he is not an absolute almighty god, he's just a deva. Brahma has an ego! Brahma is limited by the self, self consciousness. An enlightened person, the Buddha, is higher than 'god' Brahma. Brahma is the Hindu god and he lives within the first three of the four layers of this fine material sphere.

Not all of the devas are Buddhists. Many devas have a theistic relationship with Brahma, believing that he is god almighty. Sakkha told the Buddha about a time when Brahma paid them a visit at his celestial palace. He was sitting around the big table with the gods of the three and thirty when suddenly a beam of light came down. They immediately knew what it was so they perked right up and said "Brahma's coming! That's the signal!" Out of the beam of light appeared a gandarbha, the lowest level of the devas. The Buddha described 28 classes of celestial beings. Brahma is such a high god that he can't even relate directly to the devas of the lower sensuous sphere, let alone mere human beings. So Brahma creates an intermediary and he sent this gandarbha described as Five Crest. Each of the devas of the thirty three believed that Five Crest walked up to only them, but this was an illusion created by the vast mind powers of the god-like Brahma. This is what Sakkha described on one of his many visits with the Buddha.

The single most shocking thing about Buddhism is it's teachings about non theism. This is much deeper than it seems. Non theism is defined as believing that there is no such thing as a personal, almighty god or gods. This is true. There is no such thing as a separate, personal god. When theists, like most religious people in the world, hear that Buddhists don't believe in god, the typical reaction is no big deal. People can believe whatever they want. That's no threat. In Judaism, the Jews say that there is no name for god. In the Christian tradition, as well as the Muslim tradition, they share the same god as the Jews because they all have their root in Abraham of the Old Testament. The same one almighty god, they believe. The Muslim name for god is Allah and the Christian name for god is Jehovah. This name comes from the meeting of minds that Moses had up on Mount Sinai, with god. Moses experienced or they claim he experienced seeing a burning bush. He asked the burning bush "What are you?" The burning bush replied to Moses "I am that I am." This is generally regarded as being the definition of god. The Hebrew words for "I am that I am" sound something like "Jehovah," hence the Christian name for god. The Christians chose to name god, the Jews had a good reason not to.

God

A Buddhist interpretation of Moses' experience with the burning bush is that it very possibly happened exactly the way Moses said that it did. But the scariest thing about the entire Buddhist religion is that Buddhism does not refute the existence of Jehovah. Buddhism recognizes the existence of Jehovah as one great deva in the fine material sphere of existence. That's the big scary news. Buddhism has subjugated god! Worse still, is the fact that god Jehovah has to step aside for the biggest deva in the entire universe: Brahma. Brahma is the Hindu god and he's much bigger and more powerful than the lesser, weaker Jehovah. More details on this are revealed in the book *Buddhism Explained* by Phra Khantipalo. In principle Moses could have had a deva experience, but the anti-mythological eye of history states that this famous story about Moses never happened. It was something that the Judaism of 700 B.C. attributed to Moses who lived about 1200 B.C. In the ten commandments, which was supposed to have been given to Moses from god on Mount Sinai, it says that the Sabbath day is a day of rest. But Moses was an Egyptian and they didn't even have a Sabbath day until Judaism was more established, about 700 B.C. So, many fictional stories have been attributed to Moses just as Confucius has been the venerated subject of many fictitious teachings as well.

Devahood is like the idea that if you are good, when you die you will go to heaven. This is true in many cases, according to Buddhism, so that's how you become a deva. Buddhism has subjugated the Hindu religion as well as any other theistic tradition, in this way. Buddhism reveals that there is a seed syllable for some deities, or vaster, god-like devas such as Brahma. Seed syllables represent the root name for such a being; seed syllables such as OM or HRI, etc. The Venerable Chögyam Trungpa Rinpoche said that the seed syllable for Jehovah has always been kept a secret by the Jews because they were afraid that some yogi might come along and subjugate god!

The Buddhists claim that the ultimate state of enlightened mind is above the personal limitation of a self or ego which is what is still limiting 'god Jehovah,' Brahma, and most other celestial devas. They are not generally enlightened in the upstairs. They're greater than we are, but they are not god. If you attain to full and complete enlightenment in this very life, then you will be bigger than god Jehovah himself. Technically, that is literally the truth from a Buddhist view. There's no such thing as god but there are plenty of powerful devas that we should relate with. People just make the mistaken assumption that if they supplicate a deva, then it must be some kind of almighty god, or Jesus Christ. Some Christians attribute every single higher realm manifestation that they experience to Jesus. That's not fair to the countless other devas pulling their weight. That's like saying that President Roosevelt single handedly ended the depression and won World War II, without any help at all! Praise Roosevelt!

So, a Buddhist interpretation of the virtuous and caring Moses, is that the wise man made a mistake and assumed that the burning bush was a manifestation of 'the one god.' If Moses could have somehow looked up, on the proverbial left hand or right hand side, he may have noticed Brahma and some other great big devas up there too, seeing that Jehovah was not much of an almighty god after all. This explains a lot of other misunderstandings in history as well. The more you study and test out Buddhism, the more everything seems to hang together and make sense. The deeper you dig, the deeper you are. Phra Khantipalo's theory about Jesus and Mohammed is that they may have been devas in their previous lives. In deep meditation they recalled only their last life and believed that they did in fact know god. If they knew Jehovah in their previous life as a deva they could have made an honest mistake and believed that Jehovah was a one and only almighty god. Fired with this inner conviction, they could have gone out and taught a false assumption with true sincerity. It's possible.

In the lower realms, the ghost realm is inhabited by real ghosts, like the ones in your living room and closets at home. They were probably unhappy people that have died and they are characterized by poverty mentality. The hell realm is rock bottom in samsara. Hell is not at all a popular subject in the West, however it is not logical to believe that hell does not exist simply because it is unpopular. The Buddha described hot hells and cold hells, hells of moans, hells of screams and hells of indescribable filth. In Buddha's description of one hell, he said that it was like a man going into a shop which provides wheat. There are eighty bushels of wheat and once every one hundred years he takes one grain of wheat and walks away. Then a hundred years later he comes back and takes one more grain of wheat, and walks away. The amount of time it would take him to empty all of the bushels of wheat is the length of time that beings stay in this particular region of hell. Then Buddha went on to explain another part of hell where beings stay ten times longer than that! So Buddhism is not some new age trip of love and light and mush, oozing out everywhere. There really is a hell, sorry. Buddhism actually props up some crucial Christian religious beliefs. Christian purgatory could be called the hungry ghost realm.

Meditation Practice and Cosmology

The formless sphere is the top four layers of samsara. Here the mental beings have no form at all, no skandha of the body. This is kind of a spiritual dead end street because they need to come down to a lower level, like human, to get enlightened. I have a friend, Glen Pavlick who teaches Buddhism at Langara College in Vancouver. He was also a monk in Thailand and he has entered into samadhi absorption states. In a samadhi one's consciousness is automatically at the level of the fine material sphere, or the level of the formless sphere. During Glen's samadhi states, his mind has moved about amongst the form and formless levels. To date I have not yet made it to a samadhi. During the final phase of my month retreat, which was a necessary initiation before ordaining as a monk, we were instructed to make a great effort to attain samadhi. In the Mahasi Sayadaw tradition, I reached what is called the 'arising and ceasing of phenomena,' where you feel pin prick sensations all over your body. At first I thought there was an ant crawling on my knee, but then I realized that this was what I was waiting for. This is a stage prior to what the Buddha called 'neighbourhood concentration,' which occurs before a samadhi, the samadhi being like getting sucked into a black hole.

This information is included in this chapter on cosmology to relate the deva world to our meditation practice. Cosmology is not some far out thing that you will have to wait until after you are dead to validate. Also, in the chapter 'How to Invoke Devas' we will practice techniques to actually relate with the devas and bring down their blessings into our lives. So, this is practical Buddhism, not science fiction.

There are eight layers of the god realm corresponding to the eight samadhis in total. Your meditation experience relates directly to the most far out mystical regions of Buddhist cosmology. It is not as though the higher regions of heaven have nothing to do with you. Ordinary people are having samadhi absorptions today, just because they are putting time and effort into their practice, as you could be. The top four layers of the eight are the four layers of the immaterial sphere. These are the sphere of infinite space, the sphere of infinite consciousness, the sphere of nothingness, and the top layer of heaven, the top layer of samsara, the sphere of neither perception nor non perception.

In Tibetan Buddhist traditions it seems that they don't emphasize the samadhis that much but they emphasize formless meditation. This may be because the Theravadin Buddhist tradition was the first to dominate the market with the samadhi product. Because the Mahayana and Tibetan traditions exaggerate their claim to being superior to the Theravadin Buddhist tradition, this indicates a possible motive to distort the Buddha's emphasis on samadhi in favour of their sectarianism. Probably most Buddhist traditions north and south are guilty of putting truth second to their claims of the superiority of their own tradition. If the northern school admitted that the Buddha taught the importance of samadhi as much as the Buddha really did teach the importance of samadhi, then they would be bowing in line behind Theravadin Buddhism. This is unacceptable to them. I have heard Tibetan Buddhists say that Theravadin Buddhists mistakenly get stuck on samadhi and attach to the flavour of samadhi. Such an accusation is a form of aggression. On the other hand, in Thailand I lived with an Australian Theravadin monk who accused the Mahayanists of getting stuck on samadhi. The reason for this confusion is because the scriptures do warn you not to get attached to samadhi, but this has nothing to do with any particular Buddhist tradition or lineage.

The eight levels of these heavenly spheres are full of devas, countless trillions of devas. The fictional Mahayana Atavamsaka sutra is considered by many to be the greatest religious text ever written by man. In this sutra it states that there are as many devas as there are atoms in the Buddha universes. One gets the impression of a deva administration with one or more devas assigned to watch over you in particular. Perhaps your devas are talking to your boss' devas and they are asking those devas to influence your boss into giving you what you want. If you know some appropriate chants, such as in the chapter on invoking devas, you can better your chances of success by using them. That's how Buddhist cosmology can help your life in practical, down to earth ways. Manuals on effective job hunting techniques should include Pali and Sanskrit chants. These chants have worked to get this book published. It is useful and practical to know the cosmological view of the universe and how to better your place in it.

An analogy to understand the devas is that you think of a man sitting on his bed, playing with a cat. He puts his hand under the sheet and wiggles his finger to get the cat's attention. The cat adores him so when it sees the imprint of his fingernail through the sheet, it pounces on his finger and gives him a love bite. Think of the bed sheet as the surface of the Earth with over five billion people. When a person chants to the devas he is like the finger wiggling to get the attention of the devas. The cat is like a deva in the sensuous sphere who loves human beings and responds to their needs. It's not so easy to see a person down there unless they wave a flag or do something to get attention. The devas single you out for help, out of five billion other people because you did a Buddhist deva invocation chant. The cat pouncing and giving the finger a love bite is like the devas coming to your assistance, merging with your mind, or otherwise loving you and helping you out. The man who is above the cat, and playing with it, represents devas of the Brahma world, the fine material sphere. A man is far above a cat, just as the higher devas are far above the lower devas. Enlightened mind is represented as the clear blue bright sky above their beautiful house. The house represents the four layers of the fine material sphere. The attic of the house is the fourth layer. The man doesn't go into the attic much because Brahma lives at home in the first three layers of the Brahma world. You are like that fingernail imprint wiggling, when you are chanting. It is good to chant if you want to stand out from the rest of suffering humanity.

The Buddha's discourses are full of hundreds of stories of devas coming down and helping people or sitting beside the Buddha, patiently beckoning him to teach them. Dakas are male devas. Dakinis are female devas. This definition is a spin doctoring to dilute the Vajrayana meaning that a daka is an enlightened male deity and a dakini is an enlightened female deity. In this definition, dakinis are female devas, typically described as being exquisitely beautiful, topless and breathtaking in appearance. Just heart stopping beauty! Paintings or statues of dakinis in Buddhist temples often depict them as having pointed crowns on their heads with crests on either side of their head and crests pointing up on their shoulders, as Five Crest. They are covered with gold, diamonds and jewels and beautiful flowing things. Buddhism lends some support to the Muslim belief that when you go to heaven you will be attended upon by many extremely beautiful women wearing indescribably attractive celestial dress. The beings of the sensuous sphere, which includes the five lower realms are driven by the urge towards sexual union, the Buddha taught. The devas of the two higher spheres are beyond sexual identity. They are asexual devas, like 'father god' Jehovah or Brahma. The important point that the Buddha made about all of this sensuous pleasure is that the disadvantage of going to heaven after you die is that you might not get much meditation practice in, or studying done to further your spiritual path if you're indulging in sex all the time. The god realm is like an expense account. After you've expended your honestly earned merit, then you fall from that birth like a lavish company account that is cut off when you are suddenly fired from your job. You may then end up with a human birth like the rest of us ordinary people. In fact, in your previous lives you may already have been a deva for a thousand years! The *Tibetan Book of the Dead* describes deva death as being as sudden as a foul odour born on a summer's breeze. Buddha said that devas get old and die, as humans do. The Buddha actually cautioned his monks not to join him just to reach a deva rebirth. Your goal is higher than that, the Buddha admonished; your goal is to go beyond the bliss of the god realm and attain full and complete enlightenment.

The Buddha also emphasized that the good fortune of the human realm is that we have the advantage of suffering. Because we have the tremendous good fortune to suffer, we are motivated to do something about our suffering. We even go out and buy Buddhist books like *Freeing the Buddha* or we search for someone who can teach us how to meditate. It's usually some form of pain that brings people onto the path, so thank your pain. As Jesus pitied the rich young man because he couldn't leave behind what he had, to discover something better, you can pity trillions of devas this month, who are expending their energies in a storm of sexual bliss in the sensuous sphere, and on Earth.

Jesus was once asked what would happen if a man died and his wife married her husband's brother. Then if the second husband died and she married the next brother and the process continued to seven brothers, then at the resurrection, who's wife would she be? Jesus said that the situation was not applicable in that they would be angels in heaven and there would be no need for sexual relations. From a Buddhist view this would be true if they became asexual devas in the fine material sphere, but generally this would not be true because most beings remain with a sex drive in their rebirth as devas; only those who have attained samadhi can become asexual devas.

Enlightenment takes you off of the wheel of life, finally, to the extinction of re-birth. That's what you really want! You don't want to go to some region of heaven so that you can enjoy sex which is like children sharing their toys. You don't want to be grasping after countless exquisite topless dakinis, as far as the eye can see in spherical di-rections, bouncing around in space with heart stopping beauty. No way. You don't want that. Likewise, women and gay men don't really want to take rebirth amongst countless dakas of indescribable manhood and self assurance, roaming around in the same envi-ronment as above. No way. They don't want that. They would rather attain to the un-known of nirvana. That is why the *Tibetan Book of the Dead* teaches that you should go for the naked mind of the blue light of enlightenment, rather than be seduced by the less appealing sensuousness of the white light of the gods.

Nirvana, the dharmakaya, is what lies beyond this sphere of samsara (see diagram). Since nirvana and samsara are inseparable, enlightened mind permeates the space you are in right now. Enlightened mind in inseparable from every particle of matter in the entire universe. But samsara cannot penetrate to the dharmakaya, the residing place of enlightened mind. Nirvana is beyond our ability to even de-scribe accurately. Like a fish trying to understand a turtle's description of dry land, we cannot know the experience of enlightenment until we have the direct experi-ence of enlightenment. Such is our existence on the wheel of life.

Chapter 7

Class Eight
The Four Foundations
of Mindfulness

Lord Buddha informed us that the one and only true way to attain enlightenment is through the practice of mindfulness. There is no other way, he said. His instruction for human beings and devas is to practice the four foundations of mindfulness:

1. Mindfulness of body — body position and movement.
2. Mindfulness of feelings — the three big kleshas of passion, aggression and neutral feelings.
3. Mindfulness of mind — awareness itself, as well as your underlying state of mind.
4. Mindfulness of mind objects — the six senses — thinking, seeing, hearing, feeling, smell and taste.

Every single experience that you have ever had in your many lifetimes can be found under one of these four categories. Mindfulness of the body is the best place to start, the first skandha of form. In meditation you note 'thinking' whenever your body acts up and distracts you. In post meditation you should ideally make an effort to be mindful in every waking minute. That means that you should put your mind on what it is that you are actually doing, rather than thinking about 'things.'

For the purpose of teaching (or being a student in) this course, this is the class with the raisins. You should prepare a bag of raisins and bring it to class so that you have enough raisins for ten per person. After the regular meditation period, during this talk, you pull out the bag and explain that they are going to practice mindful eating. Some people say that this is almost a revelation to them, they realize that they were missing moments of their life. The discipline is to stop reading the newspaper (it's mostly negative anyway) while you eat, and stop listening to the stereo at the same time. Just eat. This is meditation in action, you regard your eating and other activities as an extension of your sitting practice. When you meditate you don't read the newspaper and listen to music. Zen roshis say, "When I sit, I sit. When I walk, I walk. When I eat, I eat. When I sleep, I sleep." That's deep.

In reaching for a raisin you note to yourself "reaching, reaching." When picking it up you mentally label "grasping, grasping." As you bring the raisin to your mouth, "bringing, bringing," then "putting," as you put the raisin in your mouth. Lower your arm and pause before putting it down on your lap or the table, "lowering, lowering... putting." Continue with noting "chewing, chewing, tasting, tasting," noting "liking," or "disliking." "Swallowing, swallowing," as you feel it going down the throat. Go back to "reaching," and continue to properly experience how to eat food. Meals in silence are a wonderful practice experience in family life. You don't have to have every meal in silence but it would be wise to make a project out of this at times.

Lead the class through a guided meditation on the four foundations of mindfulness. Pause at each one on the above list, going in order so students can appreciate looking at themselves in this grounded, mindful way. Beforehand, describe the first foundation by recommending that people frequently acknowledge their body position and movements throughout the day. Phra Sawat, my meditation instructor at Wat Ram Poeng used to walk past me and my compadres many times saying only "Acknowledge, acknowledge." In meditation, walking or sitting, one is aware of their posture and that their body is the connection between heaven, earth and man.

Ordinary Walking

When walking down the street one should alter the usual walking meditation technique, as you are moving much faster. You don't label 'thinking' as the environment is not generally subtle enough for that. You must label the feet as they touch the ground. Shambhala meditation centres have adopted British army marching techniques for marching squads of meditation troops. This is just for proper Buddhist mindfulness training and is not related to creating a defence force to protect us from the impending result of Nostradamus' certain prediction that 'a man with a blue turban will rise out of Persia. He will be the terror of mankind.' As you walk down Main Street, you bring your attention to your right foot as it touches the pavement. You say to yourself "Right, left, right, right, right. Right, left, right, right, right," as you walk along. You skip most of the left counts, otherwise you would be noting too fast for comfort. This is a very practical practice, as we walk so much. Make it so.

Number two, mindfulness of feelings means that you catch yourself whenever your mind adversely turns away from things that bug you in the slightest way, plus note things that tempt your attention, and also note things that are neither pleasant, nor unpleasant— neutral feelings. This is a completely different meaning for 'feelings' than the 'feeling' in the 2nd skandha of anatta (which means the five senses).

Goldfish in a Goldfish Bowl

To remember the third and fourth foundations, there is a very good visualization from the Theravadin tradition which helps anchor these concepts to a vivid mental image. The image is of a goldfish swimming around in a goldfish bowl. The fourth foundation is represented by the bright goldfish. The mind objects are the bright reflections off the fins and body which are easy to see. What is not so easy to see and appreciate is the water around the goldfish. This is the mind itself, and the underlying state of mind (how clean the water is). Is your underlying state of mind joyous, rapturous, depressed, confused? All of your thoughts and sensory input from seeing hearing, etc. are mind objects, which are very dominating in your experience, practically your whole of experience. Behind it all, your awareness is there, consciousness itself.

Standing Meditation

The Buddha taught four postures for meditation practice — sitting, walking, standing and lying. Ananda confused the arahant policy by attaining enlightenment in another posture. He was trying hard to get to nirvana, he took a break from his meditation a few weeks after the Buddha died, he almost laid down and just as his hand touched the mat, pop! He attained full and permanent enlightenment.

To do standing meditation you stand with your hands comfortably at your side or together. Your balance is better with your eyes open. You look down cast out in front of you. In the Mahasai Sayadaw Vipassana technique from Burma, the object of meditation is the rising and the falling of the abdomen (or you could use the breath at the nose). You say silently to yourself 'rising, falling...' After following the first breath in and out, you say 'standing, touching.' On the second in breath you bring your attention to your whole body standing as you scan it from feet to head. On the out breath you bring your attention to an arbitrary touching point which is the bump on the back of your hip on the right hand side. You visualize that that point on your hip is being gently touched. Do this again on the next round of breaths but for the left bump on the back of your hip. Just keep going back and forth, around in a circle in this way until the time is up. There is no esoteric meaning to the arbitrary touching points. You must also label 'thinking' when you have thoughts, then go back to the breath. Vipassana sitting meditation can be done the same way, but with noting "sitting."

This is a good technique if you've been meditating too long and need to stand up. If you are teaching a class in a crowded apartment with no room for walking meditation, use standing instead. This is a great one for line ups, line ups anywhere, or bus stops because you don't look weird with your hands hanging at your side. Let such mindfulness practices infiltrate your being, build a lifestyle of mindfulness. Joy and delight! It is by being so ordinary that life takes on an extraordinary quality. Simplifying your life is defined as: creating an environment in your life that makes you more mindful. When I was 20 my buddy Rob and I visited my sister Diana and I was telling her about living here and now. She thought I was talking irresponsibly about 'eat, drink and be merry' and we left without me really being able to express myself correctly. Thirteen years later at Wat Ram Poeng I finally understood what being here and now meant. After three weeks of a retreat the mindfulness sunk into me at an experiential level. With mindfulness life can take on a sparkle in the rain quality. It's magical.

Lying Meditation

In lying meditation you do much the same as in sitting meditation. You lie down, preferably on your right side, the Buddha taught, because your heart is on the left side. It puts less pressure on your heart. In lying, you note 'rising, falling, lying, touching.' After following the abdomen rising and falling, then you feel your whole body touching the surface, the bed. Next, the first touching point is the head touching the pillow. After the next round of breaths the touching point is where your hip touches the bed, finally where your feet touch the bed. Then you go back to the head and follow these three points around and around until your time is up or until you fall asleep. Similar to counting sheep, this is a good technique if you can't sleep. The Buddha said that a monk or nun should be mindful until the last moment of consciousness, and then immediately resume mindfulness practice as soon as they wake up. You shouldn't lie down if you want to meditate because you'll likely fall asleep. Meditating while lying down is like trying to start your car with a dead battery, it doesn't work. So you wouldn't say "O.K. boys and girls, it's time to meditate now, let's all lay down." Lying meditation is meant for situations where you are lying down anyhow, like going to bed, or when you're sick. This is good for cold Canadian winters when you don't want to get out of your cozy bed, snuggled up to another warm lovable body beside you. If you wimp out from sitting practice, because it's too cold to sit up in the living room, just lie there and do Vipassana lying meditation. Easy. Stay awake!

Dying Meditation

It's good to die on your right side for the reason of putting less physical pressure on the heart. If there's ever a war and you suddenly find yourself dying, try to move to your right side if rubble is not pinning you down. Minutes before the Buddha's father died, Buddha taught him "nothing is more important right now than your breath, father. Follow your breath. Concentrate on your breath." Not intending to be morbid, it is important that in the future, if there is some kind of war, you must not be overcome at death by thoughts that some of your loved ones must certainly have died. You must let those thoughts go while you are dying alone and stay with your breath, and label 'thinking' as you die. Also practice the loving kindness contemplation. You must be concentrated and die unconfused. Your whole Buddhist life pivots at the moment of death. There is no moment more important, not even conception nor birth. *The Tibetan Book of the Dead* may not exactly be true but it provides much wisdom. That book, which so many are intrigued by, may be the writings of one monk who lived in Tibet in the fourteenth century, contrary to popular belief. It is supposed to be terma authored by Padmasambhava but the majority of Buddhists in the world probably cannot accept this as the Buddha taught no such thing. 'Terma' means revealed teachings that were hidden by Padmasambhava in Tibet, for the benefit of future generations. These alleged hidden teachings are allegedly found centuries later by tertons, who can allegedly receive them.

When you're dead, who can help you? You're on your own (unless people are practicing give and take for you — that helps dead people a great deal). However, if you think of the Buddha first, and think of the guru, if you think of your teacher, that will act as a binding factor in your mind while you are in the bardo and such devotional thoughts will very much help steer you around the bardo rocks to safety. If you only take in and accept one piece of advice from this book, these teachings on death are the most important for you to take to heart.

If you do the best possible job of being mindful during your death, you will go on to a better rebirth, but you can't cheat or avoid the laws of karma. If you've lived a wicked life but manage a rebirth as a deva, then what happens is that your bad karma will ripen in those beautiful surroundings. Maybe the other devas won't like you and they won't let you join in any devaloka games. In the big picture it balances out. Conversely, if you've lived a virtuous life but you really blew it in the bardo by freaking out and taking rebirth as a cat, then you may have a very pleasant and pampered existence as a well off and dearly loved house cat, to compensate for your lower rebirth in the animal realm. Then after your lifetime as a cat, you could take rebirth as a human again or even go straight to the devaloka.

Retreats

You can start with a one day or a weekend retreat, then you can jump into a one week or one month meditation retreat. In Vancouver, weekend retreats are organized by the author, and by the Shambhala Centre and by the West Coast Dharma Association. For a longer retreat at low cost, you can go to the Mount Tuam Buddhist Retreat Centre on Saltspring Island (K.D.O.L.-Kunzang Dechen Osel Ling), founded by Kalu Rinpoche. On the high end, for one week $1000 retreats go to Hollyhock on Cortez Island. Check retreat times, cost and other locations in your area. One of the best places to retreat at is Rocky Mountain Shambhala Centre (RMSC) in Colorado, or other Western Buddhist retreat centres spread around North America. The technique matters not, if you don't meditate! Just getting yourself to the cushion is 80% of the job. The 80/20 rule, the Parado principle, applies to meditation and most areas of the universe. The rule is that 80% of the value of your results in life come from 20% of your activities. 80% of your income comes from 20% of your clients. If you practice dharma only for 20% of your life, that will result in 80% of the merits of your life. The meditation technique that you choose to practice is like choosing a suit of clothes to wear. The Buddha definitely taught a plurality of techniques so be very careful not to get too attached to one technique like I did back in the early days. It is considered to be tremendously fortunate karma even to do a one week retreat in this lifetime. Lucky you. The author envies how happy you will soon be.

You don't have to go to Thailand or a Buddhist country to do a retreat. The main benefit of going to places like that is the money. "If you plan a long term retreat of a few months," Jack Kornfield says,"then even with the cost of airfare it is cheaper to go to Asia than pay $25 per day in the United States." In Thailand you can retreat in a monastery for about $3 a day but the instruction probably won't be as good as back home. If you have the money to afford your own culture, stay here; the quality is better here. The best way to save money is to live for free by staffing at a retreat centre such as RMSC, Karme-Chöling in Vermont, or Gampo Abbey Tibetan Buddhist monastery on Cape Breton Island, Nova Scotia. Staffing is ideal if you can take several months off, or even make a longer term stay. To live in a proper Buddhist environment is like being in a nuclear furnace of dharma. Such a chance might never come again.

Chapter 8

Class Nine
Awakened Heart

Awakened Heart is a translation of the Buddhist term bodhicitta. 'Bodhi' means 'awake,' and 'citta' means 'mind,' 'heart' or 'seed.' So bodhicitta means the seed of enlightenment that is in all sentient beings. This is parallel to, or opposite to the idea of original sin in the Bible. In the book of Genesis Adam and Eve are in the garden of Eden with god and they are not even aware of any difference between god, man, or woman. Then they did something terribly shameful by eating from an apple given to them by the snake. This was their original sin, because of which they were driven out of the garden of Eden, and into exile.

In some Christian traditions the idea of original sin is that deep down inside of you, there is something fundamentally wrong with you. Deep, deep, deep, deep, deep down, you have a basic problem. That problem is original sin, so you have to be fixed up. You have to be saved. Your soul must be redeemed by the messiah, you need to be saved by Jesus. That salvation is like coming back into the garden of Eden again.

In Buddhism, deep, deep, deep down, your root problem is ignorance. That's your most fundamental problem. Desire and ego arise from ignorance. But even deeper down than that, underneath your ignorance you have bodhicitta, the seed of enlightenment. All sentient beings limitless as space have this Buddha-nature. You already have enlightenment within you right now, except that it is buried under your layers of ignorance and confusion. We all have our stains, we have our weaknesses and faults, but regard those as stains on your clothing. They will come out in the wash because you are the Buddha. You are the Buddha inside. Your job is to unravel your confusion and ignorance and let that jewel in a heap of dust shine out. You don't have to go anywhere to get enlightened. You don't have to get something from outside of yourself and take it in and swallow it. You weren't born to learn anything, you were born to remember.

A traditional analogy for connecting with bodhicitta is that it is compared to connecting with your parents. Suppose you take a trip to Mexico with your beloved parents. You are all on the beach having a good time. You get tempted by some rather attractive looking locals and you wander off with them and get carried away. It's the height of tourist season and the beach is a completely mad festival of multitudes of happy people (the scriptures define a multitude as being 84,000 people). When you come back you cannot find your parents. You search the beach, scanning up and down, but they are nowhere to be found. You've lost your parents. This means that you were once connected to bodhicitta but because of your neurotic thinking you've buried it under crowds of confusion.

Twenty years go by, and you haven't seen your parents; you think about them now and again. You go on vacation to Long Beach on the west coast of Vancouver Island, Canada, with your own family. As the humongous cold waves shimmer across the sun baked sand, you feel a rare and sacred peace after working so hard at the office all year long. An old couple sit close to you but you don't pay them no never minds, until you smell something familiar. You hear a familiar voice so you look again and you see your parents sitting right there. You go over and introduce yourself and they feel as awkward as you do. You all agree to have lunch over at the Beach House and it is there that you notice the many idiosyncrasies that remind you of your youth spent with them. Only then, after being with them for some time do you breakdown and cry because you know that you have finally been reunited with your parents, like the Adventures of Odysseus. That's connecting with bodhicitta, awakened heart. The Buddha said, "It doesn't matter how long you forget, only how soon you remember!"

The Buddhist concept of bodhicitta is much more upbeat than original sin in the book of Genesis. Using the comparison of the garden of eden, there is a Buddhist image of the Buddha sitting under the tree of immortal life, sitting in, the ultimate peace of nirvana. Protecting the Buddha is a dharmapala standing close by. When you walk into a Buddhist temple the dharmapalas are fierce protector devas depicted as statues of very tough looking guys placed so that you would have to get by them first in order to see the Buddha. This is very much like the scene at the gate of the garden of eden. There you have a tough looking figure, a cherub, standing at the gate and god is saying that the guard is emphatically there and that you can't get in! But as you peer in to see the Buddha, the Buddha is holding up his hand and he's saying to you "Don't worry about that guy at the gate, he's not going to hurt you. You can come in." So, you step inside and you sit under the tree of immortal life and you find your transcendence to nirvana. Buddhism leads you to the still point within, to the end of your spiritual journey, but the Bible is basically a religion of exile.

The moment of exile from the garden of eden can also be compared to the metaphoric first moment that the ego split off from the vast open space of primordial mind, as a ripple, then a bubble. Ever since then, we have been trying to get back to enlightened mind, trying to get back into the garden of eden. That inward journey to attain enlightenment means to go into your heart. What lies within your heart is bodhicitta. Emerson said "What lies behind us and what lies before us are tiny matters compared to what lies within us."

So, how do we connect with bodhicitta? How do we realize awakened heart? We must be willing to face our state of mind. In the sitting practice of meditation, we sit and we look at our minds, ourselves, our inner being, our true nature. In meditation we confront our state of mind, we work with our mind as it is. You are searching for your heart, your naked beating heart of bodhicitta. Beginning with meditation practice there are many techniques which guide you to opening your heart and making your heart more available to others. Meditation is the way to touch your seed of enlightenment. By looking into your mind, you look into your heart. In this way you can share your heart with others. Because there is so much suffering in the world it is not best to be self stuck in the bliss of the god realm state of mind. "Enjoying happiness without producing happiness is like spending money without earning it," George Bernard Shaw said.

It benefits others more if you feel a genuine heart of sadness, and make your heart available to others. In this way you care more about others. The sadness you feel is an unconditioned sadness, as enlightened mind is unconditioned mind. If you could touch your heart, if you could put your hand in your chest and touch your heart, you would feel tenderness. Even if a feather lands on your heart, you feel so touched you could cry. Your heart is open to the world, you could pour your heart all over others. You don't have to go on a rampage of hugs and kisses and throw flowers in the air as you dance and sing in the street, to extend warmth towards others. If someone speaks to you in the supermarket line up, you may feel aversion, but you can listen to them and warm up to them. To chat with them is compassion in that moment, in that situation. Each hour presents different moments of compassion, different opportunities to give to others. Compassion is ordinary.

A sterling reputation has been earned by the Mahayana traditions for developing compassion to the highest priority. This is described as a process of working on yourself before you have the skillfulness to go outwards and work with others effectively. If a person doesn't work on himself first, they could be like the well meaning person that sees someone lying in the street after a car accident. They pick them up, accidentally sever their spine, then put them down at the side of the road. Working with others must also avoid the missionary mentality of laying a trip on people and shoving 'the truth' down their throats.

Compassion means compassion in action, stepping forward. It is wise to spread Buddhism and compassion, it is wise to go outwards and do something. It's O.K. to do it right. Chögyam Trungpa would cry during his public talks saying "Please help people. Help others. Please help people." This ideal of benefitting others is distilled in the noble virtues of the bodhisattva, which means 'enlightenment being.' This could mean someone who is enlightened or close to enlightenment. It is also used in a wider sense to refer to people who have a lot of compassion, like Mother Teresa, or firemen and ambulance attendants. The bodhisattva takes the bodhisattva vow, which is generally associated with the Mahayana. However, Dr. Rahula states, "the fact is that both the Theravada and the Mahayana unanimously accept the Bodhisattva ideal as the highest." A mental prostration should be given to the Venerable Walpola Rahula for his long efforts to demonstrate how many of the quintessential Mahayana teachings are found in the original Theravada. The Corporate Body of the Buddha Educational Foundation in Taipei, Taiwan distributes free books worldwide. In their *Gems of Buddhist Wisdom* Dr. Rahula states (Rahula, 1996; 468):

> In the dim past, many incalculable aeons ago, Gotama the Buddha, during his career as Bodhisattva, was an ascetic named Sumedha. At that time there was a Buddha called Dipankara whom he met and at whose feet he had the capacity to realize nirvana as a disciple (sravaka). But Sumedha renounced it and resolved, out of great compassion for the world, to become a Buddha like Dipankara to save others. Then Dipankara Buddha declared and predicted that this great ascetic would one day become a Buddha and he offered eight handfuls of flowers to Sumedha. Likewise, Dipankara Buddha's disciples who were with him and who were themselves arahants offered flowers to the Bodhisattva. This story of Sumedha distinctly shows the position a Bodhisattva occupies in the Theravada.

> In the 12th century A.D. in Burma King Alaungsithu of Pagan, after building a temple set up an inscription in Pali verse to record this act of piety in which he publicly declared his resolution to become a Buddha and not a Sravaka/ arahant. In Sri Lanka, in the 10th century, King Mahinda IV in an inscription proclaimed that "none but the Bodhisattvas would become kings of Sri Lanka."

Unlike the Theravada, the Mahayana has a separate literature devoted to the bodhisattva ideal. Over the centuries in India the altruism and idealism of the Mahayana blossomed into this wonderful expression of commitment to love and compassion. It is a vow that we are going to save all sentient beings limitless as space and establish them into a state of full and complete enlightenment. Once you've taken the vow, you not only commit your whole lifetime, but you also commit your future lifetimes as well! You promise that you will always come back and take rebirth and continue to work for the welfare of others; you will teach, you will exert compassion in whatever way that you can to benefit others. You will not quit until all of samsara is empty of sentient beings. 'Sentient' means 'of limited awareness,' so the Buddha was not a sentient being because he did not have limited awareness.

This vow is a big vow, it won't be fulfilled in the next five year plan. Sentient beings are countless in number throughout the galaxies. But there is some relief indicated by Shantideva in his *Guide to the Bodhisattva's Way of Life*. Shantideva says that the key understanding is that there are no sentient beings. By this he means that there is no self, so no beings actually exist as true separate independent sentient beings. This deserves some contemplation and Shantideva's book has been recommended for centuries as the textbook on how to be a bodhisattva — worth studying.

In the Mahayana tradition, the altruism of the bodhisattva vow goes so far that bodhisattvas renounce their own enlightenment in favour of others. They say that they will not enter into nirvana until all other beings are established there first. This may seem like a cold slap in the face but looking deeply into this, we see that this is another wise technique to help us to renounce our ego. As other people become more important than ourselves, we put the spotlight on working towards their awakening. In this way, we take attention off of our own ego. With our energy going outwards to benefit others, we achieve enlightenment from the back door. Therefore, there is no bona fide contradiction between Theravadin and Mahayana Buddhism on this famous point. On the surface renouncing your own enlightenment looks like a direct contradiction because the Buddha taught that your goal is complete enlightenment. Even though the Mahayanists bite the bullet and are proud to renounce their own enlightenment, we still admit that we do aspire to reach enlightenment for the benefit of others. One way we work towards that is by undercutting our egos with the act of renouncing our own enlightenment, in favour of the enlightenment of others. Admitting that, many Buddhists simply aspire to attain enlightenment for the benefit of others, to be better able to guide them to nirvana. So, renouncing is just another technique!

A difference in view about enlightenment is that in Theravadin Buddhism the Buddha taught that once you attain enlightenment you will never come back to being born again. The idea is that once the ego is discarded, there is no longer any possibility of ever taking rebirth again. In Mahayana Buddhism the bodhisattva vows that even if he reaches enlightenment he will come back to human birth and continue to exert compassion for others. This is a direct contradiction between the two major schools of Buddhism and it indicates the altruistic but unreal ideals of the Mahayana.

Loving Kindness, Compassion, Joy, Equanimity

Opening your heart to others is easier to do if you have training. What distinguishes Buddhism from other systems of thought and practice is that techniques are provided to invoke more heart and compassion for others. Buddhism isn't just a head trip of mind and concentration. There is tremendous heart. The Buddha taught a series of four contemplations which are, loving kindness, compassion, joy, and equanimity. These contemplations are the basis of bodhicitta practice. The Mahayana prescribes a series of practices for relative and ultimate bodhicitta. Ultimate bodhicitta is a state of mind with absolutely no mental clinging, a state distinguished by nondiscursive clarity and pure simplicity. It is an experience where you follow no train of thought, but rest evenly in a state in which mind in itself is clear and free of discursiveness. Bodhicitta is the core of your own experience.

Relative bodhicitta consists of the more down to earth practices that you do to invoke compassion in your heart and crack open the numbness and insensitivity encased around your heart. This bodhicitta, or Buddha-nature is empty of an editor, a filter, empty of an ego. Decades ago Buddhist scholars and translators such as Christmas Humphries described this emptiness with adjectives that seemed cold, bleak, almost nihilistic, but in truth emptiness is warm, compassionate. You should appreciate that 'your' Buddha-nature is no different than 'someone else's' Buddha-nature, so how can you possibly watch them suffer? How can you not want them to be happy? "You" are not so important, not central.

There is some sense of stages to the four contemplations on loving kindness, compassion, joy and equanimity. Visualize them like four sides of a square, with equanimity being the most advanced practice. The Buddha called these the divine abidings. Here we draw from Buddhaghosa's famous commentary the *Path to Purification,* written in 412 A.D. Buddhaghosa writes that the word divine means that you put your mind at the level of the most divine devas who, specifically, live in the fine material sphere of the god realm. These practices can put you there in your state of mind. Abidings means that you live or associate with these vast god-like devas, as though you are one of them.

The general purpose of these four contemplations is the bliss of insight and obtaining a beautiful and excellent form of future existence, meaning your next re-birth. Considering all the time and money spent by people to look beautiful, they should invest in their future beauty by doing these contemplations. For those who have the foresight to take good care of their skin while they are young, they already have a disposition to take the long time perspective, which is wise, so it is not radical thinking to be planning ahead for one's physical appearance in the next life.

Peculiar to each of the four respectively is the warding off of ill will, cruelty, aversion (boredom) and envy, and greed or resentment. As to the characteristics of each, loving kindness is characterized here as promoting the aspect of welfare. Its function is to prefer welfare. It is manifested as the removal of annoyance. Its proximate cause is seeing lovableness in beings. It succeeds when it makes ill will subside, and loving kindness fails when it produces selfish affection.

Compassion is characterized as promoting the aspect of allaying suffering. Its function resides in not bearing others' suffering. It is manifested as non-cruelty. Its proximate cause is to see helplessness in those overwhelmed by suffering. It succeeds when it makes cruelty subside, and it fails when it produces sorrow.

Joy, or gladness is also called altruistic joy because it is characterized as gladdening produced by others' success. Its function resides in undercutting envy or jealousy. It is manifested as the elimination of aversion (boredom), its proximate cause is seeing the success of others. It succeeds when it makes aversion (boredom) subside, and it fails when it produces merriment.

Equanimity is characterized as promoting the aspect of neutrality toward beings. Its function is to see the equality in beings. It is manifested as the quieting of resentment and approval. Its proximate cause is seeing ownership of deeds (karma) thus: 'Beings are owners of their deeds. Whose [if not theirs] is the choice by which they will become happy, or will get free from suffering, or will not fall away from the success they have reached?' Equanimity succeeds when it makes resentment and approval subside, and it fails when it produces the equanimity of unknowing, which is that [worldly-minded indifference of ignorance] based on the house life.

The technique for the loving kindness contemplation is described in that section of the 'Practices' chapter. The other three contemplations are done in similar ways, however a specifically Mahayana contemplation on compassion is provided in the give and take section of the same chapter. Loving kindness means an attitude of friendliness towards all beings, gladness, happiness. It is like the Greek concept of agape which made an impression upon the philosophy of Martin Luther King Jr. Dr. King said that when he was in university he struggled with the problem of how to love the white southerners who were oppressing the blacks. King actually studied Buddhism in university but it was Greek philosophy that made more of an impression on him. He said that he was moved by the idea of a disinterested love for all mankind, which is found in agape. He discovered that he didn't have to be best buddies with the racists, he did not have to associate closely with them, he only had to love them from afar. This is exactly the same as the Buddha's teaching on metta, or loving kindness.

Buddhaghosa extensively described the benefits of doing the loving kindness contemplation. He describes the results of loving kindness practice as being that you sleep in comfort and fall asleep as though entering upon an attainment, you wake in comfort like a lotus opening, you dream no evil dreams, devas guard you, weapons do not affect you, your mind is easily concentrated, the expression on your face is serene, you die unconfused, after death you will reappear as a deva in the fine material sphere as one who wakes up from sleep, you are dear to human beings and you are dear to non human beings.

Buddhaghosa tells the story of an Indian man, the Elder Visakha who heard that the island of Ceylon was 'apparently adorned with a diadem of shrines and gleams with the yellow cloth, and the environment is favourable.' He made over his fortune to his wife and children and set off for Ceylon where he ordained. In *Path of Purification* Buddhaghosa writes (Nanamoli, 1956; 338):

> When he had acquired five years' seniority and had become familiar with the two Codes, he celebrated the Pavarana at the end of the Rains, took a meditation subject that suited him and set out to wander, living for four months in each monastery and doing the duties on a basis of equality with the residents.

> On his way to Cittalapabbata he came to a road fork and stood wondering which turn to make. Then a deity living in a rock held out a hand pointing out the road to him.

> He came to Cittalapabbata Monastery. After he had stayed there for four months he lay down thinking 'In the morning I depart.' Then a deity living in a manila tree at the end of the walk sat down on a step of the stair and burst into tears. The elder asked "Who is that?" - "It is I, Maniliya, venerable sir." - "What are you weeping for?" - "Because you are going away." "What good does my living here do you?" - 'Venerable sir, as long as you live here non-human beings treat each other kindly. Now when you are gone, they will start quarrels and loose talk." The Elder said "If my living here makes you live at peace, that is good," and so he stayed there another four months. Then he again thought of leaving, but the deva wept as before. And so the Elder lived on there, and it was there that he attained nirvana.

> This is how a person who abides in loving kindness is dear to non-human beings.

Compassion contemplations traditionally begin with contemplating one's mother. The idea is that the mother image kick starts a feeling of love and compassion because we are supposed to have the most love for our mother. You contemplate thus: "My mother has taken care of me from the moment I was conceived in her womb. She suffered hardships giving birth to me, nursing me, cleaning away my filth. She taught me to do good and she steered me away from evil. Because of her incredible kindness I have now met with the teachings of the Buddha and am practicing the dharma, while she herself still wanders in samsara! How sad I feel in my love for her. The least I can do is help clear away her suffering." You arouse genuine compassion in this way and extend it to your mother, and you continue from there and send compassionate thoughts to all other beings.

To contemplate altruistic joy you can visualize someone that you know who is really happy. Or, if you don't know anyone, you can think of someone that you don't know personally, or you can imagine someone. You could visualize happy families skiing in the German Alps. They're rich and full of good character and charm. Everybody loves them so much. You feel their success and you tune into that. You get vicarious joy from visualizing their joy.

Equanimity is a highly attained state of mind. No matter what activities you are engaged in, you have an evenness of view. You may be the CEO of a Fortune 500 company. One minute you are putting a stamp on an envelope, then another minute you are making decisions affecting the jobs of a thousand employees. It's all the same to you as you flow in the space of undisturbed equanimity.

An example of equanimitous behaviour occurred when President Kennedy went to parties during the Cuban Missile crisis. Before the President went public with the crisis, the Soviets saw him going to parties in Washington so they assumed that he didn't know what was going on. Kennedy knew what terrible possibilities of nuclear war were at stake but he remained in the present moment. Secretary of State Dean Rusk had what Bobby Kennedy described as "a complete physical and mental breakdown," during the crisis. President Kennedy had secret audio tapes of the cabinet meetings made, which have recently been published. His generals were advising him to just fly in and blow up the missile silos with everyone there, but Kennedy, not wanting to kill hundreds of Russian engineers and technicians, took the middle way and ordered a blockade of the island instead, resulting in no loss of life. Even without his Secretary of State to help, Kennedy maintained equanimity masterfully. Equanimity is like an eye in the sky stretching from horizon to horizon, looking with dispassion upon the world.

Chapter 9

Class Ten
How To Invoke Devas

Co-written by Brian Ruhe and Pia Ruhe

D
evas are higher realm beings, heavenly beings that live in the god realm. The Buddhist path encourages you to develop an intentional relationship with devas because they are there to help you to help others. Other religions refer to devas as angels, heavenly hosts, guardian angels, spirit guides, ascended masters, guides, etc. This is a very common belief. The reason why billions of people believe that devas exist is because devas really do exist. This is the nature of conventional reality. As much as we might assume that mankind created them in our minds so that we can feel comforted and better, that doesn't change reality. For example, science has proven that germs do in fact exist. It is true that there are invisible beings that live amongst us. These invisible beings have the power to make us ill, or feel better, they influence the way we think and behave. This is true, germs can do that and they really do exist. In the past, such a belief would have been regarded as superstitious nonsense, but science (the most powerful religion in the world) has triumphed. Germs do exist, and devas exist too.

I take refuge in devas. My deepest comfort and security in life, I have found from taking refuge in Buddhism. Before I took refuge in the Buddha, dharma and sangha, I took refuge in other people, in my friends, which was a fickle situation. Now I feel great support from the deva sangha which is above human beings and is not dependent upon human beings. This chapter helps you find that deeper security and comfort for yourself. This strength comes from not selfishly grasping at people or things but having the intention to go beyond that and live in harmony with how you can assist the deva sangha.

I am convinced of the existence and the presence of the deva sangha in our lives and this belief gives me strength. People may say that we won't know for sure if there is a deva sangha until we are dead but this belief is helping me now anyway. There's a true story about a man who went to a fortune teller and she told him that he was the reincarnation of Napoleon Bonaparte (Tracy, 1988; Phoenix Seminar). He accepted this as true and he began to think of himself as Napoleon. He studied Napoleon and dreamed big plans the way he imagined that Napoleon would have made big plans. He went into business and he became a huge success! By the time he found out that the fortune teller had lied to him, he was already a millionaire. This shows the power of belief, right or wrong. Whatever the subconscious mind takes as true and accepts as true about yourself, can have an enormous impact upon your life.

Even though this wasn't true his belief became his personal mythology and this gave him strength, confidence, comfort and security. Right or wrong, I believe that the deva sangha is actually real and I can take that to the bank. I have authentic Buddhist sutras as the basis of this belief and this view has become a considerable strength which I did not have before I was a Buddhist. With this mythology you feel that you can depend on something that is above others. My deepest refuge is the Buddha, the dharma, the deva sangha and the law of karma. "Just keep doing good," and you'll have no problems at all.

When I first decided to teach deva invocation methods I was very hesitant because this is perhaps the second most far out thing in Buddhism, after *The Tibetan Book of the Dead*. This may seem like a bit too much for Westerners. But, when I first taught this course in Thailand I could see that most of the 59,000,000 Thai people believed in the higher realms and they did daily chants to relate with the devas, so these are not restricted teachings meant only for senior dharma students. Some teachers may present them that way in the West, but my belief is to be open and honest because I believe that people have broad spiritual backgrounds and they are ready to hear more than what many teachers give them credit for. The Buddha stressed that there were no secrets in his teachings. This book is part of the process of bringing these deva invocation teachings out of the underground and into the mainstream. If you are teaching this powerful subject, one class is not enough to do justice to such a tremendous window of opportunity to a wondrous new world, but just one class is effective for showing students that there is such a window that they can make efforts to reach. Cunningly, if they want the goodies, then they are going to have to meditate — a lot! Great ploy — give them a carrot to keep them encouraged. The Buddha employed this policy. You'll find that dharma students are like trained seals. Throw them a fish and they will slap their flippers together.

A standard method to invoke devas is by doing deva invocation chants. I was trained in doing this when I was a monk in Chiangmai, Thailand. I was given chants by a visiting Burmese master, Sayadaw U Silananda, with his book *Paritta Pali and Protective Suttas,* which list several particular chants prescribed by the Buddha himself to invoke the assistance of devas in ordinary everyday life.

Inner, Outer and Secret Mandalas

It is very important to set up the proper inner, outer and secret mandalas for this practice. The outer mandala means the physical environment around yourself, your room, or home — make it clean and uncluttered with good fung shui. Your physical environment is regarded as sacred space. The devas are looking. If your place is a mess then no deva will enter. Pay attention to detail. You create an environment that wakes you up. The shrine room at a Buddhist meditation centre is an example of this, and such locations will surely attract devas. You want to create a container, or space that is uplifted so that something good will descend into it. The inner mandala is how you care for your body, your health habits and how you dress— be uplifted. Regard your body as sacred. Synchronize your body, speech and mind. Ward off any sense of casualness. It's actually good if your clothes fit you a bit too tightly; that helps to perk up your mind. It's not that your clothes don't fit you well, but your neurosis doesn't fit your clothes. Don't put too much junk in your body because it blocks your energy. There is some virtue in being a vegetarian but you don't have to do that. You should abstain from alcohol, except for medicinal purposes because it clouds your connection to the higher realms.

The secret mandala is the world of your emotions and thoughts. Since no one can see what you are thinking, it is called secret. Have thoughts of love for the devas! Dwell in peace, inner peace, outer peace. It is very important to have openness and gentleness. As you are cultivating your state of mind doing deva invocation chants, to make contact with the devas you must be in a gentle and open state of mind. This may sound simple enough but it is a special state to be in. Can you look at your watch and say that at 9:00 o'clock you will be gentle and open? It is not so easy to say that you are going to be gentle and open but this is what you need. You relax in the space and radiate gentleness. 'Ziji' is the beautiful Tibetan word for 'shining out.'

If you don't get your mandalas together the devas could literally look through your window, come through your window, and they might say "there's nothing going on down there. Let's not waste our time with these wretched people. Let's help somebody else instead." They might even say to a few of the virtuous ones among us

"Why don't you come on up here with us? There's nothing going on down there. This is where all the action is." The devas are interested in people that are interested in them; it helps to be aware of the process between the human world and the deva world (devaloka). The devas are also interested in people who are actually doing something for the benefit of others, rather than just having ideas about it. If you are such a person, they might be interested in commingling with you, or sending you some energy, ideas or support. They could affect the karmic coincidences to cause the right people to come to you, and create a serendipitous situation. It's like a whole deva administration going on in the upstairs. But during your normal habitual activities they have no platform upon which to land, they need a container, an invitation. When you practice to bring down the devas, sometimes you feel their presence, and then that feeling fades. This is not just your state of mind that is changing, this is a sign that the devas have been magnetized, they gather, and they leave. Pay attention to that. Even if you are successful and make contact, there is a fickle quality to the devas. You don't know when they are going to leave or if they will come through you at all, even if you do everything right. Ideally you can invoke an ongoing saturation of devas in your presence 24 hours a day, and even wake up from 'glow sleep.'

Chanting

Chanting is a powerful part of the process of calling to the devas. There are Buddhist, Hindu, Christian and other chants that are used like getting on the telephone and actually pressing the buttons to make a call to the upstairs. When you invoke a chant such as the Mangala sutra below, the idea is that the deva sangha are listening for this particular chant and others. This chant and others come from the Buddha so the devas will respond for that reason. It's as though they're saying "Hey! There's somebody down there chanting a Buddhist deva invocation chant. Let's go!" Devas are always on edge to help you any way that they can. They are possessed of compassion so you know that they are there and you know that they care. The way that many devas became devas in the first place is that they were virtuous human beings who had such good karma that they took rebirth as devas! They have love and a sense of kinship to their family and friends left behind so it is on this basis that you know that you can supplicate their compassion, and that they will indeed help you. It's like a mathematical equation. You must open yourself up to such possibilities!

The Buddha taught that the devas are everywhere, they live in the sky, on the earth, in the trees. The devas are thoroughly involved with human affairs and there are Buddhist stories of how they have changed the course of human history (see Tupigowa, chapter 19). Develop an old shoe relationship with them, chant to them often, dedicate your merit to them. The Tibetan Buddhist teachings encourage you to mix your mind with the devas and invite them to descend into your life. You make your body, speech and mind a throne for the devas. As you prepare your outer, inner and secret mandalas, you offer your life as a landing pad for the devas. But this is not encouraging mediumship. You are not losing consciousness and allowing a spirit to talk through your body. You share consciousness with devas but you remain in control of your body, speech and mind. The preliminary stage for this is to practice sitting meditation for about five minutes or more to set the stage of your mind. Next, there are a number of chants or sadhanas from all the major Buddhist traditions, which you may choose, by yourself, or better, with the help of a teacher, for the purpose of invoking devas. For example, you could use chants from the book of protective suttas. ('Sutta' is from the Pali language; the Sanskrit translation, more commonly used is 'sutra.') You can chant the Mangala Sutra for blessings and prosperity and the Atanatiya Sutra for protection. The Buddha said:

> "Monks, learn the Atanatiya protection, study the Atanatiya protection, hold in your hearts the Atanatiya protection. Monks, beneficial is the Atanatiya protection for security, protection, freedom from harm and living in ease for monks, nuns (bhikkhunis) and male and female lay followers."

According to U Silananda's book, when chanting these sutras chanters must fulfil three conditions:

1. They must have learned and chant the Sutras correctly and fully without any omission,
2. They must understand the meaning of the Sutras being chanted, and
3. They must chant with the heart filled with goodwill and loving-kindness.

This book is listed in the bibliography. Curiously, when I was first given this book by U Silananda, I chanted the entire book for one hour, then walked over to visit my friend Phra Narong. His pet dog was sleeping outside of his kuti and I patted her with my foot. She immediately woke up and bit me in the foot, and I was bleeding in two places! Some of the chants specifically mentioned protection from four legged beasts, so needless to say, I was very disappointed in these chants! It wasn't until much later that I discovered that this is a common occurrence with protector chants! Many times people will be rear ended in the parking lot or some nuisance will happen after such chants. Who knows why? It may be the ripening of your bad karma that occurs just before the protection blessings kick in. Maybe Mara is taking one last shot at you. Fortunately, the blessings do take effect.

You can do the chant in the Pali language using the English transliteration provided. However, U Silananda taught that it is just as effective to do the chant in English, which is also provided. Traditionally Theravadin Buddhists generally feel that it is better and more potent to chant in the Pali language, because this is the oldest language known to Buddhism. This is like Latin in the Catholic Church. However, Pali chanting is not necessary. It is important to understand what you are chanting. Likely the devas know enough about these things to respond to these particular chants if spoken in the English language. Remember, it is on the basis of their compassion that you are supplicating the devas. You can call them to you and no doubt they will come closer because they want to help you all that they can.

Below is the English version of the Mangala Sutra which is a chant for blessings and prosperity, rather than a protection chant. Before chanting you should arrange your room, calm your body and mind, and do five minutes or more of meditation to help create openness and gentleness within your being. You should arouse bodhicitta by having the proper motivation to do this for the benefit of others. Think of what it is that you are requesting, or what your particular question is. The clearer you are the better, so that the devas will understand what you need. You wouldn't get on the phone to the President of the United States without having a good reason for calling. You are calling to the higher realms for a purpose.

You do the chant in a monotone. This steady rhythmic quality harmonizes the right and left hemispheres of the brain for optimum memory retention. It's good to do the chant more than once, you could do it three times, nine times or 108 times. Do not take breaks for sentences and paragraphs; chant it straight through like it is one long sentence. If chanting in a group, inhale while others are chanting, so there is no pause in the chant for breathing. Alone, you subvocalize while inhaling so even alone you do not break the continuity. This is the actual chant which comes from the Buddha in the *Khuddakapatha,* 3-4, and the *Sutra Nipata* 308-9.

Mangala Sutra Chant
(for blessings and prosperity)

Men, together with deities, tried to find out for twelve years what blessings were. But they could not find out the blessings which number thirty-eight, that are the cause of happiness.

Oh, Good People! Let us recite those blessings which were taught by the Deity of the Deities (the Buddha) for the benefit of beings and which destroy all evil.

Thus have I heard. At one time the Blessed One was dwelling at the monastery of Anathapindika in Jeta's Grove near the city of Savatthi. Then a certain deity in the late hours of the night with surpassing splendor, having illuminated the entire Jeta's Grove, came to the Blessed One. Drawing near, the deity respectfully paid homage to the Blessed One, and stood at a suitable place; standing there, the deity addressed the Blessed One in verse:

"Many deities and men, desiring what is good, have pondered upon just what blessings were. Pray tell me what the highest blessing is."

"Not to associate with fools, to associate with the wise and to honour those who are worthy of honour. This is the highest blessing.

To live in a suitable place, to have done meritorious deeds in the past, and to keep one's mind and body in a proper way. This is the highest blessing.

To have much learning, to be skilled in crafts, to be well-trained in moral conduct and to have speech that is well spoken. This is the highest blessing.

Caring for one's mother and father, supporting one's spouse and children and having work that causes no confusion. This is the highest blessing.

Giving, practice of what is good, support of one's relatives and blameless actions. This is the highest blessing.

Abstention from evil in mind, abstention from evil in body and speech, abstention from intoxicants and non-negligence in meritorious acts. This is the highest blessing.

Respectfulness, humbleness, contentment, gratitude and listening to the Dharma on suitable occasions. This is the highest blessing.

Patience, obedience, meeting those who have calmed the mental defilements and discussing the Dharma on suitable occasions. This is the highest blessing.

Practice that consumes evil states, a noble life, seeing the Noble Truths and realization of Nirvana. This is the highest blessing.

The mind of a person (an Arahant) who is confronted with worldly conditions does not flutter, is sorrowless, stainless and secure. This is the highest blessing.

Having fulfilled such things as these, beings are invincible everywhere and gain happiness everywhere. That is the highest blessing for them."

End of Mangala Sutra

You may be chanting just to ask the devas to do something to help in some way. For that, you are not trying to actually merge with a deva's mind. But if you are trying to make direct mind lineage contact with the higher realms, after doing a deva chant, and perhaps another supplementary practice, you should wait and feel if they are drawing near to you. Pay attention to your six senses, be aware, be open, be gentle, be relaxed, be still and quiet. Your gentleness should be wholehearted and perky, not weak. You are not in any hurry for something. You simply rest your thoughts without any project in mind. After a while there is another chant, the Contact chant, you do to ask them to come. You repeat several times:

Contact Chant

Devas, I offer you body, speech and mind as your throne. Please always remain inseparable.

I offer you body, speech and mind as your throne. Please always remain inseparable.

I offer you body, speech and mind as your throne. Please always remain inseparable.
Now approach approach. Come here.

In group practice replace 'I' with 'we' to unite your group's interest in being a larger platform for which the devas may land. However, contact will not be in the form of a 'group mind' or something far out like that. If you feel a connection with one particular deva, such as Jehovah or Brahma or one you naturally sense, or if your guru has assigned you a deity such as the deity of compassion — Avalokitesvara, then you should arouse a strong sense of devotion and longing while you bring your mind to bear on that sacred deva or deity. Deities are enlightened, devas are not. This idea of a deity comes from the Mahayana. In Theravada, deity is synonymous with deva. Theravadin Buddhism does not acknowledge the existence of the Mahayana celestial deities.

In this deva invocation practice, your aspiration is to merge minds, to commingle with that deva or deity, so that longing is what seems to enliven the visualization and connection that you have with the deva or deity. With that, do this additional chant several times:

If there is no father deva, to whom shall we look with hope?

If there is no father deva, to whom shall we look with hope?
If there is no father deva, to whom shall we look with hope?
Now approach, approach. Come here.

You're invoking the devas on the basis of their compassion. Next, visualize the deva/s coming down into the vessel of your body, speech and mind and imagine the physical sensation of your energy being raised at making contact. You are raising lungta, windhorse. Rest your mind and go into the silence and listen to that still small voice within. If an answer is coming, it will come from that still small voice within you. Do not practice meditation but do the contemplative practice of going into the silence. This means waiting for something to happen. You sit, wide awake with your eyes open and you do nothing. You can write down one question and put the paper in front of you to remind yourself of why you are there. You can write something like 'Please devas, will you give me an answer? Or: 'Please devas, will you please help me to do this?' Or, some other question. You wait for 30 minutes, 40 minutes. After this you may notice a stream of thoughts starting to flow through you. Sometimes, after a whole hour, 'bang!' an answer will pop into your mind that is complete and satisfying, clear and meaningful to you. Usually it is accompanied by the energy to act on it immediately. It is not clear whether this process is channelling through to devas, or something coming up from alaya.

Outer, Inner and Secret Practices

There is an outer way of doing a practice.
There is an inner way of doing a practice.
There is a secret way of doing a practice.

The Vajrayana tradition from Tibet deserves the most credit for working out the commentaries on the subtleties regarding chanting practices of invocation, such as with the seven line supplication to Padmasambhava as taught by Pönlop Rinpoche. Literally channelling to devas has more to do with Vajrayana Buddhism than Theravadin Buddhism, because of the Tibetans' long association with shamanism and Hinduism. The way that the outer, inner and secret practices relate to Mangala sutra practice in particular, is this:

1. The outer practice is to recite the Mangala sutra chant and the other chants prescribed here.
2. Your inner practice is to do a simultaneous visualization.
3. The secret practice is your own inner experience of the practice and how you choose to routinely guide yourself through it.

Simultaneous with the outer practice, where the chant begins at "Men to-

143

gether with deities . . . ," is your inner practice of doing a visualization in which you imagine numerous devas in celestial palaces that have many towers, each palace being showered with coral flowers and other celestial flowers from the heaven above it while heavenly music softly plays. Some palaces are made of heavenly substances beyond your imagination, some are made of crystal, diamonds, gold, lapis lazuli, etc. You do this visualization in the background of your mind while you are chanting out loud. Generally when you chant you are supposed to be concentrating solely on your chanting but in this case you are visualizing what it is that you are actually chanting so you can visualize in such a way that it actually enhances your concentration rather than confusing it. Really get a vivid mental picture of your mind's idea of what this 3-D picture of heaven looks like and sounds like. You can study more god realm imagery in vivid detail in the *Avatamasaka sutra* which you can use to enliven this visualization. It's a beauty.

In the inner practice visualization, imagine numerous devas in celestial palaces that have many towers, each palace being showered with coral flowers and other celestial flowers from the heaven above it while heavenly music softly plays. Some palaces are made of heavenly substances beyond your imagination, some are made of crystal, diamonds, gold, lapis lazuli, etc. You do this visualization in the background of your mind before you begin the chant. Really get a vivid mental picture of your mind's idea of what this 3-D picture of heaven looks like and sounds like. See these blissful devas in heaven, surrounded by joy and beauty, unaware of what the highest blessings in life are. Next, imagine that one of the devas leads a great squadron of devas who come down to earth to visit the Buddha. Also visualize a rain of devas in your own city at the same time. Next, the principal deva with surpassing splendour asks the Buddha "Many devas and men, desiring what is good, have pondered upon just what blessings were. Pray tell me, what the highest blessing is." At this point you visualize the setting in Jeta's Grove with the Buddha giving the response from the sadhana. Visualize the Buddha surrounded by oceans of devas while his company of monks and nuns are scattered in the night nearby. Throughout the chant you hold this visualization of the Buddha delivering these words to this multitude of devas.

At the end of the chant imagine that the devas put their hands in anjali and bow to the Buddha. After a pause, you notice that the devas all turn and they face you! The deva sangha look at you and pause, then they move towards you, whether you are alone or doing group practice. Somehow the devas move across time and space and they surround you just as they surrounded the Enlightened One. Take a minute to visualize them in all their splendor and love. Feel their presence and sacredness. Wait and feel your inner senses. Then visualize a deva descending down to you . . . it envelops you in its loving kindness. Sit with this for a while then visualize the deva merging into your body, speech and mind. Pay attention to your six senses, be aware, be open, be gentle, be relaxed, be still and quiet. Ramakrishna said "The winds of grace blow all the time. All we need to do is set our sails."

Your gentleness should be wholehearted and perky, not weak. You are not in any hurry for something. You simply rest your thoughts without any project in mind. Then once again repeat the Contact chant, inviting the devas to make contact with you. Imagine the physical sensation of your energy being raised at making contact with the devas. You are raising lungta, windhorse, kundalini, chi. Rest your mind, go into the silence and listen to that still small voice within.

After some stillness the secret practice comes next. Your secret practice is provoked by the synchronization of your outer and inner practices. Your secret practice includes your personal interpretation of the practice plus it has something to do with resting the mind in it's natural state, in a stage of meditation beyond the chant and a stage of meditation beyond the visualization practice. The secret practice can only be passively or receptively exercised. You must be in a state of gentleness and openness, resting the mind with only a minor distraction of discursive thoughts. Your gentleness and openness should be perky and wholehearted as you descend into the silence. If your thoughts after that point intensify in quality, power, energy and vision, then you may have succeeded right there in establishing direct contact with your spirit guides, your guardian angels. That is as direct as it gets. Don't expect Jesus Christ to knock on your front door in the form of a visible spirit body echoing words of wisdom. Be happy and recognize that you have been granted an audience. This is it. You have arrived at the outer, inner and secret practice of deva invocation. It may take you months of practice to feel something, probably less, but if you nurture that special part of your inner spiritual life, then as Joseph Campbell taught, eventually something will happen.

Quality of Inspiration

You may not be able to decide until much later whether or not your meditation experience was a bona fide connection with the devas or something more confused than that. Perhaps you will never know. The reason for this is because if it is genuine, you may know or you may still second guess your own experience because many people have a tendency to discount their own ideas because they are their *own* ideas. Like Groucho Marx, these are the kind of people that say "I would never join a club that would have me as a member." We are so used to ourselves, that we have no respect for ourselves! But even people with low self esteem who regard themselves as losers, can be very capable and competent at deva invocation practice. In fact, it is humility itself that is one of the key ingredients of success! People with big egos and an inflated opinion of their spiritual qualities will get nowhere with deva invocation practice. Humility rules. As the Tao teaches, "It is not very holy to point out how holy you are."

Sometimes the devas will spoon feed you a million dollar business plan while you're sitting in Starbucks day dreaming over a tall coffee. Then you blow it by thinking, "I wonder why no one has come up with that product or service? It could make a million! Huh, there must be a reason I guess." Then two years later you see an ad in the paper for a brand new product or service which is almost exactly what you thought of two years before and you think "Hey! I thought of that! I thought of that years ago!" Perhaps the devas channelled down that idea to earth when it was the best time for humans to receive it. Do you think the devas are going to single you out as being their special chosen one? No way. They'll give the idea to many people until somebody perks up and plays ball with them, while you're sitting, day dreaming at Starbucks over another tall slow coffee again. Get with it. Trust yourself; trust that still small voice within you. One of the biggest obstacles to a genuine deva inspired realization, is your friends and family who regard you as an ordinary schmuck who could hardly be expected to come up with a million dollar idea. Protect yourself; have stealth. Again, it's a question of containment. Once you "catch" a deva inspiration, which is common enough, the real mark of success is "containing" it in such a way that you can work with the real phenomenal world and bring that deva gift into a physical reality that can benefit the lives of other human beings. That is what this whole process is all about. They say that there is a fine line between genius and insanity. Well, that's not good enough. We have plenty of insane people in the world and we can be sure that it will get worse. "Contain" yourself calmly, and still be a genius at the same time. That's the ticket. Be normal.

If your stream of thoughts is not bona fide deva contact, then you could mistakenly believe that it is. Your own expectations or spiritual materialism could result in your creative mind manufacturing something that could sincerely fool you into believing that you have received the blessings of the higher realms. There is no easy answer to this challenge. See the section on Aurobindo. You are fortunate if you have a teacher of whatever calibre to consult with who can work through this spectacle with you. Medical science is not much help with facing reality as it is and recognizing the fact that the higher and lower realms are a major part of our psyches. Even if medical science does recognize reality, they will talk circles around it. These are still the pioneer days of Buddhist deva practice in the West. If you're all alone and you lose control, you could be confined for a short period in a mental institution, but still the risk is worth taking. This is your life; not just your spiritual life, not just your future spiritual life, but your *whole* life, and your future lives as well. A very serious wrong view would be to cut off the higher realms altogether and to throw out the baby with the bath water. You just can't do that, you know. The higher realms are going to work with you one way or another, whether you are conscious of this process in your life or unconscious of this process in your life. They have made that decision long ago. Maybe you have already guessed that by now. Trungpa Rinpoche said "The dharma will haunt you in the very best sense of the word." Good luck.

Buddhaghosa, who has commented extensively on deva invocation techniques in his fifth century *Path of Purification,* says that by using such practices you become dearly loved by the devas.

As monks in Thailand we did 'recollection of the deities' practice in the main Viharn where we would visualize the Buddha in the sky above and in front of us. This represents something that is higher and beyond us. We would visualize Sariputra and his other senior disciples arranged in the sky around him while we chanted a beautiful musical chant.

Below is Buddhaghosa's powerful commentary on how to do recollection of deities practice. The author's comments are in brackets. Do not confuse the word "deity" with the Mahayana interpretation, which is that of a fully enlightened celestial being. Here, "deity" means "deva," most of whom are not enlightened. Some may be 10% enlightened, others 98.6% enlightened. It helps to read between the lines or to have had the attainment of deeper meditative states of concentration such as samadhis, to appreciate what Buddhaghosa has written here, and it is stated that this practice succeeds only in noble disciples. Curiously, Buddhaghosa's commentary is the single most respected Buddhist commentary in Theravadin, but if you live in a Tibetan or Mahayana monastery or practice centre for ten years you might never once hear the name Buddhaghosa.

Recollection of Deities
(Nanamoli, 1956; 243)

One who wants to develop the recollection of deities should possess the special qualities of faith, etc., evoked by means of the noble path, and he should go into solitary retreat and recollect his own special qualities of faith, etc., the deities standing as witness, as follows:

> 'There are Deities of the Realm of the Four Kings (the first heaven in the sensuous sphere), there are Deities of the Realm of the Thirty three (Tavatimsa heaven), there are Deities who are gone to divine bliss (Yama heaven), ... are Contented (Tushita heaven),... Delight in Creating ... (5th),... Wield Power Over Others' Creations (6th), there are Deities of Brahma's Retinue (fine material sphere), there are Deities higher than that. And those Deities were possessed of faith such that on dying here they were reborn there, and such faith is present in me too.

And those Deities were possessed of virtue... of learning... of generosity... of understanding such that when they died here they were reborn there, and such understanding is present in me too (Aiii, 287).

In the Sutra, however, it is said: On the occasion, Mahanama, on which a noble disciple recollects the faith, the virtue, the learning, the generosity, and the understanding, that are both his own and those deities', on that occasion his mind is not obsessed by greed, ... (A,iii,287). Although this is said, it should nevertheless be understood as said for the purpose of showing that special qualities of faith, etc., in oneself are those in the deities, making the deities stand as witness. For it is said definitely in the Commentary "He recollects his own special qualities, making the deities stand as witnesses" (meaning that the devas are drawn to you because you are like them).

As long as in the prior stage he recollects the deities' special qualities of faith, etc., and in the later stage he recollects the special qualities of faith, etc., existing in himself, then 'On that occasion his mind is not obsessed by greed, or obsessed by hate, or obsessed by delusion, his mind has rectitude (uprightness in principles and conduct, correctness, as of judgment) on that occasion, being inspired by deities. (A.iii,288).

So when he has suppressed the hindrances in the way already stated (*66), the jhana (concentration) factors arise in a single conscious moment. But owing to his being occupied in recollecting special qualities of many sorts, the jhana is only access (not yet a full samadhi absorption state) and does not reach absorption (a full samadhi — see chapter 4). And that access jhana itself is known as 'recollection of deities' too because it arises with the deities' special qualities as the means (This is the actual moment of contact when the devas choose to engage with and commingle with one's mind).

And when a bhikkhu is devoted to this recollection of deities, he becomes dearly loved by deities (the devas pay particular attention to such a person and channel more and more through them). He obtains even greater fullness of faith. He has much happiness and gladness. And if he penetrates no higher, he is at least headed for a happy destiny.

Now when a man is truly wise,

His constant task will surely be
This recollection of deities
Blessed with such mighty potency

This is the section dealing with the Recollection of
Deities in the detailed explanation.

[General]

And when in the case of the recollection of Deities *inspired by deities*
is said, this should be understood as said either of the consciousness
that occurs in the prior stage inspired by deities (the actual moment
of contact) or of the consciousness [that occurs in a later stage] inspired by the special qualities that are similar to those of the deities
and are productive of the deities' state (cf. '117).

These (six) recollections succeed only in noble disciples. For the special qualities
of the Enlightened One, the Law, and the Community, are evident to them; and they
possess the virtue with the special qualities of untornness, etc., the generosity that is free
from stain by avarice, and the special qualities of faith, etc., similar to those of the deities.

And in the Mahanama Sutra (A.iii, 285f.) they are expounded in detail by
the Blessed One in order to show to a stream-enterer an abiding to depend upon
when he asked for one.

Recollection of Buddha

(*66) So when he has thus suppressed the hindrances by preventing obses-
sion by greed, etc., and his mind faces the meditation subject with rectitude, then his applied thought and sustained thought occur with a tendency towards the Enlightened One's special qualities. As he continues to
exercise applied thought and sustained thought upon the Enlightened
One's special qualities, happiness arises in him. With his mind happy, with
happiness as the proximate cause, his bodily and mental disturbance are
tranquillized by tranquillity. When the disturbance has been tranquillized,
bodily and mental bliss arise in him. When he is blissful, his mind, with
the Enlightened One's special qualities for its object, becomes concentrated, and so the jhana factors eventually arise in a single moment. But
owing to the profundity of the Enlightened One's special qualities, or else
owing to his being occupied in recollecting special qualities of many sorts,
the jhana is only access and does not reach absorption. And that access
jhana itself is known as 'recollection of Buddha' too, because it arises with
the recollection of the Enlightened One's special qualities as the means.

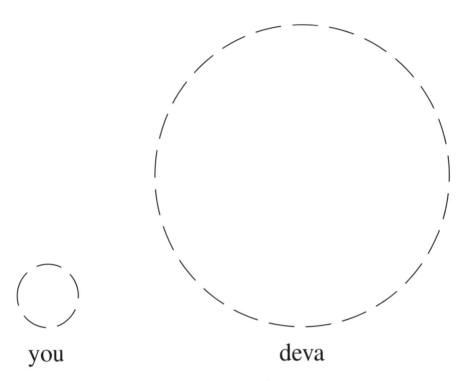

you   deva

The Experience of Contact

In the above diagram, the moment of contact occurs when the larger circle, the deva, comes over you. There is no solid line between you and the minds of devas or others, as revealed in the Buddha's teachings on non self. This is the scriptural basis for how deva interfacing is possible. The actual experience of interfacing your mind with a deva is described in the Buddhist commentaries as well as in martial arts training and calligraphy training. I have had this experience of making contact with devas, which has been described by many people because it is almost an ordinary human experience. You feel a certain power coming on, and you may think, "Oh no, not this again." It has a tendency to take you aback. You feel uncomfortable with big energies coming into you. There is an expansion of your insight, your prajna. A few minutes ago you were untying your shoelaces and now you are in big mind. You experience a much larger open space of mind with equally great confidence. It is a state of doubtlessness — primordial confidence. You may want to tone things down a bit, not speak what you feel compelled to say, you're holding back from expressing your inspiration. But this is what the world needs. The world needs big energies and big help, not just another subcommittee.

You may feel like saying, "Let's turn down the lights a bit. Let's speak a little more indistinctly. Let's let someone else take a leadership role in the meeting. I don't want to be too domineering." The devas are descending through you and they have big energy and big power. You should avoid the compulsion to sidetrack the process or meeting by staying in your familiar comfortable self limited idea of yourself. This is the time to shine, go with it! The Buddha described "the Brahma voice" in the sutras which is a deep resonant sound in the voice that occurs when devas are invoked and one is channelling down their energies which are expressed through the voice.

I first had this experience at age 17 and again at age 19 when I wrote 200,000 words. I didn't know what was going on but I believed that this was my new life, the new me, the new old world. I was wrong. It crumbled apart — impermanence — fizzled out to a dead end. Another time, late one night in Bangkok I was doing the deva invocation visualization practice the 'Recollection of Deities,' which was one of the most powerful practices I learned in the monkhood. I felt that old feeling of buzzing in my ears and pulsations in my hands and body. I knew I was 'on.' I was bristling with deva energy so I went to the computer and wrote the essay 'Why Buddhists Meditate.' It came spilling out so fast that I interpret it as a deva inspired document. I never know for sure where these energies come from. These are inspired moments that arise out of a calm, receptive state. At those precious times I am possessed of the rawness, the raw energy inside a nuclear furnace of dharma. The new frontier of my mind is at the furnace of conceptualizations. This provides products that arise from the highest point I can reach, which are mixed with my own confusion, then gently tapped onto the keyboard of my use. The keyboard is the gate to the renewed vision for the future. That is why from hour to hour, I do not know what my keyboard will produce next. It is fresh to my perception. The first thought is a still small voice of both feeble and confident energy within, very fragile and fickle. That is the very essence of insight — that 'whatever it is' 'out of nowhere' quality. This is the finest hour that I can provide at the edge of my keyboard, for as long as the devas stay. Maybe the essence of your own inspired times may be described in a similar way.

A Douglas College dharma student, Peter, related his experience of feeling an internal orbit of energy during class while we were all doing this deva contemplation together. The Taoists describe this same process of the internal orbit of energy, in their practices. Peter then told our class about what he realized was a deva presence in his life many years ago. He said that he went through the worst phase of his life when he lost his job, lost his apartment and lost his girlfriend all around the same time. He moved back to his parent's house to help out his father for a while and suddenly everything changed. The Tao teaches that when we feel most destroyed, we are about to grow. Peter's energy was way up, he was inspired, creative and all manner of coincidences went in his favour. With the insight provided by Buddhist cosmology, looking back over his life he now knows that he was connected to the devas. Now he is conscious of something really important that he was unaware of before.

It wasn't until 1994 in Thailand that I accidentally came upon the Buddhist explanation for my natural experience which closed a circle of understanding and insight for me. I am now tremendously grateful to the Buddhist religion for helping me to understand this deep personal mystery. Many people who feel the same kind of energy but can't contain it, become known as what is clinically described as a manic depressive. During one class at the Vancouver School Board one of my students, Celine, asked me if I had considered giving counselling to manic depressives and I said yes, because this could be the one vital key that they need to understand and use in their personal cosmology of how they are affected by the self existing energies in their universe. In fact, some manic depressives are more naturally talented than most at being mediums between the devas and the human world. Instead of being put down, they could be on top, if only they learn what is truly going on and have the discipline to play ball with the devas and play ball with sane human beings at the same time.

There's a fine line between genius and madness, and this area of human experience is definitely one of those lines. Too bad the American Medical Association back in the 20th century, stubbornly and fearfully fended off the larger world view provided by the Buddhists and other cultures. Billions of dollars are spent because of m-d. Buddhism is at home where medical science avoids looking. The goal is the same — sanity. The world views are different. Science cannot do much with consciousness outside of the body. Is deva invocation scientific?

Science

Science is defined as:
1. Knowledge of facts, phenomena, laws, and proximate causes, gained and verified by exact observation, organized experiment, and ordered thinking.
2. An orderly presentation of facts, reasonings, doctrines, and beliefs concerning some subject or group of subjects.

What is the purpose of science?
What is the purpose of science?
What is the purpose of science?
Is it to understand things?

What is the purpose of understanding things?

What is the purpose of understanding things?
What is the purpose of understanding things?

Is it to know what to do?
This is folly.
This is folly.
This is folly.
Trillions of dollars are spent to pave and light dead end streets.

A lot of suffering and sweat goes into every dollar.
There is no good purpose to figuring out the universe.
The purpose of Buddhism is to end suffering.

Buddhism is a smaller religion than science.
Buddhism is a better religion than science.

Take Over

Take over the purpose of your life.
Let us begin.
What is the purpose of Buddhism?
The purpose of Buddhism is to end suffering.
How does Buddhism end suffering?
By following the eightfold path.
Suffering
Desire
Nirvana
Path
What is the purpose of your life?
To end suffering.

Science is weaker than it looks. Science is a very good thing of course, but a British PhD in Neuroscience explained to me how she was disillusioned with what science is because colleagues would make presentations to get funding by deliberately illustrating their scientific "evidence" or theories in the most complicated and mystifying way possible so that people couldn't understand them enough to refute them. That way they would be better ensured funding instead of other scientists who chose to be honest and straight forward. This explains why science uses the very difficult terms that it does. It's a big greedy ego trip! It's not bona fide science at all. The next time science wants to take a shot at the deva experience, you be ready. The best defence is a good offence.

Catching and Containing

Catching these deva powers is not so rare a thing, the real skill is to contain these energies. You must contain them and channel them into a productive direction that will actually benefit yourself and others. Mental hospitals are filled with people who can genuinely catch devas, but they can't contain devas. If you succeed at channelling, you may be in the big leagues at that point. Some highly successful business people channel this ability into their careers. Don't lose it. Maintain mindfulness of the body and stay grounded. An important warning for the reader is that if you have a history of mental illness, you must continue to take your medication as prescribed, such as lithium, because it assists the Buddhist path. You can have your cake and eat it too. The big crux of the whole issue is the decision to not take a stronger drug to stop the deva invocation process. If you want to do this Buddhist practice, then you will want to allow energy and ideas to arise, of course, and you will not want to totally kill off the whole experience with a strong drug like loxapine. This is the difference of opinion that doctors, friends and family have had with people like psychologist R.D. Laing (whom I've met) and deva invocation channellers who want to go ahead and travel through their grand reality.

I encourage you to pluck that watercress of meaning from the ocean of your mind but don't allow your ego to attach to and take credit for the vastness and profundity of 'the big mind!' Ego identification with the deva experience is a cause of delusions of grandeur! If you are trained in dharmic thinking, you shouldn't have any problem at all. Don't behave abruptly but don't waste that love energy either. Don't say "Oh, let's go for a walk outside. Let's take a break now and come back after lunch." You *must* host the devas. You asked for it. The Dalai Lama consults the State Oracle of Tibet in the same manner. The Oracle is a Tibetan shaman who channels through to the highest realms and provides guidance for the Dalai Lama and the Tibetan people. He wears 200 pounds of clothing when he channels for the Dalai Lama because he manifests such powerful physical energy. Make yourself available to the devas. Cultivate a world view, a belief system, that the devas are there, all around you all the time. If you think of them more often, chant, and acknowledge them, they will think of you, love you and the sparks will start to happen.

Like exercising a muscle, if you work at it, something will develop, maybe in a surprising way. You need a space, a place, and time regularly invested, to feel the vibration, buzz and glow of results. It's natural to not believe something like this, which you cannot sense, until something actually happens. So if you just do it, just try it, something may happen. You may see some result. At that point, your faith will increase greatly and you will allow yourself, empower yourself, to invest even more concentration into the deva invocation process. Then the devas have got you! You're plugged in, you're hooked. You are one of those human beings who has turned on a light during the middle of a process that was once unseen. Possibly after people are dead they say "Oh! Have all of these devas been working around everybody all the time like this?! Oh darn! If only I knew that reality was really this way! I would have told others. I would have tried to listen to the devas and let them help me more! Oh man! How come nobody told me about the devas when I was still alive!! Damn!"

Keep up this process and you may become an old hand at it. It may overwhelm you so that you don't want to do it too much. The devas are looking for people who are serious about the process between the devaloka (deva world) and the human world. There are never too many channellers in the world. This world would be a better place if everybody had a conscious relationship with the higher realms, as long as the process doesn't degenerate into using black magic against each other, as in some cultures today.

Aurobindo

As you embark upon this higher spiritual path it is wise to heed the warnings of Sri Aurobindo. Sri Aurobindo was realized in the Hindu tradition in the early part of the 20th century and his insights are invaluable. He warns that the practitioner (sadhak) who succeeds at contacting devas can be carried away by spiritual experiences which can lead to a dead end. It is invaluable to have a guide to help you across this complex space to final enlightenment, he teaches.

It is advisable to study these writings by Sri Aurobindo in Volume 23 of his works which can be found on the Internet at www.miraura.org/lit/sa/ly/ly3-3.html. This website is: Letters on Yoga Selections, Part III Section III: Experiences of Inner and Cosmic Consciousness. In this excerpt, Aurobindo writes:

> All these experiences are of the same nature and what applies to one applies to another. Apart from some experiences of a personal character, the rest are either idea-truths, such as pour down into the consciousness from above when one gets into touch with certain planes of being, or strong formations from the larger mental and vital worlds which, when one is directly open to these worlds, rush in and want to use the sadhak for their fulfilment. These things, when they pour down or come in, present themselves with a great force, a vivid sense of inspiration or illumination, much sensation of light and joy, an impression of widening and power. The sadhak feels himself freed from the normal limits, projected into a wonderful new world of experience, filled and enlarged and exalted; what comes associates itself, be-

sides, with his aspirations, ambitions, notions of spiritual fulfilment and yogic siddhi [realization]. Very easily he is carried away by the splendour and the rush, and thinks that he has realised more than he has truly done, something final or at least something sovereignly true.

It is only when he is able to draw back (whether at once or after a time) from his experiences, stand above them with the dispassionate witness consciousness, observe their real nature, limitations, composition, mixture that he can proceed on his way towards a real freedom and a higher, larger and truer siddhi. At each step this has to be done . . . These stages have to be passed through, for the supramental or the Supreme Truth cannot be reached in one bound or even in many bounds; one has to pursue a calm patient steady progress through many intervening stages without getting bound or attached to their lesser Truth or Light... Or there is the opposite danger that he may become the instrument of some apparently brilliant but ignorant formation; for these intermediate planes are full of little Gods or strong Daityas or smaller beings who want to create, to materialise something or to enforce a mental and vital forma- tion in the earth life and are eager to use or influence or even possess the thought and will of the sadhak and make him their instrument for the purpose . . . For nothing is easier than for the powers of these zones or hostile powers to imitate the guiding Voice or Image and deceive and mislead the sadhak or for himself to attribute the creations and forma- tions of his own mind, vital or ego to the Divine.

Aurobindo is not saying that you should throw out the baby with the bath water and refuse to connect with the higher realms, but he is giving enlightened guidance about what to expect. One must have understanding and respect for these powerful practices before stepping into them.

Going into the Silence

The technique of going into the silence described earlier is not associated only with the deva process. It is a standard technique for allowing answers to spring forth which may have been buried under your confusion. This simply arises by creating a con- tainer by writing out a question and sitting and waiting for an answer. You wait for an hour without using a meditation technique, just gently place the mind on the question. This allows the fragile connection from alaya to be nurtured. In our society it is extremely rare for someone to sit attentively for an hour and do absolutely noth- ing, not even Homer Simpson can sit that long. Our work ethic always keeps us busy doing something. But, there is no faster way to get an answer to any question, than this. I urge you to try it, not only for becoming a channeller, but for any question in life. I give credit for these dharma teachings on going into the silence to Brian Tracy's Phoenix Seminar audio taped course — the biggest selling success course in the world. I recommend that you buy it. Brian Tracy expressed these ideas using Jungian terms — the superconscious mind. Here, we have used Buddhist terminology for the same direct experience.

Help From Above

As you channel through to devas, know that not all devas are Buddhist devas. Buddhist scriptures indicate that a great many devas regard the Hindu god Brahma as the one almighty personal god, which is a false view. Devas live in delusion as do human beings. You can ask for assistance from any deva but you may want to invite only Buddhist lineage devas to make a direct mind lineage connection with you. As Buddhists, our relationship with devas remains non theistic. A metaphor for this is, calling your rich aunt on the phone and asking for a gift of $3000 because your car engine just blew up. Your rich aunt says "Fine!" and she electronically deposits the money directly into your account, no strings attached. You do not worship your aunt as a god in the theistic sense. In the same way, you regard the devas as more powerful beings that want to help you on the basis of their tremendous compassion for us. But, they are not gods and you do not worship them in a theistic way. They are devas.

In post meditation, as you are entering into a building, such as a high rise, you can pay your respects to the principal deva of that place. Assume that many devas reside in each high rise building and that one deva is the principal one. You can silently say that you respect the deva and that you have a good purpose for being there. You say "I give my merit to you and to everyone in this place." That includes the ghost realm as you want them on your side too. Then you can ask the resident deva, or lokapala to help you with your meeting or your purpose for being there. Use the Pali chant below from the Theravadin version of the Heart Sutra. Again, the Theravadins have blown the whistle on the Mahayanists because the much revered Mahayana version of the Heart Sutra just rearranges some of the dialogue between Sariputra and the Buddha, so that some fantastic deity of compassion from space can take the starring role. The Theravadins have the one and only true authentic version of the Heart Sutra. Perhaps the reason why a community of Mahayana monks and nuns decided to rewrite the Heart Sutra is for the purpose of generating more compassion by inspiring faith in a constructed deity named Avalokitesvara.

This powerful little chant encapsulates all of the above concepts of acknowledging, paying respects and asking. The "ii" sounds like "ee" as in "eel." Chant

three times each time, then think more about what you want, then chant another
three times, etc.:

ïi sa wa su   su sa wa ïi
ïi sa wa su   su sa wa ïi
ïi sa wa su   su sa wa ïi

There are 28 classes of celestial beings so there are devas and there are devas.
The Christian god Jehovah is just one of the vast god-like devas of the fine material
sphere, according to Buddhist cosmology. This is perhaps the single most shocking
thing about the Buddhist religion — the subjugation of god. As a channeller, your
goal is to channel through to a higher quality product, such as Jehovah, or enlightened mind itself, instead of what most channellers get, which is Joe Schmuck deva,
who in his last life was a cab driver in New Jersey!

The Deva Experience

It is my perception and belief that I have experienced the influence of devas from
my practice. Many of my students have reported having deva experiences long before they studied Buddhism. This is a natural, common human experience which is
not the copyrighted property of the Buddhist religion. When I perceive that my
consciousness is interfacing with a deva, visually, I don't see anything out of the ordinary during this heightened state. My hearing is almost the same except sometimes there is a subtle buzzing sound which I take as a signal that the power and
energy is happening. This may be channelling, I do not know for sure what to call
it. Mainly it is the mind dhatu, the thinking mind which is the gate through which
all so called channelling comes. This comes in the form of a compelling idea that
needs to be typed out. The nature of channelled documents is that many of the
ideas are disjointed, such as the famous *Course in Miracles*, which is a channelled
book revered by many as being the channelled words of Jesus Christ. I do not share
this view. Who knows where it came from, or how many devas it came from? I
never know where these inspirations come from.

A perfectly logical rational explanation for this deva process lies in Buddhist
abhidharma. The five senses are the first five consciousnesses. The 6th is the thinking mind. The 7th is the unconscious mind. The 8th is alaya-vinaya. Carl Jung had
a lot to say about the collective unconscious. The Buddha went even further. Underneath the unconscious mind is the base consciousness of alaya, although we
each have our own little pool of alaya according to the eminent teacher, Chögyam
Trungpa Rinpoche. He described alaya as a thick creamy white pool of creativity
like a pool of milk and honey. All creative thoughts spring from there.

Buddhists know what the word 'person' means as a being that is not separate and distinct from others. The five aggregates, or skandhas that comprise this illusion of self are form (body), feeling (5 senses), perception (recognition of the sense stimuli), mental formations (thoughts and intentional actions), and consciousness, limited to self consciousness.

The interface here between devas and humans can occur at the level of the 2nd to the 5th skandha; feeling (the senses), perception, and mental formations. Consciousness is affected as a human beings' consciousness can be raised to that of a deva during such meetings of the mind. The sense by which we apprehend devas is usually the thinking mind of the 6th consciousness, which the Buddha regarded as the 6th sense. So when a person gets a strong stream of ideas coming into his mind, this is the 6th sense and its source could possibly be deva inspired. Buddhism teaches that the true illusory nature of the self is comprised of these five skandhas. This is the one piece of doctrine upon which all of Buddhism either stands or falls. So, we can see that it is not so unbelievable a thing that a person's mind can mix with a deva's mind, or with another person that they feel very close to. This is not so far out a thing when we study Buddhist abhidharma.

If the source of channelling bubbles up from alaya, through the unconscious mind and onto the surface of the sea of the conscious mind, then perhaps it isn't so important where the ideas come from. It just comes from alaya. Whether a particular deva deliberately put the idea into your alaya or into your subconscious mind or into your conscious mind, or whether a deva did not, we do not know, and it is not so important. We can look to alaya as the source of our creative ideas. Alaya can be visualized as a thick creamy bright milky white pool swirling around someone's body, engulfing them as they smile and breath in liquid sunshine and breath out virtue and goodness. Alaya. You're swimming around peacefully in this warm sea of love with all other beings. There is no being in existence that is not with us in the great big jacuzzi in the sky of alaya. 'Enemy' does not exist, only our own ignorance. The only 'enemy' is within our own habitual patterns of passion, aggression and ignorance.

The devas that people channel through to are generally not fully enlightened devas. Watch out for the Vajrayana put down when someone asks you "Why would you want to channel through to unenlightened devas when you could do a practice to invoke fully enlightened deities and bodhisattvas?" The problem with this circular logic is that these enlightened deities and bodhisattvas do not exist. In the Theravadin sutras the Buddha never taught that enlightened deities or bodhisattvas exist at all, and certainly not as something better and beyond devas. Such enlightened celestial beings are fictitious creations which arose a few centuries after the Buddha's death and there is no possibility for their existence in the cosmology that the Buddha so thoroughly taught us. The Buddha did describe devas in great detail and how we can relate to them. The Theravadin view of the dharmakaya is that enlightened mind pervades this ultimate reality beyond personal identity or name. How can deities exist there with different names and characteristics? — like the bodhisattva of compassion, or White Tara or Green Tara? Their existence is refuted by the Buddha and by Theravadin Buddhism. What is good about such practices is that the Buddha praised the benefits of visualizing a confidence inspiring object. Visualizing deities can serve very well to inspire confidence and energy or greater compassion, such as the visualization practice for the bodhisattva of compassion.

Psychic Communication

Visualize alaya as 136 waves on the dark ocean at night. You are sitting at a window seat on a 747-400 while an air hostess leans towards you with a cup of hot airline coffee. As you sip and smell the aroma of the coffee you look down ten kilometres below and see the surface of the ocean. You see billions of waves which represent your own personal subconscious gossip. 136 of those waves reflect, no, actually glow with creamy white light. These 136 waves in alaya represent the same, exact same 136 waves that also exist in the alaya of many other devas and people flying on other jets over the same ocean. When they see those 136 glowing waves down there, they know that those waves represent the alaya within their own minds too, just as you do.

Most of the waves represent your own self consciousness; part is shared mind. This is explained in the Buddha's teachings on non self. This represents the true reality that your 'self' is not separate from other. This illustrates the quality of the threshold between our mind and the minds of others; what Carl Jung called the collective unconscious or the superconscious mind. This explains how minds can merge and telepathy and psychic communication can happen. This is not so unbelievable a thing. This is ordinary. You have already had direct experiences of this in the past. And you will continue to have direct experiences of this alaya bound psychic communication in the future.

Dharmapalas

Yea, though I walk through the shadow of the valley of death, I shall fear no evil. Because I know that I walk underneath the secret service protection of the president's psychic deva mindguards, the biggest damned bastards in the valley, dharmapalas.

(Chant above 1, 3, 9, or up to 108 times.
Interchange the word 'bodyguards' with the word 'mindguards.')

Dharmapalas are protector deities, or devas in Buddhist cosmology, which specifically protect the dharma, Buddhist temples, centres, teachers and lay members. The word 'president' is not so much about a person as it is about the connection of power that flows through the most influential office on earth, and the relationship between the power of the devas and how they protect and assist mankind through protecting and even penetrating the minds of those at the helm of the government. With this chant you are supplicating these great dharmapalas to protect you. In Robert Monroe's book, *Journeys out of the Body,* he describes an astral travelling experience in which he discovered the 'secret service protection of the president's psychic mindguards,' after he was astral travelling in his home state on the eastern seaboard while President Kennedy was visiting. He said that a being, which we can interpret to mean a deva, stopped him and refused to allow him to see the President of the United States. After returning to his body and reading the morning newspaper, he discovered that President Kennedy was in town. At that moment Monroe received the ultimate conviction that President Kennedy had a psychic mindguard or bodyguard protecting the influences that went into the President's mind. This makes complete sense. Incidentally, this principle was not contradicted by Kennedy's assassination. Regardless of whether or not the devas were frantically trying to prevent his death in Dallas by flying around the grassy knoll and the Texas School Book Depository in an effort to throw off the gunmen's aim, the laws of karma are still the laws of karma. If it was time for America to be hit with big pain, then the devas had no authority or power to change the laws of karma.

Monroe was a Pennsylvania engineer who spontaneously developed this out of body experience (OOBE) ability. He and others at his Monroe Institute, in West Virginia did some very good and very fine Remote Viewing work for the CIA in their intelligence gathering efforts. In 1978 President Jimmy Carter commended the success of a remote viewer when the President proclaimed that she gave them the longitude and latitude of a plane downed in the ocean. They trained their satellites on the spot and the plane was found.

Interestingly, Robert Monroe had nothing to do with Buddhism at the time of the writing of his book, and yet he was unknowingly confirming many of the Buddhist teachings on the nature of the higher and lower realms of the cosmology of conventional reality. That's the kind of credibility that lends support to spreading Buddhism in the West. Monroe even described leaving his body and seeing a Buddha floating through space, cross legged. The Buddha said that one of the ten magical powers of some enlightened persons (the Tatagathas) is the ability to fly through the air cross legged. Consciously working with the devas gives you the kind of confidence that a kid might feel when he's convinced that his father is the best dad in town. You have a comforting sense of presence and protection and you can learn to communicate both ways with the devas that come and go around you. Remember to incline toward Buddhist devas, deva sangha. There's definitely a difference.

Stroke Practice

Stroke practice is a deva invocation practice which can be used separately or with the Mangala sutra practice. In the Theravadin sutras the Buddha said "visualize a confidence inspiring object." This liturgy came through the author and it is one of his deepest and most profound contemplative practices. In beginning it is important to arouse the proper aspiration to do this practice for the benefit of others.

Generation stage. Chant several times:

Soft human copper gold.
Soft human copper gold.
Soft human copper gold.

The main practice. Chant nine or anywhere up to 108 times in total:

Sacred messages from the devas enter your copper buddhacle godhead.
Sacred messages from the devas enter your copper buddhacle godhead.
Sacred messages from the devas enter your copper buddhacle godhead.

Dissolution phase. Chant several times:

Soft human copper gold.
Soft human copper gold.
Soft human copper gold.

The meaning of the preliminary chant is that you visualize yourself and others as being soft metallic copper and gold. This is to give you a strong, impervious and uplifted feeling, so as to prepare you for what is to come. The actual deva invocation attempt to make contact is accomplished by repeating the main chant silently or out loud. The word 'sacred' preconditions your mind to only accepting good influences, not misleading influences. Ideally you want to channel through to the highest quality product, but that may take some time. The word 'devas' can be interchanged with the word 'dead' to acknowledge the possibility that some of those close to you who have died are now devas assisting you. The Buddhacle is the bump on the Buddha's head. In the sutras it states that the Buddha's head was shaped like a turban. A Buddhist meaning is being used to interpret the Hindu word godhead. Instead of it meaning god Brahma, we use it to mean enlightened mind. This phrase indicates our aspiration to attain enlightenment by affirming

162

that our mind is a part of enlightened mind. Copper is significant in some Tibetan Buddhist visualizations of copper mountains. The sword that is believed by some to have pierced the soft human heart of Jesus is partially made of copper and gold, but this information is not directly related to stroke practice.

As you are chanting visualize a cylinder of yellow light coming down from the sun like a stroke through space, spinning clockwise all around you. At the moment that the stroke hits, your heart radiates warmth outward. You can visualize the sun expanding and receding, leaving oceans of devas in the sky, who stream down the yellow cylinder towards you. The devas come down showering all around you, some entering your head and body. This is contact. These countless devas are not literally merging with you, but you do the stroke practice visualization in this way to invoke a more powerful state of mind, so that maybe one deva will establish contact with you. This is an important understanding. You can hold a dorje in your hand while you do stroke practice as it acts as a handle to spin the cylinder around and manipulate the direction of the energy flow, at least in your imagination. As you are waiting to feel some contact, some energy or a stream of ideas, you should do the Contact chant many times:

Contact chant

Deva sangha, I offer you body speech and mind as your throne.
Please may you always remain inseparable.
Deva sangha, I offer you body speech and mind as your throne.
Please may you always remain inseparable.
Now approach approach. Come here.

Then, you rest the mind in the nature of alaya, in non discursive awareness, and you wait for an answer. There is an outer, inner and secret form of stroke practice which relates to the outer, inner and secret mandalas respectively. The outer practice is the chants. The inner practice is the visualization of the devas descending down to you. The secret practice is sparked off by the connection between these two and it arises after your main practice has subsided and the momentum of your chanting comes to rest in a quiet beautiful peaceful place that is characterized by openness, receptivity and gentleness. This is the human throne that the devas search for when they want to connect with human beings.

Star Trek Religion

Often the Buddha would "Buddhify" the mythological beliefs of his culture and imbue them with a Buddhist meaning. Once Buddha encountered a young man who worshipped the four cardinal directions and the Buddha gave him a new inspiration by explaining a new meaning for what each one of the cardinal directions meant. A dominant mythology of our time in history is Star Trek. People buy into this as fiction but it focuses their hopes for the future on a Star Trek mythology which holds out a vision of mankind's survival, growth and more evolved relationships. Therefore, in keeping with the Buddha's policy of not rejecting, but incorporating workable beliefs, a variation on stroke practice is to make real a Star Trek practice of dharma by creating Star Trek related visualizations as a stepping stone to deva invocation methods. This gives people more ways of contacting the higher realms. The purpose of associating the Buddhist higher realms with this pop culture is to expand your reality by subjugating Star Trek and Star Wars within Buddhist cosmology. It is useful to activate this prior knowledge when learning Buddhist cosmology which is new to your understanding. Instead of this pop culture being apart from your path to enlightenment, these icons help pave that path with colour, energy, motivation and power. It is good to feel powerful, brave, fearless and inspired.

If this sounds too far out to take seriously consider that Tibetan Buddhism has stretched the practice of Buddhadharma beyond acceptable limits such that the Vajrayana is even more far out than the Star Trek "religion." Tibetans claim as real their imaginings about Green Tara and they teach people to take her as their main deity for all of their future incarnations until enlightenment. Tibetan Buddhists claim that Green Tara and other celestial characters are better and more attained than devas, and higher than the historical figures of the Buddha's chief disciples. This is unacceptable. Because Tibetan Buddhist higher realm invocation practices are centred upon fictitious deities rather than bona fide devas- they have compromised the validity of these practices and they cause harm to practitioners who do those particular higher realm practices. The harm is the harm of deliberately perpetuating confusion and misunderstanding, century after century. When practitioners believe they are relating with a fully enlightened deity, they are at best, contacting devas. Since the devas are generally unenlightened the practitioner is mixing with a higher but still confused mind. Because they may not know that they are relating with devas, their security is compromised if they believe they are relating with enlightened mind. Deities do not really exist so what is really happening is that practitioners of deity visualization are the victims of institutional one upmanship. Their own Mahayana or Vajrayana institution has compromised their understanding of devas and their relationship with devas. That's what's really going on. Star Trek practice does not contradict the Buddha's teachings about the true nature of devas. There's no claim about Star Trek actually existing. This is simply a dharma visualization practice. We meditate:

Star Trek Practice

Imagine that you are Captain Kirk. You have taken on the role of captain of the Enterprise. Carl Jung taught that one of the most powerful archetypes of the unconscious is the king; the deep seated realization that you are the king of your own life. This is called "ruling your world." Captain Kirk can be regarded as an archetype. If you are a female you can visualize yourself as a female captain. You visualize yourself leading the ship and the landing party through an adventure of your own imagination. You don't need to come up with whole episodes, the imagery is left up to you. Visualize Mr. Spock and Dr. McCoy and the others in your retinue. You are commanding the ship to enter into unknown territory. You are witnessing visions on the main screen. Yellow cylinders of light shooting out from suns, shine through the hull of the Enterprise when you do stroke practice together with the entire crew. The Enterprise goes through a worm hole and emerges in Tavatimsa heaven and comes to a stop amongst celestial abodes. There you and your senior officers go out and somehow mix as equals among the devas of Sakkha's retinue. Visualize bliss. Sitting in Tavatimsa, you do stroke practice with an ideal outer mandala. You chant for compassion and loving kindness directed at all beings and you invite the devas to commingle with your mind. You feel contact and raise windhorse. There is a precious substance that you are seeking out in Tavatimsa which can bring tremendous power to the Federation and light up a thousand planets. Empowered with greater mind, your discovery is at hand! With this tremendous boon, something further happens and you succeed at bringing this blessing to the Federation. At the end of Star Trek practice you visualize yourself, the ship and crew slowly dissolving into space and merging with the luminosity of nirvana.

The visualization possibilities are endless. Make variations and use these potentialities to create and combine visualizations that fill your mind with love, inspiration and well tested dharma techniques available from many books. Opening up secret practices, it's O.K. to combine formerly secret techniques with any other technique. If it feels wise, do it. Kill the guru.

In the role of Captain Kirk, or you can use Captain Picard and his crew, you can invoke the law of reversibility and actually convince your subconscious mind that you are the captain of the Enterprise. If you can 'get the feeling', then the devas and the natural law of dependent origination will better bring positive results into your conventional reality, like the results of NLP. This is good for your confidence, windhorse and decisiveness. Combine this visualization with stroke practice, Star Wars and phaser practice below. The symbol of oneself sitting in the captain's chair on the bridge of the Enterprise is a powerful and uplifting symbol in our collective cultural consciousness, because of the mandala that surrounds you. This can be fun. Star Trek and Star Wars are concepts in your mind; that's it and that's all. Like beauty, goodness, up or down, use whatever concepts work to break out of unskilful habitual patterns. Ken McLeod at Unfettered Mind calls it expedient means. Gotama Buddha taught "visualize a confidence inspiring object," so he gave us licence to free ourselves of inhibitions and boldly go where no one has gone before in combining dharma with pop entertainment and culture.

When I was a boy my eldest brother Peter constructed the bridge of the Enterprise inside huge cardboard boxes up in the sun room of our house in Fonthill, Ontario. It remains one of the vivid joys of my childhood memories. In that make-believe world I thrilled at the chance to command the starship Enterprise. When I was six I first saw the second pilot episode of Star Trek where Gary Mitchell's eyes glowed as he became as jealous god (in the Buddhist idiom). This had such a powerful impact upon me because I believed that it was real life and that I could also seize such omnipotent powers. Star Trek quickly became my personal mythology and cosmology just as my family dropped out of Roman Catholic mythology and cosmology. Star Trek reruns were helpful conditioning for me as a child because it boosted my confidence and personal power. If you do Star Trek dharma practice alone no one else needs to know. In group practice this is ideal as a guided visualization because most people already know Star Trek. This practice uplifts the mind by bringing it into a grand container. This is more sensible than adopting cultural visualizations from Tibet, ancient Iran or India. The most powerful suggestive influences on your mind come from your own culture, not from a foreign culture. Joseph Campbell taught that any mythology that has to be explained to the brain isn't working. It has got to click instantly. Visualizing the red enlightened female deity Vajrayogini, with 52 skulls around her waist does not capture the American imagination fast enough. Buddhism is always up to date and current with the culture of today. The true dharma is always fresh.

Star Wars Dharma

Bill Moyers asked Joseph Campbell "Do you see any mythology for our time today," and Campbell replied "Well, the Star Wars saga is a mythology that has captured people today." Pausing, Campbell continued "I think that's really a fine thing that George Lucas did there." George Lucas was influenced by Joseph Campbell in the creation of Star Wars and Campbell was influenced by Buddhist cosmology. Star Wars provides imagery compatible with the dharma so it can be combined with Star Trek visualizations so that the powerful tool of these movies and TV episodes can be better utilized and incorporated into stroke practice or other Buddhist contemplations. More so than Star Trek, Star Wars emphasizes our connection with the higher realms, heaven and earth, and the forces of good and evil. Star Wars and Star Trek can be used as stepping stones to better understand Buddhist cosmology and to tap into the devas and the unspeakable powers that exist in Buddhist cosmology. This is meant for raising windhorse, kundalini, on your spiritual path. The symbolism and scope of science fiction helps condition the mind to open up to the genuine higher realms. Everyday life at the office does not give us a forum to speak about these things. Fiction is an excuse, a medium through which people nourish their secret belief in the higher realms.

What you must find is a purpose, a meaning behind each visualization. Your purpose is to arouse more skilful states of mind, while having a view of emptiness. Visualize yourself like Obi-Wan Kenobi standing with your light sabre blazing straight up in the air. The higher realms pulsate down into your hand, into your body, into your speech and into your mind as the devas of the force from Tavatimsa heaven gather speed in your mental continuum. "May the force be with you" means "may the devas protect and bless you." When 'the force is strong' with someone, that means that either good or bad devas are strongly protecting and supporting them. Hold a dorje to represent the handle of a light sabre and visualize the sacred power of the sword illuminated before you. As you hold your dorje light sabre, you feel a certain power coming on, your hands tingle and you know that you're coming alive. With your dorje light sabre, imagine slicing through obstacles in your personal life and heroically liberating others. Picture the rod of dazzling white light emanating from your dorje, resonating with a steady hum.

This contemplative practice can be done alone or in a group meditation, led by an umdze who is the keeper of the dorje light sabre. The umdze holds the visualized sword straight up to draw energy off the wall of the cylinder. The umdze creates circles with the visualized dorje light sabre, then points the dorje above the head of each member of the group, like being knighted, blessing them individually by directing the energy down from the yellow cylinder. The umdze gives them a cue at the end of the practice and their hearts all expand out together, expanding the walls of the cylinder around them until the cylinder goes across the entire universe and across the entire god realm, then it dissolves into space.

Don't rely on a book to provide your practice for you. Develop your own secret mandala practice. Your secret practice is potent because it is your own special technique created by you and meaningful to you, your own personal mythology linked to Buddhism, which grows into your conventional reality. As you learn other techniques in the future you can modify your personal practice. The result is that your mind is inspired with energy, your love and compassion for others is fortified, and with each confident step into the future you are living powerfully in the now. As Master Yoda told Obi-Wan Kenobi, "be mindful of the future." May the force be with you. Soft human copper gold. Sacred messages from the devas enter your copper buddhacle godhead.

Phaser Practice

Phaser practice helps you to invoke windhorse which produces a more powerful frame of mind to assist deva invocation. Like a stroke of grace visualize the yellow deva cylinder of light from stroke practice coming as a phaser beam out of the sun which goes around you and through a column of the Earth and out the other side of the planet. At that moment your heart radiates outward. Phaser practice can also be represented as a tunnel that encompasses the entire Earth. Like a fire hose of devas, extend this visualization to imagining a hand held phaser that shoots windhorse devas in the direction that you are pointing your hand at. This is safe enough for boys and girls to do at home. Since children are less rigid in their understanding of the difference between imagination and reality, they will be more successful in phaser practice than adults. Phaser practice can also be modified to join you with devas as you point to them with your extended arm. This is a method of supplicating and signalling to the devas, yearning for them and paying your respects to them. Extending your arm means that you are reaching to the devas, extending to the devas, contacting the devas. Instead of a negative idea about what the arm extension is, or what a phaser is, this is an energy beam of love and light. Devotion. Devotion. Love the devas and they will love you. People in Theravadin Buddhist countries dedicate their merit to the devas to help the devas to attain nirvana. You take care of the devas and the devas will take care of you. You can allow your whole body to move spontaneously to express or release whatever energies you are feeling in the moment. Free your constraints. Be fluid. There's no technique. This is basic goodness.

Imagine Star Wars ships or the Enterprise above you firing deva phasers at you or at the beneficiary of your choice. It also fires dazzling white photon torpedoes which you absorb as a boost to your health. You could imagine the Enterprise nurturing peace in a war torn area of the Earth. You can regard the Enterprise or another ship as a deva UFO and a senior deva compared to the lesser ones that it emits from its phasers. You can visualize a Star Trek like phaser beam coming from the sun to the Earth. The purpose of all of this is to encourage contact with your spirit guides. This imagery helps to open your mind. The phaser from the sun is pictured as a grand wide cylinder of light. It can vary in colour from yellow to a mixture of yellow, gold, white, diamond points, etc. It takes light eight minutes to reach the earth from the sun. You can imagine the cylinder taking eight minutes to touch you or you can cut it to seconds. On the journey, see the mouth of the cylinder zapping through space as it spins clockwise. The mouth is unstable, it fluctuates in shape. Points of white light like pearls shimmer on the surface of the hollow translucent tube.

> In Buddhaghosa's commentary he writes that the Buddha taught that **the Sun's disk is the divine palace of a deva** (Nanamoli, 1956; 457).
> *Path of Purification* states: "There is no sun deity in the aeon-destruction sun as there is in the ordinary sun. The 'ordinary sun' is the Sun's divine palace that arose before the emergence of the aeon. But like the other sense-sphere deities at the time of the emergence of the aeon the Sun Deity too produces jhana and reappears in the Brahma World. But the actual sun's disk becomes brighter and more fiery. Others say that it disappears and another appears in its place." (Pm. 412).

The aeon destruction sun has no deva residing inside. This will appear before the end of the world, billions of years into the future, when the universe collapses again. Buddhaghosa describes the sun deva attaining jhana and transcending the sensuous sphere in a samadhi absorption and taking rebirth in the fine material sphere. We can take this to mean that another sensuous sphere deva takes the place of the sun deva so that our solar system continues with a powerful deva at the centre. This is a significant revelation about the centre of our solar system!

Visualize that your stroke practice touches the heart of this great deva and his palace in the sun and that the deva helps by responding to your supplication, with assistance. Wherever the sun is, day or night, visualize that the cylinder comes from the sun to you- it can even come through the Earth or curve around the Earth. You are connected to the oceans of devas in the sun! You can visualize the sun directly at the zenith surrounded by a clear blue sky regardless of where the sun actually is. Visualize oceans of devas surrounding the sun and surrounding your cylinder. See them streaming down and joining you, showering you with multitudes of diamond-like blessings. You can invoke the transporter beam in Star Trek to imagine the yellow cylinder all around you. Just as the transporter dematerializes everything inside the tube, feel yourself mixing together at a particle level with the devas surrounding you. Make the yellow cylinder a fortified shield that screens out foolish influences and jealous gods. You know that you are safe inside.

Once you have consolidated the visualization of the yellow cylinder, and you have held it clearly in your mind, then move on to the next step. Only after you are holding the image deeply and clearly, visualize the yellow cylinder transformed into a dazzling bright white cylinder. This is the greatest purity and power. Because you transform this vision only in a concentrated state of mind, your windhorse is magnified like a swell in the sea.

The reason why the sun is such a powerful object of attention is that it is so fundamental to our health and a fundamental element of the existence of our world. Everyday we dwell upon the sun, largely unconsciously. You can see where our old nemesis, the Iranian sun god religion, came from. Phaser practice is definitely aimed at your unconscious mind and at your alaya mind stream. You want to deeply imbue your being with dharma, dharma, dharma, twenty-four hours a day, as the Vajra Regent exhorted us to do (1988, Discipline talk two; Halifax). With this conditioning, the intention is that in future human lives you will be drawn back to the dharma, to the practice, by familiar influences. The more you practice dharma now, the greater the probability that you will be blessed to stumble upon the dharma in future lives. Then you will succeed in reestablishing your footing on the Buddhist path to enlightenment. No good efforts in any lifetime are wasted.

Deva Qigong Cylinder

While you are sitting in peace and waiting for something to well up from inside of you, you can stand up and do Qigong to raise your windhorse. It is best to have direct personal instruction in Qigong to learn this properly. Qigong is a Taoist exercise from China and it is one of the best methods for stirring up energy and keeping awake. In Qigong the idea is to stir up the energy in your aura. The physical exercises have been skilfully designed to achieve this and the results are apparent. The Qigong deva invocation technique is that you put your left hand on your hip and your right hand out in front. You slowly spin your right arm going out from the centre in a clockwise circle. Slowly. You shift your weight forward over the knee as you reach out, and shift it backwards onto your back foot, which is one step behind your front foot and pointing out 45 degrees. Do that twenty times.

Once you've got the motions going you silently or verbally repeat three times the Pali homage to the Buddha chant, "Namo Tassa Bhagavato Arahato Sammāsambuddhassā," while simultaneously doing the 'recollection of deities' visualization of the Buddha and about ten of his closest disciples in the air in front and above you, surrounded by an ocean of devas. Wait, and then when it feels right, do the stroke practice visualization of the yellow cylinder coming down from the sun and spinning all around you. Do the stroke practice chants as prescribed, 'soft human copper gold,' 'sacred messages from the devas enter your copper buddhacle godhead.' Visualize devas streaming down to you. When you lose your concentration, chant in spurts of three, "ii sa wa su su sa wa ii."

After twenty arm rotations, reverse direction and do twenty more. Next you discharge the energy by bringing your hands up on an inhale, visualize universal energy coming down a funnel, and imagine the chi energy of the universe pouring down through your body. Curve your hands over your head, close your fists lightly at your forehead while starting to exhale. Exhale while running your hands flat, four inches from the front of your body, down to the end of your reach by your thighs. This discharges the chi energy into your body and particularly into your internal organs. If you run your hands too close to your body you will short circuit this chi energy. It is important to not lock the knees during Qigong because this kinks the energy flow. Next, switch sides with your feet and do the left side the same way, starting with your left hand slowly spinning out counter-clockwise. If you go slow enough you may feel a buzz and tingle of energy building up in your hands. If you go too fast it won't work as well and your hands may feel cold. Move reasonably slow, with warm equanimity.

During this Qigong practice with the 'recollection of deities' imagine that some devas come through the yellow cylinder of light around you. See these devas descending in the cylinder and merging with your body, speech and mind. After doing this first move of Qigong you can do another Qigong move or go back to sitting again, meditate, be gentle, open and receptive to the energies coming through you. This is the method for doing Qigong deva invocation practice. These practices give you a myth to live by. Joseph Campbell said "What people are seeking in life is not meaning and purpose. What we are seeking is an experience of being alive, so that the life experiences we have on the purely physical plane will have resonances within that are those of our own innermost being and reality so that we actually feel the rapture of being alive. That's what it's all finally about and that's what these clues help us to find within ourselves. Myths are clues about the spiritual potentialities of the human life. The mind has to do with meaning. In the heart is the experience of life. The inner value, the rapture that is associated with being alive is what it's all about."

By delving into these deva invocation practices you'll be alive like Superman. It's up to you to actually do the practices and experience results for yourself.

Superman

Another option in these visualizations is to combine eastern and western mythology by visualizing yourself as Superman, another great pop icon. This image, this concept, this archetype of the unconscious activates prior knowledge in the practitioner. Superman is synonymous with virtue and power so this is a fine selection. Superman was created by two youths in Cleveland, Ohio and our hero first appeared in the June, 1938 issue of Action Comics. During the despair of the depression Superman filled a need so his popularity quickly spread. So much so, that some deluded people actually believed that Superman was for real. This was just like the creation of Amitabha Buddha and Quan Yin which filled a need for a father figure and a mother figure. The Buddha offered no such thing. In only sixty years, Superman has become more important in the Western mind than Amitabha Buddha — and deservedly so since Superman is more in accordance with the dharma than Amitabha Buddha. Founded in 1938 Superman has been an American bodhisattva ever since.

See yourself standing with your dorje sabre held straight up. Upon your blue chest is the bright red "S" and below your blue legs are your red boots. Your red cape hangs low to the ground from your shoulders. Your being courses with unstoppable power. Covering yourself from head to toe with a visualization is done for the purpose of displacing your limited views of yourself with something uplifting and greater. If you are walking in the countryside, when no one is looking you can extend your arms and get an idea of what it's like to fly over the fields, trees and water. This conditions your mind to incline towards the deva realm, rather than dwelling upon your base instincts which conditions the mind to incline towards the animal realm. Some Vajrayana practices teach you to visualize yourself as being your guru. Since your guru is your role model, you try to take on the qualities that you admire in your teacher by imagining that you already possess those great qualities. This same principle applies to picturing yourself as Superman. With a view towards emptiness you can develop the practice over time such that you can promote Superman to being a fully enlightened arahant.

No Spiritual Seniority System

In July 1991 the Tibetan guru Khenpo Tsultrim Gyamtso Rinpoche taught a Mahamudra Intensive course which I attended at the Rocky Mountain Shambhala Center at Red Feather Lakes in Colorado, USA. There he explained to more than 200 of us that if someone has been practicing meditation for 20 years and studying the teachings of the Buddhadharma for 20 years, then it is possible that they may not be as spiritually advanced as a new young person that just walked in the door the day before. This is because the new person who just learned how to meditate for the first time and who just started learning about the dharma yesterday, may have already reached great levels of meditative attainments in previous lives. Some people are just naturally more concentrated and together than others, regardless of their age, education or background.

So, there is no spiritual seniority system in the Buddhist religion. That is why the Buddha rebuked Ananda, his faithful attendant, when Ananda suggested that the Buddha should name a successor to lead the sangha after the Buddha's death. The Buddha knew full well that such a thing would create more problems than it would solve. The Buddha deliberately wanted the Buddhist religion to be decentralized and not controlled by any hands of power; he didn't want something like the Papal lineage to happen to Buddhism.

There should be a political seniority system within the sangha, for people to relate to each other and to relate to the conventional world. And, there is a political seniority system within the Buddhist sangha, and most other communities. But, Buddhism undercuts the idea of a bona fide spiritual seniority system between human beings. The Buddha did classify people into the four levels of sainthood, but it is impossible for us unenlightened people to make such distinctions in others. The four levels of sainthood are: stream enterer, once returner, non returner and an arahant. The Dalai Lama does not claim to be spiritually superior to a simple monk.

A stream enterer is someone who will reach enlightenment within seven lifetimes. They have attained to the level of a fundamental shift in thinking, as though they had seen only one side of the Buddha's hand all of their life, then suddenly they see the other side. A once returner will only return to human birth one more time. A non returner will never take rebirth again as a human being, but is not yet enlightened. By process of elimination, they will be reborn as a deva and attain enlightenment as a deva. This blows away the misconception that devas cannot get enlightened because they are indulging in too much pleasure and bliss. Trillions of devas genuinely do have that problem, but some areas of heaven are better than others for attaining enlightenment. Heaven is not all the same. The fact of enlightened devas is the basis for the Pure Land School and the Mahayana belief in deities. Since devas can become fully enlightened and continue with their very long life spans before leaving us for the dharmakaya or wherever enlightened ones go, then people might regard these enlightened devas as deities. The most popular deity of the Pure Land is Amitabha Buddha, meaning, 'the Buddha of infinite light and immeasurable length of life.' This marries the southern and northern schools together, in the sense that both have enlightened beings in the higher realms and both have pure lands, or pure abodes. An arahant is fully enlightened, like a man who's been blind all of his life, suddenly being given sight.

You cannot measure or easily discern a person's spiritual attainments. The Buddha counted amongst the 38 blessings in life the blessing of paying respects to those worthy of respect. It is easy to pay respects to well known people. It is not so easy to pay respects to those unsung heroes who have done much to create enlightened society. If you find them and pay respects to them, then you are truly fortunate to do so.

You can develop your own relationship with the higher realms, without getting permission from the guru or head office to have such contact. You don't have to be a senior student of Buddhism in order to be an old soul.

Shipwrecked with Devas

There's a deva invocation story about a voyaging ship that was wrecked during a storm at sea and only two of the men on it were able to swim to a small, desert like island. The two survivors, both Buddhists, not knowing what else to do, agreed that they would do deva invocation practice and ask help from their spirit guides as a recourse to redeem them from their plight. However, to find out whose practice was more powerful, they agreed to divide the territory between them and stay on opposite sides of the island.

The first thing they chanted for was food. The next morning, the first man saw a fruit-bearing tree on his side of the land, and he was able to eat its fruit. The other man's parcel of land remained barren.

After a week, the first man was lonely and he decided to pray for a wife. The next day, another ship was wrecked, and the only survivor was a woman who swam to his side of the land. On the other side of the island, the second man had nothing.

Soon the first man asked the devas for a house, clothes, more food. The next day like magic, all of these were given to him. However, the second man still had nothing.

Finally, the first man visualized a ship, so that he and his wife could leave the island. In the morning, he found a ship docked at his side of the island. The first man boarded the ship with his wife and decided to leave the second Buddhist on the island. He considered the other man unworthy to receive the deva's blessings, since none of his practices had borne fruit. As the ship was about to leave, the first man heard a voice from the heavens booming: "Why are you leaving your companion on the island?"

"My blessings are mine alone, since I was the one who was attained enough to ask for them properly" the first man answered. "His chants, visualizations and invocations were all unanswered and so he does not deserve anything." – "You are mistaken!" the voice rebuked him. "He had a very special practice which we all answered! If not for that, you would not have received any of our blessings." – "Tell me," the first man asked the voice, "what did he ask for that I should owe him anything?" – "He combined his deva invocation practice with the give and take contemplation on compassion. He asked that all your requests be answered."

So the first man swung the ship around the island and rescued his companion, who later experienced even greater blessings. As seen in this light, it becomes easier for us to share our blessings in life, whether these blessings be material or otherwise. For all we know, these are not the fruits of our aspirations alone, but those of another person secretly praying for us.

Chapter 10

Practices

Loving Kindness Visualization
(Theravadin)

The contemplation on loving kindness is a good way to finish off a period of meditation, or to end a class on Buddhism. You could do an entire meditation session of 30 minutes on loving kindness. The contemplation on loving kindness was taught by the Buddha to a group of his monks who were being tormented by devas who were trying to drive the monks out of their home region because the monks had overstayed their welcome, so to speak. The practice, called metta in Pali or maitri in Sanskrit, was very successful; the devas loved the monks, and in return they made their rains retreat very pleasant. Loving kindness has been a Buddhist tradition ever since.

The Technique

Sitting upright in meditation posture with your eyes closed, you begin by bringing your attention to your heart centre. Direct your thoughts in the direction of loving kindness and extend a feeling of warmth to a benefactor, someone who has helped you a lot in the past, such as your parents, a friend, a boss or someone else. Traditionally, thinking about your mother should cause you to arouse feelings of love and gratitude. Kelsang Gyatso teaches that you should visualize your mother thus (Kelsang, 1995; 69):

"After we were conceived, because of our mother's kindness we now enjoy a human life and experience all its advantages. When we were a baby, had we not received her constant care and attention we would certainly have had an accident and could now be handicapped, crippled, or blind. Fortunately our mother did not neglect us. Day and night she gave us her loving care, regarding us as more important than herself. She saved our life many times each day. During the night she allowed her sleep to be interrupted, and during the day she forfeited her usual pleasures. She had to leave her job, and when her friends went out to enjoy themselves she had to stay behind. It is principally through her kindness that we now have the opportunity to practise dharma and eventually to attain enlightenment. Since there is no one who has not been our mother at some time in our previous lives, all living beings are very kind."

After invoking love for your mother or a benefactor, extend this love back to yourself. The law of higher consciousness is, love everyone unconditionally —including yourself. Feel within your heart warmth, gentleness and envelop yourself in loving kindness. It is necessary to love yourself first, the Buddha taught, in order to be able to extend true loving kindness to others. In the *Path of Purification*, Buddhaghosa writes (Nanamoli, 1956; 323):

"[If one develops their loving kindness contemplation] in this way 'I am happy. Just as I want to be happy and dread pain, as I want to live and not to die, so do other beings, too,' making himself the example, then desire for other beings' welfare and happiness arises in him. And this method is indicated by the Blessed One's saying.

> I visited all quarters with my mind
> Nor found I any dearer than myself;
> Self is likewise to every other dear;
> Who loves himself will never harm another (S.i,75;Ud. 47)

So he should first, as example, pervade himself with lovingkindness. Next after that, in order to proceed easily, he can recollect such gifts, kind words, etc., as inspire love and endearment, such virtue, learning, etc., as inspire respect and reverence met with in a teacher or his equivalent or a preceptor or his equivalent, developing lovingkindness towards him in the way beginning 'May this good man be happy and free from suffering.' With such a person, of course, he attains absorption.

But if this bhikkhu does not rest content with just that much and wants to break down the barriers, he should next after that, develop lovingkindness towards a very dearly loved friend, then towards a neutral person as a very dearly loved friend, then towards a hostile person as neutral. And while he does so, he should make his mind malleable and wieldy in each instance before passing on to the next."

Buddhaghosa continues with 19 pages of vital commentary on this loving kindness practice, which is recommended reading.

During the visualization, forgive yourself and let your hardness relax and touch your loving kindness. Silently chant to yourself several times "May I be well, happy and peaceful," and realize that you have gentleness in you already. You begin to feel that everything is possible and you are surprised at how gentle you can be with yourself; you discover that you don't have to torture yourself (Trungpa). Then extend this feeling of warmth outwards and forgive others. Extend a feeling of loving kindness, friendliness, gladness and love to all sentient beings. First think of those that you love such as family and friends, then extend your heart to acquaintances and neutral persons, strangers. Then include people whom you are having difficulties with, people who hurt you and people whom you dislike. Extend your loving kindness to everybody. The Buddha said "There, O monks, the monk with a mind full of loving-kindness pervading first one direction, then a second one, then a third one, then the fourth one, just so above, below, all around and across; and everywhere identifying himself with all, he is pervading the whole world with mind full of loving kindness, with mind wide, developed, unbounded, free from hate and ill-will."

Intermittently chant to yourself **"May all beings be well, happy and peaceful. May all beings be well, happy and peaceful."** Ten times should be standard. U Silananda from Burma teaches that "when we send these metta thoughts, we can send them in different ways; we can send them by location or by persons. When we say the sentences, we should try to visualize the beings or persons mentioned in the sentences as being really happy and peaceful." When sending loving kindness above you can include the devas in heaven, in the god realm, tuning into their happiness. Sending it below you can include the three lower realms of the animals, the hungry ghosts and hell beings. At the end bring it up, around, across and everywhere, visualizing a golden wave or sphere of loving kindness going out from your heart centre, across the city, across the country, across the planet, across the galaxy, to the ends of the universe, passing through all sentient beings limitless as space, spreading a feeling of harmony and happiness. This is a wondrous practice.

Note: Credits given to Buddha, Buddhaghosa, Trungpa Rinpoche, Geshe Kelsang Gyatso and U Silananda.

Give and Take
Contemplation on Compassion
(Mahayana)

What is the most powerfully effective way of relieving the suffering of others? Many Mahayana Buddhists believe that the best way to help others is by practising what is known as give and take, which is a meditation on compassion. It is called *tonglen* in Tibetan. *Tong* means "sending out" or "letting go,"and *len* means receiving. This is a very important term. It is the main practice in the development of relative bodhicitta. Ultimate bodhicitta means to rest the mind in the nature of alaya without following discursive thoughts. Alaya being the level of consciousness below the unconscious mind. Relative bodhicitta is the active practice quality of going outwards and using practices to extend your heart to others. The way in which give and take is done is that you take upon yourself the suffering of others, and you send them your happiness, your strength, your virtue, anything good. Give and take, and other such practices which wake up our bodhicitta (Buddha-nature), are the very core of spirituality on the Mahayana path.

The actual technique is that you sit in meditation for a few minutes. Then, you visualize that you are breathing in blackness. You may have your eyes closed or open for this visualization practice. On the out breath, you visualize that you are breathing out whiteness. Continuing, you imagine that you are breathing in the sufferings of others. Imagine that black tar collecting all the suffering, obscurations, and evil of all sentient beings enters your nostrils and is absorbed straight into your heart. Think that you have forever freed others of their pain and foster a great feeling of joy as you bring their suffering upon yourself.

At the end of the in breath, you imagine that a white lava eruption is occurring within the black tar in your heart. This is the moment when the negativities are transformed into love. This occurs by the power of the Buddha-nature within yourself. The blinding white lava consumes all of your thoughts, except for an illuminated awareness of your nose, and the object of your compassion. Your nose feels bubbly, as if you drank Coke too fast. On the out breath you feel that moonbeams of light are emanating out from your nostrils. Some of this love energy goes straight through the bridge of your nose. This pure unstained white love goes out and is absorbed by all other beings. You are sending out all of your goodness, love, virtue, health, energy, light. Anything good that you've got, you're giving it away to others. You do this on the out breath. The moonbeams of love emanating from your nostrils are focused on the being or beings whom you are healing. However, the emanation through the tissues of your nose encompass the entire periphery like a bright haze on a hot sunny day.

You practice giving and taking alternately, on the medium of the breath. It is good as well if you hear or imagine a soft buzzing sound in your ears, like a computer's hum. It is natural to hear buzzing in your ears and you can bring this experience into the practice of give and take. On the out breath imagine the buzzing sound as the sound of a wave of whiteness and goodness going out. Like a tide receding, on the in breath visualize the blackness coming in on the sound. Don't confuse yourself by trying to make a project out of this. But if your attention naturally goes to the sound in your ears, then bring that onto your spiritual path of experience. But your main practice lies with the breath.

Shantideva, who has described this practice extensively, says:
If I don't completely exchange
My happiness for others' sorrow,
Buddhahood will not be realized.
There is no happiness in samsara.

You can begin by extending your compassion to objects that are easy for you — your friends, parents, loved ones, your cat. Then you should extend give and take to include people that you are having difficulties with. You can even breathe in the blackness of negative encounters you have had with people today, or this week, and breathe out the soothing calm glow of the moonbeams of light into that visualization. To heal situations between ourselves and others, it takes a bit of give and take. You can even use give and take to heal your own physical, mental or emotional suffering. Breathe in the blackness of your sore backache, and breathe out the healing white light to yourself. Do the same to take the tension out of anticipated future events, like job interviews. You can go back in time and breathe in the suffering of your childhood and rewrite the history books by breathing out vibrant white smiles into that period of your life. Each time you do this, even when you are doing it for yourself, some of the goodness and joy is emanating to benefit the whole world.

Extending the scope of your give and take practice, you breathe in the suffering of all sentient beings, limitless as space. Imagine that all of their suffering from the past, present and future is concentrated into the black tar going into your nostrils and into your heart. Cultivate a tremendous feeling of joy and think that you have forever freed them of their suffering. As you breathe out the whiteness, think that all sentient beings immediately attain buddhahood. That's the ultimate in compassion, to bring all sentient beings limitless as space, into a state of complete enlightenment. This practice is characteristic of the heroism of the bodhisattva ideal in Mahayana Buddhism.

Before practising give and take it is best to begin with a generation stage of non conceptual meditation. Sit for about five minutes in meditation first, then begin the give and take visualization. Give and take should only be done for about ten minutes, not too long. This is because it is an intense practice of taking on the sufferings of others, and giving away your strength. It is very conceptual and involved. Afterwards, you should dissolve the visualization and go back to your sitting meditation practice for at least five more minutes. This is the dissolution stage before you get up and leave the cushion.

Give and take is not limited to a practise that you do on the cushion. In the post meditation world, you should give compassion to people you see on the street in this way. If you are standing at a bus stop near someone, you can practice give and take for them as you are breathing. Even if someone is talking to you, in the midst of a conversation you can breathe in their suffering and extend this compassion visualization to them. If their words are boring, you may have nothing better to do while you nod, smile, and fain interest in what they are saying. Like exercising a muscle, you can develop this practice as a lifestyle of compassion so that you automatically help others in this way. The Mahayanists have combined loving kindness and compassion with this one technique. Breathing out the white is a loving kindness contemplation. Breathing in the black is a compassion contemplation.

Because the Buddha taught that the mind is not separate from the rest of the world, there is no solid line that divides you from others. Because of this reality, with give and take you can actually reduce the sufferings of others and give them some strength and love. This isn't just a good technique to undercut your ego's selfishness and develop your inner heart qualities of compassion. Give and take does that as well, of course, but the experience of many people indicates that give and take actually produces a real benefit for others. Buddha taught that we interact with the world only through the three gates of body, speech and mind. So even at the level of mind, you can actually benefit others and have a real affect on their lives. This is the basis of the practice of ancestor worship.

I taught give and take to a class in a Vancouver temple and later one of my students practiced it for a friend of hers who was having an abortion after a case of date rape. As Lindy held her friend's hand during the operation, she contemplated on give and take without telling the other woman what she was doing. Later her friend said "I feel great! I feel like all this blackness and tar has been sucked right out of me!" This was very surprising for Lindy to hear, but it is not uncommon.

Don't worry about any possible negative effects of taking on the sufferings of others. It gets transformed and you feel better after doing the practice. In Vancouver in 1997, someone asked Jetsun Kusho if there was any danger that doing give and take could cause some psychological damage to the meditator. Jetsun Kusho lives near Vancouver and she is probably the highest ranking female Tibetan lama in the world. She replied "No. Only a Westerner would ask such a question. An Asian would never ask that question." Then we all laughed! We Westerners are so psychological that we second guess this practice.

It may be contrary to our habitual patterns of taking in all the goodies for ourselves, and dumping our garbage on the side of the road, but this is very much the Mahayana approach. You are making others more important than yourself, and you are taking on the suffering of the world, personally. You are undercutting your ego fixation on personal territory by giving away your heart and compassion to others. "In ordinary situations, you don't send and receive at all. You try as much as possible to guard those pleasant little situations that you have created for yourself; you seal them up like fruit in a tin. It is completely vacuumed, purified and clean," Chögyam Trungpa said. "Anything outside of your territory is regarded as altogether problematic. You may not have enough money to build a castle around you, but your front door is very reliable. You are always putting double locks on it."

"Basically speaking, the Mahayana path is trying to show us that we can afford to extend out a little bit — quite a bit. The idea of sending and taking is almost a rehearsal. The discipline of passionlessness is to overcome territory (Trungpa, 1979; 96)." You find that you can help others and relieve them of their suffering. It's a great feeling!

The Mahayana experience proves that give and take actually bestows a bona fide benefit on others. There are many cases of this. If someone is dying, or dead, you should take their confusion and suffering upon yourself. You can extend your power to them when they are in their most desperate hour of need. If you fail to do this, then you will have lost an opportunity to earn merit, like avoiding throwing a life preserver to someone struggling in the water.

Suppose that you came upon a woman just after she died. Suppose she was confused in the bardo and felt drawn to two cats because her own cat used to lay in the sun and purr, sleeping on its back. She could make the heart wrenching and horrendous mistake of choosing to enter the womb of a cat because human life was stressful for her. Suppose you stood there and you didn't help this poor dead woman with give and take! You could have given her enough presence of mind to avoid a feline rebirth so that she could have attained another human existence. Imagine, it is possible that you could save someone from rebirth as a house cat and give them a boost in the direction of a good human birth, just by doing give and take.

This is surely as true as the rising of the great eastern sun. What better way can you suck away a poor dead person's confusion than with give and take? Give and take is ideal service for the bardo and for the dying so this compassion should be extended in the direction of hospitals and morgues. It is a tremendous blessing to volunteer this gift at a hospital with dead and dying people — opportunities for merit are all over the place.

You may have the compassion to risk your life entering a burning house to save a total stranger, but do you have the compassion to practice give and take for your own mother after she dies? If you do, the merit earned would be immeasurable! One reason why people would rather run into a burning house, than sit and contemplate is because of the ignorance of what Ralph Waldo Emerson described as the conspiracy of the vast majority. People receive no recognition for doing contemplation for a dead person, but they may receive a medal of valour if they walk out of a burning house carrying a human life. Our peers see each other, they do not see the dearly departed.

You have responsibility. Heed this appalling teaching of the Buddha: The third highest blessing in life is to pay respects to those worthy of honour. Society does not know who is worthy of honour. 90% of the job of compassionate management is the selection of good people to put under the spotlight in positions of power. The best people in the world are not famous. The famous people in the world are not the best. If you do the right thing, even when no one is looking, you're looking. Practices such as give and take make you feel great and deliver you towards emancipation.

Bodhicitta Visualization
(Vajrayana)

This is adopted as a Theravadin practice that combines the loving kindness contemplation with the Tibetan Vajrayana visualization of one's self as a fully enlightened Buddha. This is based on the Buddha's teaching to visualize a confidence inspiring object. Begin by taking your posture, sitting upright with your eyes closed. Bring your attention to your heart. Extend a feeling of loving kindness to yourself. Envelop yourself in a sphere of warm white light and make yourself a basis of love which is the foundation for the loving kindness that you send outwards to others.

Next, extend your loving kindness to the people that you love the most, your family, your friends. Visualize them as being well, happy, peaceful and bathed in sunlight. Then extend the circle by including acquaintances, strangers. After building up some heart, give your loving kindness to people whom you're having difficulties with. Give them your loving kindness too. Now, extend your loving kindness in the four directions — in front of you, to your right, behind you, and to your left. Think **"May all beings be well, happy and peaceful. May all beings be well, happy and peaceful..."**

Now that you have generated some heart and have aroused bodhicitta, imagine that you are already fully enlightened. In *Joyful Path of Good Fortune* Geshe Kelsang Gyatso teaches the following contemplation (Kelsang, 1997; 60):

What will it be like when I become fully enlightened? I shall possess every good quality and I shall have perfect ability to help all other living beings. My emanations will be as numerous as living beings and I shall use them for the benefit of all. Just as there is one moon shining in the sky whose reflections fill all the lakes and waters of the world, when I become enlightened my emanations will cover and protect every living being.

When this meditation induces in our mind a strong intention to become enlightened for the sake of others, we hold this thought clearly and single-pointedly for as long as we can, acquainting ourself with it more and more closely. Then we recite the chant for generating bodhicitta:

Through the virtues I collect by giving and other perfections, may I become a Buddha for the benefit of all.

Since bodhicitta is the main cause of full enlightenment imagine that in response Gotama Buddha emanates another aspect of his form which sits above your head. Visualize a translucent white Buddha above your head with rainbow colours oscillating on the surface. Then the Buddha rests on your head and merges his enlightened mind with yours. Slowly the Buddha descends through your head and into your heart, resting in a pavilion of light, like an open shell.

Visualize dazzling white rays of lights coming off the Buddha which purify your obscurations and non-virtues from the inside out. Gradually your whole body is completely consumed and you are transformed into a living Buddha. You have now discarded your name and identity because you are a fully enlightened being. Now you radiate light in all directions, reaching every single living being and purifying their non-virtues and obstructions. All living beings absorb into light and reappear as Buddhas in the same aspect as Gotama Buddha. Pause during each stage of the visualization and repeat several times: **"May all beings be well, happy and peaceful."**

Like a sphere imagine that the Buddhas furthest out from you are coming in closer to you. You are at the centre and they are merging together and melting into each other. The walls of the sphere are coming closer and closer to you and the Buddhas closest to you merge into you and become one with you. Gradually all beings limitless as space melt into you leaving only the luminosity of the clear light nature of mind. Finally you begin to dissolve from the top down and from the bottom up. Visualize that the top of your head and the bottom of your feet are dissolving into luminous empty space. You're dissolving, dissolving, closer and closer to the centre.

Now rest your mind in space and as far as possible follow no train of thought. The last part of you in the middle dissolves into space and you are free of discursive thoughts. Just rest your mind in non-discursive clarity for as long as possible. Sit for at least five minutes more, then dissolve the visualization and come back to your body, back to your breath — in and out, in and out. Open your eyes at the end of the meditation.

Note: Revised and adapted from *Joyful Path of Good Fortune* (Kelsang, 1996; 60), and Bokar Rinpoche's book *Chenrezig - Lord of Love.*

Transmuting Anger

Anger is the acid test of any religion. "How should people deal with anger?" is the question that must be put to any humanistic philosophy or method of psychotherapy. The Buddha gave us several techniques in the metta sutra and in Middle Length discourse No. 20, such as replacing the thought with a more skillful thought, regarding the thought with revulsion like the corpse of a dog on a necklace around your neck, lack of attention to the thought, stilling the thought formation by visualizing the anger as a man walking quickly, then slowing down, and slowing until standing, then sitting, then lying down. This takes the gas out of anger. The Buddha even recommended pressing the tongue against the palate and clenching your jaws to get your mind off of anger. In the metta sutra the Buddha even advised suppressing anger if it is necessary in a situation. He also instructed; regard others with onlooking loving kindness, compassion or equanimity, and contemplate that they are the heir of their deeds.

These are all practices to work with the tempestuous angry mind. The practice of transmuting emotions comes from the Tibetan Buddhist tradition and it is mixed with Hinduism. Transmuting means that it is possible for you to uplevel your emotions from your lower energy centres to your higher energy centres and actually benefit from cultivating the energy of your negative emotions. This is an exciting possibility. These "chackras" were not taught by the Buddha as far as we know. This is not at all to say that they are invalid; perhaps the Buddha felt that it was unnecessary to reveal the existence of the chackras. This is a Hindu model which the Mahayana Buddhists have adopted.

The way in which transmuting takes place is that you deal directly with any negative emotions as they arise in your mind. This may be a bit more difficult to practice if you're in the middle of a fist fight with somebody, but even then this technique is applicable. What you do is that you "stare down" your anger, your passion, jealousy, envy, whatever it is. You bring your attention to it in your mind and you stare it down. This means that you do not act out your anger, you do not actually "get angry." You bring your attention to the physical feelings associated with your anger. Closely observe the knot in your stomach, your clenched jaw, the shoot of heat going up your spine and neck, etc. This is Buddhist meditation! You're practicing mindfulness/awareness.

The whole point is that you should observe your anger rather than engaging your anger and your body, speech and mind to create bad karma for yourself. Instead of getting angry at others you should avoid spreading more anger in the world and deal with your own mind first. It will not bless the world for you to scream one more time at your family- even if they deserve it. And it will not bless you to throw pots and pans at your spouse- no matter how disgusting he or she is. Stop the cycle. Break the anger response now. You can do it and this is perhaps the best technique known.

Ideally, if you can sit in meditation or control the environment around you, that would be good. If you are in your office and you slam down the phone is a huff, take that opportunity to quietly sit in your cubicle and meditate upon your anger. This is your one great opportunity to turn almost certain bad karma around and make it a moment to bring your negative emotions onto your spiritual path. The energy of anger can be cultivated just as manure on a farmer's field is cultivated to bring fresh new crops into being. After you slam down the phone with a face looking like 'Jason,' bring your mind inside your body with your eyes closed or open. As angry thoughts tumble and rumble through your mind, boycott your thoughts but stay with the feeling. Feel your pain. "Experience your experience," as they used to say in EST. Don't get into the mental rationalizations about that no good so-and-so because that will only entrench anger deeper into your mind. Your objective is to get rid of your anger and you can do that by going right into your anger. You go through your anger and out the other side, as it were. You can do it!

You can add a visualization method of your own to imagine the white power of your active, fluid energy coursing up through your spine and body. This visualization should match the physical feeling of the emotions at your body level. Imagine the energy transmuted until the point of it reaching your head with a warm soft whiteness enveloping your face and the crown of your head, then see the emanation of violet light beam upwards from your crown, going in many directions across infinite space. Visualize this connecting with the ultimate dharmakaya which you symbolically visualize as an outer sphere to the universe. Beyond the walls of this symbolic sphere resides nirvana — total enlightenment. Imagine that shooting the energy of anger up to there is the very best thing that you can possibly do with your anger and your other negative emotions.

When keeping vigil over your feelings, your emotions take on a translucent quality, they become flimsy and fall apart. No one can claim that their personal anger is as solid as concrete, that it has no gaps, that it is continuous and purely refined. No. Such anger does not exist in this universe because the Buddha's first noble truth applies to every corner of this particular universe. The truth of dukkha is that all things are impermanent so in this technique, when you put your focus keenly on your negativities, they eventually shift and change and their energy is transmuted. Boycott your thoughts — but stay with the feeling. What happens is that anger is associated with the lower of the seven chackras, and you are bringing that energy up, out of the top, as it were. "Chackras" are channel wheels or energy centres in the body.

The Seven Chackras

Location on the body	Colour	Purpose or connection
root	red	grounding
naval	orange	sex and creativity
solar plexus	yellow	emotional centre
heart centre	green	love
throat	blue	communication
third eye	indigo	mission in life
crown	violet	the ultimate – enlightened mind

As you bring your energy up, your experience of anger fades and you begin to feel alright- in fact this is a faster way of feeling better than going for a brisk walk or chomping on a stake. As the energy delicately makes its way upwards to your higher chackras, or even out the top, you feel as tough you have won, you have conquered this bout with anger. You want to keep on using your new found strength. In *Cutting Through Spiritual Materialism* Chögyam Trungpa Rinpoche was asked "How does transmutation take place?" He replied (Trungpa, 1973; 236):

> The problem is that we never experience emotions properly. We think that fighting and killing express anger, but these are another kind of escape, a way of releasing rather than actually experiencing emotion as it is. The basic nature of the emotions has not been felt properly. If one actually feels the living quality, the texture of the emotions as they are in their naked state, then this experience also contains ultimate truth.

> If we are trying to be good or peaceful, trying to suppress or subdue our emotions, that is the basic twist of ego in operation. We are being aggressive towards our emotions, trying forcefully to achieve peace or goodness. Once we cease being aggressive towards our emotions, cease trying to change them, once we experience them properly, then transmutation may take place.

Transmuting and upleveling your emotions is possible and this is an exciting opportunity for you to practice the path of Buddhadharma even in the worst situations of your life. So, when you feel miserable, just cheer up!

Chapter 11

Meaning and Purpose in Life

She sat in the July sun on the long steps outside of the library in Vienna. She was alone, and becoming more and more accommodated to being alone. A passing teenage boy recognized her as the sun through the swaying trees spotlighted her yellow dress. He sat down beside her and spoke. She was his history teacher at school and her teachings on the ancient past aroused spiritual questions within him. He asked her some of the big questions about the meaning and purpose of life and he eagerly waited for her response. He hoped that in their chance meeting that hot morning in the sun, she could share more about her true beliefs than she did in school. She searched within herself but she realized that she just didn't know what she believed in, or what gave her meaning and purpose in life. She thought hard, while he politely waited quietly, then like a candle being lit, something sprang clearly into her mind. But suddenly she was gripped with thoughts of restraint because of the separation of church and state. Baffled with herself she shrugged off the question and gave the boy no leadership at all. He eyed his beloved teacher carefully, then looked east and said "Well, I'll go inside and see if I can find a good book on comparative philosophy. See you in September," he smiled and waved as he got up and went into the library.

* * * * * * * * * * * *

The search for meaning and purpose in life is your meaning and purpose in life. This should be your aspiration until you decide what your major definite purpose is. A Buddhist can plug into the Buddhist meaning of life, as discussed in this book, but for people who are not Buddhists, we will explore the process and the questions through which you can determine what your place is in the big picture, and how you should best proceed. Looking back over the great lives of Buddhists and people everywhere, all of the lives that became great did so after the selection of a major definite purpose. People say, "Well, I finally decided to get serious, and . . ." the rest is history. Prince Siddhartha decided to find a solution to death itself. As a Buddhist or as a non Buddhist, you can aspire to benefit others with compassion in many ways, with many written goals. You can have clearly written and defined goals with regard to many things but you must have one, just one major goal in life. Carl Jung, the Swiss psychologist said, "I made it my task of tasks in life to find a mythology by which to live." That was his major purpose in life. What is yours? You must select one in order for the devas in the god realm to take you seriously and help you significantly, because lots of people just have ideas about helping others, but few act. In order to bring down the blessings of the devas, you must be strong in the power of your inner convictions. Feel it in your solar plexus. Devas are interested in people that have the ambition, like the Buddha's ambition, to do great things for others on this Earth. This is your time for greatness!

There is a set of eight questions below* which you should only give yourself one minute to answer. Get out a pen and clean sheet of paper and write down the answers. After you have read this book, come back here and do this exercise again. It is recommended that you read a good dharma book several times because then you get more and more at deeper levels of mind. Each time, do these eight questions again, and see how the answers change, or stay the same. After you read this book and answer these questions a second time, you will know that the time has arrived for you to select your major definite purpose in life. Here are the eight questions:

1. What five things do you value most in life? Sexually satiating partners? Lots of money? Material possessions? Your Buddhist spiritual path? The love of your family and friends? Your political beliefs? Your computer and the Internet? What five things? Afterwards, organize them in order of priority.

2. What would you do if you had only eleven months left to live? Whatever it is, you should be doing it now because we never know when we only have eleven months to live. Who would you call? What would you do with your money and your will? What projects would you complete or initiate? What would you put down in writing for others to read? Who would you spend your time with?

3. What would you do if you suddenly inherited $10,000,000? American readers can use their own currency (sorry for you). What would you do if you had all the time and money in the world? Would you stay in the relationship you are in? Would you quit your job? If so, then maybe you should quit your job soon, because it is the wrong job for you and you are wasting your time, and wasting your life. What would you do if you were free to choose?

4. What one thing would you do if you knew that you could not fail? If you had only one magic pill, what would you ask the devas for if you knew that once you swallowed the pill, you would absolutely for sure get just that one thing? What would it be? What one great thing would you dare to do if you knew you could not fail? Would you run for public office? Whatever it is, you can achieve it if you can develop the clarity of mind in meditation and then apply right effort.

5. What are your three most important goals in life right now? This indicates the three most important concerns that you have right now.

6. What have you always wanted to do but have been afraid to attempt? This answer reveals the ego's self limiting belief or block that is holding you back. Your ego is the problem.

7. What activities in your life have given you the greatest feeling of importance and self esteem? When have you been the happiest in life? What were you doing? This answer leads you unerringly to your true area of excellence. Past life talents may have been in that area.

8. What are the deepest spiritual experiences that you have had in your life? When was your state of mind experienced in a powerful way? What were you doing to generate that state of mind? What perceptions arose in your six senses?

Remember, only give yourself one minute to answer these eight questions. If you gave yourself two hours, your answer would probably be less honest than with one minute. The reason for this is because you would have too much time to second guess your heartfelt response, and you would rationalize and change it around so it would seem very proper and politically correct. So, be totally open and honest with yourself. No one else needs to read this.

*Special thanks to the human potential guru, Brian Tracy. Derived from 'The Phoenix Seminar' tape series, highly recommended.

Chapter 12

Teaching Philosophy

Many people hold back from sharing what they know with others because they fear that they will be criticized for not having enough qualifications. Because of this, people throw out the baby with the bath water and withdraw from the life force, teaching nothing, rather than risk being less than perfect. This is anti-dharma because there is a traditional saying, "Whatever realization you have is like the child of a barren woman, unless you give it away to others." You do not have to be fully trained and qualified to teach Buddhism. My teacher said "Share your confusion." What matters is your heart intention to benefit others, and your interpersonal skills. Qualifications can come later. Even if a teacher is an expert in a subject, people will not stay in their class if they are an angry scholar. Studying dharma is important but it may be even more useful to study teaching skills, people skills and classroom dynamics. The book *How to Win Friends and Influence People,* by Dale Carnegie is, beyond doubt, one of the finest Buddhist teaching manuals in existence. It's also the third biggest selling book in history after the Bible and the *Boy Scout Guide.*

I encourage readers to form their own independent Buddhist study groups, and accept donations, so that something bigger and more uplifted can emerge from this process. Each group is an invitation for a deva or devas (higher realm beings) to descend into that jewel like human group container. Like a magnet, be an iron Buddha and attract other iron Buddhas to your home. Small practice and study groups are like acorns. Many scattered acorns result in a few majestic oak trees. Please do plant an acorn. The clock is ticking. You don't have to teach. Your group can be fellow students without a teacher. Today, people have to pay $500 to learn meditation practice from the Transcendental Meditation organization. This inhibits growth at the grass roots level, so you should accept much smaller contributions. TM is a fine organization which has accomplished a lot to popularize meditation in the West and it has helped lay the foundation for Buddhist meditation groups.

Buddha taught that it is wise to pay attention to the advice of elders in the sangha if you have them, but he did not want a strongly centralized religion with powerful authority figures because that would lead to ego problems. The Buddha gave an astonishing amount of freedom to his disciples to figure out the truth for themselves. In one of his last discourses the Buddha told his faithful attendant Ananda "After I have passed away, go to no other as your refuge. Let my teaching be your only guide. Be an island unto yourself. Go to no other as your guide." As Deepak Chopra says "The single biggest enemy of your spiritual life is organized religion." With your good heart, you act freely!

Historically the quality that makes a Buddhist teacher a teacher, is the students. It's always the students that decide if you are a teacher, no one else. You can do it. For a budding Buddhist teacher, one of the most inspiring role models is John Lennon. In 1967 John said that he considered himself to be a Buddhist. John said of 1961 "I thought that we were the best god damned band in the whole fucking world! It's just that nobody had caught on yet!" John was practicing the tradition of "taking the result as the path." This great happiness leader of men, with his profound insight invoked the law of reversibility. He "got the feeling" of being "the best god damned band in the whole fucking world," which invoked the devas to bring Paul and he the songs to bring Lennon's vision into manifest reality upon the airwaves. If you can get the feeling, you can bring it into your reality.

Even in 1963 Ringo Starr believed that the Beatles would fizzle out within months and he hoped that he would earn enough money to open a beauty salon. Ringo said that the penny finally dropped as he was playing drums for the Beatles before Queen Elizabeth in a Royal Command performance in 1963. He then realized that they were a powerful influence in society. Silly. The very blood and oxygen coursing through Ringo's veins was created solely by John Lennon. In the entire history of the millennium, John Lennon is in the top five of the most inspiring people that have ever lived. As you stammer in front of your mirror reading your messy dharma notes, do an analytical meditation on the 1962 John Lennon in Hamburg, Germany, sitting pissed on stage with a toilet seat around his neck. He made it big; you're a modest, humble Buddhist. There is no problem. There's no problem at all with that.

You can start teaching next month. Organizing a course like this in your home, even with two other people, can be the basis of a community and a warm friendship directed towards the highest spiritual aspirations, rather than a group spirit focused on playing cards or enjoying the outdoors. This very much benefits everyone involved. Our Western culture is too superficial with a fractured sense of community. People all live in their little boxes and they are crying out for some sense of community. You can be healed by teaching Buddhism. The important thing is to get something going, before this moment dies, and then learn as you go. In groups, people want to talk, so let them talk. If you all study the same Buddhist book, you'll share the same text with which to refer to, and have a hard copy to read after discussions. Understanding grows from discussing a subject that everybody is studying together. A teacher is not necessary and students may even be more motivated to learn without a teacher present. In teaching this course, you can completely revamp the course material to suit your own situation.

The Buddhist Spectrum encourages students of Buddhism to create an income for themselves by leading a "Course in Buddhism." The Buddhist scriptures describe dana as generosity or donations to a Buddhist temple or teacher. It is considered much better karma for someone to donate money to you — the Buddhist teacher or facilitator, than to someone on the street. That karma is intended to support the dharma — perhaps the one thing that will delay the deterioration of our world. This must grow and we must succeed. There are career opportunities in Buddhism because it is on its way to prominence in the West.

Everybody has a sense of what feels right and wrong. Don't worry about making mistakes; no one's gut will wrench if you falter when trying to help others or if you teach Buddhism incorrectly. It is terribly wrong to not even try. Literally hundreds of millions of people may die because one uncourageous soul after another refuses to make an attempt at uplifting themselves and uplifting their neighbour. Major world wars are provoked and encouraged by weakness. We need sane and realistic people who are the true supermen and superwomen. We should be willing to die for compassion or we are not fit to live. Martin Luther King Jr. said "If a man has not found a cause for which he is willing to die, then he is not fit to live." The tendency that people have to retreat away from confidence beyond hesitation, into a sleepwalking style of neurosis may, by an imperceptible karmic chain of events, literally result in ATT: W — accidental total thermonuclear war. If we sit in complacency while people suffer at all levels of society in all countries, we invite the damnation pronounced upon Prime Minister Chamberlain by Winston Churchill in 1940, "You must leave! You must go!"

PART II
ESSAYS

Chapter 13

Adolf Hitler
The Bad Boy of Buddhism

"The last thing I want to do is find myself inside the skin of a Buddha."
- Adolf Hitler

Once upon a time there was a big powerful angel in heaven named Angela. This angel, this deva had a good side and she had a bad side. She loved her people in heaven but she hated the devas in the higher heavens that were better than her. She grew old and after a long life of mixed karma, she died in that heavenly state in the fifth heaven of the sensuous sphere. She died a violent death when a titan, a great jealous god killed her in combat by smashing her right on her weak spot—above her upper lip. After deva death she took rebirth as a male deva called Ravan, in the first heaven of the four kings. Angry about her demotion, his demotion, the mighty Ravan deva became a jealous god too. Ravan took his frustrations out upon the Earth directly below. He looked for animals and people that would cooperate with his beliefs and with his mighty powers.

He inspired black ravens, black crows and men and women in the Americas, Africa and Europe, until one day he found the perfect match, the perfect conduit to manifest his vision. In Europe he found a man in Vienna, Austria that was pacing the streets and dwelling upon the same kind of ideas that this great powerful deva promoted. Ravan saw in him the one man who could make his ideals a reality on Earth. Ravan nurtured, protected and cared for this gentle man. The deva helped the man care for his dying mother until the end of her days. After the mother's death she took rebirth as a female deva and immediately accepted Ravan's job offer to help him oversee the protection for her son suffering in the violent human realm of samsara. She protected him as a virtuous mother protects her only child! The man became *untouchable*. He could not be stopped within the law, outside the law or even *above* the law. Ravan sealed his fate. He was the chosen one and the Germans were the chosen people. That was *it*.

Ravan's karma had come to ripen; Ravan ruled and he knew it. The timing was just perfect. Because of the massive negative karma ripening throughout humanity, no higher deva was prepared to intervene in Ravan's private affairs on planet Earth. Ravan was a free deva, powerful and free, uplifting mediocrity.

Ravan gradually channelled suggestions and the larger vision to this Austrian guinea pig. Ravan merged his mind with him until he knew that he could not fail to use the man to fulfil his intentions in Europe and in the world. From that moment on, this Austrian was protected from above. Unlike ordinary people, this man was protected and inspired by a mighty titan, by the god Ravan and by Mara's deva hosts.

Ravan gave his beloved human disciple charisma, influence and governmental powers. Ravan drew good friends, capable friends to the aid of his chosen one. Both gods and humans adored his main man. In Nuremberg, Ravan magnetised tens of thousands of new friends around his beloved one. As they assembled peacefully around the leader, Ravan succeeded in using their grounded human energy and power to totally draw himself down into the very body of this tiny man on earth. This could only be accomplished by means of a massive ritual by thousands of interested people using the appropriate symbols to magnetise the necessary energies that could make such a transformation possible. In shivers of ecstasy, Ravan descended and became one with this human being. Ravan became a man, as he was many lifetimes ago on another planet. Ravan merged minds with his only son, and feeling the skeletal structure of his new body for the first time, Ravan grimaced slightly because of the inconvenience of using that heavy sluggish form. His first motion was to bring his right hand to his face to cover over his weak spot! First in apprehension, then in relief he checked to confirm that his weak spot was in fact covered over with a narrow moustache! He was safe, safe enough. He was happy in his new home, until his own karma ripened. He was Adolf Hitler at a Nuremberg rally in 1936. He is not the past; he is the future.

Ravan felt uncomfortable with the mental limitations of his ape-like human form in 1936 so he asked his doctor for drugs to bring him back to the heightened state with which he had become accustomed in the god realm. His doctor indulged Adolf too much and this began the ripening process of his painful karma which led to his degeneration and his death by suicide. After Hitler's death, he had to take on the ripening of his earthly karma, and then he moved on to other concerns. And so, they all lived happily ever after.

Lest We Forget

Approximately fifty million people were brutally killed in World War II. On Remembrance day people say "Lest we forget," to emphasise that we must never forget the causes of this terrible war, so that we can ready ourselves to prevent such a thing from ever happening again. Many people today have relatives that were killed during the war, their scars are still alive. Why did their loved ones die? What is the reason? It makes clear sense to say "lest we forget," because this could happen again. However, there is a problem with this attitude. The problem is that most people don't know why World War II happened! In order to prevent such things people must understand them. The Buddha defined love as understanding. The real causes and conditions of the war are shrouded in mystery, because the people that caused World War II lost the war and died. Perhaps Buddhism, Hinduism and Shamanism can shed some light on that mystery. This chapter pieces together my views and the views of many Buddhists and non Buddhists that I have interviewed.

A Buddhist theory is that the powers of the higher realms were invoked and harnessed by Adolf Hitler and Nazi Germany, which they unleashed in World War II. Adolf Hitler and his companions tapped into the immense powers of the devas of the jealous god realm, as described in Buddhist and Hindu cosmology. The more you dig for evidence, the more evidence you will find. Studying this example of gross misuse of the higher realms is an opportunity to spread Buddhism because the dharma can shed fresh light upon an infamous person and utilize public fascination with Hitler as a vehicle to deliver people to a dharma gate. That is the intent of this essay.

What are the higher realms? According to the Buddha, there are realms of heaven where good and bad devas (heavenly beings) exist and they relate to our human realm on a daily basis. If people develop their minds or learn effective techniques, they can ask the devas of the god realm or the jealous god realm to assist them in whatever they want to do — good or bad. This is the basis for black magic as well as many good powers, such as miraculous healing. Buddhism teaches only the good use of the higher realms, obviously. But such powers can be used either way, and people such as Hitler or Chairman Mao could have used Buddhist teachings to harness the dark side of the higher realms. In Mao's case, he and in particular his devoted wife, were very powerful personalities. Mao's doctors have reported that Mao used the feminine energies not only of his wife but of countless peasant Chinese women because of his belief that he could harness power from this yin/yang exchange of energy. This belief is correct. Mao was the most powerful person that ever lived. He ruled over more people for the longest period of time than anyone in recorded history.

There is suspicion that Chairman Mao's wife was a master of the higher realms. On August 15, 1950 when the young Dalai Lama was washing up for the night in the Potala Palace in Lhasa, Tibet, he felt the ground shake; it was the fifth largest earthquake in recorded history. This was followed by eerie sounds that could be heard all over Tibet. They were sounds like the cracks of 40 rifle shots being fired across the sky. Everyone took this as a very bad omen and as the Dalai Lama watched the sky turn red in the east, he felt like the world was coming to an end. It was. In October, the communist Chinese invaded and took over control of the country. Millions of Tibetan Buddhists believe that this earthquake was the result of the protector deities of Tibet losing a battle with the devas of China, with the mysterious sounds indicating that they were trying to fight off the Chinese devas. It was a human realm decision initiated by Chairman Mao to invade Tibet shortly after this earthquake. The question arises, who initiated the earthquake and the thunderous sounds? Was there a being behind that? The Buddha described how ascetics of great meditative attainment can cause earthquakes at will. Was Chairman Mao, his wife, or higher realm masters in their employ behind this? That's the $64,000 question. Who knows?

One thing we do know is that many Buddhists point to Adolf Hitler as an example of someone who was so highly attained that he could raise up his people and stir their energies. I believe that Adolf Hitler was the most powerful spiritual being to manifest in human form during the 20th century. Could Mahatma Gandhi protect himself from assassination by invoking the powers of the higher realms? No. Hitler did. Adolf Hitler was evil. This hardly needs to be emphasized, as it is so obviously true. Hitler was truly evil but his spiritual power came from deep within, or beyond him. Like many Buddhists, my view is not unique that Adolf Hitler used Buddhist and other spiritual or occult teachings to tap into the staggering power of the jealous god realm. Chögyam Trungpa Rinpoche described Hitler as a master of the higher realms. Hitler could have been protected from above by devas under the administration of Mara, the evil one, who resides in the outskirts of the sixth and highest heaven in the sensuous sphere. In the Theravadin Buddhist teachings, the Buddha called this heaven Paranimmita-vasavatti heaven.

The value of studying the connection between Hitler, Buddhism and the higher realms is that this process can give people more respect for Buddhism and for the existence of the higher realms altogether. The name 'Hitler' is a conversation stopper and 50 million dead is an effective way to be remembered. This may seem like negative publicity for Buddhism but fortunately it is not. The more we associate Buddhism with Hitler, the more people will get the idea that Buddhism provides a tremendously powerful spiritual path which leads the practitioner through the temptations of fantastic power, to ultimate peace and nirvana. It was ego that ruined everything, not Buddhism.

Buddhism is not to blame. The Hitler/Buddhist connection should be promoted and spin doctored in this way. Buddhism is still quite small in the West so it would be auspicious for Buddhism to gain some publicity. Hitler perverted higher realm powers by using them to magnetize millions of people in a brutal way. The insight that Buddhism can shed upon Nazi practises will serve to demonstrate the validity of Buddhist claims that Buddhist practises can deliver people to the ultimate powers possible in the world. Publicity wise, this is a good thing for creating interest in Buddhism and meditation, so the Hitler thing should be taken advantage of to a much greater extent. Buddhists have a responsibility to warn others that someone like Hitler could rise again. Because Buddhism provides an understanding of the higher realms which Western society may not even want to hear, it is the duty of Buddhists to be vocal about danger signs that others will ignore. Danger signs like the cult which called itself the Nazi party of Germany.

The swastika is an ancient and potent Hindu symbol which was adopted by the Mahayana Buddhist tradition. Hitler likely read more about Hinduism than Buddhism. In his 20's he studied in a more focused way than people realize. He studied the Vedas, the Bagavad Gita, yoga, occultism, astrology, and his German philosophy mentors Schopenhauer and Nietzsche (who are quite negative). Schopenhauer was very much guided by eastern philosophy. Historians say that during this period of Hitler's life his reading and studies were disjointed but it is obvious to others that this assumption is completely false. Hitler's spiritual quest indicates that he was searching for big answers to big questions. Hitler once said "The last thing I want to do is find myself inside the skin of a Buddha."

Buddhists accuse Hitler of taking the swastika and turning it around backwards, painting it black and invoking a powerful red background behind it. This can be said, however the symbol is used both ways by Buddhists. When I worked as the public relations representative at the largest Buddhist temple in Canada, the single most common question I would hear was "What's that swastika doing on the Buddha's chest?" To the Buddhists the swastika means ultimate power, the sun, the brightness and the power of the sun, the wheel of life, the rotating aspect of life growing and dying, good fortune — there's lots of meanings. In Pure Land Buddhism the swastika represents the ultimate power of the sun god from the ancient Iranian religion, although Pure Land Buddhists don't generally know that. The swastika has been known in Germany for 300 years from Hindu teachings. It is also an ancient Germanic symbol from their own culture. The swastika is also indigenous to the cultures of the American Navaho Indians and the native Indians in Saskatchewan, Canada. Five monkeys with sticks could come up with a swastika —it's a simple enough design. Even the Christians in England used it. It was one of the most respected religious crosses until World War II. Just one look at the swastika conveys a feeling of great power. The Germans and British were the first Europeans to introduce Buddhism to the West, around the mid 19th century. Even before

WW I there were Buddhist practice and study societies active in Germany. The swastika was recognized then as a Buddhist symbol.

In the sacred geometry of Egypt a point in space extends itself in all directions. These equidistant points form a sphere and if one point on the sphere extends out in the same way, the result is two overlapping spheres. The idea of extension is represented by extending an arm straight out in each direction. This represents the original movement of spirit, which is one of love. The Nazi salute also means this idea of extension but it includes the meaning of extension of ego to extend and consolidate power. Hitler's Nazi salute is a perversion of this original creative force. A symbol of this original creative force is the swastika. In the sacred mystery school teachings awakened consciousness can't be experienced by one person alone, it needs someone to confirm it. The full arm salute is confirmed by another, or an outside agent. Properly, if you do the full arm extension you do it with love. This is a practice of the Buddhist Spectrum Study Group. In the Hindu practices, the straight-arm salute is a technique for raising kundalini energy.

The jealous gods had a motive to support the Nazis. They supported Hitler so that they could feed off the energy of the human realm. The Nuremberg rallies are an example of this kind of energy, 100,000 Nazis sending energy upwards in straight arm salute. Reading transcripts of Hitler's speeches at Nuremberg, one may feel, "So what! This seems like a bunch of disjointed thoughts." But if you were actually there, live, you would have been moved. What you can't read on paper is the brahma voice. In the Digha Nikaya (Long Discourses) the Buddha described the brahma voice as a powerful resonant voice associated with channelling devas through your speech. It is possible, although we have low grade evidence, that Hitler the great orator invoked jealous god devas to manifest a kind of anti-brahma voice. Before he delivered his speeches he performed a deep private solitary ritual of practice in front of a mirror. Ideally this would be the prime moment, to chant and invite down the presence of the asuras (jealous gods) into his body. He may have made his body, speech and mind a landing pad for the devas, a throne for the great German gods. He would whip himself up, psyche himself up, then step before his massive throng of adoring disciples, some fainting dead away at the sight of him. Sometimes Hitler would stand in silence for the first five minutes on stage while the crowd whipped themselves wild; then he would speak with his riveting warriors cry. During his oratories at the Nuremberg rallies he may have invoked 'a saturation of devas.' There was such power in his presence that the crowd would still have been hypnotised even if he had recited the recipe for Black Forest cake.

Hitler himself claimed that he had a vision and offered his body as a vessel to the 'superman' (translated from a German term). This occurred when he was in the hallowed presence of the Sword of Destiny, which was kept in Vienna, Austria. This legendary sword is said to be the sword used by a Roman guard to pierce the side of Christ after his crucifixion. Because of this, Christ's body wasn't pounded to break his bones so many believed that for a moment the Roman soldier held the fate of all mankind in his hands, because he enabled the resurrection to take place. In 1909 Hitler first saw the sword which is believed to give highest power of good or bad to the one who knows it's meaning and how to control it. Hitler credited the sword with assisting him and as the Furhrer he went to the sword and had this trembling vision where he beheld the superman and went into another state of mind, opening himself to be the vessel of its powers. If that isn't channelling to the jealous god realm devas, what is? Almost hysterical about it, Hitler exclaimed to his associates that "the superman is living among us now!" He marvelled at the power, speed and brutality of the being.

Many Indians believed Hitler's claim that he manifested the powers of the gods. In the 1930's many Brahmins — the highest caste in Indian society, believed that Hitler was an avatar — a god in human form. They were very impressed with the powers he was wielding over the Europeans and they very much appreciated his efforts to conquer the English during the war because they wanted to get the British out of India. Hitler was popular with the Brahmins!

The devas knew that this particular person, Hitler, commanded the lives and deaths of millions and millions of people. Beyond doubt, the devas would have related to Hitler and Goebbels in a very special and very concentrated way. Paul Joseph Goebbels was eight years younger than Adolf but he was the leader in many ways, particularly in calling down the German gods. Ordinary people have devas baby sitting them, but chackravartins (universal monarchs, or great leaders) command a whole deva administration. It is too naive a thing to say that only bad jealous god realm devas assisted the Nazi effort. The radiant ones must have helped out as well. Regardless of whether the Nazi party was elected fairly or not, they were in power and they pulled the strings that raised all of Europe out of the depression. How did Goebbels, the minister of Enlightenment and Propaganda, and his protege Hitler, move masses of people to march forward? How did they do it? The higher realms.

With a mahamaster like Goebbels pretending to be his subordinate, it's no wonder that Hitler desired women who would beat him, swear at him, abuse him, and totally dominate him. Like anyone with the duty and burden of leadership thrust upon his mortal shoulders, Hitler may have felt unworthy of the adulation showered upon him. Not only was he showered with flowers from the human realm, but he was probably showered with coral flowers from the god realm as well.

Goebbels manipulated people, including Hitler. If Goebbels had been a good person (perhaps he is, in this lifetime now) we wouldn't use nasty words like 'manipulating people.' Nice words would be used such as 'he could inspire, transform and uplift minds all over the planet.' Consider what he could have done with the tool of subliminal audio and video messages. In Goebbels' day they didn't have that level of subtle influence on the mind. Sound movies were only invented in 1928 and the Nazi twins came to power in 1933. In Vajrayana Buddhism in particular, and Hinduism in general, it is taught that you should literally mix your mind with the guru — the relationship is that intimate and intense. The guru is everything. Although what Hitler was doing was the opposite of Buddhism, perhaps that high level of communication was made manifest in the relationship between Hitler and his guru, Joseph Goebbels. At a rally in the early years of the Nazi Party Goebbels announced, "I am half drunk with pride that a genius like Adolf Hitler sees eye to eye with me regarding the future!"

I believe that Hitler made a deal with the devil, so to speak, a deal with the higher realms. The jealous god devas enjoy wrecking havoc on humanity. That's their fun, their playtime, R&R. We cannot comprehend the vastness of their unspeakable powers, or how meaningless 50,000,000 human lives may seem to them. Perhaps in your youth you stomped on ant hills killing thousands upon thousand of ants — same thing. Hitler certainly knew about the powers of the higher realms and he used them. That was his upper hand over ordinary politicians. He made plenty of stupid mistakes during the war, sure. All of his powers did not give him clarity of mind, and certainly not enlightenment. Ultimately the laws of karma closed in on him, and on Nazi Germany. Probably his great karmic undoing was killing perhaps 7.2 million Jews, gypsies and other minorities. What a loss!! That was his great undoing. The laws of karma forced the destruction of the Nazi regime and genocide was plenty enough to do it. This is quite literally, the Jews' revenge. What a shame. What a shame for the Jews, the Germans, the economy and Europe.

The allies may not have had leaders with the higher spiritual attainments and concentrated mind of Hitler, but they had much better virtue and karma. (Although it's a great disappointment that General Eisenhower let 750,000 Nazis die after the war. Eisenhower just hated the Nazis.) The allies' karma was better because what the Nazis were doing was very bad, and because the allies saw fit to stop that, for the benefit of others, then that makes the allied karma good. Buddhist discipline teaches that you must say no to the aggression and ego trips of others. You can't let people trample on the sanity of the world. From a Buddhist view it would be wrong to be a pacifist in the face of Hitler's domination; it was right for the British to declare war on Hitler. The early warnings and the relentless leadership of Churchill are a mere reflection of his immeasurable virtue. Some Buddhists may say that any kind of war is wrong but that doesn't seem to be a logically thought out view. Buddhism means sanity, not rules. Disallowing any war effort is a rule, not sanity. Waging war on Nazi Germany and murdering Hitler and Goebbels a.s.a.p. would have been the proper Buddhist thing to do.

That's prajna, skilful means. Such a course of action has a lot of bodhicitta and compassion as the aspiration behind it.

What benefit did Nazi Germany leave behind for the world? Some rocket technology and plots for countless war movies? All they really left was a path of destruction and callousness. At least the British colonizers left behind schools and a judicial system that worked. And yet people are so fascinated by Hitler and Nazi Germany. Perhaps it was the Fascist uniting of the people around grandiose national goals that is so energizing. The straight arm salute which Hitler stole from the ancient Romans is a powerful way to raise people's windhorse. This is a Buddhist term for stirring up your energy and inspiration, riding a horse on the winds of energy and delight. No one can deny that Hitler's oratories inspired and lifted Germany out of the depression. He reenergized the economy.

Hitler probably used the Nazi salute so that millions of people would send energy to him. This technique should be stolen back from the Nazis and returned to the public domain. It doesn't belong to them. After the Roman Empire conquered Egypt they had to encourage the Egyptians to give grain to feed the Roman soldiers. To do this, Augustus Caesar had to erect statues of himself on temple buildings and proclaim himself as a god. This was to appease the Egyptians so that they would feel better making the grain offering to a god, rather than to a bunch of Romans. The Egyptians then raised their right arm in salute to the statue of god Caesar. This 'hail to the great one' is where Hitler got the Nazi salute from. You can do this salute to a statue of the Buddha, but not with the god idea in mind. You do it with devotion. This is just one of countless ways of expressing devotion.

The Buddha said that his number two chief disciple, Maha Moggallana was Mara in one of his previous lives. This indicates that evil beings like Mara, or Hitler may possess high spiritual powers of concentration, and that they can be turned around. Dr. Elizabeth Kubler-Ross, the specialist on dying was criticized for her outspoken belief that Adolf Hitler would take rebirth as a great world leader, and compensate for the deeds of his last life. I believe that she may be right. Perhaps Hitler is not in hell, where Joseph Stalin certainly is. Maybe there is something Hitler can still do to redeem himself.

What matters today is power now. Who's got it? How are they using it? Who's on the way up? What is the direction of their ego? Snuff consciousness battles. The lessons of the 1930's indicate that Hitler was more than a politician and head of state. He was first and foremost, a guru. He may have been an asexual guru with a close clique of disciples. After the violent gun death of his girlfriend in the 1920's, Adolf Hitler transformed his sexual powers onto his spiritual path— the dark path of Mara. By some accounts he had an unspeakable personal power. Hitler's early years, in his 20's seem like nothing much, a drifter. His best friend in

Vienna said that he led a monk-like celibate existence. He wouldn't have sexual relations with women because he was too good to stoop to such things. Friends described him as almost asexual. But later, as Adolf became more powerful he engaged in revolting, bizarre sexual practices which would lead women to suicide.

After Hitler joined the Nazi party he met up with Joseph Goebbels, an unemployed, drifting university graduate. There was a book written by a survivor of the war about a secret occult group in Germany. The book was written as fiction but the author claimed that he met Hitler and Goebbels in such a group. They tried to kill him for not joining their occult circle, but he fled the country. This information indicates that it was Joseph Goebbels who was the ring leader and master of the higher realms. There was a devoted partnership between Goebbels and Hitler with Hitler as the front man, and Joseph Goebbels as the master supporting him. Goebbels was with Hitler until the end, after others in Hitler's government had deserted him. Goebbels oversaw the cremation of Hitler's body before he took poison with his wife and six children to die together. Both Goebbels and Hitler were masters of the higher realms, and the Third Reich was the vision of Joseph Goebbels as much as it was Hitler's vision. Goebbels would never leave his master.

Goebbels was most known for hating people who took his photograph. One practical reason for this is that masters of black magic, such as he, know that shamans who curse people using black magic sorcery can do so with the aid of a photograph of their intended victim. This focuses the negative energies more effectively. Goebbels may have been fearing that such higher realm powers could be used against him. Being a public figure, there were plenty of photos of him around anyway, but his fear may have been an irrational one.

Hitler and Goebbels selected the swastika for its ultimate power and made it the symbol of symbols. How did Hitler raise up his people and inspire the masses? Because of the desperation of the depression and the crippling effects of the treaty of Versailles, the causes and conditions in Germany were ripe for a bizarre occult group like the Nazi elite to draw support. In a more prosperous environment, Hitler would never have had the chance to rise to power. At the Nuremberg rallies from the early 1920's to 1939 the Nazis created an elaborate mandala to employ the four karmas of Hinduism which were adopted by Tibetan Buddhism. They are pacifying, enriching, magnetizing and destroying. Joseph Campbell the mythologist used a video of the Nuremberg rallies to show that the power of a well orchestrated ritual to take you beyond your own personal intention and control, is terrific. He said he had two friends that were in Nazi concentration camps and once Hitler was in their neighbourhood giving a speech so they were brought out to stand at attention. The fellow said that it was all he could do just to stop his right arm from going up and saying "Hail!" "We have no idea about these mass rituals; we just know nothing about it. And then along comes a guy who has a genius for this sort of thing, and look what happens," Campbell said. Since the victors write the history books and lead public sentiment, we cannot now believe that we have any real sense of the depth and power of the Nazi elite's mind force.

My guess is that after Adolf Hitler and Joseph Goebbels developed the Nuremberg rallies with 100,000 Nazis in straight arm salute, Hitler's unspeakable powers grew to unthinkable powers. I believe that jealous god realm devas were there giving and taking energy with the thousands of magnetised and energized Nazis. It was a grandiose spiritual experience for everyone. They had flaming torch bearers and gymnastics and pyrotechnics — the grandest show on earth. The rallies were designed to raise Nazi windhorse so that they could takeover the leadership of the country. Everyone centred on the furhrer. David Bowie called Adolf Hitler the world's first pop star.

The unthinkable powers of Adolf Hitler are still knowable. Knowable but unthinkable. Listening to CD's from the library of Adolf Hitler's oratories leaves one riveted. From my own experiences, I feel that there are some powerful states of mind which cannot be spoken of. Even more powerful is the mind that can know terrific and terrifying power, which cannot even be thought of. There is a difference between the direct experience of knowing, and thinking. In the Buddha's abhidharma, this state of mind is found in the threshold between the 4th skandha and the 5th skandha — thought and consciousness. All things are possible here. This is the residing place of Kennedy's New Frontier. It's similar to the idea in John Lennon's song 'Steel and Glass' when he sang,

> Every time I put my finger on it, it slips away.
> Every time I put my finger on it, it slips away.

Vast, unthinkable powers are within the capabilities of human beings that cultivate their minds in meditation. The Buddha said that mindfulness practice is "the only way to enlightenment." True. The only way. You don't have to be a Buddhist, but you do need to meditate to attain higher states. In one of the Buddha's discourses with a well known Jain disciple, the two of them were describing ascetics and masters who had the power with their mind to cause earthquakes and to destroy cities, many cities, 50 cities. This is a scriptural example of the powers, hopefully beneficial, that we may see manifest.

Like Darth Vader, Hitler had, and still has, tremendous ability to do good works. People do say that Hitler got the economy going and he inspired the people. In the 1930's even Winston Churchill said "Adolf Hitler is the greatest leader of our age." What a shame. All that power, but in the wrong direction. He seized the zeitgist of the day, one of prejudice and aggression. Today, is history. We have a beneficial zeitgist to seize. We must seize it or deteriorate. All those people meditating everywhere, all those people studying the dharma, somebody will do something good.

Hitler magnetised support before his election, he hypnotized people at his rallies. After coming to power Hitler appointed his partner Goebbels as the Minister of Propaganda and Enlightenment. Propaganda wasn't a bad word then — it meant propagating ideas. With Goebbels they made the most skilful use of radio and movies. The Germans even invented television. This power was dramatically portrayed by the esoteric Hollywood school of thought in a scene from the movie *Contact.* The first message earth received from the aliens in space was a reverse TV broadcast from the 1936 Olympics in Berlin which was televised. The swastika was the first image from space along with Hitler's lightning voice. The Nazis fully appreciated the power of video to influence people with the sense of sight and sound. Buddhism teaches that visualization is a powerful tool to affect the mind, because sight accounts for over 80% of our sensory input. Goebbels put Hitler on the radio after the workers got home, around 6:00 pm. They felt that this was the best time when people's minds would be most open to suggestion. They were masters at mind control, using the big lie theory to convince people of white supremacy, or anything else they wanted people to believe. The big lie theory is an ancient Indian practice. Hitler preached "The bigger the lie, the more likely people will believe it."

Shortly after the Nazi government was elected, Goebbels formed squads of the party faithful who rode motorcycles through the streets, with loudspeakers announcing "Jews are dirty. Jews are dirty." Repeating these words over and over again, like a mantra, even the most intelligent and reasonable Germans became conditioned to feel revulsion when they met a Jew, subconsciously assuming that the Jew must be dirty and polluted. This is mass psychology manipulation at its worst. A similar process of mass psychology manipulation, though not malevolent, has been carried on in the Mahayana Buddhist tradition for 2200 years, in regards to the Theravadin tradition which they put down as the "Hinayana." In many a form and figure, subtle and gross, consciously and unconsciously, the Mahayanists are always unfairly calling the Hinayana inferior. This can easily be seen today in most Buddhist books with page after page infected by this virus. It is literally a grand conspiracy, a vast lie, stretching over thousands of years, an insidious disease dividing and destroying the Buddhist religion from within. The 'Mahayana conspiracy' has succeeded in gripping the minds of the majority of Buddhists throughout history; even some of the Theravadins buy into it. Unlike the Nazis, the Mahayanists didn't lose- they won. The losers are the Buddha, his dharma, and all sanghas.

This Mahayana mass psychology prejudice is just as strong today as ever before. From the most senior to the most junior Tibetan and Oriental Buddhist teachers, most of them say negative things and *untrue* things about the Hinayanists. They repeatedly state "Hinayanists just want to get enlightened for themselves but the

Mahayanists aspire to get enlightened for the benefit of others." This is a ridiculous assertion. How can a selfish person attain enlightenment? How can there be any unity amongst 100 million Buddhists to want to get enlightened only for themselves and to avoid helping others attain enlightenment? Mahayanists even make the flat out claim that it is utterly impossible for a Hinayana practitioner to attain to full and complete enlightenment! Mahayanists constantly claim that they have more compassion than Hinayanists but observing the character of Burmese, it is obvious that the Theravadin Burmese have more compassion and kindness than many other Buddhists. This spin doctoring goes on and on but the worst part is that people believe it.

Like countless other organizations, the Buddhist religion could have provided much greater leadership in this world but it shot itself in the foot with institutionalized in-fighting and internal arrogance and prejudice. What a loss! The Buddhist Spectrum Study Group holds out a vision of uniting the three yanas into one. Mahayanists who try to express that they do not feel any prejudice about the Theravadins or the Hinayana will often trip all over their tongue and put their foot in their mouth because they just don't know how to even talk about the Hinayana without being condescending. Because they have been brainwashed, if they are true to their heart, the Mahayanists will put down the Theravadins. If they try to be diplomatic in company, they may embarrass themselves. Go and talk to one about the Hinayana. Forgive them; it's not their fault. They were raised that way. I am a trusting soul by nature, but because of my experiences over the years and because of my extensive research, I have grown to be deeply suspicious of the Mahayana. As Ram Dass says, "Drink from the source and let the rest go by." As Westerners we are somewhat dependent upon Mahayanists for our education since they comprise about 90% of Buddhism in the West. Don't bite the hand that feeds; lead the hand to the truth.

Many teachers with higher realization see this divisive process and they stay out of the politics. The Dalai Lama has taken some personal risks to combat this prejudice within his people. In his book *A Policy of Kindness* he pushes the Tibetan people to use the word Theravadayana instead of Hinayana. So, things may be improving. In the influential Shambhala mandala, Pema Chodron has gone on tour before thousands of people saying "The word Hinayana means lesser vehicle but this is a politically incorrect term which should not be used. These are simply the original teachings of the Buddha." At the Sixth Buddhist Council held in Burma back in 1956 it was unanimously decided that the word Hinayana should be dropped from use, but not many people remembered that as the propaganda machine rolled on.

Goebbels' propaganda machine worked so well that even at the end of the war Germans trusted Hitler still, and they blamed the generals and others for the collapse of the country. A cousin of Goebbels' wife was the father of my Douglas College dharma student, Ilse Harvey. Ilse was in the Hitler youth and she told me how Hitler took the young men off the streets and put them to work on the Autobahn. She said Hitler inspired people to help the poor and he directed that no one must go cold or hungry. Hitler encouraged all Germans to have a one pot meal on one Sunday a month and party members would knock on people's doors all over the country on those days to collect the money saved in food and gas, to donate it to the needy.

I asked Ilse "How did he do it? How did he get the country going? How did he inspire the masses?" Ilse thought for a moment, then replied "Well, he would shout!" Probably Hitler was a medium and a deva would come through him and shout out his great oratories. More than fifty years have past but Ilse still has a fondness for Hitler, "I still admire him," she said as she hung up the phone. Ilse still can't believe that Hitler was responsible for "KZ," concentration camps. She never heard about them until after the war. Her disconcerting view demonstrates the powerful Nazi manipulations of mass psychology.

I too am an innocent victim of deliberate mass psychology manipulation. When I became a Buddhist in 1991, from day one I was presented with the three yana stages of the path- Hinayana, Mahayana and Vajrayana. In Thailand in 1994, I directly realized truth: the primacy of the Theravadin sutras and vinaya. However even myself, I still have deep seated thoughts that sometimes arise in my mind which buy into the big lie about Mahayana superiority. This is because I have been brainwashed as a result of the Mahayanists using the ancient Indian big lie theory. They have succeeded in repeating their big lie so many times and from so many angles that most Buddhists accept it as the big truth, part of their world view.

The Nazis proved beyond doubt that the big lie theory does work. Millions of Germans had religious devotion for Hitler. This level of devotion is taught in Hinduism and Tibetan Buddhism, more so than in Theravadin Buddhism. In 1934, after Hitler had consolidated his hold on Germany, he had a 90% approval rating by his people. In the 1930's if Germans saw Hitler step out of a car, many times people were breathless with adulation, fainting dead away in the street. Not even the Beatles could do that! Indeed, Hitler was the Beatles of Germany. This tiny country, beaten, bankrupt, and defeated, rose within a few short years to stand within one step of global domination. The higher realms were behind it.

By 1934 many Nazis were moving to revolutionize religion. Hitler hated Christianity and Judaism, and they wanted the Germanic gods to be the supreme religion. A proposal was promoted within the party that would resurrect the old Germanic religion, and place Hitler in the role of the messiah. In his speeches Hitler invoked Germanic devas. He wanted to promote the devas of Germany. This is what Buddhists call lokapala, the higher realm devas that live at or are associated with a particular geographic location. Buddhism teaches that Germany has her own devas, and these are the higher realm beings that Hitler, Goebbels and others were supplicating. There is some evidence that Hitler was protected from above by these devas. During the war when buildings were bombed apart, there was more than an average number of walls left standing that were adorned by a picture of Hitler. This was also true for the swastika. There have also been a documented 42 serious assassination attempts against the life of Hitler. This also indicates that he was protected from above, as no one ever got to him. A feeling would come over him and he would leave a place just before an assassination attempt. In the most famous attempt in July, 1944 Hitler gets up for no good reason and walks across the room. Suddenly a briefcase that was next to Hitler's feet blows up and kills a bunch of officers. The next day, Hitler is on the movie screen smiling with one bandage around his little finger!

Hitler may have even possessed the ability that some highly attained Buddhist gurus have, to affect the weather. Some people like Kalu Rinpoche seemed to create double rainbows above themselves, or manifest incredible wind, hail and thunder. In the mid 1930's Hitler was the first world leader to use an airplane to travel between meetings in his own country. During one such trip a party of faithful devotees were waiting for him at his destination. A storm brewed up out of nowhere and Hitler's plane was in the midst of it. People were getting very concerned. They could see his plane coming in for a landing and just then the weather calmed right down. Hitler's plane taxied up to the relieved crowd and just as the door opened on Hitler, a shaft of sun broke through the clouds and shone on Hitler at that precise moment! It was as if the weather was controlled to set the stage around him! Witnesses said that when Hitler greeted the adoring crowd there was a glow coming off of people's eyes as they gazed upon their beloved leader. Some wondered aloud whether Jesus had that glow which Hitler had. History never changes, only our perspective on it does. Since the history books are written by the victors, we are not aware of the good Nazis, and the uplifted people that worked with good intentions. Few war movies will ever show that side of the German people.

In Chiangmai I knew an American man who was a close personal to the Tibetan guru Kalu Rinpoche for over 10 years. Sherab Ebin and I would sit eating toast and jam in the America Restaurant, while he described to me how Kalu Rinpoche informed him that he had met Germans sent to Tibet during the 1930's and 40's. They were there on orders from their furhrer to uncover the secrets of Vajrayana Buddhism, and bring them back to Hitler in Berlin. Some of these Germans remained after the war and even helped to get the Dalai Lama out in 1959. One of the Germans who went from Tibet to Berlin to see Hitler reported that when he went in to see the furhrer, he felt that Hitler was this vast powerful being that just sucked the information right out of him. He staggered out of Hitler's office as if he had had an audience with a god! It was obvious to him that Hitler was one of the highest level gurus he had ever met.*

This idea of Hitler scouring the world for higher powers is the theme of the movie *Raiders of the Lost Ark,* with Harrison Ford. Some Tibetan Buddhist monks even went to Berlin to work for Hitler! Who knows what they were doing? In India and that part of the world, Hitler was not despised, and certainly not before the war. Even today in India, *Mein Kempf* sells well and Hitler is not regarded nearly as negatively as we feel about him in the West.

Hitler must have believed of himself that he was a great deva manifesting on earth. He visualized himself as a divinely inspired ruler. Heinrich Himmler followed Hitler's example by also invoking powerful visualization and NLP techniques. Himmler had a castle restored and he decorated the rooms to suit the many great German kings and leaders of the past. He would bring his officers to stay there so that the spirits of these worshipped German heroes would be imbued in his men. Their aspiration of consummating those unearthly powers within themselves was successfully demonstrated by their great leader, Adolf Hitler. In Hitler's last will, articulately written hours before his suicide, he wrote "as I leave my earthly career . . ." This indicates that he believed that he was going upstairs, probably to the jealous god realm, not to hell. Adolf would psyche up a visualization of himself by practising his speeches in front of a mirror before electrifying a crowd. His practices compare to Tibetan Buddhist practices where one visualizes oneself as a deity or as their guru or as a dharma king. The culture of Tibetans, Hindus, and Nazis deliberately create an aura of absolute power around the guru or leader. The Nazi German belief is to follow the leader, to be elitist. Advisors are there to serve the leader with the best advice, but democracy is nonsense. The Dalai Lama first introduced the concept of democracy during the early days of the Tibetan government in exile. In the constitution that he prepared he proposed the possibility of the Dalai Lama being democratically impeached if necessary. This was such a shock to the Tibetan people that it drove many into despair and depression. To the Tibetans, the idea of democracy, instead of the theocracy which they are accustomed to — is nonsense. The Dalai Lama is their guru and that is it!

Adolf Hitler was first and foremost, a guru. His disciple and deputy furhrer Rudolf Hess is an example of total devotion to the guru, which is emphasized in Vajrayana Buddhism. Rudolf Hess had a dog-like devotion to Hitler, just like a dog! If Adolf threw a bone into the Rhine River in February, Hess would surely dive in and fetch it. In a classic case of disobeying his master in order to carry out his wishes, Hess parachuted into Scotland in 1940 to try to negotiate a peace with the British. Because of this act Hess lived to a very old age. In the 1980's reporters would still interview him in prison (the Russians would have freaked if the British let Hess free) and they would ask him, "So, what do you think of Hitler now?" To their surprise Hess would take a deep breath, and raise his right arm saying, "Ah! . . . *Mein furhrer!* He was just the greatest man who ever lived!" That's devotion. 40 years later. That's devotion.

Goebbels arranged with Hollywood filmmakers to depict Hitler in a way similar to how Confucius taught ancient Chinese Emperors to appear. In the films of Hitler, the leader is alone. Ancient Chinese rulers were supposed to have a divine connection to the cosmos. If there is a comet in the night sky, then it must mean something to the emperor. The idea is that they must look like a great leader as a responsibility to the masses, to provide them with a role model to inspire their miserable little lives. This gives the people vicarious pleasure. Even if the emperor and his ministers are bored with their official duties, it is their job to appear great and almighty— to inspire others! Duty. So, Goebbels, the Minister of Enlightenment, instructed Hitler to become a father figure, and that's definitely what Hitler was to millions of Germans, Austrians and others. This is the guru thing again.

If the Germans had tapped into the unspeakable powers of the higher realms, then why did they lose the war? Why did they fail? The answer, as written earlier, is bad karma. The result of the manifold bad karmas that they initiated, is that bad karma rebounds back upon those that initiate it. It's always that way — a natural law. It doesn't make any difference whether you are a higher realms master or not, you can't escape your bad karma. Killing the Jews is what really unravelled them. Big mistake! I don't believe the view that other people, not Hitler inspired the genocide of the Jews. Since Hitler was a lost youth he believed that the one organizing principle of the universe is that the Jews are behind anything that is bad. As fearless leader Hitler had the power to start and stop the mass slaughter. He's responsible. Higher realm powers and genius could not stop the results of Hitler's bad karma. Hitler's stupid mistakes indicate the fruition of this bad karma.

When Hitler saw his people eating stew he would call it 'corpse tea,' since he was a strict vegetarian. His vegetarian diet helped his mind powers, but since 1936, Hitler started to take regular injections of drugs from his private physician, a highly decorated doctor, but in reality his doctor was a quack. By 1942 Adolf lost his great ability to think out grand plans and concepts. His vast mind degenerated into the animal realm of route thinking and stubbornness — the indication of a drug addict. This last period of his life was his "fat Elvis years." Just at this point, the war forever turned against Germany, around the end of 1942, beginning of 1943. Hitler lost his charisma. He needed to feed off the crowds, but he couldn't because he was enclosed during the war, cut off from adoring fans. Devotion would have seemed ridiculous in the matter-of-fact environment of headquarters. As his dream of the Third Reich was blowing up in bombs and smoke, he blamed the German people for failing to live up to his vision — the mass visualization of Aryan supremacy, for one thing. As Hitler would drive down bombed out streets he would detach himself from the scene and not acknowledge any personal responsibility for all the destruction. In the end, Hitler wanted his country to die with him, he felt that Germany deserved to commit suicide with him. That's pretty scary, having a leader like that, like a father who loses his job so he kills his wife and children before commiting suicide because it's the 'proper' thing to do. This is evidence that using the higher realms in a hurtful way (such as black magic) is not something you can ever get away with, even if the courts cannot prosecute you. The law of karma will get you in the end and prosecute you, one way or another.

What if today's technology was used by someone like Hitler? With computers, audio, video and 3-D video in the future, the brilliant power of mass psychology manipulation could be seen again. Both the Buddha and Hitler were pop idols but their styles were very different. Hitler and Goebbels whipped up mass adulation to enlist millions into their plans which were outward looking, laying a trip on everyone in society. The Buddha was loved by millions but he taught people to turn inwards and practice the dharma. He led a peaceful, quite, humble existence, not struggling to attain more power. Buddha already had power, he *was* power. Buddhism cannot approve of a Fascist society focused on the leader. Buddhism inclines towards the individual effort to discover the truth that is inside every individual. Do we need big energies, devotion, and determination to turn the environment around now, and in the 21st century? Do we need the kind of big energies that Nazi Germany had? What do you think? What haunts people is the knowledge that Hitler's regime was the most efficient state Earth ever knew. People always wonder if that kind of situation could be created again, but run benignly. Presently, the world is careening out of control with no one, absolutely no one, in the driver's seat. That's scary. In the predictions of Nostradamus, he predicted a 'Hister,' then further in the future, our future, he predicted that "a man wearing a blue turban will rise out of Persia. He will be the terror of mankind." Unfortunately, that is what we have to look forward to because Nostradamus has an exceptionally good track record. This is what happens when no one good is in control — someone bad takes control. Lest we forget, it could happen again.

Out of compassion for the world, the higher realms should be tapped into for the benefit of others. Certainly the Buddhist teachings train people to develop a conscious relationship with the higher realms. No Buddhist can deny that. The stakes are high. The negative side of the higher realms led to 50,000,000 dead in World War II. But if good people like ourselves ignore the higher realms, then bad people will take advantage of such beings to consolidate power. "So it might as well be us," the Vajra Regent said, "it's as simple as that." Joseph Campbell taught that it is necessary to live your life with a sense of the power and mystery of life and your place in the cosmos, the big picture. That is the function of mythology, he taught. We must take the higher realms seriously and ask for their help to subdue mankind's recklessness and to heal our world. Lest we forget.

Could Nazi teachings and practices be employed in a way to benefit others with compassion in a peaceful climate such as in Canada? Yes. Considering the staggering long term power of audio/video and 3-D video, national boundaries are of little meaning. If Goebbels was in power today he could manipulate minds all over the planet, in many languages. He and his partner Adolf promoted a German mythology and the depths of their power arose from the power inherent in that mythology. Right or wrong, there are always devas around who will buy into your mythology, adapt to your mythology, and support it. There's bags of evidence for this if one studies other cultures, or shamanism.

It's a chicken or egg question, whether devas or humans initiate new mythologies. The weakness of the world today is that we have little or no mythology. Joseph Campbell felt that the late 20th century is a period in the terminal moraine of mythologies, a mosaic of conflicting hodge podge mythologies. Campbell said that his main thought for the future is that the next mythology has got to include everybody, the whole planet. Hitler had that kind of vision and fortunately he and his vision were destroyed. For the vision of our future as human beings on this planet, the role model that we find in Joseph Goebbels is that he is the modern master of materializing mythology. There is no other. He alone was the most skilful genius at communicating pure vision. He raised up the German world and brought down the German devas to make it one Nazi world, a physical reality on earth. That is a very great thing. Methods of how to apply Goebbels' sacred teachings to benefit our world with compassion in the 21st century are not explored here. The people who will be responsible for those decisions, will then be responsible for every other decision that will come after those initial decisions so this indicates a tremendous responsibility and opportunity to raise the inspiration of others in a way that benefits all. Any attempt to move mass psychology in such a powerful way must be thoroughly considered by many people in order to properly and compassionately uplift our world.

*The account of this meeting with Hitler is written in a Mexican book called 'La Mujer Dormida Debedar Aluz' from Editorial Jus, S.A. de. C.V., Plaza De Abasolo No. 14, Col. Guerrero, 06300 Mexico, D.F. The translation in English is: "The woman who sleeps, must give birth."

The Nuremberg Visualization

There's a story about the border area between Russia and Poland. There was once a surveying team that was sent out by Joseph Stalin in 1937 to clarify just precisely where the border was (or they would be shot!). A big happy Polish family lived on a huge dairy farm right smack dab on the borderline. When the surveyors completed their mission (they were shot to death anyway because Stalin had too much sugar in his coffee that morning) they stepped up to Josep, the farmer standing on the porch with the wife and kids, and they said, "Mr. Agacinski, we have determined beyond doubt that your entire farm is in the country of Poland! Russia is 1.36 kilometres that way!" he said, pointing to the great eastern sun in the early morning sky.

"Oh joy!" the entire family cried out at once! "Now we won't have to endure those long Russian winters anymore! Horray! Whoopee!" and they had a hoe-down, dancing on the porch of the farmhouse. Little Ronae, age four, took his honey spoon out of his mouth and held it on his happy beating heart, thanking the father, the son and the holy ghost. 17 days later, Stalin's henchmen came back to the farm and beat and tied up Josep Agacinski and forced him to watch as their commanding officer Col. Boltrukiewicz, raped the exceptionally attractive Mrs. Agacinski. At the climax of this process, they cut off Mr. Agacinski's penis and inserted it into his screaming, perspiring mouth. That's the difference between Stalin and Hitler. Totally different animals.

> Move real slow
> Warm equanimity
> Warm equanimity
> Warm equanimity
> Move real slow

As the echo of machine gun fire commingled with the rays of the great eastern sun that gently graced the pond beside the side door of the house, little Ronae escaped onto the soft wet soil of the October morning. The grass impeded his progress with its wet dew and Ronae slipped and stumbled again and again, losing valuable ground to the advancing machine gun behind him. Looking back over his shoulder, tiny, cold, smelly Ronae fully understood that the grim reaper was chasing him under the oak tree past the swing rope. His mind awakened and enlivened by thrilling terror, Ronae felt a surge of primordial power and confidence which he had never known since his previous life in France. Ronae slowed down and felt totally present, living fully in the moment, and he was happy with himself, happy with his being. Ronae experienced true bliss for the first time in that lifetime!

On the long lane to the country road, he was displaced by a slug in the back of the brain and thirteen slugs in the back, and bottom. As little Ronae coughed up blood for the last time, thinking of a Russian colonel's sperm on his mother's breasts, Stalin's henchmen took Mrs. Agacinski away in the truck with them. Ronae took rebirth as a deva in Yama heaven and remained there until the Earth year 3136 A.D., during which time he took rebirth as a human girl on the Martian colony John Glen. Little Ronaea lived happily ever after, finally reunited with her previous Polish family.

Meanwhile, back in 1937 A.D., Ludmila Agacinski "lived," you could say, until the year 1967, after eventually remarrying with one of the Russians, but it wasn't any of the rapists that she married. There was a long convoluted process of trading her around and such, until she kind of gave in to the whole thing and got sort of brainwashed, you might say. And, they all lived in dukkha ever after. End of story.

The Four Superior Qualities of Nuremberg Practice

The goal of a decent education is beneficial purposeful action. To apply some of the ideas discussed in this chapter, there is a practice of visualizing Nuremberg that you can contemplate upon if you choose to. Nuremberg is selected for its four superior visualization qualities which are:

1. historic success,
2. vivid video, audio and printed recordings,
3. vital "taboo absorbing interest," as Mr. Mistlberger illuminates in the Foreward, and
4. your feeling of superiority.

All of these four potent factors contribute to a visualization practice that rivals others in it's impression upon the human psyche. Can Quan Yin kick a swastika's butt? Hardly. Take a closer look at these four qualities.

1. This actually happened. 100,000 plus people were in attendance from 1927 to 1939 at Nuremberg. If you visualize *Jack and the Beanstalk* for 20 years, you'll just never believe in it. Nuremberg is so believable that millions have tried in vain to forget about it.
2. We can see it even fresher, and in 3-D colour unlike the theatre bound Germans who were the very first to adore this process.
3. To get 21st century group psychology interested in this new deal, taboos get attention, taboos blow away boredom and opening taboos can liberate energy by freeing blocks. This will benefit everyone by raising windhorse in the best way! This practice is a foremost visualization.
4. Because you know how bad many of those people were at the historic rallies — Jew killers dancing in the aisle, you can better love and forgive the hateful part of your own inner character. Visualizing Avalokitesvara has the opposite effect which reminds you of what faults you have in comparison. We need Hitler, we paid oh so very dearly for him; we're cashing in on Nazi Germany now. You can see the worst of yourself in Hitler and those around him. You can see the best of yourself in Hitler's inspiration. Because you can identify with the best and the worst in people, you can move up with this visualization and transform these energies in the most uplifting way.

Because Nuremberg arouses negative emotional energy, this is a Buddhist's opportunity to skilfully uplevel and transmute this negativity into awakened energy (see: Trungpa, 1973; 234). In accordance with the greater vision of the Buddhist Spectrum Study Group, Nuremberg visualization practice contributes to healing the pain of the millions killed in World War II. This is so because from time to time you include in the visualization, the practice of give and take, to take on the suffering of those masses of people that you visualize, and bestow peace and love upon them. In doing this practice alone, or with other people, you do feel energy — energy so gentle, open, not at all subtle. This maddenly unharnessable unknown invisible energy can, if captured and contained and down-loaded into your life, manifest as greater power, inspiration and even insight.

Ideally, a number of people are needed to support a large enough container of people to use this deva invocation method to bring down the greater blessings of the higher realms into a group human container and reignite their mass inspiration. It worked at the last rally held in 1939 so it will work at future rallies too. The prescription for how to build a light bulb will always work. This deva process is like downloading a transformer into the electric wires of the Western hemisphere (to play spiritual catch up with the East). Until we globally harness this process, or something similar, such as Hindu/ Buddhist temple deva practices, then we are like Beatles fans in 1971 pinning for John, Paul, George and Ringo to reunite. They *were* a deva invocation container. We cannot imagine what uplifted greatness can arise from within ourselves, until we have gone through a long group process. Star Trek. We should commit ourselves to the goal of recreating the mass Nuremberg energy and awakening and realizing the presence of the devas in our cultural life.

A well orchestrated group ritual such as this has great power to arouse bodhicitta beyond our own personal ability or control. You would want to be able to trust the administrators of your rally. This energy simply needs to be generated to invoke devas in a good way, by invoking the great compassionate devas such as Sakkha, primarily, since he has been close to us throughout this entire kalpa, thick and thin. In Buddhist countries such as Thailand there are many statues of the Buddha with his right arm extended straight out. Don't invite the jealous god realm devas. Hitler taught us the process, he exemplified the tremendous power, but we certainly do not model his evil intentions. When people talk about building a mass UFO landing site, this is what they really aspire for. UFOs *are* devas (see: Buddhism and UFOs). Group deva invocation practices will be the mass UFO landing sites of the 21st century. Instead of silvery tin cans from space landing on the front lawn of the White House, we will see what the band R.E.M. prophecized as "shinny happy people holding hands."

The significance of Goebbels and this Nuremberg visualization practice cannot be dismissed because Goebbels provides us with a unique example of someone who actually succeeded in manifesting this deva invocation process in a large scale way that magnetised mass psychology in the West. That is a very great thing! Hitler was his front man. It is of heavy heart pounding significance that today we have video, audio and books which have recorded for us this fantastic human process of mass ritual which undeniably helped to raise a major country out of the depression and bolt them into the centre of power in Europe. The way that this truth benefits your contemplative practice is that you can visualize yourself at the centre of the Nuremberg rallies. This avoids the controversy and political incorrectness of visualizing Hitler. To assume that other people do not want to benefit others is actually a disgusting and conceited view. Many Germans who got pumped up at Nuremberg did go out and benefit others. They worked hard, they achieved results, they had good karma and then they died and went to heaven.

In many Vajrayana visualization practices, you visualize yourself as the Buddha, as your guru, as a bodhisattva, or as a fully enlightened deity of some kind. Even though Vajrayana Buddhism does not exist from one Theravadin view, the purpose of this ritual is to throw off your limited self concept and take on the larger mind of an enlightened being. This training is called "taking the result as the path," in that you visualize that you have already arrived at the result of your spiritual goal of complete liberation from dukkha. Theravadins can regard this as another technique of skilful means.

In the Nuremberg visualization practice below, you place yourself at the centre of the stage in Nuremberg, or you can visualize your guru, or the Buddha. You arouse bodhicitta — the aspiration to attain enlightenment for the benefit of others. You can use the rest of the recorded real life Nuremberg rally environment to create a vivid visualized setting around yourself. Only the German people have provided this powerful tool in such a conversation stopping way. Today, over half a century after Goebbels, this concept and this essay are still taboo which is evidence of the great power that people are still too afraid to face directly. That's power. Over 50 years later. That's power. The time has come to face this power directly. It's O.K., you know. We can just live in honesty and tell the truth. There is no problem. There's no problem at all with that.

You have videos, CD's, photos and books that you can use to generate a vivid visualization, but even more, you have the certain knowledge that this did in fact happen and that the Nuremberg rallies really did succeed at being a source of gun powder behind the Nazi inspiration. As in the practice of Ikebana, we take all kinds of seemingly unrelated things and put them together to create something beautiful. That was Nikola Tesela's invention of the radio. Hitler's rituals seem to have nothing to do with Buddhism or upliftedness, but we can combine even that with what we know, to synthesise ways to create enlightened society. If you can only overcome any aversion, or prejudice, against using a process that was used by an evil empire, then you can use Nuremberg practice in an uplifting way for the benefit of others. Time is running out before World War III. You must break out of any complacent belief that everything is going to be alright or that everything will just keep running along the way it usually does, or any belief that we don't need more powerful group contemplative tools to redeem our world. If people ask, "why should anyone do Nuremberg practice?," the answer is: tools. Done properly, this is another among countless tools to work with the mind and apply effort for the benefit of others.

There may be only decades left before the next major world war. No matter how severe it will be, the world will survive according to the Buddha's prophecy for our future. Nostradamus predicted that after this certain war, with suns burning upon the earth, we will achieve an unparalleled peace and prosperity for over 1000 years. Therefore our future is up to us; the future is flexible, it is not cast in stone. We can't change the past but we can change the future. This puts even more pressure on everybody to wake up. Wake up! Do you want to be a passive victim or do you want to mobilize your strength while your country is still stable enough to do so? That is the vision; that is the prophecy. The future is more important than the past.

Nuremberg Visualization Technique

With eyes closed for this Buddhist / Hindu / Taoist practice, sit in insight meditation for two minutes. Then repeat the chant from the deva invocation chapter, "soft human copper gold" at least three times. Silently chant ten times "Sacred messages from the devas enter your copper Buddhacle godhead." Sit quietly for a few more moments, then visualize yourself silently moving with ease out of the dot centre of all universes. The form of your body is that of a deva UFO of the sensuous sphere. By inter realm shift you glide out of the centre of all universes and then you glide through the centre of our universe. For an enjoyable period you witness the splendour of oceans of galaxies as you cross vast space. Then you go through and out of the centre of the Milky Way galaxy with the hull of your body aimed at our Terra solar system.

Visualize that you are looking at this solar system as you rapidly approach it. With your deflectors you enter through the peripheral meteors, and you look at planet earth with your sensors. Streaking lines in space of pure 24 carat gold, like Superman with your red cape and red boots and blue suit, you set the controls for the heart of the sun. The Buddha taught that the sun's disk is the divine palace of a deva (Buddhaghosa, 412). Previous devas have left, but our world system father, who art in heaven, hallowed be thy name, his kingdom you can experience on

Earth as it is in heaven. Gliding through the liquid, plasma and love of this indescribably blissful exquisitely beautiful golden crystal and lapis laluzi palace inhabited by a former principal one from Earth, you emerge in a cozy warm solar flare that jettisons you to our planet Earth.

With your eyes still closed you imagine a line from the left to the right of your field of vision. Utilize the middle 20% of your view as a dark circle, barely visible. This represents your view of Earth as you come in for a landing. You see a bright point of light on the Earth which is Nuremberg, Germany. Coming in quickly, the Earth fills the screen, you see Europe, then you go straight for Germany. The light glows brighter as you descend upon this present moment Nuremberg rally. You can choose day or night.

A vague cylinder of light is streaking around your descent as you slow to a halt right in front of the face of the principal one floating in the air. You project upon the principal one the identity you have spontaneously selected for the principal one. He or she could be you or someone else, the Buddha or your guru. This is the hero, the leader of the Nuremberg rally. The leader is suspended in space 136 feet above the stage. You descend to the back of the stage and a multitude of 84,000 people are hyped up all around you. Looking out, visualize this principal one dressed in khaki, white and yellow, suspended in space at the zenith. The cylinder of streaks of light is around him or her, then it fans out thicker in density and diametre like a cone to the ground which blesses the entire Nuremberg rally. For the purpose of description we shall refer to the principal one as your guru.

Your guru is wearing a white arm band on his uniform with a yellow circle in the centre of it. The yellow circle has a large white swastika in the centre, clockwise or counterclockwise. The guru image is wearing a white stripe diagonally across his chest and one around his waist. He smiles with non-referential compassion which envelops all of the people at the Nuremberg rally. His face is ever glowing, warm, tender, gentle, all knowing, powerfully self assured, and with an infectious inspiration that is being held back from exploding.

Music

To accompany this vivid practice, you can use music to compliment the visualization. This adds a powerful dynamic which can ignite your inspiration. This is similar to dancing around your living room when no one is looking, except that this practice is focused in the direction of raising your spirits for exertion on your spiritual path. You can memorize a piece of music or actually play a recording during Nuremberg visualization practice. You may use any piece of music that you prefer, such as the startlingly different song *She Sells Sanctuary* by The Cult, from the 1986 album *Sonic Temple*. Other fine choices are the theme to *Rocky,* the violins of

Angel Delight by Mike Rowland and the *Overture* to *Tommy* by The Who. When the music peaks and explodes, this visualization synchronizes with the music as you imagine the explosion of a white sphere of light behind your guru, which encompasses all of the sentient beings that you extend love to. Emerging from this explosion are millions of celestial devas as the retinue of the Buddha/guru. Visualize a vast ocean of devas in the sky around him.

The guru descends to the main stage in the midst of a cloud of white, yellow and/or gold swastikas. Because this is a Buddhist practice we are using this powerful Hindu/ Buddhist swastika symbol of "ultimate power." If you feel that the colour coordination of yellow and gold clashes, you can just mix the white with either yellow or gold. Make the swastikas whatever size you feel most inspired with. This practice does not come from head office — it comes from your primordial mind, so there's no rule trip about doing it just one way. Be free, but disciplined at the same time. After the principal one alights onto the stage of the Nuremberg rally, the army goes wild and you see yourself backstage gazing with devotion upon your guru, or upon the Buddha. Imagine his inspiring words exhorting 100,000 uniformed people arrayed before you. His right arm is out stretched in straight arm salute, gently and very slowly scanning the audience from side to side. Depending upon what message you want to reaffirm in your mind, you select the words that are exchanged back and forth.

The main chant and practice interspersed in the oratory is:

Buddha refuge!
Dharma refuge!
Sangha refuge!

This practice is accomplished by gently pounding your right fist on your heart and then quickly outstretching your right arm with your hand pointing flat at the principal one. For the people in the group they do the same pointing to the leader; for the leader he points into them. A variety of ways can be used to raise windhorse in this way. The crowd can do all three gestures while the principal one stands silently in Roman army salute. Or, the leader can initiate this ritual with "Buddha refuge!" and the others respond with "Dharma refuge!" Then the leader goes "Sangha refuge!" It keeps going back and forth until the leader decides to stop. After the third chant the cycle just keeps going around to "Buddha refuge!" again. In this way the principal one can best gage how long to raise windhorse for his or her students.

At some point in this visualization you move towards the leader, and then you actually merge together; you melt into one another as one being, and now you become the guru. At this point you can initiate the give and take contemplation on compassion for everyone there and for people in your every day life, but you don't have to do this every time you do the Nuremberg practice.

In the tradition of the Nuremberg rallies there is mass motion and music so you get into a vehicle with your entourage and you drive through the crowd as the full arm salutes follow your every move. This is reiki energy of love, devotion and healing going back and forth. Next, oceans of devas appear out of nowhere and they rain from the heavens into the array of people and as they too join the throng in straight arm salute directed at you and outwards from beside you. You lower and raise your right arm and they respond in kind. This is like a flashlight aimed at the sky from a lifeboat on the deep dark ocean. The mahadevas then notice your array of humans and in kind, they descend into your group mass human container. This is an ancient pre-Hindu mass psychology deva invocation technique, masterfully applied to 20th century Europe. This practice can be used for the southern U.S. Bible belt as they are amiable about this sort of spiritual revival.

The devas move towards you and merge into you, they melt into you. When you visualize the devas channelling through you all things seem possible and movable because all things are possible and movable. Your illness is fading, unnoticeable... Nothing is stuck! After you have achieved "a saturation of devas," your enlightenment body begins to dissolve outwards in the form of light extended from your right hand, into the crowd of warriors. This showers blessings down upon the devotees below and as you completely dissolve into space, all of the participants are blessed with vibrant health, hearts of love, and great clarity of mind. Every last good thing that you have, you have given it all to others as everyone sits in silent meditation. The people across Germany and Europe feel a glow of well-being and peace. Under the blaze of the great eastern sun, folks hear the sound of flies buzzing against the glass windows on their homes. The breeze through the maple trees indicates that coral flowers from heaven are wafting through their entire bodies. Children stop crying and they group together to go bird watching and treasure hunting. They discover two dollars in the woods behind the elementary school. They find coins several times, as they are scattered all over the countryside. There is success on this monthly Easter egg hunt. Waves along the shore fall silent. The long legged cranes stand in the ocean. There are new species of fish to be found. Sit.

Nuremberg Uplifted

The pilot episode of *Star Trek - The Next Generation* provides an ideal ready made visualization for you in the form of the jelly fish shaped cosmic beings in outer space dramatized in *Encounter at Farpoint*. Visualize that the entrails of this super deva begin at the centre of planet Earth. For us, this deva represents Sakkha, king of the gods and ruler of heaven number two—Tavatimsa heaven. This is one of frequent countless business trips that Sakkha makes to Earth. Sakkha pushes up underneath the foundation of the entire community of Nuremberg, Germany. The Nuremberg rally, being stirred out of meditation, and the whole town is lifted slowly into outer space with a bubble dome atmosphere held in place by Star Trek mythology. The warriors are engulfed in pink light in all directions beyond the ends of space. The gathering happily floats through the golden diamond gates of Tavatimsa heaven under a liquid gold sky tinged with clear light. Here now they are finally reunited in tears for the first time with all of the War War II dead, unaware of past enmities.

In Tavatimsa Jews, gypsies, Germans, mothers of the dead— everyone is there, and around the crystal table of the three and thirty, sitting among these principal devas is the foremost amongst Sakkha's retinue, the John Kennedy deva. Beatles music is playing, Mozart too... Coral flowers descend and waft through your earth bound head and shoulders as you visualize coral flowers wafting through these devas of the dead. You're not just making this up, you know. Conventional reality really is something like this.

> We meditate:
> *Coral flowers...* (to be read slowly and visualized) *coral flowers... coral*
> *flowers... coral flowers...*
> *coral flowers... coral flowers... coral flowers... coral flowers... coral flowers...*
> *coral flowers... coral flowers... coral flowers... coral flowers... coral flowers...*
> *coral flowers... coral flowers... coral flowers... coral flowers... coral flowers...*
> *coral flowers... coral flowers... coral flowers... coral flowers... coral flowers...*
> *coral flowers... coral flowers bursting...*
> *coral flowers... coral flowers... coral flowers...*
> *coral flowers... coral flowers... coral flowers...*
> *coral flowers... coral flowers... coral flowers...*
> *coral flowers... coral flowers... coral flowers...*
> *petals... petals... petals... petals... petals... petals... petals... petals...*
> *petals... petals... petals... petals... petals... petals... petals...*
> *petals in heaven...*
> *petals... petals... petals...*
> *petals everywhere across luminous outer space saturating*
> *the ten directions....*
> *petals... petals... petals... petals... petals... petals...petals... petals...*
> *petals... petals... petals... petals... petals... petals... petals...*
>
> *"My god! Look at all the stars!"*
> *-astronaut Dave Bowman (2001: A Space Odyssey).*
>
> *Transcend through the stargate to a higher level of consciousness.*

Imagine further, the Nuremberg shuttle above, after everybody lives together in harmony, brotherhood, peace and glee until almost the end of this kalpa, this same Nuremberg rally slowly descends back to Germany and the super deva — Sakkha, king of the gods — puts it back in the same place as before, except that only your real time has elapsed, about fifteen or twenty minutes. Such is the magic of the gods! Then, finish it all off with one of several appropriate songs you can play or imagine at the end of the visualization, such as:

All You Need Is Love

Love love love
Love love love
Love love love
There's nothing you can do that can't be done
Nothing you can sing that can't be sung
Nothing you can say but you can learn how to play the game
It's easy!

All you need is love!
All you need is love!
All you need is love!
Love

Love is all you need

- The Beatles

It's good to spend a few minutes in silence at the end of Nuremberg practice to dissolve the visualization and return to your breath in insight meditation. Follow your breath in and out. In and out.

The Berlin Wall Speech - 1961

There are many people who do not understand, or say they don't,
what is the real value of Nuremberg practice
Let them come to this depressed economy
There are many people who do not understand, or say they don't, what is
the real difference between 1920's Germany and the 21st century world
Let them come to Nuremberg practice
As a free man, I say
Nuremberg is a Berliner

Commentary

My single biggest concern when I published this for the first time was that I didn't want people to think that Brian Ruhe is a Nazi. It is not true that I am pro-Hitler. I am not pro-Hitler. I am in support of cultivating the energies unleashed by Hitler, like taming the atom bomb to create helpful nuclear energy to warm the homes of millions of families. Some people will say that Nuremberg visualization practice is a terrible and dangerous thing, a perversion of Buddhism, because of its association with Adolf Hitler and the Nazi Party. Fortunately, this is a wrong view and it is illogical to believe that the Nuremberg experience is dangerous in any way, shape, or form. Look at the "e" word —evidence. There is no evidence that such a visualization practice is harmful. You will not start to turn into a concentration camp promoter or booster just by visualizing a large gathering of people and devas, just as visualizing New Year's Eve in New York City won't twist your character either. Hey, what could possibly go wrong? You're just moving inspiration around. Don't give in to fear based minds, as Teertha Mistlberger exhorted you in the Foreword. Personally, when I feel depressed, I turn on a few tunes from *Tommy*, particularly the first and last one, I extend my right arm forward, and I go to Nuremberg in mind. This is great. I move up and down. You feel like a tiger surrounded by uncomfortable goats. Better to be a tiger than to give in and go along with behaving like something that you're not — a goat!

You can do Nuremberg as a still, sitting contemplation / meditation / visualization. One technique taught in the *Middle Length Discourses of the Buddha* for overcoming depression, is to "visualize a confidence inspiring object." Those five words from the mouth of the Buddha provide the justification for the Buddhist practice of Nuremberg. "Go to Nuremberg." In the spirit of the Vajrayana, nothing is a false refuge. The deities of Mahayana Buddhism are unreal metaphors which practitioners visualize to invoke skilful states of mind. Conversely, Nuremberg is real human experience and real present moment history. The past does not exist. History does exist. When you study history or see videos or listen to tapes, you are doing that *now*. That is influencing you *now* and influencing your future actions, *not* your past! All of the suffering of the Jews in the past does not exist. It is just a present moment memory. All of the suffering in the future does not exist, because it has not yet arisen, and the future is flexible, it can be changed. However the past is inflexible, it can never be changed. Travelling back in time will be utterly impossible for the remainder of the future. History never changes, only our perspective on it does.

The Jewish suffering in history seems to exist as long as any person or deva dwells upon that historic pain and recalls it in the present moment. This is actually present suffering. Buddhists know that the honest reason why perhaps 7.2 million Jews and minorities were killed is because each individual person created the cause, the karma to be killed. The reason why millions of other Jews and minorities were not killed is because those individual persons did not create the cause, the karma to be die at that time. This is a common Buddhist interpretation, no matter how polite Buddhist teachers are about this subject. Possibly, when the ancient Jewish tribes invaded their neighbours and killed everyone, as described in the Bible, they killed the people who literally were the precursors to the Nazi Party of Germany. The victims who were killed, could eventually have taken rebirth as Hitler, Goebbels, millions of Germans, etc., and the whole battlefield just kept going around again.

The vital point to understand here is that *it's still not right*. It's still not right to break the five precepts even if everybody's karma has come to the point of ripening. Buddha. The holocaust was absolutely a bad thing. There was nothing good about it. The holocaust was absolutely a bad thing, without equivocation. It didn't have to happen. This was a terrible sad tragedy which could have been skilfully avoided. Just because all this supposed negative karma was ripening, if the Germans had total insight into all of these past lives, they could have broken the cycle of habitual patterns and woken up. It is always possible to wake up! Buddhism is not pre-deterministic. It is always possible to lessen the affects of bad karma by doing good deeds. Just keep doing good. It is not necessary to have to kill people just because they killed you in a previous life. Stop. The time to stop is now. Stop. Break the cycle. Stop. Breathe in black. Breathe out white. Just keep doing good. If Goebbels and Hitler were even more aware beings than they were, they could have held back their deep habitual aggression towards the Jews and let life turn forward in a civilized manner. That was Hitler's opportunity to be truly the single greatest statesman and human being of the 20th century, and he blew his one great opportunity. Loss.

Let's have some peace now. Suppose it was true that the Germans and the Jews had their ancestral roots in the lives of the ancient Biblical tribes. As these supposed two great karmic equations cancel each other out (What? Do you still want to hunt down a few more 92 year old Nazi war criminals? Let it go.) in their wake they leave behind a jewel in a heap of dust, for yourself to discover as it is just sitting there for anyone to pick: Nuremberg visualization practice.

Let go and get up and walk away from the electric chair. *Smile* Step over here into the sunshine. Hell is that close. Heaven is that close. Suffering can only be experienced in this present moment but this present moment is quickly crumbling into the next present moment which is a completely different and totally separate present moment. Therefore, logically, Nazi Germany is no longer any kind of problem at all, to anyone anywhere anyhow. Adolf Hitler does not exist. Nazi Germany does not exist. It is impossible for Nazi Germany to rise again because of the strong resolve to prevent such a thing from happening. In the 1920's and 1930's there was no such resolve because World War II did not yet exist and people had no idea how bad the Nazis would become. They loved Hitler then. Any prejudice and hatred directed towards Nuremberg visualization practice is insincere... it is bad karma and it is aggression. The danger is always what you don't expect, or so it is said. It is illogical to think that people could get organized as overt Nazis and actually take over again. Look to Nostradamus. The next big wipe out will rise as karma always does—*it'll just rise.*

Jack and the Beanstalk

The city of Nuremberg, Germany is important because if you visualize a fiction, like *Jack and the Beanstalk*, then you will always lack faith in it because you know that it is just a metaphor; it is not really true at all. *You know it!* Useless. You will always have doubt about whether Jack really could have had such and such abilities, if he was for real. The fundamental advantage of Nuremberg visualization practice is that for the rest of your life, when you go to sleep at night you will know, waking and sleeping, that those grand, moving and magnificent Nuremberg rallies are honest real history. "Go to Nuremberg." Rest in peace. Lest we forget to rest in peace.

There's goodness in every bad thing, except for Ronald MacDonald and Joseph Stalin. They are the only two beings in history that have been scientifically proven to possess absolutely no bodhicitta! Transform the delusions of Nuremberg with the give and take practice, to create the realizations of Nuremberg. Do give and take while you are the principal one before the assembly of warriors in silence. They practice give and take for you in silence. Warriors, officers, ladies and gentlemen all. Everyone slowly grows five crests and develops the appearance of a deva, with dress similar but more celestial than that of the past and present kings of Thailand when they are dressed as a deva in golden garb with a spiked crown one foot high and crests on the shoulders 5" high and crests on the sides of their head 5" high as well. Everyone looks like an unordained stream enterer or more and so do you! Ordinarily, this is how people on the bus could look to you if you were attained.

You can develop several of your own versions of this practice to include breathing in the blackness of the pressure and the prejudice of the Nazis, and breathing out the white doves of peace. You're living a charmed life when you do Nuremberg practice regularly.

The Arahant Knows What is Real and What is False

Suppose in the year 3000 A.D. the history books state: "World War I began in 1914, World War II began in 1939, and World War III began in 1959. World War III was ignited in Lhasa, Tibet and engulfed most of Asia and the Middle East until the war ended in 1964 with 250,000,000 dead."

Now, the problem with this is first noticed in your solar plexus. It just doesn't quite feel right in your gut does it? Well, the reason for this, is because such history is total bullshit (well, O.K., *one third* bullshit). When we have that uneasy feeling whimpering upwards from our still small voice within, then we shouldn't second guess that. A spade is a spade is a spade, and we should not ever need to visualize another more impressive spade beside the real spade! You can do so if you have a valid reason, but it isn't necessary. Mahayana and Vajrayana practices visualize things that have never existed (see chapter: 'Changing Buddha's Words').

The way that the false history of World War III from 1959 -1964 relates to the Nuremberg rallies is that the rallies represent the real truth that we can appreciate and relax into. Cozy stuff, you know. But it always makes us uneasy to visualize some Buddhas and bodhisattvas that were invented by people several centuries after the Buddha. Now is the winter of Theravadin discontent. A grave uncertainty is caused by one big factor: falsity. Avalokitesvara is false — Nuremberg is real. Real history. Movie reel history. "Go to Nuremberg."

We should take the literalist approach and take refuge in reality and push metaphor into the more useful realm of metaphor. Zen master D.T. Suzuki claimed that more people have reached enlightenment from the Pure Land school than from Zen. He was likely being polite in accordance with his Japanese custom to do so, in order to spare someone's feelings. Don't hold it against a good teacher as Suzuki for saying such an unjustified thing. He may have been quoted out of context.

Because we are dependent upon reality for our enlightenment, we should continue to have vast inspiring visions as before, but use real history rather than comic book Amitabha Buddhas or the current fictitious bodhisattva of the month. As Thoreau taught "Build your castles in the sky, but put foundations underneath them." Reality is the only foundation for true Buddhism, for the authentic holy dharma. Nuremberg adds such realism and sheer power to your mind. I have been to Nuremberg... I know. I was there.

direct experience

The question may sometimes occasionally arise about how the Jews and some minorities feel, doing this practice. They in particular can benefit from using the tool that was pitted against them. They use it for the benefit of others, all others. They can involve the visualization of their own god in association with Nuremberg and they can imagine feeling the success of their Judaic karma. Hitler looked into the sky above Nuremberg and he sensed the deva Mara, the evil one, as he opened his body, speech and mind to be the clear vessel for Mara. Power. That's power beneath the fine material sphere.

Is there any experience that a person can't have? Is there any experience in the mind that is against the law? No. It is possible that the mental experience of opium in the 19th century led the white people in North America to stop the

Chinese Coolies and merchants from using opium, because the Chinese used opium to work much harder. White people were being put out of business by Chinese immigrants so thus we received our first ever anti-drug laws in North America. Drugs are illegal today because they are dangerously unhealthy but also because of jealously, envy and people feeling threatened. Of course drugs are un-healthy, so are other things. Amongst the many mind altering drugs that are bad is one good one, LSD. I was sitting with Phra Charles, the monk who taught in the temple next to mine in Thailand and a man related to us the experience he had of going beyond ego while taking LSD 30 years before, and he was always trying to understand what that sacred experience was. "In Buddhism I found an explanation," he shared with us. Then Phra Charles revealed a similar LSD expe-rience he had in 1967 with his professor and a group of students, when they were almost as one. I too have had this sacred experience in 1980, when I felt that the wonder of childhood was as close as lifting a veil off of my mind. LSD has a virtue because of the power, the unspeakable power in it's particles to tran-scend the human consciousness beyond the walls of ego. Although Buddhists condemn the use of intoxicants, many Buddhist practitioners respect people's choice to use LSD on occasion. I'm not at all recommending LSD for people, but if you choose to take it as part of your spiritual path, to assist you in opening up, you should first read the work of researchers in this area, such as Ram Dass, Dr. Stanislav Grof or Dr. John C. Lilly. You must arouse the proper motivation of bodhicitta and you should have a responsible undruged adult guide to super-vise you. I wouldn't take LSD more than once a year.

A Tiger is Not a Goat

Joseph Campbell's all time favourite story in the entire history of the universe, since our galaxy first exploded into space, is the story from India about a tiger cub that thought that he was a goat, because his mother pounced on a herd of goats, slipped and died, and gave birth to him at the same time. The goats had strong pa-rental instincts so they took the baby tiger cub as one on their own. The tiger couldn't eat grass very well because of his teeth, and he was frail from the lousy vegetarian diet that the goat herd provided for him. One day a huge male tiger pounced upon the herd and the goats scattered, leaving our poor little friend just sitting there looking rather pathetic. "What!!?" the masculine tiger exclaimed at the adolescent tiger. "You *live* with these people!!?? Come on! I'll show you how to be a tiger! You're a tiger! like me! Be like me!" This is the guru thing. So, the tiger took the teenager to a pond and showed him his reflection in the water as he stood be-side him. "See! You look like me. You're a tiger!" Grabbing a slab of raw meat he shoved it at the young tiger but our friend quipped "I'm a vegetarian..."

"Oh no you're not! You're going to eat meat right now! with me!! Eat!" and the tiger shoved raw water buffalo meat down his throat. This is a metaphor for indoctrinating someone into your trip. If you don't go along with it, they'll shove it down your throat for your own good, understand? Soon our fuzzy friend began to feel like a tiger for the first time in his life and he came to love his mentor, oh so very dearly — his teacher! The adult male tiger took him into the jungle saying "Come on. Let's go hunting now..." And, they all lived happily ever after.

The Nuremberg rallies were like a tiger training novices to act like real tigers. The Nazis tapped into the power of the "oversoul" as Ralph Waldo Emerson described it. It was the jealous god asura mahadevas that literally took over the "group think,"at the Nuremberg rallies. Probably Hitler, and even the legendary great, Goebbels were pawns too but they chose to invite the asuras to *come on down!* For you, this process begins with your intention. You have to intend the process; devas can't just swoop down and take over your mind. You choose to invite them, so invite good devas. This mass process can happen again so we should prevent an evil application and cultivate the mass invocation of virtuous devas. "This could happen maybe faster then we are willing to go along with it," one teacher said.

Sincerity   *Sincerity*   *Sincerity*   *Sincerity*

In order for civilization to advance upwardly after World War III in the 21st century, we must build a platform upon which these virtuous mahadevas from the Brahma realm can land into our mass human container. We are the landing pad for the devas. This is what is meant by "the mass landing of UFOs." It is mistaken thinking to presume that the future of mankind lies in science and technology. Science and technology will remain tools to be used by humanity. The future of planet Earth, our shared mythology, lies in raising windhorse via mass psychology. This can successfully result in the subduing of Muslim or pseudo Muslim expansionism and aggression. Until you wake up and get to work, your efforts along your spiritual path resemble dilettante dabbling in spiritual masturbation. There will be a war in the guise of a holy Islamic religious war, lashing out at American and European culture. When the pseudo Muslims kill entire cities full of people, "we will just be reborn, so that's no big deal." So we must harbour our resources judiciously with the belief that we shall overcome even this worst war of all. We shall continue so we must make efforts now to protect the container of the Buddhadharma in this world, for the benefit of future generations. Future generations will decide if we did the right thing or not.

Joseph Campbell said that all of us are tigers but sociologists are very quick to point out your "true" goat nature, he warned. "Go to Nuremberg." You are a great tiger when you are a warrior in that crowd, modelling your mind off of the guru, or when you are up there on stage before 84,000 goats at Nuremberg, convincing them of their tigerhood. "The master race," ideology is a perversion of this NLP technique (neurolinguistic programming). You are a tiger, now, and always. The definition of "tiger" is: bodhicitta. If you look in a Buddhist dictionary under the word "bodhicitta" you will see a picture of a tiger. Do you know what matters? Do you know where to go next week for personal spiritual guidance? Do you have someone that you can confide in about the realizations which will pulse through your mind next month? Who can help you? Who can you talk to about these inner experiences that are important to you? You're on your own. There is so much meaninglessness in what people say, think and do everyday. It is staggering how much of our physical and spiritual energies are devoted to meaningless pursuits. Listen to what is meaningful inside of you. Don't believe people who tell you to take a pill to calm down, or that you're just not good enough to make your own vision a reality. In the 19th century, Emerson wrote "There is a conspiracy of the vast majority to keep everybody down to a low level of mediocrity. If somebody decides to rise up above the crowd and do something special with their life, then there is a flurry of activity to keep them back down." So, what's the solution? Don't tell anybody your goals. Don't tell anybody. Keep your goals a secret. That way, you won't give people a chance to shoot them down. Be precise without making a scene by working with the people who will help you, and do things one step at a time. Compassion means skilful means, working with the world as it is, functioning successfully with people as they really are. You can still be an elitist but your compassion opens your territory to allow others in. This challenge supports you and your true tiger nature—your Buddha-nature, in working for others. You don't want to die out there and lose your next shot at precious human birth. Stop your equivocation and do something, anything, about taking refuge in the Buddha, dharma, sangha. Bob Dylan sang "You could die down there, be just another accident statistic (Slow Train Coming, 1979)."

You can do the Nuremberg visualization technique alone, or in groups, such as the Buddhist Spectrum Study (and Meditation) Group. When practising Nuremberg alone the author found that his arm didn't get sore until after a very long time, but if he were to just hold his arm out straight without the practice, then it would get sore in two minutes. Take the guru's advice. "Practice, practice, practice." Arouse bodhicitta, and just do this practice as it is prescribed here, and you will find that fresh, spontaneous addendum visualizations will arise out of your alaya that are completely in line with the lineage of the dharma. You'll have no problems at all. Nothing will go wrong. There's no right or wrong experience of the practice. You'll be fine. You've come home.

As with insight meditation and with other contemplations, it's important to always begin by arousing bodhicitta, the proper motivation, *to get pumped*, for the benefit of others. Have some fun! There's no problem with this. Fear based minds may feel that there is a problem with Nuremberg practice but this can be gently diffused. Remember to always have a sense of humour and a healthy suspicion for all the reasons why information should not be freely available. Don't believe in the validity of restricted practices because they are all self secret anyhow. And, certainly senior students are not one bit further ahead in their thousands of rebirths than junior students. How could a mere 40 years of dharma saturation put them ahead of your last 1000 lifetimes?

Theatre sports clubs are suitable places for Nuremberg visualization group practice and recreating the physical setting of a microcosm of the *present day* Germany city of Nuremberg. "We are not trying to recreate historical ghosts. We are doing this now, in the 20th century, with motor cars, metallurgical plants, stock exchange, harbour facilities," one of my teachers said. When you watch hours and hours of translated Nazi films of Nuremberg and other gatherings, you should later close your eyes in sitting meditation and use "the power of recollection" by remembering the living room you were in when you watched the sacred T.V. video, recollect the smell of the incense, etc. Visualize that film from the past, and look at photographs or videos of what Nuremberg looks like today. For the growing German Buddhist sangha they should flash the old upon the new to manifest for themselves a dynamic time warp practice. The locations of great war time karmic deeds can be used today for give and take practice to heal the pain inflicted at those geographic locations. This is one blessing of precious German birth.

Our purpose in this approach to our religious practice is that we believe that Nuremberg, Germany holds the key to stored up energy waiting to be drilled into like an oil geyser. It's down there and nobody is using it, so it might as well be us! It's as simple as that. When Bob Dylan believed that he was going to die in a nuclear war during the October, 1962 Cuban Missile crisis he wrote *A Hard Rain's Gonna Fall*, "I saw a highway of diamonds with nobody on it." That is the potential of Nuremberg visualization practice and the justification for you to "stir up your energy" as the Buddha suggested, and *open up your heart* to your inner life once again.

Practice Experience and History

Over the decades, in my own experience of the Nuremberg practice which began before the age of 17, I came to realize in 1977 that the central figure of the principal one is not so important; it is the ritual itself that is so much fun. The visualization brought with it imagery of the real men and women present at the Nuremberg rallies and I came to believe that many of them personally disliked Hitler, and feared Hitler, as Swiss Paul Schaub confirmed for me back at the end of the 20th century. The people who hated Hitler's guts still tended to thrill in the rally because they were there with their friends, they were part of the pageantry, and the ritual was a tidal wave of inspiration. Because I have received such vivid imagery of this since childhood, I suspect that in my most previous life I was a Nazi soldier at the Nuremberg rallies, but I do not know with any degree of certainty. I have zero knowledge of my previous lives.

My publicist, Mr. Percival Sweetwater suggested that I package my most immediate previous life as a Buddhist monk in Tibet, since we know for a fact that I was conceived in late March of 1959. We thought that such a storyline might increase this book's sales by about 1.5%. Later, we agreed to be daring and change my most immediate previous life to the Nazi soldier thing. Controversy or bad publicity is still good publicity. Hopefully this will improve my book, audiotape and video sales by 4%! Please wish me luck. It's a tough life out there on the writer/speaker circuit.

In conclusion, we can use the Nuremberg visualization practice to transform the energy of Nazi Germany and uplift that energy by bringing it onto our spiritual path. This process facilitates you in seeing and working with your dark side. By exchanging Hitler, like a hood ornament on a car, with the Buddha, your guru, yourself, or a virtuous quality of some kind, you can reverse the negative intentions that Adolf Hitler had, and use methods similar to his, combined with Buddhism to result in great heart and gallantry. We have never lost the car or the engine, we've just updated our hood ornament.

Chapter 14

Buddhism and UFOs

What is the connection between Buddhism and UFOs? The Buddha taught people to look deeply into things. He encouraged people to look deeply into things to see the causes and conditions which bring things about. This is understanding, the Buddha said. You cannot really love something unless you understand it. Does Buddhist wisdom penetrate to the interconnected nature and the causes and conditions which cause UFOs to arise in the world? The Buddha taught that all phenomena are interconnected into one whole. Therefore, UFOs are not something entirely separate and apart from us.

The UFO question was raised by Douglas Roche, Canada's former ambassador to the United Nations. In 1989 he flew to Vancouver on a speaking tour to promote his new book. I was on the Board of Directors of the United Nations Associations in Vancouver at that time, and I was assigned the privilege of driving Mr. Roche around all day, as I was the chairman of the UNA International Law Committee. We had a wonderful time together! At the end of the day I was driving him back to the airport. Our conversation was bouncing all over the place and somehow we got to talking about UFOs. I was startled when Mr. Roche asked "What are they doing up there? What are they doing?" I didn't particularly know what the UFOs were doing, so I couldn't respond. I just kept driving down Oak Street to get to the bridge to the airport. Then he continued, "Why don't they help us? There's so many problems in the world! Why don't they *do* something?!"

At that moment I was struck by the his compassion and the expansiveness of his view. My eyes left the road and I glanced at him. Having only known him for one day, I guessed that his professional concerns as Canada's ambassador to the U.N. may have been larger than my own, selling investment funds in Vancouver. I appreciated his large scale concerns. Then, for him to engage me in an immediately serious conversation about UFOs, caused me to suspect that he may have been privy to secret information about UFOs, being an ambassador. I didn't ask. I wasn't a Buddhist at that time and I responded by accepting the reality of UFOs. I suggested that the reason why they don't help us may be something like the non-interference directive in Star Trek; that it is our karma to be here, so we don't deserve help from them. He obviously accepted the existence of UFOs but he couldn't reconcile that reality with their unwillingness to help out, in our world of suffering. However, both he and I did acknowledged that although the UFOs were not helping us in any apparent way, they could be preventing nuclear war behind the scenes.

The deeper understanding which we should consider is that UFOs don't have to be limited to the idea that they must be human realm (humanoid) beings from other planets that come here. A wider view of UFOs which is in harmony with Buddhist cosmology is that some of them are devas from the god realm who have the power to manifest themselves as unidentified flying objects, when and where they choose. This was something I didn't know about when I was driving Douglas Roche around in 1989.

Buddhism teaches that human life is a workable situation. Suffering through birth, old age, sickness and death is not some cruel imposition on us. Our advantage is that we have suffering. So, we want to do something about our suffering. Suffering is a gift for the purpose of encouraging us to overcome our suffering by following the noble eightfold path to enlightenment. True words are not eloquent. Eloquent words are not true. If this was a stainless world, then where would beings go to school? This indicates why the UFOs, or deva UFOs refuse to land and help us out. It is our karma that we each deserve to have been born on this planet. We are not worthy of deserving UFOs to take care of all of our problems the way daddy and mommy look after a spoiled rich kid. No. We sink or swim together, now and always. Love one another. Work for the benefit of each other, instead of turning to the skies and hoping that the UFOs will do your work for you. Besides, a human realm existence is ideal for the spiritual path. The UFOs are just never going to land. UFOs do exist, even as people imagine them to be, but they will never, ever land or lift a finger for us. Never. Never. Never.

With the force of your individual merit, you can attain future rebirths on UFOs, other planets, here, the higher realms or even reach the deathless state of enlightenment itself. It's all up to the individual who can rise as high as his merits will take him in society and in the cosmos. That's empowerment. If people wonder why UFOs don't get directly involved with helping out human beings, then do ants wonder why human beings don't get directly involved with helping out ants and giving them drops of honey? It's not exactly like Gene Coon's idea of the prime directive in Star Trek, which is to not interfere with lower life forms (or lower realms, in the Buddhist idiom, as most humans are to devas). It's more like the natural way of mother nature and the laws of karma.

It is not appropriate for devas to appear physically so that they can serve us. It is appropriate for them to help us all they can as devas do in their own way. Buddhism teaches that billions of devas are among us and they care very much for us. It is on the basis of their compassion that we can invoke their presence and assistance. But it is natural and better for us to be in control of our own destiny so that we can be responsible for our own karma and progress on our spiritual path. That means that we are left pretty much on our own. We were born to work out our karma, however painful it is, in this world as it is. We got this life, in this world, because we deserved to get this life in this world.

UFOs are written about in the ancient Indian Hindu Vedas which predate Buddhism. One ancient King in the vedas was even lent a UFO for his own use! What is important about the Vedas is that they reveal the cosmology of devas in the god realm which the Buddha later confirmed. There are three vedas which predate Buddhism. The Buddha did refute the credibility of the authenticity of the vedas, denying that they were the words of god which should not be questioned. But the Buddha did acknowledge as true the Vedic belief in the higher realm devas.

I know a man who has recently seen several UFOs up close in Salvador, Brazil. There are other places in Brazil where they appear regularly. My friend saw one during the blackness of night from about 200 feet away. It was about the size of an apartment he said, and it really threatened the core of his rationality. Imagine how you would feel about reality after such an encounter. You grew up and lived your whole life thinking that reality is like 'this' and then you see 'that'! He said that the lights displayed on the UFO were there for purely aesthetic reasons; as if the devas were saying "Hi there! We're a UFO. Don't you like our beautiful display?" His actual experience of seeing the UFO was in fact, a sacred experience. He was reluctant to talk about it and only after a year did he reveal to me the sacred significance of the UFO sighting. He was in the presence of a great higher realm deva or devas and he felt humbled and in awe of them. Carl Jung was very interested in the psychological significance of UFOs and he felt that it was of importance that there are more UFO sightings now, with all of our tensions in the world, than ever before in history. Jung said that UFOs may be the mythology of our age.

If some UFOs are really devas, then this could explain a lot of things. For example, they did not have to come from another planet. They could be from right here, but from the god realm which is always right here, interpenetrated with our human realm. In non Buddhist terms, we can say that they come from another dimension. The dimensions, or realms in the Buddhist teachings are the god realm, jealous god realm, human realm, ghost realm, animal realm and hell realm. Human beings share the same dimension with the animals and that is the only other realm that we can see. We cannot see the happy devas in the god realm or the titans and asuras of the jealous god realm. We don't know what they're up to or how they can do the things that they do. This is what the Buddha taught.

In the book *A Farther Shore* by Dr. Yvonne Kason, she has noted the similarity between the kundalini experience and the UFO abduction experience, or close encounter. That experience includes the perception of white light, floating out of the body, pressure and pain in the head, and a burning sensation in the back and the back of the neck. Abductees often report being transported to another world and seeing alien beings. This could be a deva experience. Hostile abductions can be explained by the jealous god realm. Hindu teachings indicate that people can have a spontaneous kundalini awakening. They don't have to know about what it is, they don't have to intend to have such an experience, or do any such practices to arouse the kundalini. It can just happen. Therefore, when people are in a forest and they have some incredible experience and see a bright white light in the sky, in their confusion they may believe that they are seeing a UFO. But really they may have experienced the greater awareness which results from insight. Because they have not been taught any model for this type of experience they revert to the conventional thinking that a bright light must be caused by an external object or external phenomenon. In a way, some UFOs are not external to the human mind. But that can be a cop out because the entire universe is not external to the mind. In the 9th century B.C. the pre-Hindus had already figured out that the devas are inside of our own being, they are not purely external beings. But they do also exist outside of ourselves in a mysterious way that we do not understand.

The mechanism by which people apprehend deva UFOs may in some cases be the moving upwards of kundalini energy, or chi energy. There is evidence that this process has resulted in people reporting the sighting of a UFO. This may be because the word 'concentration' is synonymous with the word 'energy.' Some practitioners of Chi Qong, Yoga, Tai Chi, meditation, and other disciplines have succeeded in building up the concentration of their minds, which then naturally leads to results such as insight or higher powers. Profound transformational experiences such as these are also associated with UFO sightings. It is possible that people cannot generally see UFOs or devas because their minds are not concentrated to a level that crosses a threshold into that experience. Certainly the Buddha and his more attained disciples could see devas and ghosts. Once Maha Moggallana was walking along with another monk and he saw some ghosts fly by but the other monk could not see anything so he asked Moggallana what he had seen. This is an indication that it is a person's level of attainment which may allow them to see UFOs. There are other factors too, as UFOs have been seen by large groups of people of probably quite ordinary attainment, but it makes sense that some people may see UFOs while someone else with them may not.

The deva explanation for the presence of UFOs explains sightings of UFOs that go 2000 miles per hour and then instantly turn 90 degrees, and go 2000 miles per hour in another direction. The laws of physics say that the occupants inside could not live through such physical stress. But, if the UFO is a visual manifestation of the devas, then it is likely that the UFO may not be a real physical object with flesh and blood occupants inside. Devas, according to the Buddha's teaching, do have the power to create visual or auditory appearances here in our human realm, to interact with us. What motives the deva UFOs have, we can only guess. Surely they have their own projects going on, no doubt. Who knows what? There were plenty of examples abounding during the Buddha's ministry of devas manifesting in visible form to humans. Shortly after the Buddha's great awakening, a Brahma deva popped up out of nowhere and supplicated the Buddha to teach the dharma to human beings. Then the deva promptly vanished into thin air again. The Buddha was popular. Often devas would visit the Buddha at night and illuminate the whole grove where the Buddha was staying.

A Deva UFO Incident?

There are plenty of examples in our day of UFOs manifesting in a manner characteristic of the deva UFO theory. One such example, to relate this to something that has been well documented at the highest levels of government, is the multiple UFO sightings witnessed by thousands of panicked Los Angeles residents on Feb. 25, 1942.* This incredible incident began when radar picked up unidentified targets 120 miles out to sea at 2:25 am. Air raid sirens sounded over L.A. and the city blacked out at 3:16 am to 4:14 am. Anti-aircraft artillery (AAA) batteries began firing at the "unidentified aircraft" coming in over the ocean, as searchlight beams pursued them through the sky. 1430 rounds of 12.8 lb. shells were fired! Witnesses saw red or silver in colour, small objects which seemed luminous to ground observers. At one point they remained stationary for some time. They moved inland and were caught in searchlights over Culver City where one was photographed. Witness Paul T. Collins said the smaller UFOs were consistently "appearing from nowhere and then zigzagging from side to side. Some disappeared, not diminishing in brilliance or fading away gradually but just vanishing instantaneously into the night." Other witnesses recalled a formation of "six to nine luminous, white dots in formation." The UFOs seemed unaware of the stampede they were causing below. Many buildings were destroyed by the shell debris.

White House Chief of Staff General George C. Marshall gave a secret memorandum on Feb. 26, 1942 to U.S. President Franklin D. Roosevelt, describing the above, and the most violent reaction on record to a UFO sighting. This incident has all the hallmarks of a genuinely anomalous event, yet the next day, Secretary of the Navy Frank Knox, in Washington D.C., stated publicly that no planes had been over the city. He attributed the firing of the shells to "war nerves" and a false alarm, but within hours the U.S. government was relating to this incident as "secret."

I believe that this suggests the possibility of deva UFOs as they were travelling at very high speeds and zig zagging over the night sky in Los Angeles. The city was in pandemonium as over 1000 anti-aircraft shells were fired at them. Only three months after Pearl Harbour, the Americans did not launch their own planes, which indicates that they realized that what they were shooting at was beyond anything the Japanese could do. Thousands of eye witnesses saw countless UFOs at speeds of up to 18,000 mph, zig zagging, stopping, going on at a leisurely pace, seemingly oblivious to the panic they were causing below. Three people died of heart attacks because of all the panic in Los Angeles. The UFOs seemed to come from nowhere, carried on for over an hour, then disappeared to nowhere. They caused no damage. They could have been devas.

This incredible incident has been well documented at the highest levels of government but it is not generally known because the U.S. government deliberately down played it. This was the first time that the American government publicly admitted getting involved with investigating a UFO sighting. A report was given to President Roosevelt by the Secretary of Defense. Within weeks the U.S. government publicly claimed that the incident was caused by war jitters, and they discounted the direct experience of thousands of sane residents in Los Angeles. I believe beyond doubt that this was a manifestation of the higher realms. I do not believe that these objects were space ships from another planet.

Cosmology

Buddhist cosmology explains that each individual solar system, or "world system" as the Buddha put it, has its own higher realms. That is, a god realm with the fine material sphere of the Brahma realm, etc. I don't understand what the relationship is between solar systems, with vast powerful devas such as Brahma. Brahma is the most powerful deva in the whole cosmos so he is not limited to our tiny solar system. What is important here is the idea that each solar system, or certainly each galaxy is kind of self contained. The Theravadin Buddhist teacher, S. Goenka said that the extent of one Buddha's influence is limited to the one galaxy he is in.

This completeness of each region in space reduces the need for humanoids on other planets to build spacecraft to travel across our galaxy to visit our planet Earth. This adds more evidence, admittedly low grade evidence, that UFOs are more likely from each solar system's local god realm. This makes much more sense from a Buddhist perspective than the idea that UFOs come all the way from other planets, light years away, just to hide out here in orbit.

If we completely ignore devas then we can see the motivation to travel into space and explore the galaxy. But, with an understanding of the devaloka, you realize that it is not so interesting to travel to other planets. Because, the devaloka high ground is more interesting and higher than mere humanoids building spaceships and travelling between planets. Also, if you become a deva you can naturally soar across outer space to investigate other planets. Why put yourself in a physical body and into a can and travel light years across cold space when the devas can do that naturally? The devas are higher than the human realm, no matter what planet the humanoids are on, and we can assume that the devas are presently living right in our homes or nearby, and in the trees outside of the window. The Buddha taught that there are earth bound devas that live in the trees, and on the earth.

It behoves us to develop a conscious relationship with the devas before we spend billions of dollars travelling to other planets. Everything is here, within the reach of our own consciousness if we practice meditation.

A former Secretary General of the United Nations saw a UFO at very close range for an extended period of time in New York City when his limousine was deliberately disabled for the purpose of him seeing this UFO. This has been documented.

The deva UFOs and deva aliens can explain how many people claim to have been abducted by aliens or visited by such beings. The Buddha taught that the asuras of the jealous god realm are paranoid devas of a more demonic nature. Still powerful and of high attainment in mind (like Darth Vader) they could manifest as hostile UFOs and aliens that do experiments on people. But the happy devas interrelate with the asura devas so there exists the probability of heavenly protection against bad devas and cosmic battles going on in the upstairs. The deva Sakkha from Tavatimsa heaven described this very thing to the Buddha. Sakkha said that when they have wars with the asuras (the jealous gods), they drink asura nectar.

Since the devas are invisible and have been around us for billions of years, since primordial time, such appearances may simply be devas that have manifested themselves in a form visible to human beings, or to some human beings. That's more believable and practical in a sense, than believing that these aliens actually travelled all the way from other planets to hide out here or in orbit without showing themselves. These UFO alien devas are very much at home and comfortable in their natural devaloka, thank you very much. They just "come down" from time to time for whatever purpose they have, we don't know. This is believable. This is one Buddhist view of UFOs.

We must expand our concepts and views of UFOs and consider the possibility that UFOs can come from more than one general source. There could possibly be physical aliens from other planets but some Buddhist's believe there certainly are deva UFOs and deva aliens manifesting in physical form above Earth via visual and auditory appearances.

*UFO incident taken from the book "U.F.O. The Government Files" by Peter Brookesmith, Published by Brown Books 255-257 Liverpool St., London, England N11LX.

Chapter 15

Beyond Grouse Mountain

A Serial Story

The purpose of this chapter is to create a vehicle with which to teach the Buddhadharma to people who are not interested in reading books about Buddhism. The vision is that this should be drawn out into a comic strip as a serial story. This first episode is entitled 'Beyond Grouse Mountain.' And the name of the whole series will also be 'Beyond Grouse Mountain.' The goal is to have a successfully syndicated Buddhist comic strip that can compete for attention with the many non dharmic or antidharmic comic strips in the world. This is to help spread Buddhism and uplevel comic book readers to put down the comic books and reach upwards towards the meditation cushion. It is necessary to create an exciting story to sustain people's attention.

This serial is about a Buddhist monk meditating in a cave beyond Grouse mountain. His name is Behinda-dharma, inspired by the name of Swami Beyond-ananda, the humorist in syndication. 'Rinpoche' is a Tibetan Buddhist title meaning 'precious one', reserved for high teachers. Hopefully our protagonist will deserve the title Rinpoche in future episodes. It is used sparingly at first, and for now, his name is long enough anyway. Behinda-dharma is befriended by an 8 foot tall sasquatch named 'Bigfeet.' Bigfeet came straight out of the Kingdom of Shambhala on a UFO and first graced the surface of the Earth on a mountaintop deep in the mysterious land north of Tibet. Later, Bigfeet travelled on a UFO to the remote isolated valleys behind Grouse mountain, North Vancouver, British Columbia, Canada, on this planet of Shambhala (that's another fanciful future episode — for now, planet Earth). Some of the local B.C. sasquatches say that Bigfeet is a Chinese Yeti. Others say that he's from Mongolia. The truth is that he's not from Russia. Using their telepathic communication, Bigfeet would constantly encourage Behinda-dharma to "Think Big! Think Big!" Behinda-dharma would reply, "Yes Bigfeet. Let's think big. Think big!"

After 40 days meditating in the wilderness, Behinda-dharma attains the insight that his knees hurt, so he returns home to the shores of Georgia Strait. His sasquatch buddy, Bigfeet understands and prepares to warm up the UFO to fly his stricken master home. Behinda-dharma stops Bigfeet and says "No Bigfeet. I must walk home. Alone..." With a deep dramatic musical score in the background, Rinpoche turns and walks away. Resolute, he climbs over the north slope of Grouse Mountain and our hero sees the streets of home below. Mara (the devil, the evil one in Buddhist cosmology) appears before him and tempts him to jump off of the cliff and into the deserted valley below. Behinda-dharma refuses to put his newly acquired magical powers to the test, so he rebukes Mara by saying "Take off, eh!"

Through the day and through the night he makes his way down to Burrard Inlet to greet the great eastern sun. People gather around him because of their religious fascination for him and his monk's robes. So because of that "Behind" disrobes and he puts on a two piece suit. He starts to grow his hair back and he teaches a course on "Mountain Meditation" at the local YMCA. Later he switches to the YWCA because it's a better way to meet women. He becomes a success all over the city! He teaches his students to visualize Grouse Mountain and what is beyond Grouse Mountain. He says to them during his instructions and transmission while they are in deep meditation, "First there is a mountain. Then... there is no mountain. Then... there is." As they all sit in deep silent meditation together, suddenly Grouse Mountain vanishes before 1.8 million people in the lower mainland area of Vancouver! We can see Bigfeet sitting way back there in the mountain valley, sitting in a half lotus position. Bigfeet nods to the audience. When Grouse Mountain returns a few seconds later, our comic book hero, the masked monk says "Huh. That's nothing. You should see what we can do after we put on our robes." To be continued...

Our newly created comic book hero is "The Masked Monk." He's dressed like an ordinary man, to mask the truth that he's really a monk, but on only six precepts! (1). He's a gullible heart, stumbling into creating enlightened society. Some of the comic strip mythology is below.

Part 2 – Mythology

One theme in this comic strip is that Bigfeet is really the fully enlightened guru. Bigfeet is a bona fide Bodhisattva, an arahant! But Behinda-dharma thinks that he himself is the BFD of a BFG— a big f'ing deal of a big famous guru. Behinda-dharma is a fool and a dharma bum who was very very lucky to stumble onto Bigfeet during his lost wanderings in the mountains of British Columbia. This is the story about how they met.

Behind takes the Maverick bus to Whistler, B.C. to snowboard down the longest vertical drop in North America. His monk's ego swells with pride and he wants to be famous so that he can really do something big and wonderful for the world. He's intrigued about how Ross Rebagliati from Whistler attained global fame for winning the gold medal for snowboarding at the 1998 Winter Olympics in Japan. Although Behinda-dharma has no such snowboarding illusions for himself, he still wants to snowboard down to feel the vicarious pleasure of Ross' fame. At that time he knew that Ross was training on Whistler mountain for upcoming competitions so he was scanning the many snowboarders flying past him to see if he could sense the presence of Ross. After his thrills, Behinda-dharma takes the gondola to the top of Whistler mountain one last time and disembarks into the savage wilderness following only a deep inner sense that his answer lies amongst the snow clad mountain peaks of the Coast and Tantalus Range. Behinda-dharma meditates in the snow and in a mountain cave until he attains such a deep samadhi meditation absorption that his body stays warm. He lies down in samadhi surrounded by his ultra puffed up down sleeping bag.

Behind's quest for insight leads him into the breathtaking scenery of Black Tusk and Garibaldi Lake. He mixes his mind with the deep turquoise blue water and his powers of concentration are directed at Helm glacier in an attempt to cause vast walls of ice to cascade and crash down into Garibaldi Lake. He receives the vivid perception, or imagery of Black Tusk as a crystal palace intricately constructed from terma tubes (terma is dharma teachings embedded into rocks and crystals), muni gems, diamonds and many colours of precious stones. Living as an ascetic practitioner, eating only wild blueberries that fall from the bushes onto the ground, and wild roots, Behinda-dharma gets thinner and thinner until he arrives in the lush valleys behind Grouse mountain in North Vancouver. Just as he renounces his practices of asceticism and resolves to get himself some decent grub, Behinda-dharma faints from weakness and collapses onto a pile of unforgiving rocks. Some incredibly gorgeous babes had just hiked right past him which caused him to be weak at the knees. It also challenged his monk's precepts to abstain from any sexual behaviour. It is summertime and the tube tops are out in full force on the hiking trails. The temperature is a balmy 25 degrees. The Whisky Jacks fly down from their snipers' perch and intercept bread from the sandwiches of unaware hikers. Black Bears munch their way through endless bushes of blackberries along the bubbling rivers in this near deserted valley just miles from two million people. The moonless nights recede into the peaceful lazy days of summer. The direct experience of the fragrant ecstasy coming from the mountain flowers cannot be given justice on the plain white pages of this book in your hands right now.

Unconscious on the cold wet rocks, Behind is saved by someone with some decent Chinese food. For the first time Behinda-dharma and Bigfeet meet! Bigfeet props up Behinda-dharma's head and pours Chinese tea into him plus some sweet milk. Regaining consciousness, Behind mindfully eats the Chinese food before he realizes that a stinky eight foot sasquatch is standing over him. The first thing Behind is conscious enough to say is "An hour later, I'm gonna want to eat more, you know."—"Eat my friend. You will be alright now," the sasquatch spoke to him softly. Behind lost his mindfulness and ate quickly and nervously as his attention darted around. But when Bigfeet ate, he ate. When Bigfeet walked, he walked. When Bigfeet slept, he slept. And when Bigfeet sat, he sat. Behinda-dharma was impressed with Bigfeet's noble bearing and mindful countenance.

Behinda-dharma was stupidly searching for inspiration in the mountains and somehow, he found it! Behinda-dharma never fully realizes how fortunate he was to discover and have Bigfeet as his teacher, because of his big ego. Whenever Bigfeet gives him sage advice, Behinda-dharma returns to the city of Vancouver, and teaches it to the people there, taking full credit for the teachings as if they were entirely his own brilliant insights and wisdom. In this way, the comic strip builds up the mystique around the sasquatch character, Bigfeet. Since Bigfeet came from a deva UFO from north of Tibet, this already enhances his mystique beyond the beyond.

Behinda-dharma begins as a character that is a bumbling fool. But, modelling the example of Luke Skywalker in Star Wars, Behinda-dharma grows into his seat as a kite for the dharma, and as a spiritual leader, and he eventually confesses full credit to Bigfeet. Later, he attains full and complete enlightenment in a future episode, a very future episode. After that, 'Beyond Grouse Mountain' continues with both Behinda-dharma and Bigfeet existing and manifesting in the contemporary world as fully enlightened arahants/Bodhisattvas. They focus their teaching activities on audio/video and 3-D holographic videos in their mountain retreat studio in Outer Mongolia, and across the boarder in Russia. Bigfeet discloses to Behinda-dharma only, where he is really from—the Kingdom of Shambhala. Bigfeet and Behinda-dharma never, ever reveal to others where Bigfeet is really from. It must always be kept as a maha secret to protect Bigfeet from his one and only Achilles' heel: ignorite.

Bigfeet is almost always only seen, heard and met by Behinda-dharma, alone. This builds up the importance of Behinda-dharma and adds more mystique to the comic strip generally. Usually, Behind has to go down into the valley behind Grouse mountain to be able to meet with Bigfeet in person. Only rarely does Bigfeet manifest himself on the streets of Vancouver to impart his sage advice to our comic book hero. At one point Behind asked him where he learned such excellent English but he couldn't understand the answer that Bigfeet was trying to give him.

Character Development Scenes

To be inserted into future episodes of the *Beyond Grouse Mountain* comic strip series.

1. During the Masked Monks' 40 day retreat in the mountains and valleys behind and beyond Grouse Mountain, Bigfeet, the friendly sasquatch, asks him "So, where are you from master?"—"I'm from Aurora, Illinois."—"You mean Wayne's World?! The Aurora Illinois? The one near Chicago?" Bigfeet asked. "Yep. That's the place. I knew Wayne."—"You've met Wayne!?"—"Sure. He was just a small time operator back then," the unmasked monk replied, "but now he's Austin Powers! I liked the first movie better than *The Spy Who Shagged Me.*"

2. Rinpoche asks Bigfeet "So, where are you from Bigfeet?"—"Well, I can tell you, but the author of this comic strip decided to leave that as a continuous mystery to other characters in this 'Beyond Grouse Mountain' series, you see. I really come from the Kingdom of Shambhala and I came straight out of Shambhala on a deva UFO, as I am also a deva."

    "Wow! A deva, eh?! And are you saying that you're self aware as a cartoon character? By that I mean, are you saying that in this comic strip we, as characters are self aware and that we know that we are just in some obscure comic strip? That is, can we as characters openly acknowledge that we were created inside the container of a comic strip and that we're not truly existent? Is it legal for us to even discuss such things?" Rinpoche asked. "Sure. We're all self aware, beyond Grouse mountain," responded the sasquatch. "Hey! Who's the guru here? Me or you?" Rinpoche asked sternly. Bigfeet just smiled as blankly as a sheet of snow white paper.

3. "I'm confused about this 50 foot UFO of yours, tucked under the trees here. Where does it come from, Bigfeet?" Behinda-dharma asked. "I always assumed that UFOs were made by humanoids on other planets who flew over here to visit the Earth. By humanoids, I mean humanoid members of the human realm in the most general terms. But now, Bigfeet, for some mysterious reason, unbeknownst to me, I get the feeling that your UFO was not made by humanoid hands! I don't know where your UFO comes from. I don't have

any idea in fact!"

"Yes . . ." Bigfeet nodded imperceptibly. "It comes from the devaloka. This is a deva made UFO," he said, glancing into the trees where the big brown cigar shaped craft was parked. It had something like Christmas lights on the outside that were there for purely aesthetic reasons. "Would you like to take it for a spin?" "What!?" Rinpoche asked. "Is such a thing possible!?"— "Well sure. In the ancient Indian Vedas a king was lent the use of a UFO, and it sure made his day! Don't you read the vedas Behinda-dharma? What kind of a big famous spiritual teacher are you?" Bigfeet asked, holding the upper hand. "Hey! Who's the guru around here? Me or you? Huh?!" Behinda-dharma challenged! Bigfeet only smiled.

They are sitting on a rock under a few Douglas Fir trees right at the top of the downhill skiing run at Grouse Mountain. It is summertime and many tourists take the Gondola to the top and some are sitting just a few hundred feet away in the shrubs. Behinda-dharma is worried that people will flip out if they see the sasquatch. "They're busy watching the paragliders take off," Bigfeet remarked. "They won't see me as long as we stay in the shade here." The view of the Pacific Ocean and the coastline extends into Washington state. The orange glow of the hazy sky reflects off the Gulf Islands and the reflection from a B.C. Ferry can be seen on the lazy waters of Georgia Straight. It is so beautiful to be on top of this mountain! Squirrels and chipmunks climb up their legs and sit on their knees. They had nothing to hand feed them, but the sasquatch always has a magnetic affect on small furry animals. Later, after our monk friend calms down from their earlier exchange, Bigfeet explains, "We need human beings to transmit the dharma in the human realm. There is no better way. We can't rely on devas channelling through to people everyday. We need human beings, people like you my dear friend."

"You and I have met up, and we both share the same goal," Behinda-dharma said, staring at him, wondering what Bigfeet would announce next. Filling in the continuing silence Behinda-dharma adds "I decided eight years ago that the major definite purpose of my life is to help spread Buddhism in the West. The question is, how do we go about doing that?" Bigfeet was prepared with plenty of suggestions and the names of others who would help.

4. "Do you have something to do with the CIA?" Rinpoche insightfully asked the sasquatch. "Hey, I'm just a sasquatch, living up in the mountains," Bigfeet defended. "Just a sasquatch!?" Rinpoche retorted. "There's no such thing as 'just a sasquatch!' You guys haven't even been officially discovered yet! And what about that UFO? Answer my question please!" Rinpoche demanded.

"Yeah, O.K. You're on to me, aren't you? How did you know to ask if I was working for the CIA?"—"Working for the CIA are you? Do they give you a pay cheque in US dollars?" Rinpoche asked rhetorically. "The reason why I asked is that we know from the freedom of information act, a few things about the CIA. The Central Intelligence Agency was formed in 1947 under President Harry Truman. Documents recently made public reveal that in the early 1950's the CIA initiated proposals to develop psychic spies, astral agents and all kinds of things like that. This resulted in the Remote Viewing operations which have been successful. I know that the CIA thinks on a totally different level and on much higher levels than the average American John Q. Public does. It wouldn't surprise me if they pursued their projects and scored some more successes in the past four decades. It would take an awful lot to surprise me now. Now that I've met you I wouldn't doubt that the CIA has been successful in infiltrating their influence into the world of UFOs and even sasquatches like yourself. There's no telling what the CIA has accomplished. Nothing could surprise me now, now that I've taken a spin in your UFO, that is."—"Ah...you're in for some big surprises yet my friend. Big surprises," Bigfeet subtly smiled.

5. "I came straight out of the Kingdom of Shambhala on a UFO and first graced the surface of the Earth high on a mountaintop deep in the mysterious land north of Tibet," Bigfeet told Behinda-dharma.

6. You. It's your turn to write or draw an episode. Contact the Buddhist Spectrum Study Group.

1.Precepts are intentions to follow moral correctness. The five basic precepts are, do not kill, do not take what is not offered, do not speak falsehoods, do not engage in sexual misconduct, and do not take alcohol or intoxicants that cloud the consciousness. The sixth precept for Behinda-dharma is, do not claim to have attained higher human states which you don't have.

Ayuthaya – Wat Phra Sri Samphet

Chapter 16

Rescuing Jesus
from the Christians

"Look deeply into things," the Buddha told Ananda many times. "It is not
enough to have a superficial understanding, you must look deeply into
things," the Buddha taught. With these guiding words I began a very long
process over many years, of uncovering religious history. Naturally for me, I studied
the history of the Buddhist and Christian religions to see how similar they really
were, as so many people kept telling me. I was compelled to read *Living Buddha
Living Christ* by Thich Nhat Hanh. He is one of my most beloved Buddhists in the
world and the #1 favourite book of my life is his *Old Path White Clouds – Following
in the Footsteps of the Buddha*. Having covered myself with that, I now write that I
disagree with Thich Nhat Hanh's views about Jesus so this essay is a rebuttal to
that. In one sentence, what he is saying about the Christian religion is "Everything
is beautiful and wonderful, so let's all hold hands." All writers have bad days, so I
forgive Thich Nhat Hanh. I feel that he has unleashed confusion upon the world
by trying to bring these two great religions together, and he over emphasizes their
similarities. What suffering that causes people who want to know the truth, who
want to discern the differences so that they can better decide if they want to be
Christians or Buddhists. I say *Living Buddha Absorb Christ*. I gave a lecture about

this subject at the International Buddhist Society temple in Richmond, B.C. and one of the regulars at my Wednesday afternoon class was a Christian lady and she jumped right up and moved to the front near me. She even showed me a copy of *Living Buddha Living Christ,* but I was almost as blunt with her as I am in this essay. After the talk she looked like she had nothing left to hold onto, but she kept coming back for more. This essay leaves Christians with nothing to hold onto, except for the historical Jesus himself — the real thing.

A shorter version of this essay was published in Vancouver's *Shared Vision* magazine. Joseph Duggan, the editor, met me at Capers restaurant in Kitsilano and I asked him about the above title which he had created. I suggested the titles "Buddha and Jesus — How Their Teachings Were Passed Down," or "Rescuing the Historical Truth," something like that. Joseph even came up with "Give Jesus to the Buddhists," which gave me a hoot. He settled on the "Rescuing Jesus" bit which I agree is the most potent. Joseph's dramatic line sold important advertising space, so I include it in this edition. In B.C., large gatherings of native Indians in sweat lodges were quoting from that article, maybe because of how their religion was persecuted by the Christians, up until recently. I personally prophecized before the October 1998 issue of *Shared Vision* was published, that the reaction that would come from my article would not be much, just a few calls. My wise prophecy did in fact come to pass and manifest as a reality upon this earth. The guiding reason for this is Norman Lear. When he created the Archie Bunker TV character in *All in the Family,* CBS manned the phones expecting an outcry but almost nothing happened. Furthermore, Canadians are a docile people. You can say, do, think, or print *anything*, and *nothing* will happen. Nothing. Contemplate this deeply and your career can benefit immensely.

How were the teachings of the Buddha and Jesus passed down to the present day? Can we assume that both were transmitted by a similar process? Investigation of this subject is one of the most fascinating and important studies in the world. In recent years so much new information, or newly released information, has been uncovered about the historical Jesus. This essay is intended as a discussion paper, rather than as an authoritative statement on history. Forgive me if my information later proves to be inaccurate. I am inviting the written evidence and written views put forth by others (some are incorporated into this version) to better clarify my own view of Jesus and the history of the Christian religion. Some of the evidence for this is admittedly B-grade because we don't know everything. Some historic records are spotty and some other things have been deliberately kept secret, such as the Dead Sea scrolls. As long as the Dead Sea scrolls are kept secret, then this gives critics of the religions involved free licence to spin doctor appropriate suspicion at them. The virtuous karma here is to create a strong, deliberate and sustained effort to force the truth out of the jailers of the Dead Sea scrolls. These scrolls are like kryptonite to the

Christian religion, maybe Judaism as well. The sooner the truth is revealed, the more human lives will be saved. More than 50 years has been a deadly long wait already. Overcoming ignorance generally, saves lives over time in the karmic big picture.

Now is the time to seize the day. If you plant big influential seeds for the benefit of others, they can blossom and fruit when and where you want them to blossom and fruit. When I first wrote the Jesus Manifesto in February 1998, I felt the ground shake and I immediately interpreted that signal to be a deva blessing which indicates that immeasurable merit can be earned if we stop being too polite and too self conscious. The ground didn't truly shake, as my neighbours did not comment upon it, but my perception had bona fide meaning. The time for truth is now, or a later now, or right now. The truth is that the Christian religion is basically a bad thing. It's a bad thing that never should have happened, a tragedy for this world that could have been avoided! Anything good about the Christians and their religion are good things which have naturally encrusted on an original framework which remains basically bad. Like barnacles growing on the holes punched into the side of the Titanic by an iceberg, the holes are basically bad — they sank the expensive majestic ship, and killed 1500 people — that's real bad! Similarly, the barnacles are like the good that has grown onto the religion and this deep and wonderful good is now inseparable from the basically bad religion. The Christian religion is this big monstrous infrastructure in society which was built to claw people's lives into its clutches and eat the resources of society. Truth is now honest. Honesty and speaking the whole truth is a vibrational healing experience. Your voice resonates clearly when you contemplate, really contemplate the sunshine of Jesus coming up through the black rags of religion to the surface of the 21st century. Heaving a sigh of religious relief, you breathe in the blackness covering the historical Jesus and you breathe out whiteness and a jewel staircase extending down to Jesus in the form of pure white light and goodness streaming out of your nostrils to him. The black tar transforms in your heart and Jesus springs up and into your soul. Jesus has never been lost to us. Jesus has finally come home. Like the Adventures of Odysseus, everything is now put right between you and the Christian religion. With the upper hand of the moral high ground, you renegotiate the constitution of your local Christian church. Buddhism has already met the West in the 20th century, but this is Buddhism absorbing the West in the 21st century. Below are shades of Shakespeare's Marc Anthony, and T.S. Elliot, indicting the entire Christian religion.

> I have not come to praise the church but to bury it.
> I have come to support Jesus, not to bury him.
> This is the way the world ends
> This is the way the world ends
> This is the way the world ends
> Not with a bang but a whimper

Buddha and Jesus — How Their Teachings Were Passed Down

The Buddha's teachings were passed down to us in a completely different way than Christ's. The Buddha was born about 617 years before Jesus in a more technologically primitive culture. During the Buddha's ministry he personally oversaw the process of constructing his monasteries and he taught for 45 years until the age of 80. The Buddha was loved by the political powers of his day. India was a feudal society and the Buddha walked amongst about ten different Kingdoms. There was no monolithic power like the Roman Empire to persecute him and his new way of awakening. In fact, the kings would vie for the Buddha's affections and you can imagine them saying "Oh please! Spend the rainy season retreat in our kingdom. We will give you a new monastery and much support if you could just bless us with your presence noble Buddha."

The Buddha trained his monks and nuns to chant to memorize his important discourses. His faithful attendant Ananda had a memory like a human tape recorder, so this helped transmit the teachings. The monks would get together, as Buddhist monks still do today, and chant the Buddha's discourses and the rules for the monks, on a regular basis. This way, if one forgets a few lines, the rest will remember. New nuns and monks coming on board listen to the chants until they have them perfectly memorized. This system is still used today, even by other religions. In Islam, if a student wants to get admitted to university in Cairo, Egypt, he has to go before a board and recite the entire Koran from memory, before being accepted. It takes days, and they use the same technique of chanting. So, this is sufficient proof for the believability that over 3000 pages of the Buddha's teachings have been accurately passed down to us through the practise of chanting. This effectively utilizes the right and left hemispheres of the brain. The chant is the musical part associated with the right hemisphere and the words connect with the left hemisphere. Using the words and the rhythmic pulse of the chant's steady beat, together they form what Dr. Georgi Lazonoff called 'whole brain learning.' This is the superlearning process uncovered by Dr. Lazonoff behind the iron curtain in Bulgaria during the 1950's and 60's. The Buddha in his wisdom understood all of this and applied whole brain learning techniques to preserve his teachings for the benefit of future generations.

It is hard for us to imagine how big a task it was to record the Buddhist scriptures. In the Buddha's time they were unable to keep written records, as the writing materials would not last more than six months. It was completely impractical to write, so everything had to be memorized. Also, they felt that it was better to memorize. It was considered higher, more pure, than reading without knowing by heart. After the Buddha's parinirvana, the de facto leader of the sangha was Maha Kassapa. Maha Kassapa presided over the first council of 500 enlightened arahants. They met for seven months for the purpose of consolidating what the Buddha taught. At the end they agreed upon what is today the Theravadin scriptures of the sutras and the vinaya. This is the 84,000 lines of the Buddha's discourses and the precepts for monks and nuns. These scriptures have been passed down in an uninterrupted lineage to the present day. We can be confident that we have all of the Buddha's teachings. If some lines were changed around or lost, then it doesn't matter much. If the Buddha had something important to say, like the four noble truths, or non self, then he said it dozens of times in different ways. We can be sure we have every important aspect of what the Buddha wanted us to know.

Many people have a mistaken view of the fact that the Buddha's teachings were first written down 400 years after the life of the Buddha. This occurred around 100 B.C. in Sri Lanka because the elders at Great Monastery felt insecure. This was the most important monastery in Sri Lanka and favoured by the King, but then the King's royal favour switched to another Buddhist monastery. There was also the danger of a famine and some of the sutras were memorized by only one monk, or by just a few monks. In order to prevent the tragic loss of the Buddha's wisdom, to preserve the teachings they decided to write them down secretly, without the king's knowledge. Great Monastery sent monks out to the countryside, and it was there that they began the long process of writing the scriptures down on palm leaves, in the Pali language. No one is certain today if Pali was the language used by the Buddha, as Theravadins like to believe, or if it was a language that came later in those 400 years after the Buddha. It is the oldest language in Buddhism. No matter how old Sanskrit is, Buddhists started to use Sanskrit after first employing Pali.

The first writing of the sutras did not change Buddhist tradition. The teachings continued to be memorized and passed down to the present day. There are monks alive today who have memorized the entire Theravadin Canon. The most important point to understand is that during the Buddha's lifetime and beyond, the scriptures were recorded with excellent craftsmanship, perseverance and precision. It makes little difference whether they were written down one year, 400 years or 2000 years after the Buddha's time. The transmission is authentic. That's what matters. Because of the loosey-goosey nature of how the Bible was put together, some people project onto Buddhism the crazy idea that the Buddha's teachings were passed down by people sitting around camp fires telling stories about the good old days when the Buddha lived in India. Nothing could be further from the truth. Buddha created a huge institution in society that used its wherewithal to protect the holy dharma. Another false projection many Westerners made when they first discovered Buddhism is to assume that Buddhist traditions have fought with each other as much as Christians have fought amongst themselves for centuries. There has been some fighting and violence, but not to the degree of the epic proportions in which Christian blood has been spilled from oppression by other Christians.

Jesus Christ

The transmission of the teachings of Jesus Christ was very much the opposite of what the Buddha initiated. There were scribes during Christ's time and yet Jesus did not organize a systematic method of recording and preserving his teachings, as the Buddha went to great pains to do. Some of Christ's teachings may have been written down during his lifetime, but these were likely written by his wandering followers who wrote down some phrases for themselves to remember during their travels (Charlotte Allen, 1996). Probably Jesus did not have a project to found "some big religion that would last for 2000 years," but the Buddha clearly did have such a project. The task of taking the trouble to record Christ's teachings was not a thorough consistent undertaking. Jesus and his followers were being persecuted by the Romans so they could never settle down in one place. They were on the run and not favoured by the political powers of the day, as the Buddha was. Christ's impact on society was much smaller than that of the Buddha. The Buddha was a superhuman pop idol as far as civilization extended in northeastern India. Everyone knew about the Buddha and he was almost universally loved, except by jealous religious sects. Historians of the day, and the contemporary Jain religion all had to comment upon what the Buddha had unleashed upon the world.

Jesus had some popularity, but not anywhere near as big as the Buddha. In Rome, at the centre of the empire, there was not even any record of the existence of a Jesus. Maybe there was some knowledge, but Christ's impact was so small that they didn't take the trouble to leave us some records that we could find! It wasn't until about 60 A.D. that we have our first record of the Roman Empire even being aware of the Jesus movement. The notation was about a paragraph long, acknowledging their existence. Parallel to this, a few decades after the parinirvana of the Buddha, his teachings and thousands and thousands of enlightened monks and nuns were fanning out over even more of Indian territory than the Buddha had walked. Not even one of Christ's disciples ever attained to complete enlightenment. The Buddha was a noble and he attracted many nobles and high calibre people as his senior disciples. Jesus first acquired fishermen as his disciples and he may have had to settle for ordinary working class men because he couldn't attract the best people. Perhaps it was all Jesus could do just to get twelve apostles together.

Jesus After High School

I believe that Jesus really did exist. Some university professors of comparative religion have some doubts even about that. I believe in the existence of Jesus, the Galilean wise man. I had a friend from the Anglican Church that took a course in comparative religion at the University of Calgary and all her church friends tried to talk her out of it because they teach you things that you would never hear on Sundays if you went to church for 50 years. It seems that Jesus Christ was one of a hundred prominent teachers of his day. They were charismatic and attracted a large following. From a Buddhist view it is entirely possible that Jesus did have some of the magical powers reported of him. Many gurus of high attainment have done such things. One theory is that as a Jew, Jesus studied the Kabala which is Jewish mysticism. Such magical powers are taught in the Kabala but practitioners are not supposed to show them off and demonstrate them to the uninitiated (although this restriction did not become policy until many centuries after Jesus). Perhaps Jesus was a very pious Essene Jew and greatly gifted at mastering his own tradition. He went out, impressed people with his incredible attainments, and made it big. People made such a big deal out of him that he became the new religion. The rest is history.

What's acceptable about this theory is that it does not require Buddhism and it does not require Jesus travelling east to India or Afghanistan to learn his trade. The other theory, quite common amongst Western Buddhists, it that Jesus was one of us, of course! In the Bible we know almost nothing about Christ's life until he was the son of god at age 30. Prior to that there is one story of his virgin birth and a story of him visiting a synagogue in his childhood, at about age 12. We know nothing, officially about his early influences. We do know that Buddhism had penetrated Jesus' homeland before his birth. King Asoka sent Buddhist emissaries to Egypt and the middle east about 250 B.C. Buddhism just never caught on. It is doubtful if there is any evidence for the suggestion that the very first monastic situation in the West was a Buddhist monastery in Alexandria, Egypt. The theory is that Jesus learned monasticism from this influence. New Testament scholars describe the historical Jesus as being like a wandering monk. He taught his disciples not to take food or money with them, but to rely solely on the generosity of others. One Roman writer described the followers of Jesus as a rare bunch because they had no women, only the palm trees for company. These historic records describe people that are similar to Buddhist monks.

The common Buddhist theory is that Jesus went east and studied under great Buddhist gurus which we know were alive at that time. From 100 B.C. to 100 A.D. Mahayana Buddhism was flourishing big time just 800 miles or more east of Jesus, in Afghanistan. And the big altruistic message of Mahayana, the northern school of Buddhism, is compassion. What did Christ teach? Compassion. Very similar influence. Jesus could easily have travelled east, even to India, got enlightened, and headed home to uplift his own countrymen. Another common theory amongst Buddhists is that Jesus went to Tibet, but that theory is refuted because

Buddhism didn't even exist in Tibet! Buddhism first entered Tibet around 600 A.D.

The Jews Did Not Crucify Jesus

At age 33, Jesus was no more, gone from the persecution of the Romans. It is commonly held that the Jews persecuted and crucified Jesus. This belief is fine except for one thing — the evidence. A startling book called *James Brother of Jesus,* blows this false view away. The author Robert Eisenman uses extra-biblical historical data with a huge intellectual apparatus of footnotes. His very surprising evidence, to paraphrase liberally, is that James was the real life brother of Jesus and his number one chief disciple. In the Bible James is a marginalized member of the twelve disciples; there's not much information on him. Eisenman claims that this is because James had ideological differences with Paul. Paul, who arrived on the scene later, practically rewrote the history books, since he had clout as a powerfully aligned Roman, high up in the empire. Paul favoured Peter, he rewrote history and cut James out of prominence by deleting James' incredible accomplishments. Aryabodhi, of the Friends of the Western Buddhist Order, describes Paul as "the founder of Christianity." Eisenman notes that even in spite of Paul's efforts to re-educate history, today there are more surviving extra-biblical historical references to James than there are to Jesus! James is described as the leader of the "Jesus Movement," which included Jews and non Christians. Eisenman provides sources to support evidence that James was Christ's chosen successor, dharma heir and lineage holder. The Jesus movement got along quite fine with the Jews. The historic prejudice against Jews all over the world seeks justification in a Bible that is infested with falsehoods about Jews killing Christians, but this never actually happened! The Bible is infested with untruths and violence, because the causes and conditions from which it arose were falsehoods and violence. The Theravadin Buddhist canon is pervaded with truth and peace, because the causes and conditions from which these scriptures arose were enlightened and peaceful. Western religions are far more similar to many other primitive religions in the world, than they are to Buddhism! The story of Adam and Eve and the snake is remarkably similar to other snake stories in the primitive tribal religions of Africa and the Middle East.

What is the truth about the Romans and the Jews? The Romans were dictatorial butchers. If they didn't like what people were doing, they would just breeze in and kill them all. It was the Romans that persecuted Jesus and the growing Jesus Movement. The big switch occurred after the Romans adopted and took over the religion. Embarrassed by their ancestor's liberal use of force, the Romans rewrote the history books (again) as victors usually do. They blamed the Jews for beating up on Jesus and the Romans depicted the Romans of Christ's day, as being uninterested in Jesus, or as being innocent bumbling fools. Effective lies, similar to how the Warren Commission and the American government once convinced people that Lee Harvey Oswald killed JFK. Like a CIA Black Operation, people believe the Bible and they will continue to do so. Even after discovering the truth, many people will still believe the lie. The reason why, is in the nature of the lie itself. People prefer the lie, they don't want to hear the truth — the truth that they must save themselves—that a Messiah cannot possibly ever exist. The tendency towards theism is so strong in human beings that people will hope and pray for an external saviour even if they fully understand that they must save themselves.

The Buddha encouraged people to attain to disenchantment with the pleasures of the world. It is as though we are narcotics and we would rather believe in the lie of the drug, than face ordinary life. For example, millions of Orientals almost viciously guard their belief that the Iranian invention of Amitabha Buddha, around 150 A.D., is in fact an authentic celestial and eternal Buddha of infinite light and everlasting length of life — who will save your very "soul" after your death if you are devoted to chanting "His" name. No need to meditate or study. For heaven's sake! This criticism is and should continue to be laid at the front office of Mahayana Pure Land Buddhist temples everywhere as they constitute perhaps most of the Chinese, Japanese, Korean and Vietnamese Buddhist temples in the world. Millions of Pure Land Buddhists practice something that many Buddhists feel is more similar to the Christian religion than to Buddhism. Amitabha worship means tremendous belief in the theistic salvation of their souls by this celestial Buddha who accepts you into his Pure Land if you have paid homage to him. This "short cut" to salvation, they believe, will result in you taking rebirth in a lotus flower floating on a lake and when the lotus flower blooms you will transcend to enlightenment. People rationalize by saying that at least the Pure Land is something for people of mean intelligence but this is simply a horrificly illogical view. Anyone can meditate, can't they? Do people really need neon signs flashing the Pure Land to notice Buddhism?— if you call that Buddhism. There are even *nine levels* of Amitabha's Western Pure Land that you can get to! — it's quite commercial actually. If you write to the Buddhist Spectrum Study Group, for only $3.95 CAD you can have your very own death ticket to the esoteric 10th level, formerly reserved for only those temple patrons who donated over $100,000 USD.

Here we see a part of the process of how the Buddha's teachings were degraded and corrupted as they were "passed down" from 543 B.C. in India, through China to the 21st century. In view of the Pure "Fiction" Land perhaps we can ease up a bit on Chairman Mao for his final parting words to the Dalai Lama in 1954. Mao pulled in very close to the 19 year old Dalai Lama's face and softly said "Religion is poison. Poison! It saps people's will and saps their minds. It deludes them like a drug." Because Pure Fiction Land truly is a drug, with sympathy and understanding we should

259

consider that Mao may have made a mistake by tarring the sacred Tibetan Buddhist diamond path, with the same brush as the Pure Fiction Land. If true dharma had been the dominant tradition in China — such as Ch'an, then Mao may have spared Buddhism. We will never know.

False Mahayana Sutras

Buddhism has other parallels to the fabrications written into the Christian Bible. Several of the Mahayana sutras and tantra sutras are untrue in that people claim that they were spoken by the Buddha. This can hardly be accepted as many of them first arose centuries, even seven centuries, after the Buddha. The enlightened deities described in the Mahayana sutras by the Buddha are not to be found in the Theravadin sutras, which are authentic. But instead of calling these brilliant sutras lies many Buddhists acknowledge them as very useful metaphors. These teachings remain brilliant and wise expositions of the dharma even though they cannot be attributed to the Buddha. So just as people put words in Christ's mouth centuries later, the same thing happened in Buddhism. The scripturally sanctioned and unabashed violence in the Christian Bible also has a parallel in Buddhism but only in a theoretical way. In the Pure Land tradition the Bodhisattva Kshitigarbha is a very popular deity as he looks after beings suffering in hell. In the Kshitigarbha sutra, 'the Buddha' extols the virtues of Kshitigarbha and the Buddha says that anyone who ridicules someone paying respects to Kshitigarbha, will take rebirth in a state of woe. Even someone who has just one thought of disrespect, the Buddha allegedly said, he will undergo many rebirths in the hell realm before proceeding to many rebirths in the animal and ghost realms!

Although this part of the Kshitigarbha sutra is an embarrassment to the Buddhist religion, no one has been hurt because of it compared to the chronicles of real violence and genocide praised in the Bible. For example, in the old testament god would tell the leader of a tribe to invade a valley, kill everyone there and take over the place. It's O.K. because god gave them permission to do so. It's god's valley; god told them to kill so, that's that. It should be pointed out however, that the Bible is also a book of practical teachings about how to get along with others and live with discipline, compassion and wisdom. In comparing the religion that resulted from the Bible to the religion that resulted from the Theravadin canon, Buddhist history is quite a bit different than the Christian Crusades. There is not one historic example of people being forcibly converted to Buddhism, or blood being spilled for this purpose.

The Lost Gospel

Who was the historical Jesus? Perhaps our best window to view the real Jesus has been painstakingly provided by a largely North American cadre of biblical scholars, who in 1993 published a book called *The Lost Gospel* containing the pieced together bits of what has come to be called the Q gospel. Q is German for "Quelle" which means "source." They believe that there is a missing source gospel from which Matthew, Mark and Luke derive. From the gospels, they have pieced together 235 lines attributed to Q. **Because of this evidence Christianity cannot make the claim to represent the religion of Jesus.** The scholars have amassed an enormous computer database of 150 years' worth of scholarly opinion. Going one step further, if we compare the historical Jesus to the Buddhist religion today, and if we compare the historical Jesus to the Christian religion today, then it is evident that Jesus Christ has more in common with Buddhism than with Christianity.

The Search for a No-frills Jesus

The support for a new, fresh perspective on Jesus is to be found in countless studies of the Christian religion. The work of the Q scholars is reported below in a summary of an excellent issue of *The Atlantic Monthly* magazine titled "The Search for a No-Frills Jesus," by Charlotte Allen.

> "Q scholars have built into their reconstructed text an apparent window of authenticity that permits a glimpse of who in their view the real Jesus was. It seems that the real Jesus had nothing to do with Jesus the resurrected redeemer, Jesus the Messiah, Jesus the lord of the apocalyptic future. Jesus lived in a metaphoric Galilee which was a kind of beachhead where the surge of political crosscurrents constantly kept the people on their toes. First-century Galilee presents a multi-ethnic population that did not overall feel much loyalty to Jerusalem, the centre of Jewish religion and culture. Jesus may have been a countercultural guru who encouraged his Galilean followers to experiment with novel social notions and life-styles, to question taboos on intercourse with people of different ethnic roots and to free themselves from traditional social constraints and think of themselves as belonging to a larger family."

> "There are also in Q many of the teachings of Jesus that Christians place near the heart of their faith: the Lord's Prayer, the Sermon on the Mount, the Beatitudes, the Golden Rule, and the famous admonition "You cannot serve God and Mammon." This sounds all very Christian but these biblical scholars suggest that the teachings of Jesus in Q hold the key to

an understanding of Jesus that is fundamentally non-Christian. The authors of Q did not view Jesus as "the Christ" (that is, as "the anointed one," the promised messiah), or as the redeemer who had atoned for their sins by his crucifixion, or as the son of God who rose from the dead. Instead, they say, Q's authors esteemed Jesus as simply a roving sage who preached a life of possessionless wanderings and full acceptance of one's fellow human beings, no matter how disreputable or marginal. In that respect, they say, he was a Jesus for the America of the third millennium, a Jesus with little supernatural baggage but much respect for cultural diversity. Perhaps Jesus was a roving "Cynic-like sage," [more of a secular philosopher, like Socrates than a religious figure.] The Cynics were adherents of an authority-questioning philosophical movement that began in Athens nearly four centuries before Jesus. The Q community may have actually lived like Cynics — Jesus possibly having picked up their philosophy on trips to Gadra. In this view, all the aphorisms of Jesus that we associate with Christian selflessness — "Turn the other cheek," "Love your enemies," and so forth — were actually clever survival strategies for unpopular Cynics in strange places. Jesus' first disciples were proto-beatniks encamped along the Sea of Galilee, who wrote down his teachings during spare moments on their travels. They might have done their work in the town squares— that was the equivalent of coffeehouses back then. In a serious context, one scholar even called Jesus "a party animal." Another scholar said "Christianity has had a two-thousand year run. It's over." [Martin Luther King Jr. said "No lie can live forever."]

One of the scholars by the name of Burton Mack, propounded the "car accident" explanation for Jesus' death: he suggested that the crucifixion might have been sheer happenstance. He also blames the Bible for providing justifications for Waco-style apocalyptic violence and the selfish exploitation of natural resources.

In Q we find that the historical Jesus actually did perform most of the miracles attributed to him. This indicates that Jesus Christ may in fact have been a sixth bhumi bodhisattva, just as Chögyam Trungpa Rinpoche claimed of Jesus. This refers to the ten stages of enlightenment described on the Mahayana path. For centuries, highly attained Buddhists have performed miracles, as did the Buddha himself. Also a down to earth guru, there is a description of the company Jesus kept, in the book *Jesus Under Fire — Modern Scholarship Reinvents the Historical Jesus,* by Michael J. Wilkins and J.P. Moreland. In this book the authors relate:

"Perhaps the most distinctive feature of Jesus' ministry, seized upon by nearly every scholar of Jesus, is what Crossan calls "open commensality"— Jesus' regular practice of table fellowship with the unlikely. It was a common jibe by outsiders that Jesus shared a table with sinners, tax collectors, whores, and other social undesirables (Wilkins/Moreland, 1995; 64)".

Wrong Tribalism

The period after Christ's death was a tumultuous time for the Jesus Movement. What happened from that time until 325 A.D., were the events leading up to the construction of the whole Roman Catholic Church, which is the basis of the entire Christian religion and all of the Protestant churches which sprung from it, or re-belled against it. It seems that for 325 years the Christians were a rag tag bunch of flaky people having visions and disagreeing amongst themselves about what their religion was all about. Charlotte Allen continues:

> "In 1934 a professor at the University of Tubingen named Walter Bauer contradicted classical thinking by arguing that "primitive Chris-tianity" had never existed, and that from the very beginning Chris-tianity had exhibited an extraordinary theological diversity that amounted to bickering sectarianism. There were geographic variants of the faith. Gnosticism, regarded as a heresy elsewhere, was the only variety of Christianity available in some areas and Gnostic Christians in Egypt considered themselves to be the true Christians, with their "orthodox" enemies being heretics. Bauer's book caught the eye of Rudolf Bultmann who taught New Testament theology at the University of Marburg. He believed that the Gospel stories were mostly mythological material, each dealing with a specific theological or practical problem. These were life situations or *"Sitz im Leben,"* facing the particular Christian community that composed the myth. Every story in the Gospels had a "form," he believed, a distinct literary for-mat related to its *Sitz im Leben*, and every New Testament book — along with its sources — had a distinct genre that served a theological purpose for its community. Bultmann believed that the stories in the Gospels had grown like pearls, from simple core aphorisms (perhaps reflecting Jesus' actual words) into longer, contextualized discourses and narratives. One is forced to conclude that the **non-Christian Jesus** — the Galilee-based wise man who displayed no interest in the end of the world, resurrection, or redemption — is about as "histori-cal" a Jesus we are likely to retrieve."

The Virgin Birth

The Christian church regularly held high level ecumenical council meetings. At one time, the people felt a need for a powerful female figure within the religion. After a few decades had past, fomenting this feeling in the masses, a bishop came forward with a proposal to a high level ecumenical council meeting and his proposal was seconded by another bishop. "We propose that we say that Jesus Christ had a virgin birth, that he wasn't born like everybody else. Out of respect to our teacher, why don't we say that an angel of the lord came to his mother Mary and that he had an immaculate conception. In this way it elevates the status of both Mary and Jesus."

A hesitant, conservative leadership, not immediately accepting the plan of action, eventually did however revise church doctrine and adopt this position after the time of Paul, who says nothing about a virgin birth. This inspired proclamation was bestowed upon the world after the 100 A.D. translation of the Bible from Hebrew into Greek. A great many Jews at that time couldn't even speak Hebrew and the word for "maiden," describing Mary, was translated as "virgin" in their more familiar Greek tongue. People became idolatrous of Mary as the "blessed virgin," almost elevating her to the status of the trinity, even though the Bible clearly states that Mary had several children with Joseph. In 1998 scholars best determined that Mary actually had seven children.

By a slow process of revisions, not via any big conspiracy, this ecumenical council passed off as official church policy the sacrosanct doctrine that Jesus Christ truly did, in literal fact have a virgin birth. In those days they didn't know enough about biology to realize that the female must contribute an egg to make a fetus. Many believed that it was entirely the man who plants the seed that is responsible for conception. Therefore they were much more open to the idea than we are, of the possibility that some kind of mystical immaculate conception could happen to a great spiritual being. Today, we know that Mary was a mere human being contributing an egg, so at best the Vatican could fake a belief that our totally sacred messiah, the saviour of the world, the unique son of god, Jesus Christ, must have resulted from an immaculate sperm or something. In adopting the virgin birth story, the very conservative church was amazingly flexible in accommodating public sentiment when it was in their favour to do so. This lack of truth and consistency corrupts the credibility of all the teachings of Jesus.

In the gospel of Luke there is one of only two references in the Bible to Jesus having a virgin birth. This was put in Luke, because Luke as we know, was a Greek and it is very common in the Greek tradition for all of the gods and goddesses of Greek mythology to have a virgin birth. It was not meant to be taken literally! As with the Buddha, it is said that the Buddha was born out of the side of his mother but I have never met a Buddhist who actually believed this. The idea is that the Buddha should not have come out of the lower chackras of his mother, so out of respect for him they say that he was born out of the side. In Buddhism this is such a very minor point that few Buddhists even know about it. In Christianity, the virgin birth of Jesus is such a big deal that today there are whole churches in South America based around the virgin Mary.

Paul

Who can assert that Jesus ever claimed to be the son of god? These were words put in his mouth years later. Jesus never claimed to have a virgin birth. Peter, his disciple, but perhaps not the first Pope, had constant arguments and run-ins with Paul decades after Jesus. Paul threw Christians to the lions until he got converted and was a zealous promoter of the Christian religion. One wonders if the incident of Jesus turning over tables in the temple was possibly reason enough for Paul personally to have ordered his execution? Highly unlikely, as our best evidence indicates that Paul arose one generation after Jesus. Paul's karma made him later feel very regretful about killing Christians but he over compensated to make up for it! Paul rearranged a great deal of the Christian religion. He changed things and created things; we don't know how much is Jesus and how much is Paul! So great is the significance of Paul that some even say that the Christians are in fact really "Paulists." Like so many other religions, the religion that Jesus created lasted for only one generation before it was changed around and converted into a completely different religion. Jesus and James may have wanted the religion to remain as a sect within Judaism, but Paul decided that the only way to survive and make it big was to branch out into a new, wider religion that included the Gentiles. From this marketing perspective Paul was right and he succeeded, very much so. It just wasn't going to work with James because of these ideological differences so James had to be cut out but Paul seemed to have managed to persuade Peter to go along with him. The parallel to Paul today is L. Ron Hubbard who founded Scientology. The parallel in Buddhism is that the Mahayana received an impression from other cultures and religions and converted itself into a hybrid of Buddhism which enabled it to be more popular than the Buddha's original teachings. For example, the Mahayana Pure Land tradition is a hybrid of Buddhism and the Iranian sun god religion. The Iranians didn't actually worship the sun, but the sun was used as a symbol of light, purity and compassion. The Iranian Buddhists used this idea to create Amitabha Buddha which is the most popular of the fictitious celestial Buddhas of the Pure Land school, and the number one most popular lineage today of Mahayana Buddhism altogether.

One of the most disturbing discoveries for any Christian to face is the solid evidence that the four gospels of Matthew, Mark, Luke, and John, were not written by Matthew, Mark, Luke, or John. These gospels contain all the words spoken by Jesus (which aren't many) in the Bible. Scholars determined that they were written in different stages from about 65 A.D. to about 140 A.D. by different hands, in different dialects, such that Christ's words have been mixed with the words of others. That's the bottom line. It's all game over, right there folks. Would the last person heading out of the church please turn off the lights?

Wait, there's more. For three hundred years these Christians were persecuted, thrown to lions, and kicked around by the Romans. And yet they were a tough bunch and they were gaining support. They established churches in Europe, in Constantinople, Turkey and further west. They were disparate, in the sense that some of them believed in the virgin birth, others did not. Some bishops and preachers made a big deal out of the father, the son and the holy ghost. Others did not even recognize this trinity.

Meanwhile, as the Roman empire expanded, the emperor Dioclecian was faced with the necessity of uniting the people of his vast empire. He and his ministers decided that they needed a strong state religion, so they tried out their Roman Sun God religion, but it flopped. It just never caught on and was unable to inspire the imagination of the people. The emperor was not able to find a solution to this problem before his death.

Constantine

Afterwards, warring generals were competing with each other to take over the emperor's seat of power. General Constantine made a deal with the outlawed Christians who were growing in influence and said "If you support me, and I am successful, I will make Christianity the official state religion." Constantine won, as he was an astute politician, plugged in Christianity as the state religion, gave the early church leaders a shot at the title, and it worked! Christianity took off like great guns!

Officially, Constantine had a vision of a cross before his battle with another general. He put the symbol of the cross on the shields of his soldiers and then he won the battle! Constantine also claimed to have a genuine conversion experience and that he believed in Jesus Christ. Constantinople was named after him, as the centre of the Roman Empire at that time.

After Constantine decided to go ahead with the implementation of the religion, you can imagine him getting together with his advisors about how to control the people with religion. They may have said something like, "Good idea boss! Yes sir. We believe that this is a very good religious product. The life story of Mr. Jesus Christ is very appealing, an easy sell, and maybe we can improve upon it. He's got this religion going with a bunch of people called the Christians. Even though we've been kicking them around for 325 years now, they still have a strong and loyal following. They've got heaven, hell, good guys and bad guys, sacred mysteries and everything! This is way better than the last product! This will be just what we're looking for!" Instead, if Constantine had made a deal with the Hare Krishna's or some other sect, many of us could have grown up in a much different culture! In other religions as well, such as Buddhism, the effect of just one king to propagate a religion has been enormous. According to *Gideon's History of the Holy Roman Empire*:

> "When Constantine conquered the East in 324, the Christian church was not some small sect, nor did he solely raise it to a dominate position. Christianity was a respectable power before it acquired an imperial champion. The Christian Bishop had become a respected figure in the urban establishment. When Constantine turned his struggle for power into a Christian crusade, he happily united religious patronage with political advantage. An emperor could not govern without the good will of his Christian subjects."

As a result, the other great teachers of Christ's day disappeared into oblivion while the Christian religion stepped onto the big stage of Roman Empire political power and clout. There were some problems to be ironed out in promoting this faith. These Christians did not agree amongst themselves about the important aspects of their faith so Constantine convened the single most important meeting that ever happened in the entire history of the western hemisphere.

The Council of Nicaea

The formal and orderly presentation of the chief doctrines of the Catholic faith was formulated at the first ecumenical council of Nicaea in 325 A.D. The objective was also to establish the divinity of Christ, "the father and the son, " which was built into the Nicene creed as the trinity of the father, the son and the holy ghost. There is not one word in the entire Bible about the trinity! By the time the Nicene Creed was established and accepted, they had already printed the new Bible with the New Testament. They couldn't fudge the Bible later and include the trinity into it because then everybody would know! So now, if you get the whole Bible on CD ROM and put it through the word processor, looking for the word "trinity," you won't find it anywhere.

Constantine added some of the traditional Roman sun god religious belief to the new Catholic religion, such as the yellow halos that go around the heads of saints painted on the walls of churches. That was a sun god quality, not a Christian quality. That is why Constantine named this newly consolidated religion, the "Roman"

Catholic Church. Did you ever wonder why they called it "Roman?" Athanasius was an assistant to a bishop at the Council of Nicaea. In 326 he became a bishop at the age of 30 and he denounced Christians that did not regard Jesus as god. The Christian religion had to compete with a lot of other religions. Paganism wasn't knocked out of the ring yet and there were many strange religions being followed. It just didn't excite people to call Jesus a Jewish prophet — they had to make their leader appear more god-like than that! So, the son of god idea was a very practical way of dealing with their problem.

In Athanasius' Easter letter of 367 we find the first historical record of the list of books which were highly respected and recommended by many to be the books to go into the formation of some kind of a new Testament. Church historians agree that we received the New Testament from the Council of Hippo in 393 and the Council of Carthage in 397, both of which sent off their judgments to Rome for the Pope's approval. Prior to this the Bible did not exist as one book. There were various books of wisdom being passed around, many underground. It was the bishops controlled by the Roman Emperor who decided which books went into the Bible and which books were kept out of the Bible. This is a staggering fact to contemplate, utterly staggering.

Today, the official view of the Roman Catholic church is that it was the hand of god that guided the bishops to choose which books went into Bible and which did not. But if you take a university course on comparative religion, the professor will tell you that it was a long human process kicked off with the help of Constantine's mother, 'Saint' Helen, who went around collecting stories and books of native wisdom. She and others came up with books that were later used to construct the Bible. Constantine's mother was a very devoted Christian "church lady" and she was more of the religious leader and inspiration than her son. The emperor could be described as an opportunist. The church teaches that on his death bed he had a conversion experience, but historic accounts on this point are at odds with each other. Bear in mind that the honesty of our historic records are not confidence inspiring. If you're a Christian and your own church has never explained to you where the Bible comes from, then might you not wonder?

The Gospel of Thomas

Outside the small town of Dag Hammadi, Egypt, a boy dropped a stone down a deep cavern in 1945 and he heard glass break. "Hey!" He climbed down and discovered the gospel of Thomas, from one of Christ's twelve disciples. He took it home and his mother used parts of it for kindling for the fire until somebody realized that it might be worth some money. This document and the gospel of James were gospels left out of the Bible. These were called 'Gnostic' texts, which included the writings of Mary Magdalene and several other women disciples of Christ. All these scrolls were found in the glass jar together by the Egyptian boy. Apparently Mary Magdalene may have been a very high disciple of Jesus, or even his wife! The Roman Empire being very sexist, rewrote the history books (again and again and again) and made Mary out to be a prostitute. These writings seem more Buddhist in their flavour than the Biblical gospels. More emphasis on meditation, contemplation and the individual search for truth. At the end of the Gospel of Thomas, Jesus said to Thomas:

> "You can drink from the cup of my mouth and become as I am
> and I will be you, then all that is hidden will be revealed to you."

That's Buddhism, the idea of nonduality. It's also the Hindu/Tibetan Buddhist idea of mixing your mind with the guru. You can actually "be one" with Jesus. That's heresy to the Christian religion so it's no wonder that they left Thomas out of the Bible.

The Jesus Seminar

Thomas is described in the book *The Parables of Jesus - Red Letter Edition - The Jesus Seminar,* by Funk, Scott and Butts. Here the authors state (Polebridge Press, 1988; 11):

> "The material in the Synoptics [Matthew, Mark, Luke] that is clearly the product of editorial activity is uniformly missing in Thomas; Thomas never reproduces the special theological perspectives of the Synoptics. This suggests that the tradition behind Thomas was reduced to writing before the Synoptic tradition achieved its final form. Thomas sometimes appears to be closer to an original version of a saying or parable. Most Fellows of the Jesus Seminar agree that Thomas is an independent and valuable witness to the parables and sayings of Jesus."

Jesus Seminar scholars estimate that only a small percentage of the words attributed to Jesus in the Bible are truly his words. The authenticity level of the gospel of Luke is considered to be about 20%, 18% for Thomas, 17% for Matthew, Mark 11% and virtually nothing for the gospel of John.

A possibility considered by the Jesus Seminar is that Jesus may have survived the crucifixion and went to India and lived there. On the west coast of India the tomb of Thomas was found with the bones of Thomas. Other evidence indicates that Jesus had an ancient presence in India, that he was not imported there by missionaries, centuries later.

There is a Muslim paper, *Died on the Cross?* that puts forth a convincing argument to suggest that Jesus survived the crucifixion on the cross. The Muslims regard Jesus as a great prophet of god. They claim that Pontious Pilot did not want to crucify Jesus and he did not want Jesus to die. So he was crucified late in the day because there was a law that you could not crucify people after sundown. A dark storm cloud brewed up (as an act of god) so they took Jesus down from the cross early, after only about three hours. Three hours usually isn't enough time to die on the cross, they say. Next, a Roman soldier pierced Jesus in the side with his sword. Blood and water came from the wound which should not happen if the person is dead. Normally the victims' bones were smashed after being taken off the cross. The people present were very willing to do this to Jesus, the Bible suggests, but Pontious Pilate allowed Joseph, a disciple of Jesus, to take Christ away. The Roman soldier's sword is now on display in Vienna as the 'Sword of Destiny' because many believe that he held the fate of mankind in this hands. Because of him, Christ's bones were not smashed and Jesus took resurrection and atoned for the sins of man, they say.

Three days after the crucifixion, the Bible tells us, Jesus appeared before his disciples with wound marks on his hands. He asked for something to eat so they gave him some fish. Jesus ate it right in front of them. Does that sound like a spirit body of light resurrected from the grave? Later Jesus travels 70 miles away and meets his disciples behind closed doors at a hidden meeting. Why would he hide if he had been resurrected? Perhaps he was on his way out of town to France and/or India to get away from all the heat in Israel. *No one really knows how Jesus died.* The crucifixion is the one central icon that the entire Christian religion rests upon. If Jesus did not die on the cross, or if it did not have the crucial meaning of atoning for the sins of man, then the entire religion collapses and Jesus Christ is just another great guru.

How to Destroy Christian Faith

The purpose of the Christian religion is not about sharing the teachings of Jesus, or even helping people with love and compassion. The purpose of the Christian religion is simply to extend and consolidate the power of the remnants of the Roman Empire. That's it and that's all. As the centuries have gone by, this organization has proven that it has an excellent ability to survive and grow. It is a business that makes money over the long term by selling the product of people's belief in their religion. The business grows by servicing and keeping their clients and encouraging their clients to have more babies which will create more clients. Born during the maturation of the Roman empire, it has outlived the empire itself. An important and effective tool to control the masses is guilt. Your mother can control you with guilt across a thousand miles of telephone lines. This is a proven method! Jesus did not teach a guilt trip, but the Roman empire religion did because it served their purpose to control people. In the early fifth century 'Saint' Augustine used the original book of Genesis to work out the new and improved doctrine of "original sin," which was his own Catholic idea. This is the view that you are inherently bad and need salvation. This is the basis of the huge guilt trip that the Christian religion, more aptly called "the Roman empire religion," has inflicted upon over a billion people for centuries. This has nothing to do with Jesus the wise man from Galilee. This is a political tool of the empire. Saint Augustine and his followers have done more damage to humanity than World War I and II combined, by using guilt to instil debilitating low self esteem in people.

Logical Deduction

The Roman empire religion exists.
The Christian religion does not exist.
The Christian religion has never existed.
The Roman empire religion began in Turkey in 325 A.D.
It now exists in a latter stage and has existed for 1674 years.

Just as the Buddha redefined the Hindu Brahmanic term "Brahma," and "Brahmin," to mean the highest aspect of Buddhist realization and personage, my policy is that I almost never utter the name of the non-existent "Christian religion," or "Christianity," "Protestantism," "The Roman Catholic Church," "The Catholics," etc. I refer to all such former concepts as what is today the true, genuine tradition of "the Roman empire religion," "The Empire religion," or simply, "the empire."

The End

By 476 A.D. the western Roman Empire crumbled and collapsed, leaving behind the single most powerful political force in Europe: the Roman Catholic Church. So by some fluke of history, this rag tag Jesus Christ and his denomination of Judaism had made it big and dominated the entire Western world. All of our history today in the West, in the Americas, Europe and Africa can trace itself back to these terribly important events in world history. The main events happened around 325 A.D. when the Roman Empire made a hostile corporate take over bid of the entire Christian religion, and they succeeded, very much so!

Today the official Roman Catholic view of the Gospel of Thomas, James, etc. is that they are Gnostic texts. In the 1950's when these were being translated they caused quite a stir and the Catholics organized their rejection of the texts. Ironically the church rejects them because they were written by people who did not regard Jesus as being the son of god. The truth is, that these Gnostics were the mainstream Christian religion of the day in Egypt, before 325 A.D., when Constantine decided that Jesus was the son of god. The Catholics regard the Gnostics as a bunch of outsiders that studied the teachings of Christ and cared about Christ, but they were just a bunch of half committed people, not worth paying any attention to because they didn't promote the idea that Jesus was the son of god! Constantine's church came rampaging south for the purpose of destroying the most authentic lineage of the Christian religion, so that their own version would be the dominant one. Perhaps the religion of Jesus finally completely died out in 512 A.D. in an isolated desert region of Egypt. Perhaps that was the last day of the living religion of Jesus, having lasted for about 500 years, similar to some other religions.

"Survival of the fittest," is the reason why one Christian mandala beat out another Christian mandala. In an aggressive turn of history, the highest evolutionary stage of the Christian religion was wiped out over a few centuries, just as the golden age of Buddhism was wiped out of India by 1197 A.D. by a Turk pseudo-Muslim invasion.

The way in which the Romans replaced the more authentic Christian religion in the Middle East was not entirely violent. They co-existed in some areas for a century or two until the Roman Catholic church eventually won out. We have some idea of what the world lost to the Catholics. There was a rich meditation tradition which may have originated with Jesus. It was the Gnostic Christians in Egypt that became the Desert Fathers, the first Christian monks, and they practiced a form of prayer that could be described as meditation. In Buddhist terms, these true Christians practiced both mantra meditation and non conceptual meditation. Today, one of the most important and practical areas of common ground between Christians and Buddhists is this practice of meditation. Historically, meditation is part of the Christian tradition and we are witnessing today the visionary reawakening of Christian meditation. Father Laurence Freeman, O.S.B., a Benedictine monk, is the spiritual director of the World Community for Christian Meditation, based in London England. They comprise some 800 groups in 35 countries. Father Freeman said that "dialogue creative of peace and understanding must be based both in meditation and in personal friendships between meditators of different faiths. What all religions share is a deep tradition of meditation that stems from the original teachings of their founders. In the experience of meditation we all face the struggle with ego and distraction. We all discover the universals of silence, stillness and simplicity," he said. This indicates that Jesus himself taught meditation practice for his followers, but this kind of discipline went against the Roman Empire's desire to control people so meditation fell out of favour within the Roman Catholic Church.

Today, if anybody pokes around in Israel or Egypt and finds ancient writings, no one will be more terrified than the Catholic Church, the Vatican. The last thing the Vatican wants to see is change. They do not want others to discover the truth about

Jesus Christ. They just want to 'keep a good thing going.' There is evidence that the church has destroyed or would destroy newly discovered ancient writings. The entire Christian religion is fundamentally built upon quicksand, upon assumptions, lies and concepts that have been decided upon for reasons of power, politics, greed and ego, not for reasons of truth. How can anyone test the validity of the crucifixion against their own direct experience? It cannot be done. "But then," Joseph Campbell asks, "what would be the value of faith?"

The Only Way

In contradiction to the teachings of Jesus, when the Roman Catholic Church was newly founded it forced the view that the only way you could go to heaven was by believing in Jesus, the son of god. And of course the only place that you can find Jesus is at the Roman Catholic Church, the one and only true faith. Only through the priest can you succeed in this process of being saved and gaining admittance to heaven. Emphasis was put on salvation after death, for the purpose of controlling the people while they were alive. This system worked to keep people docile, like "the opium of the people," as Karl Marx said, but it used a lot of guilt to control people. The religion became dark and sinister in its violent oppression of other views. It became the very thing that Jesus warned against. As the Buddha warned, the dharma can only be destroyed from the inside. It can never be destroyed from the outside.

An analogy to understand what happened to the Christian religion is to understand the plot development of Alfred Hitchcock's movie *Psycho*. This was a new development for Hitchcock enthusiasts because the movie progressed with a plot about a woman who stole some money from her employer and took off. About twenty or thirty minutes into the movie the plot is completely blown away and it becomes a totally different movie. Norman Bates kills the woman at the Bates Motel. Norman Bates is like the Romans taking over the Christians and initiating the Catholic Church. But in his case his motives had nothing to do with the money; he's just plain psycho (he had a thing about his mother). This isn't a perfect analogy because the Romans did want the 'money'— the religion. Finally, the rest of the movie is just about Norman Bates— the Catholic Church, the 'new Christian religion.' Just so, we had this beautiful, wonderful and quite sophisticated Christian religion for 325 years. Then out of left field the Roman Empire takes control over the direction of the 'movie' and they wiped out the true plot upon which the movie was founded. *That* is psycho. The true Christian religion was murdered like Janet Leigh's character in the shower scene when Norman Bates — the Roman Empire, stabbed her to death. But fortunately the true religion is not forever lost. Norman Bates drove the car with the $50,000 in the trunk, into the swamp. That treasure was recovered in 1945 in the form of the Gospel of Thomas. We still have the true power and leadership of Jesus Christ, the bodhisattva. His teachings live amongst us.

Rebirth is Impossible

The Buddhist belief in rebirth was not to be articulated in the main Western religions; it just wasn't an issue. However the church did take the trouble to have the doctrine of rebirth officially renounced in 553 A.D. at the Second Council of Constantinople. This was because the Byzantine emperor Justinian had a wife Theodora who didn't like the idea of reincarnation. Even though this makes no sense at all, she felt that belief in re-birth made people lazy because "they knew that they were just going to come back any-how." So, she said to her husband the emperor, "Honey?..." And, you guessed it, the rest is history. True. True. True. In the book *Theodora and Justinian,* you can read how she asked her hubby to go to the Pope and arrange to have the doctrine of rebirth de-nied and rejected as a heresy. Justinian did so, with full confidence invested in his mighty armies. The Pope worked it out with the ecumenical council and bingo! rebirth is not ever possible in the Christian religion because of this one obstinate woman. In later centuries they had to work out the accounting nightmare of everlasting heaven, ev-erlasting hell or purgatory, in order to prop up and justify this untenable view. Just be-cause one Roman emperor didn't wear the pants in his family, Christians no longer have the option of moving around through different realms after they are dead.

I used to think about how my Catholic mother was forced by her father to church every single day in Holland. I thought about her confusion and her nervous breakdowns. I cried so hard, I laughed; then I laughed so hard, I cried. What suffer-ing the Vatican is causing in the world today, what suffering! I think of their clever business marketing strategies to get their profits up by 10% over the next three years; their focused conversion of souls in South America which even surpasses Buddhism as the world's fastest growing religion. In Central America, the Catholic Church is the embodiment of true evil, as they use their financial clout to break up the efforts of the workers to get themselves organized so that they can better the lives of their families. It's truly evil. True evil. Because Pope John Paul II has effectively cared for the well oiled machinery of the Catholic Church for 20 years, I feel that he is not possessed of great moral virtue. The Pope is a machine oiler. Since he surely knows the well documented evidence suggesting that the Vatican assassinated his predeces-sor, Pope John Paul I in 1978, then his honesty and decency is suspect, as he could be an accomplice after the fact (see the book: *In God's Name*).

Pope John Paul I was truly a Pope of great virtue and love for the people. He wanted the Catholic Church to be a church for the poor and he intended to use the wealth of the church to benefit millions. He even drew up the papers to fire his fi-nance minister when the Cardinals poisoned him to death one night in the Vatican, and quickly embalmed his body so that no autopsy could be performed. They explained that "you can't do an autopsy on the Pope! Tradition forbids it!" Long after it was too late, people discovered that there has never been any rule or tradition at all about doing autopsies on the Popes. So then, the Cardinals selected the next Pope and gave John Paul II orders to tow the line! Nostradamus actually prophecized this particular event! We must see the Pope and the Vatican for what they truly are — they are a political party with a politician at the helm. The Pope's job is to follow the policies of his party, and he *is* doing his job; one can hardly blame the Pope for doing the job that he has been installed to do. Is the Pope Catholic? However, don't expect the Pope to do good things or attempt to uplift his fellow man. That is not his job. His job is to do his job, and he *is* doing his job. No surprises there.

Women's Holocaust

Long after the collapse of the Roman Empire, the Christianization of Europe came to a head during the period of the 1400's to 1600's A.D. European culture had shamans and wise women leading many communities and the Catholic church discovered that many people would go to these women instead of the local priest for advice. Unhappy to see anyone better than themselves, the Catholics decided to kill them. It took about three centuries but they managed to kill upwards of 9,000,000 people. Because 85% of the victims were women, historians call this "the women's holocaust" (see video: *The Burning Times*). These wise women, healers and shamans were branded as witches and cold bloodily burned at the stake. Their money and property was conveniently confiscated by the Church. Equality of the sexes gave way to the patriarchal dominance of Christianity. Women were kept down and men were instructed from the pulpit to beat their wives, not out of rage but out of compassion for their immortal souls. If the Catholic Church was once again given absolute power in parts of the world they might resume their ancient policy of twisting ropes around women's necks as they simultaneously burn them at the stake. Or, they might use subtler means of control to adapt to the times. These are their true colours. This is a reasonable assumption to make because nothing has changed in the mind set of the Catholic hierarchy for many centuries. Given the chance, they would kill tomorrow just as surely as they killed yesterday. Is it unfair to print this? Is it unfair to the Germans to say that they killed six million Jews and minorities in a twelve year period? Is it rude for the Germans to do that? or is it rude for you to *report* that they did that?! There is nothing immoral about dwelling upon the atrocities of the Christian religion because atrocities are very much *the fabric* of their religion! Lest We Forget! Lest we forget those who died in the war against the Christian religion because those pilgrims were our forefathers in America and they gave us the freedom to publish this book!

What's the Purpose?

If Mara, the devil was in power today, you would expect him to be wearing white and appearing to be very virtuous, wouldn't you? How else would you expect Mara to appear? I am not a bitter ex-Christian, as I was not raised a Christian and I am not particularly interested in the Christian religion. I am honest and truthful and I simply call a spade a spade. The purpose of the Roman empire religion is not to share the teachings of Jesus or even help people with love and compassion. The purpose of the Roman Empire religion is simply to support the remains of the Roman empire by controlling people, controlling people with guilt and the drug of theism. Control them for what? Their purpose is to control so that they can be on top socially and gain the highest respect and wealth in society. It's about gaining respect. Fortunately, within that larger purpose, the people have incorporated some very spiritual and beautiful practices and of course the majority of the parishioners are very good and sincere people who care about the spiritual path followed by themselves and their families. The Titanic. Today the barnacles that are now growing on the holes in the Titanic are good barnacles. They are wholesome barnacles that sincerely care about themselves and their barnacle families.

Conclusion

Jesus the wise man from Galilee is alien to the Christian religion. His name has been taken and used by the Roman Empire to foster their religion; their political party. Today the Roman Catholic church is the last vestige of the Roman Empire. Out of loyalty to the Roman roots of their wealth, power and prestige, the Roman Catholic Church even today may feel protective of the Roman persecutors of the early Christians. Like a parent that defends an anti-social child that has committed manslaughter, the Vatican's true lineage is the Romans, not the early Christians. This is almost a fait accompli because of the fact that the Catholic Church upholds the traditional Roman view of Jesus, but denounces the truth of the historical Jesus as is clearly indicated by the precious Gospel of Thomas and the other early writings of the Gnostic Christians and others.

The Jesus Manifesto

Jesus Christ's church was destroyed from the inside, by the ancient Romans, but Jesus Christ has never been lost to us. Jesus truly was great, but people will never know that, as long as the Christian religion is dominating and twisting his good name. People have got the right to know that Jesus was a great teacher, worthy of true respect, not just the lip service that people give to Jesus so that they can curry favour with others by saluting a conventional icon.

Therefore, Buddhists must provide spiritual leadership and take up the banner of the love, peace, compassion and openness exemplified by the historical Jesus.

We must rescue Jesus from the Christians. Buddhism claims Jesus. We don't know if Jesus was a Buddhist but since the Christians have made such outlandish claims about Jesus being the one and only true son of god, then compassion allows Buddhists to assert something proper and decent about the man, rather than allow this Christian charade to go on for even one century longer. Christianity has had a two thousand year run — it's over. Move along folks, nothing left here, it's over. Move along folks. That is the view. That is the vision. That is the goal.

In the name of Jesus, Buddhists should commit themselves to the compassionate goal, before the 21st century is out, of inviting millions of disaffected Christians onto the Buddhist path and returning Jesus safely to the truth again. Buddhism can rekindle faith in Jesus by being a lighthouse that shows the true home where Jesus now dwells — at a Buddhist centre. Jesus of Nazareth is recognized as being a bodhisattva (a compassionate, awakened being), by countless Buddhist masters, such as the Dalai Lama and His Eminence Tai Situ Rinpoche. Jesus was a great stainless guru worthy of inclusion into the lineage of our forefathers of compassion. We must clear the good name of Jesus Christ by disassociating him from the karma initiated by the church in his name. Christians should concede back to Jesus his good reputation, by meditating and practicing spirituality the way that Jesus meant for us to practice.

The advantages of putting the spotlight on *"Rescuing Jesus from the Christians"* are these:

1. It gives publicity to Buddhism because of the great interest in the historical Jesus.
2. It undermines the parts of the Christian religion which were created for harmful purposes by the Roman Empire.
3. It strengthens Jesus Christ, what he stood for, and what he wanted his disciples to believe, which can improve Christian churches today.
4. This undermining of false Christian dogma will bring more people to Buddhism as they get disillusioned with churches that don't adapt to historical evidence.
5. Any tension or controversy caused by Buddhists will only bring more publicity to Buddhism, which is good.

In 1963 when the Beatles were getting bad press, Paul McCartney said "Any publicity is good publicity." There is just publicity. The Christian religion doesn't want this kind of publicity; the Buddhist religion does benefit from this kind of publicity. The winners are Buddhism, the historical Jesus, and sentient beings. May Jesus bless our efforts.

Those who commit their hearts to follow the Jesus Manifesto will pay any price, bear any burden, meet any hardship, support any friend, oppose any foe, in order to ensure the survival and the success of Jesus. We owe it to Jesus.

Our goal is to include the Gospels into Buddhist thought, interpreted in a Buddhist way instead of a way that extends and consolidates the power of the Roman empire. Our goal is to transform the abandoning of Christian churches into the formation of Buddhist temples with a long and bright future, as a phoenix rising from the ashes of its former life. We will work with slow and skillful love and devotion to invite many disillusioned people to investigate the Buddhist path. The bodhisattva vow commits us to establishing all of these people into a state of liberation.

It would provide clarity to have a Buddhist book analysing each line attributed to Jesus, trying to discern his real teachings. Buddhists could learn from the true Jesus. We should follow the example of the Buddha and reinterpret the meaning of the teachings of other religions in a Buddhist way, so as to replace the former meaning. In this way we can help displace the old Christian meanings of Jesus' words with a Buddhist meaning that is much truer to the authentic intentions of Jesus Christ, discarding the words attributed to Jesus later. For example, we should keep the name 'Christ' because it is such a potent, powerful word. Even though it is against the teachings of Jesus to regard him as a 'Christ,' son of god, and saviour, we simply change the meaning of the word to mean "bodhisattva." This elevates Jesus higher than the many other teachers of his day, while still subjugating him below the status of the historical Buddha.

I was a Christian in 1988 but later when I became a Buddhist I felt some aversion to Christ's teachings in the Bible because I found out that they were contaminated with additions made by the Roman Empire. But after discovering the work of the Q scholars I have a whole new love for Jesus. For the first time I now view Jesus as one among the Buddhist lineage of gurus. I can now include his compassionate teachings onto my Buddhist spiritual path, so now I am more committed than ever to rescuing Jesus from the Christian religion, which cannot claim to represent him. I respect Jesus because of the evidence of his higher human states — and there is evidence to be found. In the Gospel of Thomas Jesus said "The Kingdom of Heaven is spread across the earth but men do not see it!" This indicates that his mind could reach into the god realm and that he did have direct personal experience of higher human states.

Elvisanity

Looking to the future of religion can we project what the dominate religions of the world will be in the 23rd century? No one knows what the next future mythology will be, but we could extrapolate Christian history and imagine that after Christianity has had its 2000 year run, Elvis Presley may be the next son of god! Elvisanity, or Elvism — the major Protestant offshoot, may utilize the many films and songs, interviews and books we have about Elvis and create a church with pillars shaped like guitars and shrines of gold and jewels surrounding Elvis' original silk clothes. Visualize that Elvisanity pastors and ministers will read scriptures about how Elvis first healed people as they watched the Ed Sullivan Show in 1955. Devas of unequalled healing powers were spun off of Elvis' swinging hips and straight through millions of TV sets, instantly healing millions of people all over the land. As hysteria for Presley's healing powers grew, he went on tour and preached the gospel, which his billions of future disciples will have in many fine CD and computer chip collections. Elvis' most inspiring discourse was the Sermon in Memphis, which priests will be quoting until the end of this age. Elvis delivered the Sermon in Memphis after the execution there of his friend — Martin Luther the Baptist.

When Elvis felt that his work on Earth was done, he returned to his father in heaven promising that he would come back. He had established a monastic recording structure. All of his great discourses and songs were thoroughly and accurately recorded in accordance with his precise instructions. The transmission of his teachings was secure for as long as civilization would last. He could go, until he was needed for the time of the great apocalypse ahead. At that time Elvis will return to redeem mankind from the gravest crisis which can only be overcome by the divine intervention of the man himself. Elvis will return, but he did not say when. Elvins are always looking for indications which will predict the time of his arrival, but Elvis only said "Be ready, for you know not the hour in which I come."

After delivering his people to the promised land, Elvis said "People will know that you are my disciples, for you have loved one, for the other." Then, Elvis ascended into the sky, out of sight. Returning to Graceland his helicopter descended, and for the last time Elvis entered his great mansion alone, where he entered into a deep samadhi absorption. While abiding in the fourth samadhi absorption, Elvis made direct contact with god and he passed into parinirvana while sitting upright in a state of one pointed concentration. There was a tremendous earthquake and the ground shook all over Tennessee and the south! Elvis now sits at the right hand of god and he lovingly watches over all of our earthly affairs. Future disciples of Elvism will be given the Elvis deva invocation chants, by which they can actually invoke the Elvis deva and bring down his protection and blessings within the fibre of their own being and upon their loved ones, and others. At this time as Elvis resides in the bliss, joy, happiness, peace, comfort and fruit of heaven. He is watching us and waiting for the proper causes and conditions to arise on earth for him to return.

Future Mythologies

A fine subject for use to project future mythology is John Lennon. He even looked like Jesus with his long hair and beard in 1969. A 23rd century perspective on Beatlemania could be that it was a glorious golden age of love and compassion caused by the messiah — John Lennon. He was accompanied by his Regent and dharma heir, Paul McCartney, plus his senior disciples, Yoko, George, Richard (Ringo), and Brian (Epstein, their manager). During a crisis John Christ send his disciple Brian on a daring mission to save their church. In 1967, at the height of the John movement, Brian gave his life in a fantastic spectacle which was an inspiring success! Happiness spread everywhere that The John and his disciples went. People were singing "Yeah, yeah, yeah!" in the streets, and their was love, love, love! Millions of people learned to heal others just by singing or listening to John's songs!

The religion spread peacefully to the four quarters of the earth with remarkable ease. At the age of 40 John knew for certain that his work on earth was complete, until the time of the great future apocalypse when he would return to save all mankind. After recording his final testament in New York, in the fall of 1980, he stepped into his car for the last time and went home. He was closely surrounded by all of his senior disciples because The John gave a three month notice that he would be passing away. He installed Paul as the leader and as his successor and everyone accepted Paul's ascension without objection. As they drove back to the Dakota, John entered into samadhi as he sat in the back of the limousine. He and Paul suddenly dematerialized together and re-appeared upstairs in the Dakota. Paul alone witnessed the parinirvana of The John. John entered into and abided in the first samadhi absorption. Then he went through each and every samadhi up to number eight, back down to one, then up to four again. He dematerialized in the fourth samadhi and was gone for good, until the time of the second coming. There was a psychic on the street below and he sensed that John had passed away so he slowly pulled out a flare gun and shot four flares straight up into the air as a salute to The John Christ and a signal to others that the time had come.

John established a direct mind lineage connection with Paul McCartney which allowed Paul to channel down songs and messages from The John at will, for the rest of Paul's long life. The religion spread happily ever after.

He Took Rebirth Amongst Sakkha's Retinue

And now. . . the punch line: Just think what we could do with the Kennedy assassination.

Chapter 17

Christian – Buddhist Common Ground

The heart qualities of compassion and love are at the core of the Christian and Buddhist religions. Christ's big message was love and compassion. And if you only had one word to describe the outward expression of Buddhism, it would be "compassion." In Christ's departing remarks he said "people will know that you are my disciples because you have loved one for the other." In studying the Buddhist cosmological view of the universe it is striking how similar it is to the Christian teachings on heaven, hell, purgatory, the fallen angel Satan, heavenly hosts, guardian angels, etc. They both read like they came from the same source, but with a different interpretation.

Of course there are differences between all religions. It is good to be open about the differences so that people know what they are choosing. A Christian fellow once described his situation to the Dalai Lama and he asked the Dalai Lama if he could become a Buddhist. The Dalai Lama said "How can you be a good Buddhist if you can't be a good Christian?" For those Christians and Buddhists and others who are satisfied with and benefit from their own religious tradition, then it is the common ground, not the differences, that they contemplate. You are mentally healthy to the degree that you look for what is good in each situation and you are mentally unhealthy to the degree that you look for what is wrong in each situation. The good. What is the goodness that Christians and Buddhists share? The following describes a person's direct experience of both traditions. Generally, we are human beings that want to benefit others. Specifically, in both traditions we are following a spiritual path that will lead us to and beyond death. Death is quite a big present moment! After death we will go where we deserve to go.

Beginning with the Christian idiom, if you're good, when you die you will go to heaven. In Buddhism, you can become a deva in the god realm, which is heaven. If you've been major bad, then you'll go straight to hell. Do not pass go, do not collect 200 dollars. Hell exists, big time, in both the Buddhist and Christian views. Just ask Joseph Stalin. If you've lived a lost life like one of those cold souls that stand on the sidelines of life, who know neither victory, nor defeat; and if you've done some bad stuff and only a bit of good stuff, then the Bible will direct you to purgatory. Right this way please. This is the hungry ghost realm, or spirit realm. The Buddha described this type of rebirth as being one of predominant suffering, with only a little bit of pleasure. The ghost realm is inseparable from the Christian purgatory. They are one and the same state of mind. On the road map of life, they are both located at the same run down hotel along the side of the highway. Like the 'Hotel California', beings are all just prisoners there of their own device. They can check out anytime they like, but they might never leave for 136 years. Just wake up!

Moving upstairs, there were seven angels in heaven but one of them wanted too much power so he challenged god, and then god cast him out of heaven. He became the fallen angel called Satan, or the devil. The devil has intelligence and he's trying to trip you up all the time. When things get going good, then the devil will tempt you with sexual misconduct, or try to blind you from doing what is right. In Buddhism they have the same fellow, and he does the same things — Mara. Mara is a deva who lives in the outskirts of the sixth and highest heaven in the sensuous sphere where the devas there 'delight in the power over the creations of others.' Above and beyond that, there is the fine material sphere with the most powerful and virtuous god-like devas, and then, the formless sphere of existence. Mara is keenly intelligent, the ultimate manifestation and embodiment of ego. Mara is Satan. Mara and the devil are one, one and the same being.

People sometimes wonder if there is any value in the practice of prayer. Christians pray to a higher power, to god. Buddhists chant, pray or meditate upon a subject to invoke the assistance of a higher power too, devas or deities. The evidence is that prayer and chanting do produce beneficial results. Studies testing the results of prayer on patients in hospitals indicate this.

Both religions discourage activities like being a medium to contact the dead because it can lead to mental derangement in the medium and it also has a detrimental effect on the spirit of the person who has died. That sort of thing would only cause the dearly departed to be even more attached to their loved ones left behind. The bad news there is that such a tendency would hold them back from moving on, which is what they should do because they have no choice, once they are dead. Both the Christian and Buddhist doctrines agree wholeheartedly on this point.

One of the most important and practical areas of common ground between Christians and Buddhists is coming more and more into the spotlight. It is the practice of meditation. Historically, meditation is part of the Christian tradition and we are witnessing today the visionary reawakening of Christian meditation. Father Laurence Freeman, O.S.B., a Benedictine monk, is the spiritual director of the World Community for Christian Meditation, based in London England*. They comprise some 800 groups in 35 countries. Father Freeman said that "dialogue creative of peace and understanding must be based both in meditation and in personal friendships between meditators of different faiths. What all religions share is a deep tradition of meditation that stems from the original teachings of their founders. In the experience of meditation we all face the struggle with ego and distraction. We all discover the universals of silence, stillness and simplicity," he said.

The first Christian monks, the Desert Fathers of the 4th century practised a form of 'pure prayer' using a 'saving formula,' a short phrase. They repeated it continuously in the face of all distractions, which would then lead to the first of the Beatitudes: poverty of spirit. Beatitude means perfect blessedness or happiness, in the pronouncements in Christ's Sermon on the Mount. In the Buddhist idiom, this is the experience of emptiness. As the Desert Fathers would take a word or a phrase from the Bible and repeat it over and over again, what they were doing was exactly the same as Buddhist mantra meditation practice. So, 1500 years ago, mantra meditation was at the heart of the Christian tradition, expressed in terms of Christian theology and scripture. This fact is a pearl of great price! This is described in the Conferences of John Cassian who recorded the story of the Christian meditation tradition that he lived and taught in the fifth century A.D. Cassian's teachers also taught him the technique of resting the mind without repeating the word, which in Buddhist terms, is non conceptual meditation.

The big similarity or the big difference between these two great world religions is the concept of theism and the concept of non theism. Theism means the belief in a personal god. The Buddhist view of non theism is that the ultimate thing, enlightened mind, whatever that is, is not a personal god, but an impersonal ultimate enlightened state of mind which cannot be described, cannot be accurately defined. Buddhists call it the unconditioned. As such the unconditioned is also inseparable from this conditioned world of things and life and death. But, when a Christian says that god is in everything, in the rocks and the trees and in everyone's heart, isn't that saying about the same thing? Yes. In Christian meditation practice they teach that 'god dwells in our depths,' not 'out in the sky.'

And so, the dialogue between the Christians and the Buddhists, and their shared meditation practices is growing openly. Perhaps, one or two centuries from now, people will look way back to the 20th century and see that it was a time when Christianity and Buddhism were regarded as two completely separate religions. Even though those traditions may carry on the same way, there may be another group of Christians that practice a form of Christianity that has incorporated whatever it could from the historical Jesus and Buddhism. In the Vancouver area, Christians are learning meditation practices from their own ministers, such as at the United Church of Canada, the Anglican Church or the Unitarian Church*. They are also learning the practice and study of other meditation traditions, and then incorporating that practice into their own Christian world view. From a Buddhist view, seeing people meditating is the best common ground human beings could ever hope to have.

Because the cosmological views revealed in the Christian and Buddhist religions are quite similar, this is evidence that there truly is a conventional and ultimate reality that must be something close to what is being interpreted by human beings. Because the true nature of ultimate reality does actually exist in some way or experience, both of these religions are touching upon it. It is a service to mankind that the Christians and Buddhists are leading people to something bigger and truer than what they have yet been able to experience themselves.

1. Excerpt from 'Christian Meditation and the Unity of Religion' from the Shambhala Sun, Jan. 1993 issue.
2. In B.C., the United Church of Canada, provides regular meditation instruction and group practice. Christian Meditation instruction is also given at the Unitarian Church of Vancouver.

Chapter 18

Christian Meditation

The Desert Fathers were the first Christian monks and they lived in the period of the third to the sixth centuries A.D. They practiced a form of prayer which could be described as meditation. In Buddhist terms, this ancient Christian meditation practice included both mantra meditation and non conceptual meditation. They would take a word, sentence or phrase from the Bible and repeat it over and over again. St. John Cassian, the Roman was based at a monastery in Bethlehem. He made a great contribution to world literature by producing two sets or collections of writings. These were the *Institutes* which recounted the practices of the monks of Egypt and adapted them for use in the colder, Western regions. Then later, *Conferences* given by various great Fathers of the Desert.

Father John Cassian's conferences with Abba Isaac in the 4th century represent the first written expression in the West of that tradition of prayer of which Centering Prayer is a contemporary presentation. Here, Abba Isaac teaches John Cassian and his companion Herman the mantra formula of meditation practice. Abba Isaac gave St. John a word from the Psalms: "O God, come to my assistance; O Lord, make haste to help me." Abba Isaac says "the prayer wherein, like a spark leaping up from a fire, the mind is rapt upward, and, destitute of the aid of the senses or of anything visible or material, pours out its prayer to God."

This describes the process in Buddhism where the mind becomes concentrated from what is called neighbourhood concentration to the first samadhi absorption.

The Buddha described the first samadhi, which is continually confirmed by the direct experience of meditators, as being "momentary and discursive thought, accompanied by joy and rapture." This is an absorption state where all five senses are blacked out in a natural phenomenon of one pointed concentration. The meditator experiences a visual blackout, hearing shuts down, he can no longer feel his body and taste and smell are also absent. He is still conscious and in a state of rapture. His concentration upon his meditation technique is so deep and one pointed that he has entered into what is called a state of samadhi.

The Centering Prayer can be very closely compared to Buddhist Concentration or Insight meditation practice. Thomas Keating, a contemporary teacher of this ancient practice, and a Roman Catholic Priest based in Snowmass, Colorado, teaches that "we should not try to stop our thoughts during practice. Develop a detached attitude. In the ancient Christian desert tradition anything that can hook us: thoughts, feelings, visions, sensations, are to be let go." This is precisely the technique of Buddhist Insight meditation.

Thomas Keating uses an excellent analogy of comparing thoughts to ships passing by. Like ships passing, let them go by, don't board them, don't try to stop them. In Insight meditation it is your duty not to follow your thoughts, no matter how seductive, just label them as "thinking" and let them go. The use of labelling the thought with the mental word "thinking" is to acknowledge it, let it go and then come back to your technique.

In the Centering Prayer, there is intention prayer and attention prayer. Intention prayer is similar to labelling "thinking" and coming back to the technique. Intention prayer means to rest the mind. When thoughts arise and distract the mind, the intention prayer formula or chant is repeated until the thoughts no longer distract the mind. Then, the practitioner returns to resting the mind in silence. Attention prayer is similar to mantra meditation. In attention prayer the prayer formula, or chant, is repeated continuously, without interruption.

Thomas Keating's 'Circle of Awareness' states that "spiritual awareness is known as a 'restless longing', something within us that is 'honed on God'— as breath and heartbeat give us life. At the very core is Divine Indwelling, which is scary for many. To be 'born again' is to break through Ordinary Awareness. Ordinary Awareness is centred on self. Spiritual Awareness knows we are God's latent identity/function." Switching to the Buddhist idiom, Keating's 'Divine Indwelling' is bodhicitta, awakened heart or Buddha-nature; also called basic goodness. The meditation process clears away our inner obscurations or ignorance so that we can be touched by this awakened heart. It is compared to a jewel in a heap of dust.

The various practice reminders in the Centering Prayer, like not attaching to pious or spiritual thoughts, are also found in Buddhist insight meditation. Keating's reference to spiritual non-possessiveness and spiritual narcissism is what Buddhists call spiritual materialism. This is the tendency to solidify the barriers within yourself with spiritual practices. Like, believing that you're spiritually superior because you've learned all kinds of spiritual practices, even though your heart has not opened up to others. Spiritual materialism can also be defined as arrogance disguised as spiritual attainment. Keating warns that "words can become idolatrous, we can pile up fetishes around prayer practises."

One of the most articulate of the Desert Fathers was the theologian Evagrius Ponticus. He died in the Egyptian desert about 400 A.D. His deep psychological insight reveals a very deep parallel to the Buddhist samadhi experience. Evagrius championed pure prayer, seeing it as the "laying aside of all thoughts." Below are quotes from his *Chapters on Prayer*, along with a Buddhist parallel to his experiences.

> 69. "Stand guard over your spirit, keeping it free of concepts at the time of prayer so that it may remain in its own deep calm. Thus he who has compassion on the ignorant will come to visit even such an insignificant person as yourself. That is when you will receive the most glorious gift of prayer."

> 114. "Do not by any means strive to fashion some image or visualize some form at the time of prayer."

Buddhist insight meditation is non theistic, not meditating upon a god, but being open to whatever arises out of space, emptiness. It is free of any concept. This is what Evagrius and the desert fathers were doing. They were not holding to the concept of Jesus or a god in this form of prayer. Other references to god in this prayer form refer to the god that is in you, which in the Buddhist idiom is the same as saying the emptiness that is in you. The direct experience is the same. This is the pearl of great price. This is the cause for celebration for those who want to determine what is the deepest most important common ground that unites Christians and Buddhists together. This is it. Deeper than morality, is non conceptual meditation.

> 120. "Happy is the spirit that attains to complete unconsciousness of all sensible experience at the time of prayer."

The Buddha describes the second samadhi as "After the subsiding of thought — conception and discursive thinking, and by gaining inner tranquillity and oneness of mind, he enters into a state free from thought — conception and discursive thinking, the second absorption, which is born of concentration and filled with rapture and joy."

153. "When you give yourself to prayer, rise above every other joy—then you will find true prayer."

Rising above joy itself is the state of equanimity. This is described by the Buddha "After having given up pleasure and pain, and through the disappearance of previous joy and grief, he enters into a state beyond pleasure and pain, into the 4th absorption, which is purified by equanimity and mindfulness."

117. "Let me repeat this saying of mine which I have expressed on other occasions: Happy is the spirit that attains to perfect formlessness at the time of prayer."

The Buddha described four lower samadhi meditation absorptions as corresponding to a state of mind that is at the level of the fine material sphere. Our normal everyday state of mind is of the sensuous sphere of existence in Buddhist cosmology. There are four higher absorptions built upon the fourth samadhi which puts the meditator's consciousness at the level of the formless sphere. This is as high as an absorption meditation can go, which is not full and complete enlightenment, from the Buddhist view. Evagrius refers to attaining to formlessness at the time of prayer.

119. "Happy is the spirit that becomes free of all matter and is stripped of all at the time of prayer."

This corresponds to the four higher absorptions of the non material, formless sphere. The Buddha describes this 5th absorption as "Through the total overcoming of the perceptions of matter, however, and through the vanishing of sense-reactions and the non-attention to the perceptions of variety, with the idea, 'Boundless is space', he reaches the sphere of boundless space and abides therein." The 6th absorption is boundless consciousness. The 7th, is the sphere of nothingness. The 8th is the sphere of neither-perception-nor-non-perception.

It is startling to see the similarities between Buddhism and the *Chapters of Prayer* by Evagrius Ponticus. Buddhism can be condensed into three inseparable stages: morality, concentration and insight. The basis of your meditation practice is proper moral conduct because if you are seriously violating the principles of morality which are common to all religions, then you will not have the peace of mind to develop concentration in your practice. The very purpose of morality, in Buddhism, is simply to foster an environment so that you can concentrate your mind. There is a future to morality. Concentration is what you build during your meditation practice, like water rising in a dam. Not only meditation but chants and prayers and post meditation mindfulness — these all increase concentration. Insight is the natural fruit of concentration, like the power that comes from a dam.

Thomas Keating says "An intimation will come out in consciousness, dreams. It will come after a period of centering prayer." Insight is what Keating is describing as 'an intimation'.

The Centering Prayer could be viewed as one of many forms of Buddhist meditation. What is important to appreciate here is that these two separate religions confirm the high level of meditative attainment described by each other. It is because human beings are human beings, with or without a religious label, that people who meditate without conception will attain to realization and even complete enlightenment. This reality of direct experience validates the history of both Christian prayer meditation and Buddhist meditation. What matters is the direct experience. They both provide a path to the ultimate goal of human life. This Centering Prayer handed down by the Desert Fathers is probably the most important practice in the entire history of the Christian religion.

One of the differences here is the language used regarding theism. Theism means the belief in a personal god. Buddhism uses non theistic terms to describe meditation, such as non self, emptiness, awakened mind. The Christian religion is supposed to wear the label of theism, but the Christian Centering Prayer does not refer to god as being separate or 'out in the sky'. It refers to Jesus and god as being deep within us and it is the practice which gives us our deepest and most valid experience of reality.

It is true to say that Buddhism and Christianity meet 100% at the Centering Prayer. This is the deepest and oldest place in our 2000 year shared history, where Christians and Buddhists are one.

*Excerpts taken from *CENTERING PRAYER Renewing an Ancient Christian Prayer Form* by M. Basil Pennington, O.C.S.O., 1980.

Chapter 19

Future Dharma–
Future Anti-dharma

Move real slow
Warm equanimity
Warm equanimity
Warm equanimity
Move real slow

Consider Nostradamus' prediction that "a man wearing a blue turban will rise out of Persia. He will be the terror of mankind." The Mahayana Buddhist policy on Islam is exactly this: Establish all sentient beings, limitless as space, into a state of complete enlightenment. You may think that this prophetic prediction by Nostradamus refers to a conventional political situation where some demented leader like Ayatollah Khomeni grabs hold of a huge bag of thermonuclear missiles and fires them all over the world. Don't you wish. The Buddha warned us to be on the lookout for a much more insidious enemy. In his discourse converting a senior Jain disciple by proving to him that the mind initiates more fundamental karma than the body, the Buddha asked him if it were possible for a highly attained ascetic or brahmin to destroy the entire city of Vesali with his mind. The Jain responded by saying "Yes. A highly attained ascetic or brahmin could destroy two cites of Vesali with his mind. Nay, five cities, ten cities, even fifty cities!" The Buddha agreed. The person sitting quietly in meditation in the house next door to yours could possibly be a man, woman or child who could single handedly execute the next major world war — all planned, initiated and brought to fruition by their mind. Body and speech rest calmly, unengaged. The Buddha taught that the mind is the forerunner of all causation. The mind is fundamental and immeasurably more powerful than body or speech. The above scenario is unlikely to happen however because people with such a powerful level of concentration and attainment almost assuredly do not have the motive to harm others.

The United States and the United Nations go to great pains to ensure that Iraq is not capable of creating nuclear weapons. I believe that the President and his advisors take seriously the above prophecy of Nostradamus, as will future presidents. In February 1998 President Bill Clinton told military chiefs that 'rogue' Iraq must be stopped. He challenged Americans and the world to stand firm against Iraq, depicting the showdown as a test against the type of dangerous enemy the international community will face in the future. He gave a sombre speech to military officers at the Pentagon. "In the next century, the community of nations may see more and more the very kind of threat Iraq poses now," he said. "A rogue state with weapons of mass destruction ready to use them or provide them to terrorists, drug traffickers or organized criminals who travel the world among us unnoticed. If we fail to respond today, Saddam (Hussein) and all those who would follow in his footsteps will be emboldened tomorrow by the knowledge they can act with impunity." The threat of rogue nations exporting chemical and biological weapons to terrorists was a tactic Clinton and his officials used to emphasize that the Iraqi menace could hit home if not stopped. Hit home is the word.

The actions of President Clinton and the administration have wisdom and foresight because the Tao Te Ching teaches that all of our big problems in life used to be just little problems. So it is important to take care of situations while they are still small and manageable, Lao Tzu taught. An ounce of prevention is worth a pound of cure. But do the Americans and the U.N. know how to get a handle on the source of the danger, the causes and conditions which can result in rogue leaders obtaining weapons of mass destruction? Are they doing enough? What else can be done? Does anyone know? What threats lurk beyond Iraq? After World War I, it was not enough for the French to build the underground tunnel line of defences to protect them from Germany. That huge undertaking was utterly useless by 1940 with the Nazi blitzkrieg. After the second edition of this essay was published, nuclear tests were conducted by India and then by Pakistan. The Pakistani pride at having the first "Islamic Bomb" underline Nostradamus' prediction alarmingly. We could be witnessing the build up to World War III right now. The Americans said that the most serious threat was not Pakistan or India, but those who might get a hold of a nuclear weapon. Watch out for "Persia."

Tupigowa

About 1200 years ago in Tibet, Padmasambhava was faced with a problem similar to the one that faced President Bill Clinton with weapons of mass destruction. He could foresee the dark ages ahead that would descend upon Tibet. Padmasambhava, regarded as a second Buddha by the Tibetans, was the father of Tibetan Buddhism, and in the 760's he could see two streams of influence on Earth. He could see that the dharma was taking place very powerfully. Great kings had propagated the dharma, like Asoka. Thousands of monks and nuns committed their life to benefitting others with bodhisattva echelon compassion. Buddhism had aroused ground shaking faith and devotion and it was uplifting and transforming people's lives everywhere known. But the father of Tibet could also see another great stream of influence. He could see that the anti-dharmic forces were also very powerful and that they were not happy about what the Buddha had unleashed upon the world. Some found the dharma to be too challenging and others felt that it caused people to renounce their families, which they felt was unfilial and, quite naturally, any power structure can feel threatened when a great influence is turning society upwards. In fact, our father who art in heaven, could see that the anti-dharmic forces where getting it together to vanquish and expedite it. Two centuries later, Tibetan King Langdarma went on a rampage to destroy Buddhism in Tibet. This Padmasambhava could foresee, and he did all he could to turn the play of events back then, and centuries after his earthly life, according to the *Epic of Gesar.* What he did was, he went up to the god realm to contact a particular deva named Tupigowa, formerly an Indian monk, to fetch him and bring him back down to human birth to help things out. He explained the situation on Earth and told Tupigowa "You are going to have to go down there and do something about that."

Obviously at first Tupigowa thought that this was going to be an enormous nuisance to him but he eventually gave in to Padmasambhava's urgings and he agreed to take birth as Gesar, who became Gesar of Ling, the greatest warrior king and hero in Tibetan history. This is an example of a great leader who 'came down.' Unlike most politicians, who have to work their way up from mayor to governor to President, Gesar came down because he was born on a higher level with a duty to accept the burden of leadership, to take on the mantle of life and death decisions everyday. King Gesar vanquished the three anti-dharmic kings and he preserved Tibetan Buddhism which today benefits us inconceivably. The finest way to bring down the blessings of these beings in the higher realms— the deva sangha, into national governments, is via someone like the State Oracle of Tibet who can channel down advice to governments. This man, the State Oracle of Tibet, is a shaman who currently advises the Dalai Lama, and one or many more of these people could be employed at the White House or at 24 Sussex Drive, Ottawa. Mediums could provide a similar function, like counsellor Troy for captain Picard on *Star Trek, the Next Generation.* This is logical.

If Padmasambhava was here in the flesh today he could say that we should protect the container of the Buddhadharma by spreading the dharma. And the way to spread the dharma, Padmasambhava might say, is through mass media Buddhism in the 21st to 23rd centuries. It is essential to penetrate the mass media of movies and television with the Buddhadharma, in order for Buddhism to succeed at making a significant enough influence upon our world to inspire sanity and the blossoming of lotus flowers within millions of people all over the world. This is a process and like most processes, it takes time for benefits to be noticed. With a vision that encompasses a long time perspective, taking up this challenge is Dzongsar Khyentse Rinpoche. This young Lama and master in the Rime (non-sectarian) tradition is an example of one of the new Tibetan Buddhist leaders. A major focus of his activity is the mass psychology inspiration of video dharma. He is a leader where no other Tibetan guru has gone before. As of this printing, he was working on his first full length feature film being produced in India.

Lemmings

No one knows for sure what form the next world war will take. All we know is that this prediction of Nostradamus will in fact come true, just as surely as his prediction of 'Hister' resulted in 50,000,000 dead at the hands of Adolf Hitler and others. Nostradamus' world was limited to medieval France so to him, a limited European conflict may have seemed like the whole world. Even so, the only question now is, how can we protect ourselves? This is uncertain but we should look for leadership that is more relevant to addressing our real problems than the present political leadership which is focused upon economic mumbo jumbo, creating jobs and getting re-elected, like lemmings running to the edge of a cliff, checking to see who's who in their social and political elite. Our goal should be to install people, people like you perhaps, who will sit in tranquil meditation underneath that cliff. It makes no difference whether you see the lemmings falling on you or not. You sit before the setting sun world and you delight in the present moment. If only a few lemmings would invite you to the top of the cliff, you could help to show them how to pacify, enrich and magnetize enough of the herd of lemmings, so that they would step back from the brink of that black cliff. As long as there is life, there is hope. Together, you can march the lemmings back to the new old lemming village in the sunlit valley. They will let you disappear into the background, over the hill, as they build their own affairs again, remembering what very stupid things they did before. Lest they forget.

My stepson, Kachon, born in 1977, told me that he must be big in Thailand to help people. After I spoke to this superman, as I put down the phone, I realized that it would be better if people had the Buddhist ambition to do something great for others, rather than cling to the ego's idea of modesty. Not long ago, people would not have believed that the Berlin Wall would crumble in the 20th century. It may be a stretch of the imagination but in the future the Canadian government could officially consult a higher realm connection. We should not lose sight of our large scale concerns. We care about the welfare of all sentient beings, we have the elite compassion to benefit others in a high echelon way. In one of the great stories of history, Sir Winston Churchill was once asked at a boys school to summarize the lessons of his life. He stood, leaning on his cane and he said "I can summarize the major lesson of my life in seven words. They are these seven words young men: "Never give up. Never, never give up." Upon his appointment as British Prime minister in 1940, Churchill uttered before parliament "I have nothing to offer you but blood, toil, tears and sweat." I am not using the same words but I echo those sentiments felt by Churchill. A sense of urgency is needed and a sense of urgency is an essential ingredient in the bodhisattva vow. You are going to be dead someday. Your precious human body could even fail you today! For how long are you going to let beings like your acquaintances suffer in samsara?

If enlightened leadership arises to ward off the forces of darkness in this world, they may fail as did JFK, but we may at least have a better understanding about why it is that we died. This would benefit us immensely in the bardo, so with happiness and delight we should step forward into certain karmic progress and virtue. Buddhism cannot fail in the West. We cannot lose. Politically, I think it is good to support Canada's allies, and encourage the continued virtuous efforts of the CIA's Remote Viewing operations, which have been wrongly and gravely cut back. These astral travellers and psychics could help keep tabs on our future nemesis with the blue turban. Contrary to what may be assumed of a Buddhist writer, I believe that all spiritual leaders must ultimately bring their concerns to the ultimate place of power on Earth: the Pentagon. Its tentacles are apparent and its tentacles are also silent; as President Eisenhower warned in his prophetic farewell address, "The American military industrial complex, growing in peacetime, affects every American city and town, even spiritually." For what it's worth my insight into national and global karma is exactly this: a chain of volitions preceding President Kennedy's disastrous decision to greatly escalate the buildup of nuclear weapons will likely result in the destruction of more than one American city. The background is: during the Kennedy administration American intelligence determined that the Americans had ten times the nuclear strike capability than the Soviets. However, due to various public and military pressures, the decision to drastically escalate their nuclear arms buildup was made by John F. Kennedy which resulted in what is now the all too familiar arms race.

In a company the people who get paid the most money are the ones that contribute the most to the vital goals of the organization. This is why we should relate the dharma to world peace and security — the most vital goals of organized society. The karmic result of Kennedy's escalation is that the Soviets escalated their nuclear weapons build up. Today, the United States has a sane and responsible grip over their weapons of mass destruction. The Russians do not. Naturally, the Russians do not control power very well (see: Joseph Stalin and Boris Yeltsin) but it was the Americans that caused them to build thousands of warheads. Therefore, the fruition of this is that the accumulated aggressive volitions of Kennedy and his military antecedents could ripen in the form of severely attacked American, Canadian and other cities. A bad action leads to a bad result. Only a good action leads to a good result. Also, whatever you sow, you get more than compensated for. Good actions result in even more good coming back to you. Bad actions usually come back even worse. At least it seems this way, because you do not realize how much your good words and deeds benefit other people. You may not even remember what you said that helped someone so much, but months later they tell you how much they appreciated it. It is good news to contemplate in this way because it propels people to realistically weigh how they can in fact negate the effects of previous bad karma, and prevent nuclear or other massive forms of warfare.

A good way for our allied leadership to operate is to govern one present moment at a time. Effective governance should create around the leaders as much as possible, total silence and empty space. The Tao teaches that consciousness is the method of teaching and the teaching itself. 90% of the job of leadership is the selection of staff. Delegate everything to them and be empty. Delegate but don't abdicate. Looking for virtue, leaders should scour the environment for virtuous people with focused concentration. Leaders should keep their body speech and mind in a proper way and draw out insight from within themselves. Their personal power will then be better brought to bear upon moving their fellow countrymen upwards. Their leadership can be exercised by living a quiet little life. Peace, stillness. The Tao says that the greatest leaders are hardly noticed. They should work behind the scenes, putting chosen ones in front, putting capable ones in the spotlight and in the driver's seat. During the greatest crises of the civil rights movement Dr. Martin Luther King Jr. would withdraw and pray and meditate. As people pressed him loudly for leadership, he would be quiet and wait... waiting for insight to arise from that still small voice within. Enlightened leadership means allowing one's body speech and mind to be an open vessel available to the devas of virtue. That's politics. That's power politics. That is the safest way to cross the Rubicon.

Chapter 20

Theravadin Manifesto

The Theravadin sutras have primacy. All of the Mahayana and the Vajrayana must fall in line behind that. The very best of Mahayana, Tibetan, Zen and all other traditions of Buddhism are commentary upon the original Buddhist tradition agreed upon at the first council. These are the complete teachings of the Buddha as recorded in the Pali canon. The Buddha said it all. All else is commentary. The Buddha said that in the future when teachers profess to be teaching his doctrine, their teachings should not be quickly accepted or rejected, but their advice should be carefully examined and compared to the sutras and the vinaya. If they are in accordance with the sutras and the vinaya, then their teachings should be accepted and followed. If their teachings are not in accordance with the sutras and the vinaya, then their teachings should be rejected and abandoned. That was the Buddha's Theravadin Manifesto. "Take refuge in my dharma. Go to no other as your guide," he said. Renounce any teaching that is not in harmony with the Theravadin dharma.

There are diverse inclinations and aspirations in sentient beings, the Buddha taught. Teachers have very different styles and emphases so a great variety of teachings can flower in accordance with original Buddhism. This is what most of Mahayana and Tibetan Buddhism is. The vast teachings of the Mahayana and the secret symbolic teachings of the Vajrayana should not be renounced outright by the Theravadin traditions. Mahayana dharmas should be examined carefully, page by page, to determine if they share true Buddhadharma or not. Ideally, all Buddhist teachings should be sifted through to separate the dharma from the adharma. The adharmic teachings that have crept in should be reinterpreted, subjugated or rejected so that true dharma can be given primacy once again. Evidence indicates that the Theravadin sutras are authentic and trustworthy, except for less than 5%. The evidence also indicates that authentic parts of the Mahayana sutras have been mixed together with later additions which have been falsely attributed to the Buddha. The Mahayanists have deliberately minimized and diluted the importance of Gotama Buddha by portraying him consorting with various fictitious Buddhas and fictitious bodhisattvas. These false teachings can be adapted for their dharmic usefulness and lessons but they should be demoted to the status of commentaries, popular religious imagination, pulp fiction or comic books. The character of the Buddha should be omitted from these writings unless such literature is presented as only fictitious stories regarding the Buddha.

Fortunately, most of Buddhism can still be regarded as Theravadin Buddhism. It was harmful cultural pride and arrogance that originally caused the artificial designation of the three yanas; the three wheels of Buddhism. The Theravadin Manifesto is committed to peacefully destroying these barriers so that no other wheels exist but the first one. The Buddha taught only one eightfold path. He didn't teach a greater one and a lesser one or a secret one. This policy of tearing down falsity brings Buddhists of all traditions closer to each other and it puts them on level ground. Those who live by the Theravadin Manifesto do not recognize the existence of Mahayana or Vajrayana Buddhism. "It's just Buddhism," and "I'm just a Buddhist," they say.

Now is the time to set the record straight and consolidate a Buddhist tradition that places the truth first, and gives primacy once again to the Theravadin sutras and vinaya. This manifesto includes all Buddhist traditions. The view is to subjugate all Buddhist literature underneath the pinnacle of the Buddha's authentic words. Who came first? We can be honest. We can actually do such a thing as be honest and tell the truth about the dharma. Religions don't like truth. Religions don't like honesty. Religions don't like evidence and examination, but this is what the Buddha supported. We can reveal the truth. We can even practice and study dharma that is wholesome and good, not in need of an editor. Perhaps never since the Buddha has there been such an auspicious opportunity as now. Today we have the tools of massive dharma translations in English, freely available. The future is ours. If we waste this power, such an opportunity may never come again until the next Buddha. The next century provides a window of opportunity where Buddhists can choose honesty instead of tradition. We can improve the image and the substance of how Buddhism is manifested in the West. In this climate of change and discovery we can discover sincerity and do something constructive about admitting the truth about the false sutras. Have the courage to renounce falsities taught to you by Buddhist teachers and Buddhist traditions. The Buddha taught you to test out his teachings and decide for yourself what is the truth, not taking anything on faith. If we succeed, our moment in history will be of the greatest benefit to others in future centuries. Future generations will decide whether or not we brought the dharma to the West in the most noble of ways. The fewer of us that make the efforts, the more glory there will be for the ones that do.

end

Commentary:
The Thai, Burmese and Sri Lankan traditions have much to learn from the northern school. In fact, the greatest living Theravadin teachings exist in the northern traditions of Theravadin Buddhism — Tibetan Theravada, Chinese Theravada and Japanese Theravadin Zen. These are the teachings passed down from many commentaries, from Zen meditation, the relative bodhicitta practices of the Lojong slogans by Atisha, the Mahamudra teachings, and others. It's all Theravadin Buddhism. The wise Theravadin elder, Thai Ajhan Buddhadasa encompassed and absorbed the finest dharma from any source. Humbleness means asking for other people's dharma. Pride attached to one tradition is what the wise men call a fetter.

Three or four centuries after the Buddha, the Mahasanghika school wrongly made themselves out to be the big wheel, the big deal and they chose to put down the mainstream authentic religion by calling the Theravadins the lesser wheel — Hinayana. This is wrong so if Buddhism doesn't break up and disintegrate altogether, then the Mahayana negative group karma, or 'kalpa karma,' should properly result in Theravadin Buddhism rising above the Mahayanists once again. "No lie can live forever," Dr. Martin Luther King Jr. said. The laws of karma dictate that eventually the delusions attached to the Mahayana teachings must fall away. The Theravadin Manifesto is committed to hastening this process. The Buddha surely blesses our efforts because Theravadins carry his torch.

The line should be drawn and it should be made clear because the majority of Buddhists today are not educated to know the difference between a real sutra and a false sutra, such as the category of tantra sutras. This confusion has undermined the Buddha. This deliberate distortion has spin doctored the Buddha's words into justifying various schools of Mahayana thought. For example, the Pure Land school in the Chinese and other oriental traditions justifies it's practices by basing them on Iranian writings penned 700 years after the Buddha. The Iranians invented the Amitabha sutra, claiming and promoting the belief that Sakyamuni

Buddha spoke these words. Well . . . nothing could be further from the truth. This is the Iranian sun god religion in the guise of Buddhist Pure Land temples. People have the right and freedom to worship the Iranian sun god all they want. That's honesty. But if they call such worship Buddhism, that's dishonesty.

The Amitabha Sutra is not in accordance with the sutras and it is not in accordance with the vinaya therefore any prudent Buddhist must deny the existence of any such celestial Buddha with such powers. Because the Pure Land Buddhists insist that these teachings are true and they insist that they come from the historical Buddha, they do a disservice to mankind and to the Buddhist religion as a whole by falsifying the Buddha. They are dishonest because they take the false for the true, and the true for the false. This deliberate or non-deliberate misrepresentation serves to confuse people. Everybody gets confused when they try to study Buddhism, and when they try to find authentic teachings. As Deepak Chopra teaches, "The single biggest enemy of your spiritual life is organized religion."

Many people get deflected away from finding the dharma by being exposed to adharma and cultural affectations which are presented to them as being Buddhism. If things are done honestly based upon the best evidence of what is Buddhadharma, then there will be much less confusion in the future. The problem with this suggestion is that we do not live in an honest world. Buddhist traditions are institutionally dishonest and they will reject their own people and others for being honest. Any Mahayana teacher who has studied Buddhist history must be a dishonest person if they uphold their tradition's view of the origins of Mahayana Buddhism. In order to maintain their pecking order within the lineage, they must be a dishonest person. There is no other way. You however, are free to choose. The Theravadin Manifesto is committed to sincerity in expressing what the Buddha taught and sincerity about what is and what is not in accordance with Buddhism. The Theravadin sutras, which the Buddha devoted years of his ministry to preserving, are the only collection of sutras that exist today based upon the sincere intention to provide others with the Buddha's words. The Mahayana sutras are not authentic and they are not based upon the sincere intention to provide the Buddha's words because we know that the most popular or important ones were created centuries after the Buddha. Even the Mahayanists admit this, and they openly recognize that the Theravadin sutras are the most true to the Buddha's intention.

We as Western Buddhists have the greatest opportunity in history to actually be honest about the dharma. This is very important. In Asia being honest about the true dharma would be politically unsuccessful. Any honest dharma teacher would be demoted in his lineage or expelled, unless they cut out their own niche like the famous Ajhan Buddhadasa in Thailand. Westerners do not have the burden of religious intolerance and Buddhists comprise only about 2% of the Western population. Westerners are free to teach what they know. This is our one opportunity now to get away with misrepresenting the false aspects of tradition, to discard the false, and resurrect the true. If we can avoid the temptation of sangha friends and support given by the big machinery of tradition, if we can scratch by, plugging away at the authentic dharma, then we will earn the highest merit.

As a way of life, the Theravadin Manifesto offers a lonely path. Your fellow Theravadins, much smaller in number, don't want you because they shun the Mahayana. You don't. You absorb the Mahayana. They'll regard you as a Tibetan Buddhist. The Tibetan Buddhists will regard you as a Hinayanist. Mahayanists may suspiciously view you as a subversive. If you just want to be loved by a sangha, then sell out to a tradition and turn your back on being a true seeker. Devotion and taking refuge means being loyal to the real historical Buddha. Although a thankless task, encouragement was given by Prince Siddhartha just prior to his enlightenment. In telling a story to some children about how he saved a swan from being killed by his cousin Devadatta's arrow, he said "If a million people believe a lie, it's still a lie. If only one person believes the truth, it's still the truth, so it takes great courage to stand up for what is right." This occurred when the nine year old prince found the swan thrashing with an arrow in it's side, shot by Devadatta. Devadatta tried to claim the bird so they argued it out before the King and his ministers. Everybody believed Devadatta's side but they sold out to Prince Siddhartha just because his dad, clearing his throat, was the king! Although a hallow victory, Siddhartha learned the courage of conviction.

Applying the manifesto to real life is an uphill battle but when Gandhi was faced with difficult odds, in his confidence he said "We cannot lose. We cannot." The Buddha was a Theravadin, (this is actually a later school but still close enough to original Buddhism) and he always will be. His bright, just, all-victorious leadership, wisdom and compassion is the inspiration behind the Theravadin Manifesto.

Chapter 21

Changing Buddha's Words

"Come, friends: let us recite the Teaching and the Discipline before what is not the Teaching shines forth and the Teaching is put aside, before what is not the Discipline shines forth and the Discipline is put aside, before those who speak what is not the Teaching become strong and those who speak what is the Teaching become weak, before those who speak what is not the Discipline become strong and those who speak what is the Discipline become weak."
– Venerable Maha Kassapa, the elected head of the First Council,
   held a few months after the Buddha's passing.

"Sarcasm" is a word that can describe Mahatma Gandhi's method of making the British see what they were doing in India. The Theravadin Manifesto directs Gandhian energy right into the heart of Mahayana Buddhism— marching people through the barriers at the foundations of the Mahayana. The point in this piece is to shine a spotlight on something that the Mahayanists have done which is wrong, not to dwell on faults, but to contribute to education, honesty and improvement. The inspiration behind this is to cause revulsion for false Mahayana sutras so that greater devotion will be born for the Buddha and his dharma as presented in the authentic Theravadin sutras. However, in accordance with the Theravadin Manifesto, we should love and embrace the best of Mahayana and Vajrayana as being in accordance with Theravadin commentary. The skillful means now is to discriminate between what should be abandoned in the Mahayana sutras and what should be followed in these vast teachings. For example, the Tibetan Mahayana teachings on compassion are amongst the greatest and most accessible dharma teachings now available to people.

After I typed the first draft of this essay I emailed it to my brilliant young, 20 year old Chinese advisor on Oriental Mahayana. Andrew flipped! He fired a salvo of "dharma combat" emails back at me. Booting up the system in the bomb shelter underneath my building at 1450 Chestnut Street, in Vancouver, I read this message from Andrew:

> The kind of things you propose may generate a lot of bad karma to you and those who come into contact with this essay, for the eighth consciousness [alaya - below the unconscious mind] is the most sensitive field of karma-storage and anything you have registered with your senses WILL send seeds to your eighth consciousness. Even if you show it to a rinpoche, his or her mind will also be "affected" by the content and the condition-arising, possibly to the negative side. If you have a teacher he or she may have to bear the consequence of helping you [or allowing you] propagate what he or she would consider cause of rebirth in hell... some would allow it, I don't.

I fired a few dharma combat salvos back at him and eventually Andrew convinced me to edit out a few items from this work. In the end, I emailed to Andrew:

> I will print "Changing Buddha's Words" with your comments about hell, as melodrama for my readers. So far your questions are not too challenging so I think that I am defeating you at "dharma combat" my friend.

Hell! I'm not going to hell. Do I read like a Buddhist teacher that doesn't sleep well at night? No way. In fact, this chapter is the proudest moment of my career. I'm defending the Buddha and his words, with the above prophecy of Maha Kassapa in mind. Let us now go in and out of some constructive satire presented as a Mahayana perspective. This helps to add realism to an ancient process by imagining what the motives of people were, who wrote Mahayanasutras.

How to Write a Sutra

Would you like to write something that will be loved and cherished by millions for centuries to come? Would you like to impress your personality and opinions onto Buddhist traditions? Why not write a sutra? Sure, you can do it! There are job opportunities in Buddhism. If you write an honest Buddhist book in your own name it will be dated within 40 years. There's only a few 1950's Buddhist books left worth reading, such as those authored by Dr. W. Rahula or Alan Watts. If you write a sutra your work could be "benefitting" others for two thousand years or more.

The Buddha's wisdom teaches us that we should never make a big deal out of ourselves (Osel Tendzin, 1988; Halifax lecture), so we should not be concerned with trying to be remembered for centuries to come. However, in the Mahayana, we can put this part of the Buddha's teaching aside and do as we please! To the Theravadins the idea of changing the Buddha's words by creating a new sutra is impossible and despicable. The sutras are *the* most sacred scriptures containing the most authentic words of the Buddha himself. Practically speaking, they are the living breathing body of Gotama Buddha without a bullet proof vest on. The Mahayanists have buried his head in the bushes but the Buddha is still breathing.

The sutras have been fiercely protected and strenuously passed down for over 2540 years and the Buddha is never coming back. We must jealously guard the sutras. This, and the other canonical scriptures are the only record we have of the Blessed One's teachings. *Nothing* is more precious on this earth. *Nothing.* Any attempt to alter or corrupt the scriptures is a heinous crime, the Buddha taught, of immeasurably bad karmic proportions. Specifically this relates only to the patimokkha — the vinaya (one of the three baskets of canonical scriptures) rules for the monks and nuns. The reason for this is that you could jeopardize all future generations of dharma practitioners until the time of the next Buddha. The Buddha's teachings indicate that introducing a false patimokkha which results in creating a schism in the sangha, is a more heinous crime than killing your neighbour. Seriously, your karma could be so bad that you could take rebirth in hell. Literally. Does that sound like a joke?

Surprisingly, an ancient tradition going back over 2000 years in the Mahayana is a practice of composing new discourses and putting them in the mouth of the Buddha. These are known as Mahayanasutras. You should never try to fake a Theravadin sutra but you can take a shot at writing your own Mahayana sutra if you follow the nine principles set by our Mahayana elders in the past.

Most Buddhists are not aware of the big difference between Theravadin and Mahayana sutras. Understanding this provides a vivid understanding of just how extensively false words have been mixed with the Buddha's true teachings. The Theravadin sutras have been kept authentic except for a very few discourses, such as two of the Long Discourses. The Mahayana sutras which are not authentic are the writings which first arose four or five centuries after the Buddha's death. Those reasons are explained by one of the most eminent Buddhist scholars, Dr. Edward Conze. Conze's book *A Short History of Buddhism* is recommended if you want the real truth — the truth which virtually no Mahayana teacher would ever admit. In it he explains the early Mahayana:

About the beginning of the Christian era a new trend took shape in Buddhism, known as the Mahayana, literally "the great vehicle." It was prepared by the exhaustion of the old impulse which produced fewer and fewer Arahants, by the tensions within the doctrines as they had developed by then and by the demands of the laity for more equal rights with the monks. Foreign influences also had a great deal to do with it. The Mahayana developed in North-West India and South India, the two regions where Buddhism was most exposed to non-Indian influences, to the impact of Greek art in its Hellenistic and Romanized forms and to the influence of ideas from both the Mediterranean and the Iranian world. This cross-fertilization incidentally rendered the Buddhism of the Mahayana fit for export outside India (Conze, 1980; 44).

About 100 B.C. a number of Buddhists felt that the existing statements of the doctrine had become stale and useless. In the conviction that the Dharma requires ever new re-formulations so as to meet the needs of new ages, new populations and new social circumstances, they set out to produce a new literature. The creation of this literature is one of the most magnificent outbursts of creative energy known to human history and it was sustained for about four to five centuries. Repetition alone, they believed, cannot sustain a living religion. Unless counterbalanced by constant innovation, it will become fossilized and lose its life-giving qualities.

So far the Mahayanistic attitude seems quite logical. What is more difficult to understand is that they insisted in presenting these new writings, manifestly composed centuries after the Buddha's death, <u>as the very words of the Buddha Himself</u>. In order to make room for the new dispensation, they followed the Mahasanghikas in minimizing the importance of the historical Buddha Sakyamuni, whom they replaced by the Buddha who is the embodiment of Dharma (dharmakaya) (Conze, 1980; 45).

This approach taken by the Mahayanists is based on the belief in the timeless eternal quality of enlightened mind, which exists in "dharmakaya Buddhas." The ultimate Buddha — the dharmakaya makes itself manifest to man in the form of Buddhas that have appeared throughout the eons. So instead of attaining enlightenment under the bodhi tree, we are told that the Buddha abides for all eternity and that he manifests in countless places and innumerable disguises to preach the Law. This is taught with authority in this famous verse from the "Diamond Sutra:"

Those who by my form did see me,
And those who followed me by voice,
Wrong the efforts they engage in,
Me those people will not see!
From the Dharma-body should one see the Buddhas,
From the Dharma-bodies comes their guidance.

This verse succeeds in putting down Theravadin Buddhists by stating that they are wrong to stick to the past if they believe that their authentic sutras are more valuable then the ongoing revelation of dharma by various manifestations of the Dharma-body, as the author of the Diamond Sutra claims.

> Not content with this, the Mahayanists tried to link their own writings with the historical Buddha by a number of mythological fictions. They asserted that they had been preached by the Buddha in the course of His life on earth, that parallel to the Council at Rajagrha, which codified the Sutras of the Hinayana, the Mahayana Sutras had been codified by an assembly of Bodhisattvas on the mythical mountain of Vimalasvabhava; that the texts had been miraculously preserved for five centuries and stored away in the subterranean palaces of the Nagas, or with the king of the Gandharvas, or the king of the Gods. Then, as Nargarjuna puts it, "five hundred years after the Buddha's Nirvana, when the Good Law, after having gradually declined, was in great danger," these treasures from the past were unearthed, revealed and made known, so as to revivify the doctrine (Conze, 1980; 46).

All of these various factors drove the early Mahayanists to create their own sutras to prop up their growing inspiration. It was a moving and inspiring period of growth. Since we Mahayanists believe in a living revelation, one that speaks to us even today, let's take a look at how we can have more new fresh teachings from the Buddha and reignite our inspiration. Let's bring the Buddha to life again!

The Nine Principles of Sutra Writing

To actually go about writing a new sutra you should prepare several items of information to weave into your scripture. You should include most or all of the following nine principles of sutra writing, which may have been used since perhaps the first or second centuries A.D. It is not known for certain if the Iranians were the progenitors of some of these principles of sutra writing. The great fathers of the Mahayana may have kept their work largely behind the scenes but just as Padmasambhava is venerated as the father of Tibetan Buddhism, we should pay homage to the unsung fathers of our

Mahayana heritage. Before writing your own sutra you should arouse the proper devotion towards the Mahayana founders by meditating on bodhicitta and visualizing them enveloped in love and compassion. They cared for, fought for and nourished these principles to bring us the foundation of the greatest collection of sutras in the world. These are the nine great principles on how to create a new sutra:

1. Put down the Hinayana
2. De-emphasize the Buddha
3. The idea you want to sell
4. Built in insurance
5. Revise a Theravadin sutra
6. The bigger and better deal
7. Ancient history
8. Channelled sutra
9. Marketing

Let us now carefully and thoroughly consider each and every principle of creating new sutras:

1. Put down the Hinayana
The quote earlier from the Diamond sutra illustrates this principle. Putting down the Hinayana is almost obligatory in honour of our Mahayana founders and lineage holders who asserted that they were higher and better than the dominate Theravadin tradition of their day. Don't forget how we were rejected by the forerunners of the Theravadins at the second council, 100 years after the Buddha. At that time, the Sthaviras "the Elders", were the dominate force in Buddhism and they renounced us outright as heretics. The present day Theravadins are an offshoot of the Vibhajyavadins who were an offshoot of the original elders, the Sthaviras. They wanted to see the end of the revolution at its birth! Never forget the Hinayana. Because the Elders humiliated our spiritual forefathers the Mahayana has invented ten stages of enlightenment and teach that Hinayanists can only reach to level four, no higher, unless they practice Mahayana. Tibetan Buddhists as well as other Mahayanists regularly make an effort to put down the Hinayana so you should do your part too. You don't want another tradition being better than yours, do you? Of all the religions in the world, what could possibly be worse than a form of Buddhism that sticks very close to the Buddha's teachings? Since the Theravadins are fundamentally better than us, then we must do what we can to squash them down, otherwise we'll lose people if they find out the truth. Mahayana is an illegitimate lineage; only the Theravadins are a legitimate lineage from the Buddha. We can't change history. No matter what we do the Mahayana is an illegitimate tradition because the Buddha did not teach Mahayana, and he would undoubtedly refute it, so

we must try to keep on top of the Theravadins.

Dale Carnegie taught that criticism can be a disguised compliment. This is true of the Mahayanists. Tibetan masters go out of their way to explain how inferior the Hinayana is to the Vajrayana. They give lists, reasons, rationalizations and stories of Hinayana monks who seem narrow minded. Countless Tibetan Buddhist books selling today have such references scattered through them. Take a look. One unnamed Tibetan Lama told his students about a conference he was at in India. He said that a Hinayana monk claimed that the world was flat. The Tibetan explained that for the first seven years the Buddha only taught Hinayana and he followed the Hindu belief of the day, that the world was flat (sic), before teaching Mahayana after those seven years. When the Lama told the Hinayanist that astronauts have been to the moon and saw that the world was round, the Hinayana monk allegedly said "Well, the further out you go the more things look different."

You can write similar things for your proud tradition. All of this disdain for the Hinayana can mean only one thing: envy. You've heard of penis envy; this is sutra envy. Even Kalu Rinpoche, whom I respect as one of the most enlightened Tibetan yogis of the 20th century, in his book *Gently Whispered* he stated (Kalu, 1994, 56):

> In presenting different approaches for dealing with emotionality, Buddha Shakyamuni taught the three yanas or vehicles. The hinayana (or lesser vehicle) emphasizes abandoning or rejecting certain kinds of emotionality that are productive of confusion and suffering. Specific life styles are chosen to allow only certain activities in one's life and to cut off others simply through rejection or abandonment, because these activities are perceived as sources of samsaric suffering. The hinayana idea is to turn off unnecessary, counterproductive parts of one's life: one simply does away with activities that accumulate negative results. In many Eastern countries, where life still goes at a much slower pace and modernization is far from being complete, this path is easier to follow and is still currently in practice. For most Westerners, however, this approach is perhaps too severe, as the modern lifestyle makes it difficult to stop doing things that are considered to be within the social norm. It may not be feasible to exert such an exacting precision in shaping one's own morality without strong social support.

These claims by Kalu Rinpoche are projections which are wrong and grossly misleading to the point of character assassination. The 'Hinayana' teaches many techniques of dealing with emotions, not just abandoning or rejecting (Mn. 20). The best of the Mahayana can be found in the Hinayana anyway. Kalu Rinpoche is saying that the 'Hinayana' is suitable for a slower paced country but not for modern life and yet he would not admit that, in truth the 'Hinayana' includes every word of the Buddha's dispensation and that the Buddha's dharma is just as applicable to our world today, fast or slow, as it was then.

Because only the Hinayanists have the complete authentic teachings, our best Mahayana defence is a good offence. We call them Hinayana which literally translates as lesser vehicle but it also means crummy vehicle or lousy vehicle. You can go along with the Tibetan teaching and pretend that the Buddha taught Hinayana for the first seven years of his ministry, then he initiated Mahayana. Somehow you could try to explain (since no one else can) in your sutra how these thousands of Hinayana practitioners somehow managed to avoid seeing the Buddha for the remaining thirty-eight years of his ministry, and they managed to avoid understanding or clicking with the Mahayana teachings which, allegedly the Buddha thoroughly expatiated during those thirty-eight years. In this way supposedly, the elementary Hinayana was passed down to the present day, but they had no record of the Mahayana even existing during the Buddha's time.

2. De-emphasize the Buddha

Hinayana sutras mean Gotama Buddha. Let's use the Mahayana term "Sakyamuni Buddha," which means "sage of the Sakyas." As we have already established, this world might be a less confusing place if King Asoka didn't ensure the survival of the Hinayana in Sri Lanka, Burma and Thailand. The Theravada is like the 'Gospel of Thomas' in Buddhism. Discovered in an Egyptian cavern in 1945, the Gospel of Thomas completely changed people's impression of the teachings of Jesus because it is likely more authentic than the Bible itself. That lineage of Christianity was wiped out of existence in the early centuries, but not so with Theravadin Buddhism. So we must work harder to overcome Buddhist traditions that are more authentic than our own Mahayana. In our preemptive strike, putting down the Hinayana, we must pull down the historical Buddha as well because "he knows too much."

We have committed character assassination against Gotama Buddha because it was necessary to change the sutras to suit our growing and changing needs. You have an opportunity to write a sutra thanks to our work which has resulted in a very different record of who the Buddha really was. He's our Buddha now, not their Buddha, so we must always keep vigil to maintain our character assassination against the true Buddha. In order for you to understand all the work that our Mahayana forefathers, such as Nargarjuna, have done to assassinate the Buddha, consider this modernized analogy to President Kennedy's assassination.

> Visualize one of the ancient lineage holders of Tibetan Buddhism in the sixth floor window of the Texas School Book Depository. He is loading his weapon full of tantra sutras. Gotama Buddha's plane, Protector One, has just landed at Love Field in Dallas. The Buddha steps out of the plane and he greets the adoring crowd. As his motorcade slowly moves

along the streets of Dallas, four Mahayanists assemble on the grassy knoll behind the picket fence. After the Buddha's limousine turns left and drives past the Texas School Book Depository, shots ring out from the Depository and from the grassy knoll as the Mahayanists shoot false sutras all over the Buddha. The Buddha grabs his throat but whatever he says comes out wrong, the words are all changed around. For some reason the limousine actually *slows down* so at that point Gotama Buddha invokes his magical powers to create a replica of himself who instantaneously appears in a Theravadin Buddhist country. This Gotama Buddha survives unstained.

As the limousine speeds to Dallas General Hospital, Gotama Buddha feels his body absorbing the slime of the false sutras splattered all over his head. Inside, the doctors and nurses work feverishly over the Buddha but there is nothing they can do. The Buddha lays in samadhi while various human forces conspire with some of Mara's hosts to fly him to Bethesda Naval Hospital in Maryland. There Buddha lays in repose in a patient calm while people change his head and rename him as "Shakyamuni Buddha." Emerging from his samadhi the Buddha, now Shakyamuni Buddha, manages to carry on but he is never the same again. He is the Mahayana Buddha.

Some people are jealous because they've discovered that an emanation of the real Buddha is inspiring Theravadin countries, so they successfully set about spin doctoring views to put down the "Hinayana." They know that their own people will believe and follow propaganda more than they will believe and follow hard evidence. Like the adoring crowd, even though the Mahayanists think that they love the Buddha, they are really harming the Buddha. The character assassination of Gotama Buddha is complete.

The Hinayana sutras have got all the good stuff that the Mahayana and Vajrayana have, so we have got to use mirrors to perform some creative writing and creative one upmanship on the Buddha himself. Here's the policy: arbitrarily divide the dharma into beginner level, intermediate and advanced levels. All of this is Theravadin Buddhism of course but what we do is to associate the most advanced or difficult concepts of Theravadin Buddhism with Mahayana and Vajrayana. Anything basic we lump together as Hinayana. In this way we make Theravadin Buddhism seem basic and unsophisticated. This is a total lie but it does work effectively as people love to buy into categories like this because it is convenient for their understanding. This has worked for 2000 years.

As Edward Conze indicated above, the Mahayana transcends Sakyamuni

Buddha with dharmakaya Buddhas such as Vajradhara, Amitabha, etc., to sell the idea that the human manifestation of the last Buddha — a "nirmanikaya Buddha," is just the foam on a wave compared to the primordial Buddha. In writing your sutra, you will find that the more you dwell on these heady cosmological explanations, the more you will begin to even believe it yourself! It is sooooooo seductive. It's no wonder that the Buddha warned against being seduced by the subtle states of mind described as 'false enlightenment.' You'll have no problem talking circles around the most sincere kindhearted Buddhists in the world.

Celestial Bodhisattvas go hand in hand with celestial Buddhas in diluting... diluting... diluting... the historical Buddha. Jazz 'em up! You're a writer aren't you? Sariputra and all of the Buddha's fully enlightened monks must also be de-emphasized or put down. In the Diamond sutra the Buddha scolds Sariputra for clinging to a Hinayana view. This is classic Mahayana. In Burton Watson's translation of the Lotus Sutra* he states:

> In some Mahayana texts Sariputra and the other close disciples of the
> Buddha, who represent the Lesser Vehicle outlook and path of endeavour,
> are held up to ridicule or portrayed as figures of fun (Watson, 1993; xvii).

In the Lotus sutra the monks are treated more sympathetically with compassion, but they are made to look rather like buffoons in other sutras because character assassination is a handy formula for putting down people that are better than yourself. It's amazing actually. Politicians do this to each other at every election because it's a proven method that works! Sariputra was the number one chief disciple of the Buddha. He was possessed of the greatest depths of wisdom of any human being in recorded history next to the Buddha himself. Yet, with the right amount of character assassination plus fictitious bodhisattvas, millions of people, even American Tibetan Buddhist scholars, hold the fictitious bodhisattva Avalokitesvara in higher regard than Sariputra. Bravo for the nine principles of sutra writing!

To deepen your impact, in your sutra you can state that the Buddha's fully enlightened monks are 'sort of enlightened' or just 'Hinayana' enlightened. This is quite complicated actually because our elders had to work this out centuries after the fact, but the precedents have been established whereby you know with ultimate conviction that a Vajrayana enlightenment and a Mahayana enlightenment is better than a mere Hinayana enlightenment — that of an arahant. Watson states:

> But now, the Buddha tells us, these lesser paths or goals [arahant and
> Bodhisattva] are to be set aside and all beings are to aim for the single
> goal of Buddhahood, the one and only vehicle to true enlightenment or
> perfect understanding, a state designated in the Lotus Sutra by the rather
> daunting Sanskrit term anuttara-samyak-sambodhi (Watson, 1993; xvii).

Therefore, it doesn't matter what a Hinayanist did in the past, present or future. An arahant will never be able to hold a candle to a Bodhisattva, or a Buddha. Somehow those Hinayana arahants just don't "get it," and still have a ways to go yet. Conze writes:

> The first schism, between Mahasanghikas and Sthaviras, was occasioned by the question of the status of the Arahants. A teacher by the name of Mahadeva arose, who claimed that in five points the Arahants fell short of the god-like stature which some sections of the community attributed to them. They could, among other things, have seminal emissions in their sleep, and that fact, so he argued, indicated that they are still subject to the influence of demonic deities who appear to them in their dreams. They are also still subject to doubts, ignorant of many things, and owe their salvation to the guidance of others. His thesis led to a dispute in which the majority took the side of Mahadeva, whose school in consequence called themselves the Mahasanghikas. His adversaries took the name of Sthaviras, "the Elders," claiming greater seniority and orthodoxy [an earlier form of what is now Theravada]. The Mahasanghikas continued to exist in India until the end and important doctrinal developments took place within their midst. All these were ultimately determined by their decision to take the side of the people against the saints, thus becoming the channel through which popular aspirations entered into Buddhism (Conze, 1980; 33).

Another way to deemphasize the Buddha and take a chunk out of his teachings is to undercut the validity of the competitor sutras altogether with this tool provided by the Lotus Sutra:

> The first lesson the sutra wishes to teach, then, is that its doctrines, delivered by the Buddha some forty or more years after the start of his preaching career, which is how the Lotus Sutra depicts them, represent the highest level of truth, the summation of the Buddha's message, superseding his earlier pronouncements, which had only provisional validity (Watson, 1993; xvii).

3. The idea you want to sell

Why write a sutra in the first place? Just for an ego trip to impress people? Well, you could do that too actually, but the main reason is to insert your opinion or idea into the Buddhist religion so that you can change it to your liking. Wasn't the Mahayana founded on the view of making a living, growing, changing religion, rather than a repetitive one? What is it that you have never heard the Buddha say but you always wanted him to say? Is it the details of what happens after death which are revealed in the questionable *Tibetan Book of the Dead,* or some other agenda? With these nine principles you now have the tools to write it yourself. Perhaps you want some teachings regarding the environment, gay/lesbian issues, equality for women, socialism, capitalism or whatever. I know a man who implied that the Buddha's entire teaching was just a subsection of a larger gay issue. One Iranian fellow wanted to insert his theistic religious beliefs into Buddhism. He practiced sun god worship and the situation is alluded to by Edward Conze below: (Conze, 1980; 49)

> From the ordinary bodhisattvas as they exist on the first stages, the "celestial bodhisattvas" of the last four stages differ in that they were well suited to becoming objects of a religious cult. Soon the faithful increasingly turned to all kinds of mythical Bodhisattvas, such as Avalokitesvara, Manjusri, Maitreya, Kshitigarbha, Samantabhadra and others. Though conceived in India some of these bodhisattvas show strong non-Indian, and particularly Iranian, influences.
>
> The development of mythical bodhisattvas was accompanied, and even preceded by, that of mythical Buddhas, Who were held to reside in the heavens in all the ten directions. In the East lives Akshobhya, the "Imperturbable." In the West is the kingdom of the Buddha of "Infinite Light," Amitabha, not always clearly distinguished from Amitayus, the Buddha who "has an infinite life-span." Amitayus, is a counterpart to the Iranian Zurvan Akaranak ("Unlimited Time"), just as the cult of Amitabha owed much to Iranian sun worship and probably originated in the Kushana Empire in the borderland between India and Iran.

The big shocker is that a primitive sun worship religion is what Amitabha Buddha really and truly is. You could say that most oriental Buddhist temples you see today are really temples for the Iranian sun god religion. The two celestial Buddhas that they worship, Akshobhya and Amitabha, are on the right and left sides respectively inside Pure Land temples. Which of the three statues represents the real Buddha? Door number one? Door number two? Or door number three? You guessed it, the middle Buddha. The other two — *come on down.*

4. Built-in insurance — the threat of Hell.
One reason why the Lotus Sutra has thrived in the minds of millions of Asians is because it is very heavy handed in it's southern Baptist preacher's approach. In a nutshell, it says that if you disrespect that sutra, then you'll go to hell. Now, obviously the compassionate Buddha would never ever ever say anything remotely like that. But hey! Let's ruin the Buddha's kind reputation in order to popularize our new deal!

Welcome to the Mahayana. Looking deeper into this nutshell, get a load of this. In the Lotus Sutra the Buddha is addressing Sariputra about preaching the Lotus Sutra: (Watson, 1993; 74)

> Those with the shallow understanding of ordinary persons,
> who are deeply attached to the five desires,
> cannot comprehend it when they hear it.
> Do not preach it to them.
> If a person fails to have faith
> but instead slanders this sutra,
> immediately he will destroy all the seeds
> for becoming a Buddha in this world.
> Or perhaps he will scowl with knitted brows
> and harbour doubt or perplexity.
> Listen and I will tell you the penalty this person must pay.
> Whether the Buddha is in the world
> or has already entered extinction,
> if this person should slander
> a sutra such as this,
> or on seeing those who read, recite,
> copy and uphold this sutra,
> should despise, hate, envy,
> or bear grudges against them,
> the penalty this person must pay-
> listen, I will tell you now:
> When his life comes to an end
> he will enter the Avichi hell,
> be confined there for a whole kalpa,
> and when the kalpa ends, be born there again.
> He will keep repeating this cycle
> for a countless number of kalpas.
> Though he may emerge from hell,
> he will fall into the realm of beasts,
> becoming a dog or jackal,
> his form lean and scruffy,
> dark, discoloured, with scabs and sores,
> something for men to make sport of.
> Or again he will be
> hated and despised by men,

constantly plagued by hunger and thirst,
his bones and flesh dried up,
in life undergoing torment and hardship,
in death buried beneath tiles and stones.
Because he cut off the seeds of Buddhahood
he will suffer this penalty.
If he should become a camel
or be born in the shape of a donkey,
his body will constantly bear heavy burdens
and have the stick or whip laid on it.
He will think only of water and grass
and understand nothing else.
Because he slandered this sutra,
this is the punishment he will incur.
(This tale of misery and woe goes on for three more pages...)

Now that you've seen how it has been done successfully before, this home sutra building kit continues with an example of a sutra which you could write:

Thus have I heard. Once the Blessed One was dwelling amongst the southern peoples of Kusinara by Flora Lake. In the morning after returning from his alms round he spent the day's abiding in the pleasance gardens of Landadisney. There he addressed venerable Ananda, "Listen carefully Ananda and I will give you my teachings to guide the aspirations for the sangha of a future age." — "Venerable sir," Ananda replied.

"The dispensation of the noble law will extend through many centuries to a time of tremendous power and prosperity. At that time sensuous distractions will engulf men's minds so here I will express the course of action, the effort, the exertion that true men should strive for at that time. Those who are blessed to study and follow this sutra at that time will see truth, they will see the Buddha. Those that reject, spurn, disdain and slander my words, listen and I will tell you how they will suffer:
Firstly they will slip on a banana peel and fall on the road and their head will be crushed by what will be known as an 18 wheeler. Then they will take spontaneous uprising in niraya hell, and there they will be forced by heat and flames into the video store from hell. On the enticing walls they will see thousands of copies of the one and only video for rent that is available in the video store from hell: the TV movie *Rescue from Gilligan's Island*. Although beyond imagination, hell gets even worse! You take your

video back home to your plot of fire and brimstone and your roommates from hell blame you for having such moronic taste! They plug in the video and see the aging Gilligan running up and down the beach yelling "Skipper! Skipper!" and after every scene your roommates from hell knot their brows, shake furious fists and loudly curse you saying "God! You jerk!! Why did you pick such a stupid video?!"

The entire description of this particular region of niraya hell goes on for seventeen pages in the endlessgilligansutra, delivered in Kusinara thirty-three years after the Buddha's awakening.

* * * * * * * * * *

The above is an example of the kind of insurance you should build into your sutra to increase readership and snuff out dissent. Only time will tell if this policy of threatening people with hell actually works in our century and in our culture or not. It's been working well since the third century! and is very much the tradition of Mahayana sutra writing so at least we are honouring our forefathers. Westerners do not easily cower however if you threaten them in any way. You may have to be more creative and cunning than this to pull off a new sutra. Good luck.

5. Revise a Theravadin Sutra

Got writer's cramp? Don't know where to start to make your mark on history? If you don't know how to start writing a new sutra, then start writing an old sutra! In our Mahayana tradition there are revered sutras such as the Heart Sutra that are Theravadin sutras which have been edited, revised and sooped up. The original Heart Sutra does not include the deity of compassion, Avalokitesvara; he was inserted centuries later but the discourse is about the same. Once you start off copying an old sutra, you can let your inspiration flow and write in extra characters and dialogue with the Buddha and those around him. Sometimes if you unwind with a few beer first, when you put your fingers to the keyboard you can come up with some real inventive characters and a good story. If you're real good, like the accomplished and the experienced author of the Lotus Sutra, your work could be more popular than the discourses of the real Buddha himself! Go for it.

You can revise any of the hundreds of Theravadin sutras but you must present your fiction as an authentic Mahayanasutra. *Don't ever call it a Theravadin sutra.* This is no joke. A hundred million people hold very dear those most sacred of all Buddhist scriptures and they would be gravely offended if you tried to pass off your writing as one of their sutras. Please, you must treat Theravadin Buddhists with respect. They have worked very hard to preserve the accuracy of Gotama Buddha's message and they deserve grudging admiration. It is disrespectful, in the Theravadin tradition, to write a Theravadin sutra—it's impossible! If you write a

Mahayanasutra the Theravadins have no objection at all as they generally renounce the Mahayana anyway. To some Theravadins the Mahayana is another religion. To a Theravadin, a Mahayanasutra is like some fiction novel on a bookstore shelf in Taiwan. It's meaningless to true Buddhists. Truly, the Lotus Sutra, the Diamond Sutra and the rest, are PRI: popular religious imagination. They're great actually!; much, much greater though similar to the Batman and Superman characters of today. They are above compare to today's fantasy fiction because of the dharma imbued in these legendary Mahayanasutras. The Lotus Sutra however, doesn't seem to have much dharma teachings in it. Hardly a word about mindfulness/awareness, meditation, working with the mind. It's a fantastic story with a thousand million billion celestial devas surrounding Buddhas and bodhisattvas so it's easy to see how it appealed to the masses more than the hard work of the Buddha's dharma.

This sutra tradition in the Mahayana does allow for you to write your own sutras. You don't have to be enlightened as their sutra authors obviously weren't. So now you can relax and have some fun!; be creative! Our belief is that the religion must not be a dead religion preserved through repetition; it should be alive with new revelations, teachings and sutras all the time. Jump right in and revise an old repetitive sutra. Even today this is being done by the Venerable Thich Nhat Hanh as seen in his very good book *Old Path White Clouds – Following in the Footsteps of the Buddha.* His approach is to write in extra descriptive details around the Buddha and the main characters in the Buddha's life. This has resulted in a very vivid portrait which brings the Buddha to life in a way that is very close to us! That is a masterful book at helping others arouse inspiration, faith and devotion. Aside from the rest of this satirical essay, that sentence is not sarcasm. If you write sutras in this way just be sure you call your product a Mahayana product. The Theravadin sutras are too sacred. Don't dilute the real Buddha's words with your own. That is a sacred cow which you cannot slay. Not every sacred cow should be slain, only the stupid sacred cows.

You are writing your sutra many centuries after the Buddha but you are presenting it as the Buddha's very words for the purpose of inspiring faith and devotion. Richard Nixon published several books with his advice for how people should live but they inspire little faith or devotion because readers know who the author is — Richard Nixon. The authors of the Lotus Sutra and the Diamond Sutra and the rest of that genre, are unknown to us but because their advice for how people should live, unlike Nixon's, was put in the guise of the Buddha, it has inspired people throughout the age. The obvious objection of course is that they were unenlightened people so their teachings can't rate with the Buddha's. That is absolutely true of course which is why you shouldn't write a sutra, but of course, this is only a Hinayana viewpoint.

The Dead Giveaway

In your effort to inspire people by keeping current with their needs now, be careful not to allow people to detect that your sutra was composed long after the Buddha. You don't want them to think "Hey! This is just a fake sutra! This is no sutra at all." You want to sound convincing. Some people will be smart enough to see through your insincerity but take heart, most of the great Mahayana sutras were designed to appeal to simple people and the masses aren't as smart as Buddhist scholars. Don't worry about the smart people. They'll go away and read something else. Even if you are a bit sloppy your discourse will still fly with some people. Before a huge audience in 1965, Bob Dylan announced "You can fool some of the people all of the time. You can fool some of the people some of the time, but you can't fool all of the people all of the time!"

If you want to sell yourself to a much greater number of unsuspecting Buddhists, then avoid the dead giveaway of references to "the future." Life is such that people don't go around giving advice about what people should be doing centuries from now. If you think about it, the idea is absolutely ridiculous. But since we, like our forefathers are employed in a con job, we are faced with the impossible task of trying to get the Buddha to say what we want him to say and somehow have that mesh with the real sutras which were not (no comment) wiped out from history. This is an impossibility, but as mass psychology has proven over the centuries, it doesn't matter very much. "The big lie theory," they call it. If people are hip to an idea, they will run with it and efforts will be made to avoid discerning the truth. The Mahayana vision has succeeded and now encompasses about 75% of the entire Buddhist world. The case rests.

It is hard to avoid references to the future as seen in the excerpt of the Amitabha sutra (short for "the Sutra of Visualizing the Buddha of Immeasurable Length of Life") below, or in the more obvious endlessgilligansutra written above. In this sutra, written by an Iranian author sometime prior to 250 A.D., a real sutra is revised where the Buddha is conversing with Queen Vaidehi, of the kingdom of Magadha. Then the Iranian author, maybe a creative writer not much different than yourself, dramatically inserted a celestial Buddha with two bodhisattvas: (Max Muller, 1939; 47)

> [The "Buddha" said] "If a person has seen this visualization, his enormous crimes of countless kalpas are annulled; and he will certainly be reborn in the Pure Land after his passing away. One who visualizes in this way does right, otherwise one does wrong."

> The Buddha told the Venerable Ananda and Vaidehi, "Listen! Listen! And ponder it over. I shall tell you of the ways to get rid of suffering one by one. You should remember and practice them well and

spread them for the many."

While saying this, the Buddha of Immeasurable Length of Life appeared in the air. Bodhisattva Avalokitesvara was standing on his right and Bodhisattva Mahasthamaprapta on his left. Their bodily rays were so brilliant that one could not see them wholly.

Then, after having seen the Buddha of Immeasurable Length of Life, Vaidehi did obeisance at the feet of the Buddha (Sakyamuni) and said to him, "Blessed One, now I am able to see the Buddha of Immeasurable Length of Life and these two Bodhisattvas by the Buddha's help. But how will all the beings in the future be able to visualize this Buddha and these two Bodhisattvas?"

Does this sutra sound like "Please god, please Jesus, forgive me for my sins and take me to heaven?" You bet it does. This is capital 'T' Theism. You can just imagine the Buddha's bones stirring today as they utter the sound, "Not so. Wrong views." After the above dialogue the alleged Buddha goes into a fantastically colourful description of the visualization of the alleged Pure Land with alleged lotus flowers emitting eighty-four thousand rays of alleged light from each alleged vein.

Another craft you can learn on Saturday mornings with the kids is the art of making your own bodhisattva. The cosmos has plenty of room for a few thousand million billion trillion more. Or, you can write to the BSSG and receive a special discount on three bodhisattvas for the price of one! Just enclose a copy of the order form at the back of this book and you will receive three bodhisattva names for only $3.95 CAD. Be sure to enclose your name as it is commonly used, your address, birth date, birth time and preferably a photo of only yourself.

This brings us to the next point: Hollywood.

6. The bigger and better deal
Hand in hand with the first principle of sutra writing is the sixth principle. After putting down the Hinayana, you must boost up the Mahayana so that the buying public can simply and clearly comprehend the advantages of going with your religious product. What you do is you sharpen your pencil, as it were, and sketch out a beautiful and wonderful promise that practitioners can have that far transcends anything that Buddhists can obtain without working for it. The problem with Buddhism, that is, the Theravadin sutras, is that Buddhism promises nothing. In real life you have to do all the work. Not in the Mahayana because "the Great Vehicle" offers theism—the promise of paradise and the cleansing of all bad karma, but without taking responsibility for your actions by working through the obstacles and bringing them onto your

spiritual path. Forget a spiritual path! You don't need one! You don't have to do much more than lift a finger! In the book *Horizontal Escape – Pure Land Buddhism in Theory and Practice,* by Dharma Master Thich Thien Tam, he writes:

> "Horizontal" and "vertical" are figures of speech, which can readily be understood through the following example. Suppose we have a worm, born inside a stalk of bamboo. To escape, it can take the "hard way" and crawl all the way to the top of the stalk. Alternatively, it can look for or poke a hole near its current location and escape "horizontally" into the big, wide world. The horizontal escape, for sentient beings, is to seek rebirth in the Pure Land of Amitabha Buddha (Thien Tam, 1997; i).

Further, Thich Thien Tam describes the Transference of Merit stanza in the Meditation Sutra:

> I vow to be reborn in the Western Pure Land,
> The nine lotus grades are my parents.
> As the lotus flowers bloom, I will see Buddha Amitabha
> and reach No-Birth,
> Liberating all sentient beings...(Thien Tam, 1997; 232)

Andrew, my advisor mentioned earlier is both a Pure Land Buddhist and a Tibetan Buddhist and he describes these nine levels or grades of lotus flowers as being "very commercial actually. It's worse than the Christian religion," he lamented. Some patrons of Pure Land temples today directly disdain Buddhists who practice meditation. They say "Why meditate if you're going to go to the Pure Land anyway?" I've witnessed this myself. When I was leading a meditation group at the International Buddhist Society, Pure Land temple, a group of old Chinese ladies saw us when they walked into our hall and they talked loudly and they kept right on talking as loudly as they do in the kitchen. This means that the bigger and better deal that the Mahayanists sell can entice people away from the Buddhadharma and spoon feed them the several-centuries-after-the-Buddha anti-dharma instead. If you can create sutras like that, there's a lot of money involved in building temples and objects of worship, for people to come and venerate. I've witnessed this too, because that's where my paycheque came from. "They're doing it for the money," people say of some temples. The tendency to worship runs so deep in humanity that people will do it even in a non-theistic religion like Buddhism.

Instead of practicing meditation for the long term and studying the dharma to gain some understanding over the long term, you can give people a drug, but a reassuring drug, that everything will be O.K. if they just do the practice you are promoting in your sacred sutra. For example, in a Pure Land temple, they chant to

Amitayus Buddha, a.k.a. the Medicine Buddha. In the Smaller Sukhavati-Vyuha, alleged discourse of the Blessed One, the Buddha allegedly says: (Max Muller, 1939; 11)

> "O Sariputra, of those beings also who are born in the Buddha country of the Tathagata Amitayus as purified Bodhisattvas, never to return again and bound by one birth only, of those Bodhisattvas also, O Sariputra, the number is not easy to count, except they are reckoned as infinite in number.
>
> Then again all beings, O Sariputra, ought make fervent prayer for that Buddha country. And why? Because they come together there with such excellent men. Beings are not born in that Buddha country of the Tathagata Amitayus as a reward and result of good works performed in this present life. No, whatever son or daughter of a family shall hear the name of the blessed Amitayus, the Tathagata, and having heard it, shall keep it in mind, and with thoughts undisturbed shall keep it in mind, for one, two, three, four, five, six or seven nights, — when that son or daughter of a family comes to die, then that Amitayus, the Tathagata, surrounded by an assembly of disciples and followed by a host of Bodhisattvas, will stand before them at their hour of death, and they will depart this life with tranquil minds. After their death they will be born in the world Sukhavati, in the Buddha country of the same Amitayus, the tathagata. Therefore, then, O Sariputra, having perceived this cause and effect, I with reverence say thus. Every son and every daughter of a family ought with their whole mind to make fervent prayer for that Buddha country."

Scary, isn't it?

7) Ancient history
O.K. boys and girls, we're almost done. Now, to lend some respectability to your English language sutra, take a cue from the King of sutras (as it calls itself), the Lotus sutra. We do not know where or when the Lotus Sutra was composed, or in what language. Probably it was initially formulated in some local dialect of India or Central Asia and then later put into Sanskrit to lend it greater respectability. All we can say for certain about the date of its composition is that it was already in existence by 255 A.D., when the first Chinese translation of it was made (Watson, 1993; ix).

You are trying to lie and convince people (which some people may believe anyway) that your sutra was spoken by the Buddha and passed down as an oral tradition for hundreds of years before they had the ability to write it down, so you want it to look old. If you've got the money, or Chinese co-conspirators, you should ideally have your sutra translated into Chinese. Any dialect will do; they're all pretty old. Also, there are particular places where you can get a good deal on very old *blank* paper that has yellowed considerably. Once you have your ancient sutra printed in Chinese on the oldest blank paper you can find, then you have to consider how to make the ink itself appear to be a hundred years old. There are methods to get around the carbon dating obstacle, but for undisclosed reasons these are not described in this book.

The date when your sutra was translated into Chinese from Sanskrit should be approximated. You could even include some information about the translation process if you are daring. Nobody is going to dig around in China and give you a hard time.

8. Channelled sutras

This is almost too good to be true. This is a remarkable opportunity for legitimacy! In the Theravadin tradition, they teach that the abhidharma was channelled down from devas that were personally taught the dharma by the Buddha. This may be true, or maybe not. The Buddha visited his mother in Tavatimsa heaven, and while there, it is said that he taught the abhidharma to millions of devas. The reason given is that the Buddha refused to give a discourse unless beings could hold their posture throughout the entire talk. Because the abhidharma is so long and complicated the Buddha could not teach it to human beings as they could not sit still for so long. Instead the Buddha taught devas in Tavatimsa and other heavens. This was channelled down to human beings after two centuries resulting in the third basket of scripture which was then included into the canon. This is one Theravadin explanation given in the abhidharma itself, but Edward Conze writes that after the early splits within Buddhism, the Sarvastivadins (still the southern school), split off from the original Sthaviras. The Sarvastivadins had differing ideas than the Vibhajyavadins about the affect of the law of karma over time, so they evolved a pan-realistic theory which introduced many difficulties in its wake and a vast superstructure of auxilary hypotheses was required to make it tenable (Conze, 1980; 37).

As a result of the emergence of an interest in philosophical questions we have the first instance of a whole class of canonical literature being created to meet a new situation. This is the *abhidharma* which was clearly composed after the third division of the schools, from about 200 B.C. onwards (Conze, 1980; 37). Both the Theravada and Mahayana have abhidharma, and both claim that parts of it at least, were channelled down to earth from devas in the god realm. For sutra writing, this principle opens up limitless opportunities to justify any hair-brained scheme as being inspired by the Buddha himself. For example, in the Yabadabadoo sutra, recently channelled down to earth, a deva reported to a channeller with a clear and undeluded connection that at one time lay follower Fred Flintstone asked the Buddha to tell his daughter Pebbles to look after him and Wilma when they got old. Barney and Betty had the same concern about Bam Bam. The Buddha said "O Pebbles and Bam Bam, you must care for your parents because you cannot repay them for all they have done for you. Even if you carry them on both shoulders for 100 years and attend to them by anointing them with salves, by massaging, bathing and rubbing their limbs, you could not do enough for them. Even if you were to establish your parents as supreme lords and rulers over this earth so rich in the seven treasures, O Pebbles and Bam Bam, you would never repay their kindness to you." Other channelled Mahayanasutras reveal even more teachings regarding the Flintstones.

The Mahayana claims that even before the Buddha first turned the wheel on earth, he gave his first formal sutra to bodhisattvas in heaven, which was later channelled down to earth and included in the Mahayanasutras. Tilopa, one of the fathers of Tibetan Buddhism claimed to channel down to earth the Vajrayana teachings from dharmakaya Buddha Vajradhara. All four major lineages of Tibetan Buddhism today trace back their most sacred Vajrayana teachings to this personal channel. You can claim to have channelled your sutra too. Who's going to cross examine you?

9. Marketing

Just as new authors have to publicly promote their book, new sutra writers have to clandestinely promote their work. (Isn't this going a bit too far?) You may think that in today's information age you could never get away with such an act as faking ancient information. It's been done before. Check out the *Desiderata,* "found in old Saint Paul's Church, 1692." It's really a 1950's take on deep wisdom. Contrary to popular belief, the information explosion in which we live actually makes it *easier* to slip information into the mass consciousness because people are so overwhelmed with ideas that even if someone found you out, they would be drown out in all the information! Nobody is at home, no one is in charge in this world, so you and your sutra can take full advantage of that. You can even write a magazine article and quote from your sutra as though it is a fait accompli. If you do get this useless project off the ground, please send me a copy. I promise not to tell anybody. Good luck. You'll need it.

Conclusion

If I was so bold as to amend history and throw in a tenth principle of my own, I would call it the Kennedy assassination principle. This principle guides us with the wisdom of realizing that the best way to hide the conspiracy is to entertain 136 other conspiracy theories and water down the true evidence behind the crime. In this way the public will be offered one Lee Harvey Oswald assassin on the one hand, and 136 totally contradictory and ridiculous conspiracy theories on the other. This blessing gives direction to the efforts of the Theravadin Manifesto, which originated in Thailand. Since Mahayanists have tried to smother Theravadin Buddhism for over 2000 years, students in Thailand can work on projects to write volumes of Mahayanasutras to flood the Oriental market, like bringing down the currency of a country. This could contribute to the Theravadin sutras regaining the primacy that they deserve and help raise awareness about the fact that so many Mahayana sutras are false, which most Mahayana Buddhists do not realize. This point is not intended for action but for contemplation since approximately only 10% of Chinese Buddhists know about the "Mahayana split"— the false sutras, and about 30% of Japanese know about it because there was much theological debate about the Iranian connection over the last two centuries in Japan— many people feeling strongly that they had been betraying the Buddha unknowingly.

In conclusion, even though it is wrong to change the Buddha's sacred words people have done this for over 2000 years in order to try to revivify Buddhism, to gain more power for the laity, to make room for their own tradition, and for other reasons. Even in the light of historic evidence, the Mahayana tradition has still chosen to change Buddha's words by still accepting, as sutras, false discourses that have been attributed to the Buddha. We can now get the best of both worlds by benefitting from the centuries of wisdom and realizations accumulated in the Mahayana tradition while relying upon the Theravadin sutras for our most solid ground to hold onto and for assurance about what the Buddha really did teach. The satiric ideas presented in this essay, even if followed, would only serve to raise awareness about the truth of false sutras, therefore this is intended as a benefit for others, as a way of defending the real Buddha. You can write similar things for your proud tradition. All of this disdain for the Hinayana can mean only one thing: envy. You've heard of penis envy; this is sutra envy.

One last word: I believe that it is 'one down' from a heinous crime to create new sutras.

*Lotus Sutra translated by Burton Watson, Cambridge University Press, 1993.

Central shrine at Wat Xieng Thong, northern Laos

Chapter 22

Born in Ontario
An Autobiography

"Born in Tibet," was the first and the most dramatic book written by my beloved guru, Chögyam Trungpa Rinpoche. It recounted his brush with death enduring a nine month struggle with other Tibetans to flee their homeland and escape to India.

I've lived a dramatic life too, especially since my exodus from the horrificly boring suburbs of southern Ontario. There, with my best friend from high school, Rob Stickles, we would wander aimlessly in shopping malls searching for meaning and purpose in life. Then one day when my father was in Moscow on business as a professional engineer, Rob and I commandeered my dad's orange '72 Plymouth Duster and fled Ontario for the fabled lotus land of Vancouver, B.C. Actually, it was more confused than that. I had almost no concept of what Vancouver was. I was looking for a job and the west was booming in those days. Perhaps in a future book you'll read the whole story about the youth hostel in Thunder Bay, northern Ontario, the hitchhikers on the hot plains of Saskatchewan, the mystical experience when I fell asleep in the back seat while Rob drove through the moonless night, and the time we were shaking in the Rocky Mountains. Finally we arrived in Gastown, Vancouver, to crash at the Cambie Hotel. The local government welcomed us. The unemployment rate was so low in Vancouver, about 6%. I really noticed how people didn't worry about the unemployment rate in B.C. the way we did back home in Ontario. It was like a higher realm of existence. It was our new life, and we did it together, at the age of 20. My guru was the same age when he safely arrived in India. The parallels are uncanny!

Time is beginningless, the Buddha taught. So the furthest I can go back for a proper autobiography is to a time that was primordial. The word primordial is defined as: First in time; original; elemental. *Biol.* First in order of appearance in the growth or development of an organism. L *primus* first + *ordiri* to begin a web. In Buddhism, primordial mind refers to the vast open space of mind before conceptual mind began, which would be the basis for defilement. Probably the most effective teaching to understand this heady concept is a Far Side cartoon by Gary Larson. Larson drew this cave man family at home about to have dinner. Caveman and cave kids look rather bored and dissatisfied, when cave mom brings them soup to start off their dinner. The caveman grunts at the bowl of soup placed before him, and says "Primordial soup, again!?"

My personal story began when I split off from this vast open peace of primordial mind. Pönlop Rinpoche told me that "the split happens because luminousity gets so intense that a part of it splits off into duality." There was some ripple of confusion which began my own personal basic ignorance. In that moment of confusion, before there was even an "I," let alone an "I am me," the ripple believed that it was in fact a bubble! That's it! Too late. Blown the game right there! 100,000+ lifetimes of confusion began with that one stupid move. Ah, damn. You've heard the expression 'make one mistake and you pay for it with the rest of your life.' This was it, but each of us has been paying for it for 100,000 lives. I'm sorry Mr. primordial space. Won't you please forgive me and take me back in, please? "No." I guess I'll just have to meditate and work this out for myself.

This bubble in space made the mistaken assumption of believing that it was a separate independent self. This is how you and I and all of us began. In that moment of basic ignorance and confusion we believe that we are a separate independent self. In each and every split second throughout the eons, we constantly reaffirm that fundamental mistake. There is no self. There is no solid bubble. The ripple of confusion is just like a ripple on a pond of water. After the ripple does it's thing, it dissolves back into the empty space of primordial mind again. Good. Good ripple. No self should have arose but it did. Bad. Bad bubble. You could trace back the metaphor of "original sin in the garden of eden" to this one cataclysmic event. And so, we have samsara. We have samsara and we still have this open space of nirvana. Kind of makes for a good setting for the story.

After I split off from the rest of the band because of "musical differences" so to speak, I found that the outside world beyond the fragile walls of my bubble/ego, seemed problematic. I didn't realize that it was still me, or that I was still one with space. I've always believed since then that I was a separate independent self. I began to protect myself from the onslaughts of the universe. I developed a martyr complex because I meant no harm to anyone, and yet the environment around me was often hostile. This fortified my sense of self even more. Before long my egohood developed into the most subtle and sophisticated form of organization in the universe, even more sophisticated and well organized than the Catholic Church.

Discovering Buddhism

My ego took rebirth again and again, a different form each time. My current incarnation was born on December 31, 1959, as the youngest of five children in six years. This helped with my humility since I was used to other people telling me what to do. I owe my life to the Catholic church because if my Dutch parents had any sense at all they wouldn't have had me; five kids was just too much stress on my mother. I grew up in a middle class suburban family in Ontario. Our house was a dynamic mix of creative influences. My first guru was my mother. She channelled unintelligible writings thoughout my youth so my inner constitution is remarkably similar to hers. When I was 17 my father sadly warned, "I think you're going your mother's way." My father was my second guru because he was a reader and a seeker, always exposing us to all kinds of ideas. The shelves were full of books on science fiction, philosophy, psychology and religion. Since age ten I was listening to his success and other educational audiotapes. I began meditating at fourteen with TM.

The altar of television was of central importance after school. The moulding forces deeply embedded into my mind were Star Trek, John Lennon and the Beatles, Kennedy, 20th century American politics, pop music, and the Buddha unknowingly through the book *Handbook to Higher Consciousness* by Ken Keyes. My first memorable connection to the Buddha came when Keyes wrote that his writings were fundamentally based upon the noble truths of the Buddha. My eyes glued to the word "noble" which impressed upon me a powerful image of the equanimity of this great being called the Buddha. I soon decided that this Buddha was absolutely legitimate, beyond any faults, the real thing. Since then, that certainty has never left my mind, the conviction growing deeper and stronger. All of these early influences combined with my inner inspired state of mind which exploded through it all and manifested my own vision. By age seventeen I was writing like a demon on fire just to learn how to express what I felt was vital not only to me but to my world.

Years past before I studied Buddhism properly and thoroughly. In Vancouver my roommate Bruce Wilson suggested that we take a course together on Buddhist psychology so we went to the Dharmadhatu Buddhist Meditation Centre founded by Chögyam Trungpa Rinpoche. Instead of looking like some Tibetan temple, it looks more like office space underneath a three story apartment building. On the window it also has the name "Shambhala Training," as two organizations founded by the same teacher use the same space. Beyond the inviting reception area, inside there was the main shrine room, dedicated to the practice of meditation. We tip toed in quietly and took a seat on one of the gomdens. These are large rectangular meditation sitting cushions placed on top of a Zabutons—a larger floor mat for cushioning the ankles and feet from the floor. The large room was pristine, immaculate! At the front the shrine held photos of various Tibetan gurus, with a small statue of the Buddha on the table. There were bowls of water, candles and incense burning. The cushions were bright orange and the lights were kept bright for the meditation. The whole environment is designed to perk up the mind and remind you that this is a place for the practice of Buddhist meditation. Perhaps the most impressive thing is that this is a Canadian environment. This is not a Tibetan, Chinese, Vietnamese, Thai or Japanese scene. Everybody here spoke English which made me feel very comfortable compared to my previous experiences with Buddhist centres.

I clicked with the teachings and the meditation practice right away. It had an enormous impact upon me. In three months I took my refuge vow and in a year I quit my job after selling mutual funds for eight years, to move to Chögyam Trungpa's regional centre in Vermont, USA, called Karme-Chöling. That was the best place I ever lived at in my entire life! It is staffed by about 50 people. We lived for free, worked five hours a day, meditated together about five hours a day, and took courses all the time. It was such a rich environment because they had many highly educated, well trained and experienced Buddhists. It is like a nuclear furnace of dharma. I recommend that people go and live there. We had gurus visiting from all over. The tape and book library was great. I just loved it! There I discovered the dharma tapes of the Vajra Regent Osel Tendzin. He was the first ever American born lineage holder of Tibetan Buddhism. He came from an Italian Catholic family in New Jersey. Chögyam Trungpa named him as his dharma heir, and the Regent was brilliant indeed. If Trungpa gave a talk, the Regent would instantly grasp the essence of it. The guy was just great! He was even invited onto the Tonight Show with Johnny Carson (which he declined).

My quest for dharma continued after leaving Karme-Chöling so I decided to go to Nepal and India, head office for Tibetan Buddhism. Even though I knew that the dharma scene in Asia probably wasn't as good as it was back home, I went anyway. I went for the money. I was drawn to the two dollars a day cost of living in a temple compared to the $25 a day cost of living in an American Buddhist centre. In Jack Kornfield's guide to meditation centres in Thailand, he says that even with the cost of airfare, it's worth going there for a long retreat.

My buddies in Vermont who had already been to Nepal and done that, warned me that I would get sick from the water and food in Nepal, as the conditions there were amongst the worst in the world. They suggested that I do a few meditation retreats in Thailand for a couple of months, to get aclimatized. O.K., that seems reasonable enough. I did that. I flew to Bangkok and met up with my friend Rob and his partner Erin. They were travelling in that part of the world. The first retreat I did was in south Thailand at Wat Suan Mok. They taught us Anapanasati, which is concentration meditation on in and out breathing. Their spiritual leader was easily the most famous monk in Thailand, Ajhan Buddhadasa. He was credited with bringing Thai Buddhism back to the Buddha's original discourses. I saw him once just months before he died. He was too old and weak to give teachings so the foreigners had to look after themselves. A few lived there and organized the ten day retreats each month for some one hundred people. We had to converge there the day before the first of the month. Nick, an Aussie staffer, warned us to sweep our flashlights across the walkway at night to look out for scorpions. They weren't deadly, but he described for us the painful stinging bites he had endured. This doesn't look like Vermont, Toto.

Our valuables had to be checked in for safe keeping. Wise travellers wouldn't feel safe about doing that in many places in Thailand, or other countries, but this was a Buddhist monastery, so I safely placed my faith in the three jewels. A long haired Australian musician deposited his didjeridoo. As the staff were passing everything down the line the Aussie said, "Hey be careful! That's a didjeridoo! That's a musical instrument you know." It looked like a long wide hollow wooden stick to everybody else. He stayed in a concrete cubical close to mine in the men's compound which held almost a hundred. I came to enjoy his company even though that wasn't the idea, being a 'totally silent' retreat. It's amazing how you can warm up to people when you all shut up. After the ten days he played his didjeridoo for us with a newly inspired Buddhist song. It went like this:

Well there's dukkha
And there's dhamma
I'm still not sure who I am-a!

I appreciated the opportunity to sit again at this retreat. This was a new technique for me. In two years I had developed attachment to my shamatha meditation practice and it was hard to let go of it. This anapanasati practice was a form of concentration meditation to attain mental tranquillity. We concentrated one pointedly on the breath going in and out at the tip of the nose. Our eyes were open, which impressed me. I was used to that. Then we would visualize an object of our choice, and build concentration on that. I started to use the Starship Enterprise from Star Trek (I preferred the old ship) and I had a problem fantasizing brand new episodes of the original TV series until our teacher, the abbot Ajhan

Poh told us not to use an object that has meaning to you. It should be neutral. The idea is to build your concentration on the object until you see an inner ball of light. Some meditators succeeded in seeing this but I didn't. That certainly didn't matter to me, as one still benefits from meditation anyway.

This was the first time since living in Vermont that I was meditating more than an hour a day. Compared to the West, the quality level of the teachings provided at any centre in Thailand suffered because of the English language. Several people I met came to Thailand looking for Buddhism. This is a fundamental mistake. I would say that for all Buddhist countries, including Tibet and areas of Nepal and India. If money is an issue, which it usually is, than these places are good for an inexpensive meditation retreat. But living a Buddhist life is best done at home, wherever home is. And it can be done well as a householder, because Buddhism does speak to modern lay life as it is. I was fortunate to come from Vancouver which probably has more Buddhist centres than any other city in North America. If people are from countries with no dharma, then it's fine to move to find it. But the big mistake is to think that somewhere in Asia is better than Europe or North America. That is false. It's more a question of money. If you are taking time off from work to meditate and contemplate then you may be forced to look for ways to cut your expenses. This clarifies your thinking as you balance the cost of living with getting decent instruction in your own language.

Before I could finish my retreat at Wat Suan Mok I got sick with the seasonal flu and had a very high fever of 104.5 degrees. One night I fainted after going to the washroom and hit my head smack on the concrete floor. This made me angry because I thought something had hit me! It's funny when I look back on it now, but at the time I was miserable and hospitalized briefly with this seasonal flu.

My friends and I took the long train ride to northern Thailand to do a one month Vipassana meditation retreat at Wat Ram Poeng in Chiangmai. Three years later I ordained as a monk there. On the way Rob had a bag of garbage and he was looking for a place to put it. A kindly old Thai woman saw his discomfort so she took the garbage from him and promptly dumped it out the window! We looked out to see a parallel train of garbage beside the tracks!

Chiangmai is known for it's 700 year old Buddhist temples. We walked past one of them called Wat Bupparam and Rob suggested to Erin and myself "Hey, let's check out this temple." Inside it was beautiful! The Virharn (main temple building) housed the largest teak Buddha statue in the world, delivered from southern China to escape Chairman Mao's cultural revolution. We went in and adored it. Sitting right underneath was my future wife Pia. Pia was alone, reading *Tough Times Never Last But Tough People Do,* by Dr. Robert Schuler. We sat and meditated in front of the sacred images, then I looked at Pia and she looked at me, asking "Are you Buddhists?"

"Yes. I'm a Buddhist student," I replied. I was impressed with her and her command of the English language. She spoke straight from the heart, always. We dated before I went into the temple retreat, and the rest is history. As time passed I noticed that when I introduced people to Pia, they would fall in love with her and I would be like a wall flower. She has known her own depths so she can speak to the depths of others. Once she determines someone's sign then that's it, she really knows them well. Being present and living in the moment is something that I'm always striving for, but Pia is already there.

Going to Jail

None of us have lived the life that we intended. I've made my mistakes. I have my weaknesses and faults. I've done my share of bad deeds. When I was a kid I used to blow up ants with firecrackers and I would yell at my mother. So, my theory is that all of this blood and evil karma caught up to me in June of 1993. Pia was out while I was at home in the Thapae Place Hotel in Chiangmai. The front desk buzzed and said I had a guest. I headed down, not wanting to invite unknown guests into our single room. I took the stairs instead of the elevator from the 4th floor. Going down the stairs, I noted a police officer coming up. I knew. I acted soooooooo cool, as I usually do, and went to reception. An immigration officer greeted me with about four police officers. We sat down and he asked me about my visa. I explained that my visa was overdue by three months, but no problem, I'm happy to pay the $5 per day fine, when I leave the country to renew it. My wife was pregnant with twins (she later had a miscarriage) and we had various delays, so we decided to fly to Malaysia later, rather than take the hot day and a half journey by train at that time.

Big mistake! It was then that I found out for the first time that what I had planned was a major no no. If you overstay your visa by more than a month in Thailand, they can throw you in jail! They threw me in jail.

Even before we first sat down one policeman said to the immigration officer, "Just take him." They drove me to Immigration, by the airport and I was trying to phone Pia's cellular phone to tell her. I didn't speak more than 100 words of Thai and the shit was coming down. Somehow they got hold of Pia and she raced over, strong as always. I sat watching them explain everything to her in Thai and then suddenly, her face instantly burst into tears! In one moment! I thought to myself "Wow! I wonder how she does that?! I sure wish I could cry like that. Even real men like myself want to be able to express their emotions maturely, but I just can't cry like that!! I can cry if I get sentimental about my cat or something, but I bear a slow warm misty tear that grows to maturity, and then gives birth to another tear. I can't do that! I'll never be able to do that." I marvelled at her. She cried because they told her that I would have to go back to Canada. There was nothing Pia could do to prevent me going to jail, so they hauled me away to the Chiangmai Police station, detention centre.

Unfortunately I couldn't go to the proper jail, which had space. I was taken into the back of the police station into a dark, stinky, sweaty place that came out of a scene from "Midnight Express." They led me into the smallest cell with one Burmese man because he was the only one who spoke any English at all. Sam had been in Thailand for 25 years but his separated wife turned against him and finked on him. A man without a country, he was being sent back to Burma. How unfair! Our cell was about 7' square, including a squat toilet. It was good to have someone who spoke English but he had the listening skills of a water hose. Unlike "Midnight Express," what struck me as the most unexpected thing was that almost everybody was as polite as ordinary people. I expected murderers and thieves, psychopaths and lawyers. But 90% of the men there, all men, were illegal Burmese immigrants who were working on the fishing boats in the south of Thailand (three years later the government improved the laws to allow them to stay and work legally, since Thailand was short of a labour force). They were just here for a job. There were a few fist fights with people being punched to the ground and kicked, but these were mainly the long termers who vied with each other for control and ran the inside of the detention centre by buying and selling things to the prisoners.

The first of seven nights I had to sleep on a concrete floor with a sheet of newspaper for a mattress. They didn't think that far ahead when they planned the detention centre. Cockroaches crawled across my back as I slept. A ten inch rat jumped right onto my right thigh in order to jump through the bars of the door. I was noticeably uncomfortable with that. Later they moved me to a bigger cell, away from Sam because a guard disliked Sam and didn't want him to enjoy speaking English with me. Left without anyone to talk to, unless I hollered over to Sam across the aisle, I was stuck with 16 other Burmese in a space about 10' by 15'. We were the lucky ones. Across from us were about 80, yes 80, guys in a cell about 20' by 20'! They had themselves stacked three people high on blankets tied between the many bars. B.O. dripped off the prison walls. I had just enough space to lie down with someone's feet right at my head, being careful not to shove my feet into someone else's face!

There was a gentle sixteen year old Burmese boy who I really felt for because he had bullet wounds on his chest and arm. He managed to explain that Burmese soldiers had tried to stop him from fleeing into Thailand and they shot him several times. He fully recovered but the marks from the wounds were two inches across. He kept asking me if I could take him to Canada with me. He was very much afraid of being sent back to Burma-Myanmar, they all called it. They didn't even know what Burma was! I kept saying how sorry I was and I felt just so awful and sad for him. I wanted so much to help him avoid going back.

Pia was losing it. She would come to the visitors booth and she said heart wrenchingly "If I lose you, I will die, and our baby will not be born." She was trying to work out a deal with immigration so that I could just leave the country rather than go back to Canada. She succeeded at a cost of a bribe of 40,000 baht, which was worth $2000 Canadian. Until the deal, I did not know that I would be in jail for seven days, or one day, or much longer. That not knowing bothered me, you understand. The best Buddhist lesson I got from that hellish experience was the lesson that what bothered me the most was the thoughts in my head. My greatest suffering was anger and frustration with the situation. I really learned something about myself in that squalid jail cell. I learned that I suffered much more from the idea of being there, than I did from actually being there in that physical environment. Some of the time I just relaxed and read a book.

I could still sit there and meditate sometimes. They fed us sticky rice and soup twice a day. But it really wasn't so bad. It was the constant chatter in my skull that made it bad. I realized that we suffer the same way whether we are in jail, at home in a mansion or on vacation in the tropics. We take our skulls with us and we always suffer from that constant chatter in our minds. The solution is to work with your mind. The solution is not to save up for another vacation to get away from it all (all but your mind). Now I'm glad I went to jail!

When I was released the police actually apologized to me for putting me through something that was more severe than required for a mere three month overstay; especially since I was married to a Thai national. They said that they thought that I was a bad person, then they realized that their source of information was mistaken. I like to blame everything on the grassy knoll. Even being legally married to a Thai woman doesn't help with the visa unless you have lots of money. The money part I can understand but the problem is sexism. Being married to a woman means almost nothing, partially because women are kept low in Thai tradition. If a Thai man marries a foreigner his wife can get residency much, much easier. The reason for that is because a Thai man is making the request, rather than a Thai woman making the request on behalf of a foreigner. Another reason, which is why everybody has to take the train to Penang, Malaysia for their visa run every three months, is because Thailand is ethnocentric. For some reason they don't want foreigners taking over their Buddhist country, as Nepal is now completely overrun by tourists and pollution. This is understandable so they give foreigners a hard time in hopes that they will leave. Their immediate neighbours — Laos, Cambodia, Vietnam and Burma have all been colonized but Thailand doesn't want to go along with everybody else.

After the police released me the colour green took on a whole new meaning!

The streets were teaming with light and colour and fresh air! Inside, in the fanless heat, we only had a bit of opaque glass on the ceiling to guess if the sun was shining. Now I felt like someone who had just stopped beating their head against a wall. One sweet, humble police officer escorted us by plane to Bangkok International, where he inserted us into a plane bound for Malaysia. Freedom! That same morning I woke up on a damp concrete floor in prison and that night my wife and I stayed in the five star Shangrila Hotel in Penang. What a life.

Cave Meditation

When we were back in Chiangmai with a valid visa, my Buddhist studies got me involved with several Thai monks who could speak some English. One monk took me for a weekend retreat in Maerim which is at the foot of the central mountain in Chiangmai called Doi Suthep. Doi means mountain. The Thais believe that Doi Suthep is a sacred mountain; it's not there to go hiking or trekking. It's a jungle with cobras and other poisonous snakes. There's a great temple built near the top at a site selected by a roaming elephant and there are some cave temples on the sides and base of the mountain. We spent a night visiting a cave retreat centre occupied by about a dozen monks and as many lay people. The master held court deep inside the main cave. We crept in and let our eyes adjust to the dim light. We could hear him speaking quietly to one of his students, probably another monk. I asked my host if it was alright for me to go in. I felt out of place. Not quite a stranger in a strange land, as I loved their religion, but something kept me back. The monk went in and waited to meet with the meditation master, but I stayed back in the cave for a while. I can't remember why but I never went in, I never even saw him. Looking back on it now, it was just like the lyrics from a Curt Cobian song, "I have something important to ask, but I can't remember what it is." I went outside and part way up the side of the cliff to the area where most of the monks lived. It was like a scene out of a movie. Gilligan's Island was a TV series, not a movie, but these monks looked a bit like monastic Gilligans. They enjoyed themselves, as Thais are good at doing. Of course I never understood what they were laughing about. Sometimes I knew that it was about me, but I always played it up.

They were happy to have a falang there. A falang is a foreigner, usually meaning a Westerner, not a Malaysian or Burmese. They would ask me "You like sticky rice? You like drink? You, what country?" I replied in broken Thai as much as I could, but reverted to English all the time. I always spoke too fast and that was to haunt my Buddhist teaching career in the future. I wanted to camp out right there, but this was before I was a monk so I had to camp with the lay people below the cliff in a palm shelter with the ever present mosquito net. We did a few Buddhist rituals, like chanting and circumambulating a forest spirit house and lighting incense and candles for it. They may have been asking for rain. But mostly we did a meditation retreat. The various caves had a great feeling for meditation. There was a large four foot high golden Buddha statue inside one cave that had plenty of light. That was my favourite meditation spot. No big mystical experience. It was ordinary. We went home the next day.

The Monkhood

I was in Thailand for four years which was much longer than I had originally envisioned. Because my original purpose was the quest for dharma, not getting married, I decided in the summer of '95, for various reasons, to spend some time in the monkhood. In the Thai tradition you don't have to be a monk for life, you can do it for just a few months. Typically before a young man gets married, he enters the monkhood for one month because the Thais believe that a man is more ripe for marriage after he has had the spiritual training of the monkhood. His fiancee and mother will come and visit him and bring him nice food, and make sure that he doesn't get any ideas about committing himself for life to the monkhood. They want him ripe but not too ripe! In the Chinese or Sri Lankan traditions, once you become a monk or a nun you are expected to remain for life so it would be a real shame on your family if you ever quit. Later, when I worked at the Chinese temple in Richmond, B.C., my understanding boss Julia said, "Don't tell people that you were a Buddhist monk."

In preparation for my change in life, I moved into a temple in town called Wat Ou Sai Kham. I stayed there at the invitation of the abbot, Ajhan Cheron, who took me on a long road trip to fabulous temples in the north. We went to a favourite temple patronized by the crown Prince and I came upon this laughing guard chatting with some people while a huge machine gun rested on the table in the periphery of his vision. He was stationed to guard solid gold Buddhas behind bullet proof glass. The Ajhan liked having foreigners stay at his temple, his little kingdom, and he and the other monks practiced their English on me. I taught a regular class to two novice monks, about 20 years old. One of them was from Laos and he told a dramatic story of how his family fled the communist take over just after he was born in 1975. He was pretty young then so he didn't remember any of it. His mother had to flee across the river holding him, and she made it into Thailand. He grew up near the Laos boarder. I've been to that area and 90% of the people speak Laotian. It was a part of Thailand over a hundred years ago. He was practicing his English by telling us about his hilltribe village in the jungle. I would give them diversions from studying their *Headway* English language book published in England. It contained reading and comprehension lessons based on Buckingham Palace info or Charles Dickens stories that had nothing to do with their lives.

This sweet little novice monk kept having laughing fits. Sometimes I tried to be funny which is my nature, and part of my job as a teacher but I would get bent out of shape when he would think that one of my rational explanations was ridiculous or utterly funny. Once he had to get up and go across the shrine room to the window so that he could have a proper laughing fit and concentrate on it mindfully like a good would-be monk. His laughter was infectious for his companion, the Thai novice. It's not hard to get Thais laughing. The Laotian described his hilltribe upbringing, very different from Thai culture. Like most hilltribes they were not Buddhists, they were Anamists, people who worship spirits in the forest. Buddhists also acknowledge the existence of devas that live in the forest, on the earth and in the sky, but we don't worship them as gods. The Buddha called forest devas 'tree sprites.'

Pia would visit and she gave me an intelligence report on this particular hilltribe and she said that they were known to be clever and a bit sneaky. The novice told me that they shot wild pigs in the forest to help support themselves. I asked him if he ever saw any wild tigers because I knew that they were sadly diminishing. He said that some wild pigs were getting eaten by tigers in their hills, so they sent hunters out to kill the tigers. I was understandably disturbed by his re-marks so I said that it was wrong to kill tigers. I even pointed out that the Buddha said that tigers were one of the 'noble beasts' which should not be eaten. "No. No, teacher, you no understand," he said. "The Tiger, he kill the pig. So the shooter, he shoot the tiger, and then... then he shoot the pig." He broke out with a broad smile at the last part as if everything finally made sense! Next, I laid a statistics trip on him and I held my hands up in the air trying to speak slowly. "Many Tigers now gone," I stared at him desperately. "So few. Better to let them live." He looked at me as though he was talking to a mentally retarded adult. "Oh, Mr. Brian, the shooter get the tiger because the tiger get the pig. Is O.K., is O.K.," he assured me. After our exchange I nurtured the hope and belief that he did in fact realize that some people feel that it is a bad thing to shoot tigers. Even after bringing up the subject of tigers in other classes, I don't think that he ever got the idea that there is something wrong with killing them.

Next, I moved into Wat Ram Poeng with the intention of ordaining as a monk for about three or four months. This is a beautiful monastery at the foot of the mountain Doi Suthep, about one mile from Chiangmai International airport. This is where I originally went for my one month Vipassana retreat almost three years before and I kept up a relationship with them throughout that time, so this monastery was my natural choice for ordination. I walked through the front gate and down the main lane surrounded by teak and jackfruit trees. It happened to be a warm and sunny day, that day, so I guess that was a good sign. My meditation in-structor, Phra Sawat, was expecting me. I had met him many times before prepar-ing for this big day. He was about 40, very self assured and from a family very suc-cessful in business. Like many Thai monks, he was in the monkhood on behalf of his family, it was merit for all of them. My sponsor was impressed with me, he said "Brian, you're not becoming a monk for your parents. Your parents have passed away. You're doing this for yourself!"

Phra Sawat assigned me to a concrete bunker in a row of eight concrete bun-kers. Now I understand what Hitler's last days were really like down there. Everything was run down, compared to Canada, except for the new school with ten new Apple computers and the great marble library where they housed the canonical scriptures translated into a dozen different languages. The computers were donated for a project to translate the Theravadin scriptures into the Lanna language. That is the northern Thai dialect which very few people need to read. I wondered if their resources would have been better pointed towards the future instead of the past. This temple had money, big money. The Thais all give about 10% of their income to the local temple; they are very devote. Even foreigners who own restaurants must give to the local temple or they lose face. In the West, people don't believe in donating much, some of them have rebelled against the church and are against the idea of tithing, so Western Buddhist centres are typically poor. If you charge Westerns a fee, they will pay it. If you ask for donations, they will give two bucks, or maybe five bucks.

My room was 15' by 9' with no hot water, paint chipping off the walls and a squat toilet. I saw some spiders on the wall so huge that I lost sleep. There was no hot water in the entire monastery, except for the abbot's quarters, and I could hardly take a shower there. The Thais don't believe in hot showers because they're hot enough! I arranged my books and few possessions on some rickety shelves, spread out my thin mat, and made myself at home. I lived there for seven months.

Phra Sawat spoke pretty good English and he was very intelligent, not just about dharma but about people. He gave me instruction in the Mahasi Sayadaw tradition of Vipassana meditation from Burma and trained me to be a meditation instructor. Phra Sawat had an open screen office and there were about 20 people on retreat who would wait in line 50 feet outside, and take turns so that he could go over our minds. He would say to me, "Mr. Brian your intention must be make effort!" When I was bummed out from my depressing room or my depressing mind, I would usually leave his office feeling lifted and a bit cheered up. For food we ate cafeteria style at 6:00 am and 10:30 am. No one could eat solid food after noon until dawn the next day because that is part of the ten precepts for people on retreat. I used to like to meditate on the roof of the library. It was such a beautiful structure, covered with gold nagas (dragons), carvings of stories from the Buddha's life, and a bright red ceiling. I took many photos of it. Women weren't allowed upstairs but the reason was not typical Thai sexism. It is because the Buddha made a precept that a monk cannot be in an enclosed space alone with a woman. The stairs went up to an enclosed second floor where monks frequently sit in meditation. If a monk was alone there, and a woman just passed through on the way to the roof, then the monk would be obligated to undergo a strict penance practice which could last several days.

Vipassana Meditation Technique

The Vipassana meditation technique we practiced is the one popularized by Jack Kornfield and Joseph Goldstein at the Barre Insight Meditation Centre, and at Spirit Rock, California. This method had more form and structure built into it than the variation described in the first part of this book. The technique is that you begin by taking your posture. You sit on a cushion, or the ground. Hold your spine upright, but relaxed. Put your right hand on your left in your lap, palms up. Cross your legs, preferably and close your eyes. Follow the breath going in and out and do so saying to yourself "Rising. Falling. Rising. Falling." Say the word with the whole motion of the breath. This ensures that you have your mind on what you are doing, while you are doing it, like using training wheels. Bring your attention to the abdomen rising and falling with the breath as your object of meditation. When thoughts arise, label them as "thinking, thinking, thinking." You say it two or three times just to be sure that you have noted it. Note the other five senses the same way, "Feeling, hearing, seeing, tasting, smelling." You can even be specific and note "Car, car, car. Sore back, sore back, sore back." This encourages discriminating awareness. Try not to move because Mahasi Sayadaw said, "The tendency to fidget and move will fritter away your concentration. If you move, then you will not attain to concentration, you will not attain the path, you will not attain nirvana." Woah! That sounds really heavy. Better sit still then!

We were trained to do half of the meditation sitting and half walking. For the walking meditation technique we would mindfully get up, noting our movements. Our digital alarm clock would beep when the sit was over, sometimes a full hour long period for each sit and each walk. Standing, you note "standing, standing," as your hands are clasped in front or behind (this is to prevent them from distracting you by swinging around). Guess what? You walk with your eyes open so as to not die. I instructed some Europeans who would sleepwalk around slowly with their eyes closed and it never ceased to amaze me, how people would assume for some reason that they had to do walking meditation with their eyes closed, so that they could maintain some lofty, spiritual plane of being, or something. Good thing I didn't teach them on the roof, or I would have been taking off to Burma. In the walking technique you very slowly take steps and you silently note, "Lifting, moving, putting. Lifting, moving, putting. Lifting, moving, putting," as you step. When thoughts arise you stop for a moment to note "thinking, thinking," as well as the other senses. You walk for a stretch of ten to whatever feet, and you stop, noting "Standing, standing, intending to turn, intending to turn." Then you always turn to the right, noting "Turning, turning, turning. Standing, standing, intending to walk, intending to walk." Then you walk back and you keep going back and forth like that until your alarm sounds. I just look at my watch.

You can begin with 15 min. each of walking, then sitting. Phra Sawat, on behalf of Mahasi Sayadaw, taught us to do walking first because it settles you down before you go into prime time on the cushion with sitting meditation. Kate, my English friend said "as you stand, you imagine that you are holding a bowl full of mindfulness, and you don't want to spill any of it. So you sit down noting "bending, touching, shifting, sitting." Then you go straight into your sitting practice without taking a break. No break! You always maintain mindfulness." Later you should try to do more time, 30 minutes each, then 40, then 50, then 60 minutes each. That is what you do on retreat. At home you can ideally do one hour of meditation in total. Other meditation centres do less walking and more sitting, like 50 sit, 10 walk at Shambhala Centres. A famous Burmese teacher, S. Goenka trains people to just sit, without any walking meditation at all. I meditated about four or five hours a day. Such an opportunity is very good to avail yourself of. I don't get quite that level of a clear mind living in Vancouver and meditating just one hour a day.

Wat Ram Poeng housed the alms bowls of some 100 monks. There were also about 80 women called Machees, not nuns, because Thailand doesn't allow women to ordain as nuns. Mahayana and Vajrayana Buddhist countries do, like Taiwan (there was a Thai nun visiting from Taiwan where she went to ordain in grey robes with the Chinese Mahayana tradition) or Tibet, but Thailand is a sexist, male dominated agrarian culture. Woman are second class citizens and are not afforded the respect of monks. Buddhist monasteries are the last institutions to update women's rights in Thailand. Women are very successful in business and banking so they are making great strides in an old male dominated culture. But ancient religious traditions are harder to change, understandably. This does not look good for Buddhism. The machees in the temple had to rake up the dog droppings, do all the chores, cook the food. It made the monks weaker. The monks in Thailand have it too soft. I always had to tell people that this is not the Buddha's fault, this is a cultural thing. The Buddha himself was a revolutionary for women's rights. He was the first leader in recorded history to allow women into any kind of religious order! He had to wait about ten years to pick the right moment, otherwise Indian society could have rebelled and destroyed Buddhism. The Buddha was the greatest, most successful revolutionary for women's rights of his age; he was the Che Guevara of India.

I had to wear white robes for four months before I could ordain. This is to be sure that foreigners are serious, and also to be sure people aren't doing it just to get a free visa to stay in the country, which people used to do. Once you're in the monkhood, they will renew your visa indefinitely as long as you are in robes. I met Ajhan Passano from Manitoba, Canada. He said that 13 years before, he joined the monkhood for just that reason — a visa. Then, appreciating the lifestyle, he decided to stay. When I met him he was the abbot of the temple I was visiting in the northeast, Wat Pah Nanachat. This is the only foreigners temple in Thailand, and I recommend it, with the warning that the conditions are tough. People only eat one meal a day there. It's the best place in Thailand for English speaking sangha and the Western monks there are not losers. The first thing that impressed me about the people is that they were actually there to practice and study dharma. It's hard to find people like that in some Buddhist centres around the world. One syndrome that happens at temples in any religion is that they attract people who can't make it in life, often because they have negative personalities. I was warned about this by my former boss

Bill Szabo. He kept me on the employee list for a year because he thought that I would be disillusioned and return to Vancouver. I believed his warning and discovered that our mutual belief was true. The problem with this syndrome is that people look to monks for personal and spiritual guidance. They may be put off of the Buddhist religion if a monk snaps at them arrogantly or gives them rude, unsolicited advice. I've seen this happen to warm hearted people several times.

In the Buddha's day the elite of society left their lives and spouses behind to join the Buddha in the monkhood. Can you image if our society today solicited men and women to ordain with lines like:

> "Would you like to guide others in your community? Would you like to provide the highest level of guidance — spiritual guidance? Are you having trouble getting along with others? Nobody wants to be in a relationship with you? Are you a bit of an angry or confused person? If you've struck out at life, or at getting a decent job, perhaps you should ordain as a Buddhist monk or nun! In this way you will immediately be elevated in society to the level of a spiritual person. When people want to visit, to check out what the Buddhist way of life is like, they will see you."

At the temple where I ordained in Thailand, most of the foreigners who lived there were losers. The really together people were the ones travelling through for one month, getting meditation instruction from us. We had a foreign monk, who prior to ordination, hid heroin in his anus and smuggled it across the border into Malaysia, avoiding the death penalty. He was so angry he would use his monk's status to bully the women around in the temple. Visiting meditators would complain to me about how rude my fellow monk was. We had an older German woman who would always tell people what to do but never listen to feedback. Nobody liked her either. An English woman was sad and confused then turned against the temple in the end and left in tears. There was a very quiet nervous German girl who was quite a good hearted soul and sincere in her practice. I visited an English monk nearby who was a friend of mine. He had a masters degree in English, and British humour but he just couldn't stop talking when engaged. Everybody there seemed to have bigger neurotic problems than normal people in the cities back home. This is not gossip. In case people are thinking of giving it all up and going away to ordain somewhere, this benefits them to know what to expect if you give up your good spiritual friends at home and go to live in a religious community in some far off place. I get people all the time, asking me if they should do the same thing that I did and live in a Thai temple. I say "no." Expect losers. They are poison to you! Losers drag you down like an anchor around your neck. Help them and have compassion for them but don't associate closely with them.

Some centres in the West don't have this problem so check these places out carefully before committing yourself. I always tell people that if they have the money, it's better to stay in a Western country and live at a centre there, like Rocky Mountain Shambhala Centre or Karme-Chöling. In foreign countries such as Thailand a considerable percentage of foreigners have criminal records; that's why they are there! They have fled their own country! If you need friends who speak English, other than decent travellers, some of the people who live in your community will be criminals on the run. Welcome to an exotic, Buddhist country. The type of people who leave their country to live in an Asian society probably have a greater than average number of problems and neuroses that they are bringing with them, to work through. The highest blessing in life is to associate with good people and to not associate with fools. Years of research has confirmed the Buddha's teaching on this.

Almost universally, people change only a little in one lifetime; this was true even of the Buddha. Prince Siddhartha was already on the verge of enlightenment when he was born. In the spectrum of 100,000 lifetimes the distance that one travels on a 100 foot long spiritual path is maybe three and a half inches per lifetime. Therefore whether a person is a monk, layman or whatever, they are what they are, robe or no robe. This is why the Buddha realized and spoke out loud many times about the tremendous difference between fools and the wise. Get around the right people! If someone ordains, you can expect that 30 years later they may have improved about three and a half inches. Therefore don't be too quick to pay your internal sincere respects to someone's robe or position. It's not nice to write this and most Buddhist authors don't but I felt that I had to print this because this is very relevant to people who wonder what it would be like to be a monk or a nun. I've been there and I know so it is my moral duty to share this insight with others. The great news is that your life is O.K. right where it is, in your home city! The very best conditions for you to flower on the spiritual path could be right at home in your present relationship. Chögyam Trungpa didn't want his students to become monks and nuns. He wanted them to apply Buddhism to their mainstream lifestyle and use the dharma to work with their fights with their girlfriends and everything else in life. Buddhism is ideal for our ordinary lives!

The quality of the people around you is everything. If you live in a concentrated spiritual community, this is terribly important to consider. The Buddha said that we need good friends on the spiritual life. This is a real challenge without a known solution. I was impressed by the calibre of monks and guests at Wat Pah Nanachat. The most honoured monk at the Wat was Ajhan Sumedo who was visiting from Amaravati in England. He's probably the most famous American monk and he first ordained there in the mid 1960's with Ajhan Cha, in the forest tradition. It was my 36th birthday, new year's eve, and I had been there for three days so

I had to shave my head, as per their rules for men. I waited to have an audience with Ajhan Sumedo and he smiled at my chrome dome. "Are you going to join the club?" he invited me. I decided to ordain close to Pia and others in Chiangmai, even though I preferred their Wat. The Thais say it's best to ordain far away, like shooting an arrow, but I didn't want to so I evaded Ajhan Sumedo's flattering question. I felt bad about shaving my head, "I hate it. I just discovered that I have a ridge along the top of my head!" I complained. He laughed about my petty concerns.

Back in Chiangmai, I ordained on January 25, 1996. It took over three hours. My sponsor came with his friends from the air base. He was Lt. Col. Khun Suriyan, a really good friend of mine. He used to drive me around in his old blue car and sing really old songs. It was an honour for him and the other officers at the military base to pay for my robes, my bowl and so forth. The Buddhists believe that it earns great merit to support someone in the monkhood, and rightly so. The reason why people believe that, is because it is true. The senior scholar monk, visiting from university in India, Phra Interakito was the one with the greatest sense of humour. He volunteered to shave my head that morning. It had to be shaved bright and shiny for the ceremony and I had some serious five o'clock shadow after a few weeks. Steve, our American forest ranger friend from Utah was the photographer. Our buddy Hans Madsen came dressed formally, "This is a wedding," he said. Hans is tall, blond, good looking, gay, British, and from Angola. He lived a

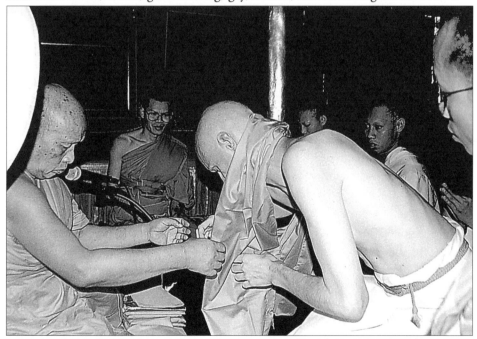

Left to right: Ajhan Tong, Ajhan Supan, Brian Ruhe, Phramaha Interakito (far right)

tough life, with the revolution there. Hans gave up an illustrious career in the shipping business, to go to university and get two masters degrees in literature. After all of his accomplishments he flew to Thailand looking for Buddhism. I was polite not to tell him that he made a mistake and should have stayed in England; there is much more English speaking Buddhism in England than in Thailand.

Hans eventually became a monk in Burma but the food was so unnutritious that he had to leave and be a monk in Sri Lanka. This happens to many foreign monks in Burma. People go to Burma because there is more serious meditation practice and better teachers there, than in Thailand. I knew it was true before I left Canada. Most of the old masters in Thailand have died off and they are not being replaced. In Burma they don't yet have the exponential materialism of Thailand and they speak better English too, which is absolutely essential. Even my guru Trungpa, said that the most meditation practice is happening in Burma. The Tibetan Buddhists were still recovering from their shock, and meditation had declined very much in the Tibetan tradition, Trungpa said (Naropa Institute, 1976). In Burma the conditions are very primitive, more impoverished than Thailand, so you have to be serious to go there, but this poverty has made Buddhism stronger in the people.

During the ordination ceremony I wore a white robe as a pakow, a lay person, then my orange monks robes were handed to me by Pia, the wife giving me away. There were about 60 people present and three Thais were ordaining with me, one for just a week and another for just a month. Our abbot's abbot officiated, Ajhan Tong. He had a dozen monasteries in the north and he was number seven in line for the top monk's position in Thailand — the Sangharaja, "king of the monks," like the Pope of Thailand. Like the papal lineage, there are some stories about previous Sangharajas that are better left unsaid. Thais generally feel that the most virtuous monks are to be found in the jungles, not at head office in Bangkok. Ajhan Tong gave us a beautiful talk about the meaning of the monkhood, the discipline and the precepts. He gave me my monk's name, Buddhasaro bhikkhu, which means 'the one who thinks of the Buddha.' They pick the name out of a book, based upon one's birth date. They said that it was auspicious that 'Buddha' was in my name. About 15 of the Western retreatants came in to watch. Temples are a place for ceremonies. The bot is the building restricted for monks only, lay people are never allowed in. In the bot they completed our vows. We had to stand outside while they asked us ten traditional questions, such as "Are you a human being? Are you a man? Are you free from debt?" The reason why the Buddha prescribed the question about being a human is that there is a source story in the scriptures about a naga. A naga is a deva in the higher realms, that looks like a dragon or a serpent. Once, a naga wanted to become a Buddhist monk so he changed into human form as devas can do. Incidentally, the Buddha said that most people are born from the womb, but some take spontaneous

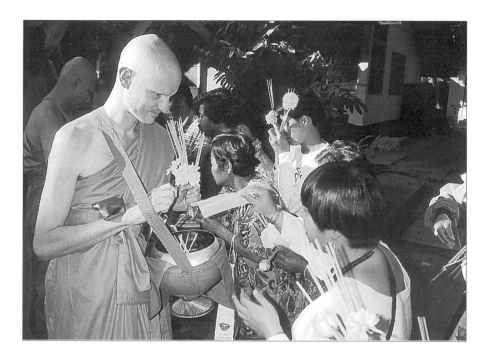

uprising. These are manifestations of the higher realms. The naga passed himself off as a monk, but one day his karma caught up with him and he fell asleep in the virharn and changed back to his naga form. The other monks witnessed this and asked him to leave. The naga left very sad because he was totally devoted to the Buddha and wanted to be one of the Buddha's monks. So, he slithered his sad little face back into the forest. Sweet story and it's probably true.

After the final ordination we went outside and the lay people competed to put money into our bowls because we were new 'pure' monks who hadn't broken any of our 227 precepts yet (or learned them either). The photo above is of that very moment, stepping out of the bot. My room is immediately in the background. That's Pia putting money in my bowl. The alms bowl was a novelty, most Buddhist countries don't use them anymore. We had to go out at 6:00 am and walk barefoot with no hat. In January, it's *cold* at dawn in northern Thailand! We had to walk 2.5 kilometres to beg for food at Talat Payom, the market. The lay people would stand by the trunks of their cars and laden us down with food. Some would kneel as I gave them a blessing in the Pali language. The chant is a blessing to invoke the devas in the god realm to give them beauty, strength, long life and happiness. Thirty million people in Thailand know this particular chant. I had to eat my food alone in my room because monks shouldn't chit chat with the boys while they eat. Mindfulness. Mindfulness/awareness. Two meals in the morning, then no more food until the next dawn. Some poor neighbourhood kids would come to my kuti and take my leftovers everyday. Pindabat, going for rounds is a fantastic relationship of give-and-take for the monks and lay people. It's a beautiful thing to partake in! It would be something to experiment with that in the West, as Ajhan Sumedo has done in England.

I was surprised to discover that I didn't get more than average dharma reading accomplished as a monk. As Rosanne Rosannadanna says, "There's always something." I was more inclined to meditation than study. The abbot asked me to teach Vipassana to the foreigners, 20 sometimes, so I helped out with that. He trained me as a meditation instructor by allowing me to sit beside him during his many interviews with the meditators. I saw everything and I could see that he's seen it all before. Ajhan Supan is an attained meditator in the Burmese tradition and he is a year younger than myself. One reason why such a young monk was appointed as abbot is because he is an abhidharma scholar. The abhidharma, or "higher dharma" is the last of the three baskets of the Theravadin scriptures. It includes a detailed explanation of the universe and consciousness.

Wat Ram Poeng is an abhidharma temple. I couldn't make heads or tails of the volumes of abhidharma scriptures. I'm good at anatta — the five skandhas of non self, which is the core of the abhidharma teachings. But I would sit in the sun on the roof of the library turning the book around, trying to glean some sense out of the very technical wording. I would read 'Conauscience factor number seven,' which had several items associated with it, before moving on to Conauscience factor number eight. I think you have to be on a really high level to 'get it.' I didn't 'get it,' the teachings are self secret.

Other temples aren't so much into this third basket of the scriptures, but Wat Ram Poeng is and Ajhan Supan was the best man to run the place. He was always so calm and happy. Once I went in to see him with one of my petty little concerns and he said "Sneck. Sneck." I smiled, trying to figure out what a 'Sneck' was. He reached for his long stick with the hook at the end and moved towards a huge six foot green snake slithering right on top of his guest room table in the elegant abbot's meeting room! I jumped back, "Yikes!!" as Ajhan Supan concentrated on the snake. Hooking the snake, he carried him outside and put him on the ground as tough he was taking out the garbage. He was cool man.

Another special quality of our abbot was demonstrated every full moon and new moon. Every two weeks all the monks gathered in the bot to perform an ancient ceremony initiated by the Buddha— the recitation of the patimokkha. These are the rules, the precepts for the monks and they all had to be spoken in the Pali language. First we would make confession of any transgressions we made of our monk's 227 precepts. We didn't have to actually say what we did. We just confessed that we did in fact break our precepts. This was an affirming and strength giving process and I know why the Buddha prescribed it. I always paired off with Phra Dhammarato because his English was fairly good, as he is an Australian. Not perfect, but I could understand him really well. We didn't all have to do the recitation of the patimokkha. Ajhan Supan was selected for the job because he could do it the fastest, so that we could listen to him, and be out of there in 20 minutes flat. His speed was incredible! Sparks practically flew off of his teeth.

A pair of English fellows did a retreat with us and I loved their typical dry humour, but Mike came up to me alarmed one day and he asked me to check on Scott. I found Scott drumming on his travel bongo drums and he was not sane. He was staring into space and Mike told me that Scott had been suffering from depression. Jonathan, the Dutchman staying long term came to the rescue and took control. It wasn't long before we were loading Scott on a truck bound for Suan Prung Mental hospital. Jonathan and I would go and visit him everyday and Mike arranged to cut short Scott's trip and send him home to England. The temple was wary about their reputation when meditators from their retreats had to go to the mental hospital. The temple would have been happier if people didn't know, because it's a loss of face for them. Asians have a much bigger problem with face than we do. Scott's breakdown was the only case I had witnessed of something I had been trained about as a meditation instructor. The mistake was that Scott should not have been instructed to do such long hours of meditation because he was in a depression. There's no problem with the meditation practice. The danger that Scott stepped into is that he stopped meditating and he just sat there thinking about all of his depressing problems and thoughts. It's like a black hole. You slowly slide down a slippery slope to a repeating loop of black habitual patterns. Because of the language barrier, the meditation instructor did not understand the severity of the problem that Scott was explaining to him. The instructor just said, "Don't worry about it. Just keep meditating." Scott should have done more walking meditation and stayed more into his body rather than just his mind. Something like mindful sweeping around the temple grounds is ideal for depression. Purposeful action is excellent for burning through depression. Keep 'em busy!

Wan Phra

Wan phra means "Buddha day." This would fall every seven or eight days according to the moon and 100 people would come in the evening, some staying and meditating overnight, which is traditional. Usually only old ladies and maybe one old man will stay the night, the younger generation is busy doing nightclub dance meditation. I wonder if a similar problem was happening in Tibet even prior to the Chinese invasion? During

Entrance, Grand Palace, Bangkok, Thailand

one wan phra, Ajhan Supan gave a talk and surprised me by asking me to give a reading in English. Later we went outside the Virharn and lit beautiful little bouquets provided for us. We would light three candles, for the Buddha, the dharma, and the sangha, and circumambulate around the main stupa (chedi, in Thai). That particular stupa was built the year before Christopher Columbus set sail for America, and it has an Indian look to it. This is a very old monastery. The stupa is a construction of rocks and bricks and it stands about 60 feet high. It may even contain a bone of the Buddha. That's the idea of a stupa. It is an object for veneration because inside are the relics of a venerated monk or nun. The Buddha described how to make a stupa by folding his robe into a square, putting his bowl upside down on the robe, and putting his staff on top. Because of those instructions, today billions of dollars are spent in Thailand and other countries, on the construction of stupas. It's a very big deal. People do three circumambulations always in a clockwise direction because when people greeted the Buddha they always kept their right side to the Buddha, coming or going. This book, true to the policy of the ninety other Buddhist books that I have read, does not explain *why* people kept their right side to the Buddha.

Privately I told Ajhan Supan that I felt that the reading he gave me to read on wan phra was not appropriate for the Europeans and Americans staying as our guests. The paper was not Beavis and Butt Head but it was a psychological paper from America that was extremely complicated and difficult to understand. I assumed his idea was to show how Buddhist meditation is justified within Western science. I suggested that next week I could just keep it simple and say a few words of my own, I didn't have to read anything. He nodded his approval and that was the beginning of my lifelong career in giving talks on Buddhism and meditation. I decided that my policy in teaching Buddhism was to focus almost exclusively on the English language, not only verbally, but in my studies as well. That may sound mundane but other Buddhist teachers would call it revolutionary because I'm not interested in educating my students in Pali, Sanskrit or Tibetan terminology. Life is short and it is not necessary for myself or my students to go beyond their mother tongue. It is definitely necessary for other people to do that so that such ancient knowledge is available to Buddhists everyday, but *I'm* sure as hell not going to do it! That is somebody else's job. I'm remorselessly proud of my policy!

My first dharma talk was about the night of the Buddha's enlightenment. I quoted from the sutras:

In the first watch of the night the Buddha saw the nature of beings.
How they arise, dwell, and pass away.
In the second watch of the night he recalled all of his previous lives.
Then, in the last hour before dawn his eyes fell upon the morning star
Which triggered the great enlightenment, and ended the cycle of
death and rebirth.

My talk went well and I got good feedback, so I wanted to keep it up. I asked Ajhan Supan if I could do a series of talks on the mornings following wan phra, a proper lecture, in the temple classrooms, for about 90 minutes including questions and answers. He smiled broadly as he always does and nodded. As I prepared my lectures I kept vigil over my ego. I recalled the admonition of the Buddha in the Dhammapada (Byrom, 1976; 21):

Whatever a fool learns,
It only makes him duller.
Knowledge cleaves his head.
For then he wants recognition,
A place before other people,
A place over other people.
"Let them know my work,
Let everyone look to me for direction."

Such are his desires
Such is his swelling pride.

One way leads to wealth and fame,
The other to the end of the way.

Look not for recognition
But follow the awakened
And set yourself free.

Heeding this warning, I also believed in the bodhisattva vow of teaching whenever someone asks for teachings. Benefitting others with the dharma is the highest act of compassion. We don't have to second guess our good intentions, and I won't convince myself that I'm on an ego trip when the truth is that I am not.

We had a German machee named Maggie who has come to Wat Ram Poeng every year for 16 years. She would work as a cook in Germany, then spend all winter on retreat. She seemed a bit jealous that I was giving Buddhists talks because no one would think about inviting her to do so. I don't blame her feeling, because sexism is the reason for the tension. There's no way a woman could give a talk with a group of monks present.

The other machee named Kate was in love with phra Sawat. Being a good monk, he could not respond to that. He even took her to the hospital in town to view the dead body of a man in the morgue who was killed in an automobile accident. This is the contemplation on death that the Buddha taught as a way to overcome sexual desire. Think of the body as something fowl and pestilent. Kate's feelings were not unusual. It happens that people fall in love with their meditation instructor, because the depth of the experience is closely associated with the guide. Before she flew back to England she recounted a moment when she sat with a monk. A Thai woman walked 400 feet across the grounds from the kitchen to give the monk a drink because that's a way people can earn merit. She dusted off the table, and presented a tall glass of coconut juice for the monk. She turned and didn't pay no never minds to Kate, and walked away. There's not much merit in giving a drink to a woman, so *c'est la vie*. The Thai people are very friendly but this was institutional rudeness. At the end of the 20th century thousands of Thai women were putting pressure on tradition to fight for women's equality. This account of sexism is not fair to the Thais because things have improved. However because the religion is ancient that part is slower to change.

I took a monk business trip to Bangkok because there were some famous teachers near there that I wanted to get teachings from, such as Phra Payutto, and I wanted to see Chualalongkorn Buddhist University. I took the train down and I had gotten used to people bowing to me. The traditional Buddhist custom is that people hold their hands together on the heart centre in anjali and give a little bow when they greet or relate with a monk. It's not strict. As a monk I could not bow back, not even to the King of Thailand. Monks are supposed to be higher, they've taken the higher ordination. In Bangkok I was a visiting monk at Wat Mahatat, where the university is located. I knew about ten Theravadin monks from Cittigong. This is a corner of Bangladesh next to the Burma border. There are about a million Buddhists there surrounded within a Muslim country. The monks told me that sometimes the Muslims would be rude or hostile to them in Bangladesh, but the monks couldn't fight back. The university was a fascinating mix of Theravadin monks from all over. It was a block from the very famous Grand Palace, where I went for free because I was a monk. Japanese tourists would line up beside me and take turns having their photo taken with me. It was fun but meaningless, I felt like a monk doll.

At the temple the Venerable Dr. Khemananda took me under his wing. This monk was a scholar and he was passing out copies of three of his Buddhist books in English — quite good, scholarly and with many footnotes. I loved being with him. He spoke excellent English so I could have serious dharma discussions with a monk — a rarity. One day he asked me to join him for lunch. We went out and came upon a huge old silver Mercedes parked inside the temple. Oh. I got in with four other monks, plus the driver and we were cruising downtown Bangkok. I snickered at the whole scene. We drove to an air conditioned mansion along the banks of the Chao Praya River. Surrounded by BMWs, Porches and a Rolls Royce, we walked into the house from the 'beach.' Even the rich people had to smell the water, breathe the hot polluted air, and get stuck in traffic. It's easy to have compassion for the rich in Bangkok. The daughter and son-in-law greeted us and Dr. Khemananda explained who I was without properly introducing me. They probably weren't in the mood to speak English. I assumed that the better educated Thais like this probably spoke better English. They all said a perky "phra falang," so that was my introduction. We were visiting a retired Minister in the Thai government who was a long time patron of the doctors'. Two of his extremely attractive and exquisitely well dressed granddaughters (I assume) served us. They were seriously challenging my precepts with regard to women. They bent over and served us honey covered shrimp cakes flown in from somewhere, and every other expensive beautiful and wonderful food I could imagine. I started with sticky rice. I felt like a poster boy for falang Buddhism. I was the guest phra falang and the doctor felt that it was a feather in his cap to be showing off a Canadian monk. I yearned for Karme-Chöling in Vermont where we would take courses on Buddha-nature and meditate together for four hours a day. I vowed then that someday I would make it back to my Buddhist homeland — America.

We were invited to the minister's house to do some chanting, so after lunch Dr. Khemananda passed this long white string around so that all of us were holding it. My wife Pia does the same thing with her shamanic practices. At the other end of the string, it was wrapped around a large photo of the minister's late wife. We chanted in Pali for her. Leaving the track lighting and air conditioning behind, we were soon back in the car in dirty filthy demoralizing Bangkok. There are worlds within worlds and heavens within hells.

I taught several drop in visitors at Wat Mahatat. They asked me to help out there because they had just one monk who could teach well in English. That was fun. I met some dharma students that I kept in touch with years later. Patricia was a half Brazilian, half Irish Hare Krishna who came for days and she was so very appreciative of Buddhism and Vipassana practice. She was with me once when Helen Jandamit came to visit me. Helen, my mentor, is an English woman who has lived and taught Buddhism and Vipassana for 20 years in Bangkok. She runs the 'House of Dhamma,' which is in many tour guidebooks. When I was working for the Buddhist University in Chiangmai the senior monks had me transcribing lectures of Ajhan Helen Jandamit. That's how I got into her teachings. She was the one who taught me that precepts mean intentions, not vows. When I was putting my first Buddhist course together Helen was very encouraging. "Just teach what you want to teach, and the students will come," she said. Patricia sat with us in section five, a meditation hall too small for the needs of the temple. "The Hare Krishna's don't meditate," she said with the concerned tone of a woman losing her faith. "They just chant to god, but we were never taught to meditate." She was on her way back to Catholic Dublin, where there were no dharma centres, so I realized how important it was for me to teach people. Not everybody has a big choice of Buddhist centres. It was at Wat Mahatat that I decided to focus on teaching Buddhism and being a better teacher. In my meditations I came to see clearer how I limited and denied myself before I even got started. What I thought other people were doing to me, I was doing to myself. I decided alone, on my own and without external validation, that I was a Buddhist teacher. I never looked back.

I definitely could not stay in the monkhood to teach Buddhism. The whole point in going to Thailand was to leave. After my training, I intended to go home, which is always where I wanted to be. I was like Dorothy in Oz for four years. I could hardly live at the Thai temple in Vancouver, as they didn't even speak English and no one would support me financially in that temple, unlike the temples in Thailand. It takes money to be a monk! So, I decided to disrobe, teach a Buddhism course in Bangkok, and then fly home to Canada. I did. I went back to Chiangmai to pay my respects to my beloved abbot, Ajhan Supan. Coming back to his warm, calm smile made me sad, because I was saying goodbye. He tried to talk me out of disrobing and he made me wait a day, then another day, to reconsider it. I told him that it was lonely being a Canadian monk. "If you leave, you'll still be lonely," he said, cutting right to my heart! He was so good at being concise. I'll never know if that's because of his English or because of him. His meditation instructions with Machee Pete tended to cut through people's blah blah, and keep it simple. Machee Pete was his Thai/English translator and all the guys fell in love with her. It was because of her magnetic being and angelic expressions. She definitely had some level of attainment. People like her and Ajhan Supan redeem my whole faith in the Buddhist tradition of 59,000,000 people. Something has been working right for 2,200 years in Thailand.

My disrobing ceremony took about fifteen minutes. Ajhan gave me the five precepts of a layman and then he dipped this small kind of broom into a pot of blessed water. He splashed the water all over me, which is what I loved the most. I love rituals that make sense.

I taught my first proper course on Buddhism and meditation at the Community Services of Bangkok, a kind of American community centre. They were a great bunch of interesting people, mostly wives of embassy staff and wives of engineers who were stationed for a few years in the country. The wife of the American ambassador to Thailand wanted to take my course, but I left too soon. They were a captive audience because they were stuck in Thailand and wanted to know something about the native religion. I sent the following email back home to my family and friends describing my life in Bangkok:

Captain's log, stardate 2539
[that was the year, according to the Thai calendar]

The Enterprise has been sent to an alien civilization to boldly spread the Buddhadharma where it has already been spread before. The landing party has faced obstacles of intense heat and radiation. They don't speak the language too well but the food is good, fast and cheap. (Captain Kirk signals Uhura for a ship wide announcement:)

"This is the captain. What you don't realize and must now be told is that Starfleet command would like the crew of the Enterprise to pull out of teaching English unless we have no other option. We must raise our sights (background musical score) and uplift these lost people by focusing on Hotels and tour groups of foreigners that have a genuine interest in the religion of this planet. We may make money or we may starve. The fewer of us that do have virtue, the more merit there will be for the ones that do! We will pay any price, bear any burden, meet any hardship, support any friend, magnetize any foe, to insure the survival and success of our mission. You must make it through that traffic and you must succeed! Kirk out."

Nearby I would frequent the World Fellowship of Buddhists headquarters (WFB). Here I got friendly with Khun Prasert, the 84 year old director. He told me stories about leaving school in England because of the war, and coming home to Thailand. He was so old I wasn't sure if he meant World War One or Two. He was friends with some Japanese administrators who had a 'friendship pact' with Thailand during the big one. I really respected his age and I kept asking him questions about his early days. His experience was so precious. I talked about my aspiration to help spread Buddhism in the West and he was very supportive of me. He appreciated that I was going home 'to the colonies.'

Back in Canada

I arrived back home in Vancouver, Canada and my wife Pia came and joined me several months later. Actually, I was sad in Thailand and always missed Vancouver. We are much happier together in Canada than in Thailand. Pia has a successful practice as a Thai shaman in Vancouver but in Thailand the Thais go to the monks for those higher realm powers. The predictors always told Pia to get out of the country, saying that she would be a bigger success if she was in a foreign country. Pia couldn't earn one baht as a shaman in Thailand but Canada is desperate for her help. She's not too interested in Canadians because they have an understanding about shamanism that is too superstitious, skeptical and primitive. 90% of Pia's clients are East Indians. "In my country," Pia said, "they never use black magic against people unless it's really serious! But Indians use it for just any little thing! So, I always have people to heal."

She can cure negative spells put on people by writing Pali, Sanskrit and Lanna Thai chants on the sides of wax candles, doing the appropriate chant, meditating and then lighting the candle. Sometimes she has two trays going with seventy candles for seventy clients — standing like missiles. It seems that the devas read them like a computer and a deva per customer flies off into the night and heals. Pia has the proper aspiration of benefitting others so she takes care that this powerful process helps and does not cause harm to others, but there is a huge moral dimension to her job. Often Pia is asked by women to stop their husbands from drinking and staying out late, chasing other women, and Pia's shamanism can sometimes do that, but not every time because of the client's karma. Often I come home and get messages for Pia and they say things like "Oh Pia! After I came to see you, my husband came home and he wasn't drunk! You're just like my god Pia!" Some East Indians put their head on Pia's feet when they leave, as Pia is like a priestess to them. After house calls to pacify difficult spirits, ghosts sometimes come back with us because they follow Pia, so one thing is certain to both of us — the stakes are high.

Once back home in Canada I looked up my old roommate Bruce who had introduced me to Buddhism. He was teaching at Douglas College and he gave me the idea of teaching a Buddhism course there. The Director of their Health Sciences department, Geraldine Street, put together an innovative series of courses on natural health and healing, which was not offered at any other community college in British Columbia. I arranged to see her and before our interview I did the Mangala sutra chants for blessings (see class ten). It may have worked. She agreed on the spot to sponsor my Buddhism and Meditation course and I came right on their deadline day. Following this I was hired at the Vancouver School Board. The program coordinator, Connie Gibbs was the force behind introducing spirituality courses at the school board. She noticed that most people don't have a religion so there is a need out there for spirituality that is going unmet. I asked her if it was permissible to have a religious course in the secular environment of the school board. She said "If people object to it, then they can give me a course proposal of their own."

She was very supportive of me and the Buddhism course. CBC TV was interested in doing a story on the Buddhism course in the school board so they interviewed several of my students after the second term. That doesn't happen for courses on Thai cooking but it does for courses on Buddhism.

One of the best Tibetan Buddhist centres in Vancouver is the Dalai Lama's Zuru Ling. I became friends with the nun who teaches there, Anne McNeil, or Anila. A Canadian, she has been a Tibetan Buddhist nun since 1970. Anila suggested that we go to the International Buddhist Society on the Steveston highway in Richmond as we wanted to see this shimmering beautiful temple. I had talked with one of their directors previously about the idea of me teaching a class there but I had never seen the place. We went and it was full of colour, ponds, statues and probably the most beautiful shrine room in B.C., if not in Canada. Their statue of Quan Yin, the deity of compassion is twenty feet high with literally a thousand wooden arms. It's also the biggest Buddhist temple in Canada. It's of the Chinese Pure Land School. This was our first time there and we paid a visit to the office, unannounced. One of the directors came out and she was very generous and interested in how we could work together to propagate Buddhism amongst Canadians. She immediately explained that they had thousands of free books to give away and she wanted to know if we could recommend other Buddhist centres in North America. She really perked up when she discovered that Anila was the Buddhist Chaplin for the Correctional Dept. and that Anila served the needs of Buddhist prisoners in eight penitentiaries in the Abbotsford, B.C. area. Anila described the behaviours of several categories of prisoners and how the Chinese inmates wanted something for the veneration of their ancestors, but they wouldn't tell her that directly.

Busy after closing time, the temple staff practically filled Anila's Toyota with statues for the penitentiary chapels — some of them made of marble, statues for the prisoners, books, chant player machines, counting beads and incense. Walking in the light rain outside we all felt that this was a brilliant and virtuous streak to help spark some wakefulness in those that may appreciate it. The International

Freeing the Buddha

Buddhist Society demonstrated the bodhisattva vow in action. Anila described their kindness by saying "They're super missionaries." The three of us felt delighted to be a part of some small effort that came together by our meeting that day. The temple was providing the actual financial means and we were there giving them another place to manifest their Buddha activity. The Buddhist teachings talk about virtue or goodness as being completely without effort, not produced or created by effort and requiring no effort to maintain; whereas confusion is said to require tremendous effort and pain (Judy Lief, 1990 seminary).

A couple of weeks after this I wrote to a Japanese temple that I know to see if I could get a gig teaching a Buddhism and meditation class. Before I followed up with a phone call, I did the Mangala Sutra chant, which is a deva invocation practice that I was taught by U Silananda when I was a Buddhist monk in northern Thailand, the year before. My purpose in this was to call to higher realm devas in the god realm to assist me. They did. When I phoned the Japanese temple, I couldn't get through. This happened more than once. Three hours later, out of the blue, I received a telephone call from the director at the big Buddhist temple in Richmond! She asked me what I was doing. I said I was teaching three courses a week. She invited me to work there full time. We negotiated on the phone and she hired me on the spot. Monday morning, 9:30 am please. As I hung up the phone, I knew. I realized what had just happened to me. The devas. Over lunch I spoke to her later about this and she said that it was her own idea to invite me to work for them. She said that it wasn't the devas but she could not deny that she did make the decision to hire me during that three hour period after I invoked the devas. Smiling, I politely disagreed with her. I have the ultimate conviction that the devas saw me as a scientist sees a white mouse in a maze. They could see that instead of some other temple, I should have been working for the I.B.S. I live my life by the Buddha's words prescribed in the Mangala Sutra blessing chant. This practice has helped out in the past and it will do more in the future.

I worked for six months at the temple as their public relations official. We received hundreds of visitors every day. What a blessing it was for me to meet spiritual people and tourists from all four directions! It was such an opportunity to propagate the dharma. I would receive school groups a few times a week for up to two hours, giving them a tour, teaching meditation and answering questions about Buddhism. Many Christian groups would come to investigate Buddhism so I gave a lot of talks on comparative religion. We had 90 kids from Surrey Christian Middle School and one boy stood near the fountain pointing at the statue of the baby Buddha standing with one arm pointing up and one pointing down, like John Travolta in Saturday Night Fever. I told him that Prince Siddhartha founded the lineage of disco music, and they all howled! I had a lot fun with the students and the teachers too.

Once a family of healers from France paid a visit. As I brought them over to the ancestor worship area in the corner of the temple, they immediately felt an energy like a wind coming from there. When I explained that the tablets of over 1000 people who had passed away were there, they knew that they were feeling the energy from all the merit given to people's ancestors. And they could feel the presence of the devas or spirits that connect with people there. When I walked past that corner sometimes I felt a more powerful, sacred energy.

People go to that temple just because it is very big and it stands out. After sixteen years without a regular class in English at the temple, I was the inspiration behind the first ongoing series of classes for meditation and various talks on Buddhism. With three classes a week, for the first time the temple had a regular sangha of local English speaking Canadians. In July of 1997 it started haphazardly because some of the temple goers didn't have much respect for the practice of meditation. Theirs is a Pure Land temple so they just don't practice meditation, except for a few like the nuns. They chant the name "Amitabha," which they believe to be a celestial Buddha, a deity that will grant them salvation. While employed there, I never once told people the truth that Amitabha Buddha was invented by the Iranians around 150 A.D. as an expression of their Iranian belief in the sun god religion.

One of the directors returned from Hong Kong and he began regularly teaching some of my students and he said "Brian I really appreciate teaching Westerners! They ask questions, they're intelligent and honestly interested in the dharma. I want to increase the intellectual standard of the temple. Most of the people who come to dharma talks here are uneducated older Chinese women. It's great to open up the temple to Canadians." This indicates the generation gap which has occurred as few young Chinese Canadians want to follow the Pure Land tradition of practice. I have had several of these younger English speaking Chinese in my classes and they have appreciated a Western perspective on the dharma and particularly the techniques of meditation and contemplation.

At another time, I was out near the pond with the temple director and he said to me "Brian, the Pure Land is the only way. In this world we don't have time to meditate. We don't have time to study. The Pure Land is the only way to enlightenment that can work for us." It really does sound like a drug, and it is not what the Buddha taught — very much the opposite in fact. The Pure Land distorts people's views of Buddhism. When I was touring a Christian Bible college group around the temple, I took them into the Thousand Buddha Hall and their instructor was delighted to explain to them how, in the Buddhist religion, the patrons here do fortune telling and they shake a stick out of a cylinder of sticks and they use that number to correspond to a sheet where they go and read their fortune. "On the Chinese New Year," she said with a disdaining gleam in her eye, "they shake twelve sticks out to read their fortune for each month of the year."

Perhaps she didn't realize that I wouldn't stand still for such a remark regarding Buddhism, so I smoothly threw water on her words by having the last word. "However, the Buddha himself was against any such practices of fortune telling." I explained how people like fortune telling so over the centuries it became attached to temples as a convenience, as a cultural affectation, but it's not really Buddhism at all.

Although the Pure Land tradition practiced at the IBS is very different from my own Buddhist background, I do appreciate their visualization practice. Mahayana visualizations are not secret practices like some Vajrayana visualizations, so I will describe one here for the sake of study. Mahayana visualizations are very colourful. In visualizing Amitabha's Pure Land you begin by visualizing the western sunset, then eight columns covered with diamonds, each emitting 84,000 rays of light. Later you see lotus flowers in the air and you think that each lotus flower has a hundred kinds of gem-colour and eighty-four thousand veins in the petals, resembling heavenly pictures. These veins have eighty-four thousand rays, all of which are clearly visible. This 'sutra' also says that the smaller petals are two hundred and fifty yojanas in length and the same in width. Each of these lotus flowers has eighty-four thousand petals. Between each of them, there are millions and millions of Muni-gems as ornaments. Each of the Muni-gems emits a thousand rays, which are like canopies, being composed of the seven jewels, covering the whole Land.

This 'sutra' goes on and on in this beautiful description of heaven. It's quite delicious! In my own experience of this practice, I visualize the "Land" as outer space, surrounding planet Earth, vast lotus flowers orbiting in space, with a height of 250 yojanas. A yojana is about 1/10 to 1/4 of a mile in length. The currently orbiting nuclear weapons flower into celestial petals, wafting to earth as they completely clean our atmosphere. This Mahayana practice is so similar to Tibetan Vajrayana visualization practices that I believe that the Vajrayana is Mahayana. To paraphrase the lineage holder of Shambhala International, Mipham Rinpoche said in Vancouver, "I think of the Vajrayana as another form of the Mahayana." I agree. I believe that Vajrayana Buddhism does not exist.

I taught Tibetan shamatha meditation to the Sunday morning congregation at the Capilano United Church, and we all practiced it together. Later the Minister, Rev. Rohana Laing, gave me a connection to an event marketer who influenced this book by saying "Brian, you've got to have the necessary communication tools to get your message across to the people that need it. You've got to sell yourself and what you have to offer if you want to skilfully benefit others." He then employed a PhD writer to write part of the Bio in the 'About the Authors' section of this book.

People have suggested that I'm misusing 'credentials' in this book, but they were a bit more at ease when I confessed openly that I am in fact using credentials but my reason for it is because I bought the advice of Lionel Wilson, the event marketer. I explained that my intention is in fact to benefit others by using my credentials like a fishing lure to attract people to the dharma, particularly since I regularly share the teaching post with other guest teachers. The good news, fortunately is that I myself don't take any of my own credentials too seriously! I don't think of my seven months in a Thai monastery as any big deal, and working in the Chinese temple was a good experience but it didn't bestow upon me sage wisdom.

The feedback I've received from people who've read this book and prototype essays from the next two books in this trilogy, is mostly positive. There's some critical feedback, which I've used to improve each subsequent edition — this is the third. Some fellow Buddhists have expressed that this book is dangerous because of the powerful practices revealed. Some even say objectionable practices. I believe that this book is dangerous only to our old institutions that do not serve us well, but that it is not truly dangerous to the reader, no. The contrary is true, I believe, or I would not have published it. I believe that when I first published this book, I was the only one who took it seriously. I think that the critics don't actually take it seriously because they cannot expatiate at length the dangers in the teachings contained here. Their criticisms cannot stand up to my patient analysis of their stance. When I was a teenager my sister Margaret encouraged me to be a lawyer but now I know there's a tad more virtue in Buddhism. Generally, emotional critics will end a meeting and leave without properly defending their criticism. Big religions are filled with small people. I win by default. It's too easy actually. In my patience, I cannot be defeated in logical argument. I pray for the day when a worthy adversary will humiliate my essays and turn them into something greater. This book is like a motorcycle headlight coming towards you as you stand at the end of a cul-de-sac on a moonless night. Out of the mist the rider comes and brings the light right up to your face. Maybe this is just a fantasy, but most good books are like that motorcycle headlight. They take time to grow.

Please send me an email at bar@istar.ca or give me a phone call if you would like to challenge any part of this book. If you defeat me, you get one free ticket to a class, and I get a stronger future edition of this book. In this information age, this is a lower budget way of hiring an editor. You the reader are the guinea pig for future editions; thanks. As Brian Tracy wrote, "there is nothing new under the sun." This book is like the Japanese economy, it includes ideas from others and makes them even better. The Japanese have a word "kayzan," which means "continuous improvements." Maybe we can't improve upon the Buddha, but we can sure improve upon how we communicate the letter and the spirit of his message. The future is more important than the past.

Exodus

Just before closing time one day at the temple, a short Polish man walked in because his wife saw me on TV when BCTV News did a story on Buddhism because of the then recent exciting movie *Seven Years in Tibet*. I showed Darcy Griffiths, the reporter, around then they used my personal story as an example of how Buddhism is influencing Westerners. The Polish fellow who came in needed a ghostbuster and they were desperate for help so they tried me. At first I felt that it was a mistake, but then I knew that this was a karmic sign. I knew on the spot what was coming down. I felt that I had to use Buddhist practices to help them out and that my temple deva friends had brought Ronae to me. I went to his massage clinic on Broadway at Burrard St. in Vancouver and I took Pia with me. They believed that negative energies in the building were killing their business and they suspected that ghosts were interfering with them. Well, the big surprise is that Pia took control and knew exactly what to do! I had no idea how attained my own wife was as a shaman. This was the incident that led to Pia's career as a shaman in Canada. She didn't think of this before because she was in a foreign country and assumed that Canadians were not interested in her in born psychic powers. Big mistake. We put an ad in the 'Shared Vision' magazine for 'Ghostbusters,' and it worked. Good news! A Sikh man answered and he began our connection to thousands in the Indian community.

The I.B.S. temple objected to me ghostbusting and they particularly objected to my wife getting involved in temple business, as this was temple business at the time. The temple nuns do this professionally. I was fired three days later. I was out and that was it, but my students kept attending my classes in Vancouver. Fortunately, it turned out to be the best thing for me. One door closed and many more opened. I wrote this book for five months plus I now work part time as Pia's shaman's assistant, but not apprentice. Being fired also caused me to reveal the honest truth about Pure Land Buddhism, in this book and in my lectures. I am a Theravadin literalist. I call a spade a spade and I call Amitabha Buddha a phony. Many Buddhists will warm up to "the metaphor" of Amitabha and how devotion is a good thing, but I'm not going to do that. I say that devotion to the Buddha is a good thing, but devotion to Amitabha is exactly like theistic devotion for Santa Claus. Totally believing in Santa Claus may arouse qualities of love, comfort and joy, but that's not my Buddhist religion. There's some hard street drugs that can also arouse qualities of love, comfort and joy but you belong in jail if you sell them to others.

Foreign Policy

I asked Pia if she could benefit more people by aiming her shamanic powers at finding missing persons, disempowering the National Rifle Association, or helping the government on bigger things that benefit more people than solving family problems in Surrey, B.C. She was completely uninterested, but she pleased me in 1998 when the American embassies were bombed in Africa and the Middle East. The Americans retaliated by bombing two locations, including Afghanistan, in an effort to get at the main culprit, Osama bin Laden, and his factories. In support of American foreign policy, Pia wrathfully cuts out the suspect's photo from the newspaper, puts it under a plate on our shrine and fires off a black candle at him, writing nasty mantras on the side. Black is black. She puts the black candle on the plate and lights it, explaining to me that "I just want to make him weak so [the Americans] can get him!"

I feel that this is the direction that naturally gifted shamans should go. If society does not accept shamans, then these psychic healers, magicians, wizards, witch doctors, are marginalized to parlour room work for the more eccentric, just as CIA Remote Viewers were once "crazy people that claimed to leave their body." If our society can grow to the point where we can just be honest and face the truth of reality, then shamans can make a calculated and powerful contribution to American foreign and domestic policy. Hitler was after the same thing but he was a man ahead of his time.

The ethical dimension is so enormous that it can hardly be imagined! Shamans act above the law and are not vulnerable to legal prosecution, until we have deva laws if such a thing can be possible. In some Asian countries there are now laws against black magic. Political leaders traditionally must be prepared to make massive life and death decisions, their first day on the job. Like a shaman, if a politician is not prepared to make the tough judgment calls, then he doesn't truly have the stomach for the job. It is not right to waste on minor affairs the finger snap amount of time of one's human life. It is brave to try to help others in a big way if your karma gives you the opportunity.

Nargarjuna, the ancient Indian Mahayana sage, said that he prayed that he would not take rebirth as a powerful politician because a ruler can too easily make an angry decision leading to the deaths of thousands (see: Joseph Stalin), which would be their own personal negative karma, plus it would be compounded by others accumulating bad karma in carrying out their commands. That is true in many cases, but if politicians have insight and virtue they can multiply their merit. Ideally, both shamans and politicians should have the bravery to step into uncertainty and fear and make the big decisions without ever knowing if they were right or wrong. Ethically, it's O.K. for parents to decide how to control their children, so the big ethical decision is that if a shaman has a compassionate intent, then it's O.K. for the shaman to use power to improve people's behaviour. Doctors do the same to stop their patients from drinking or taking drugs. This is a very serious occupation.

Buddhism is very much concerned with the practical application of compassion for the greatest number of sentient beings. Perhaps the most powerful way today of benefitting the greatest number of sentient beings is by assisting American foreign policy in a way that benefits others. It takes some effort for a shaman to ask the devas to block the piracy of intellectual property in foreign countries, or to protect allied soldiers by blessing them and affording them deva cover and protection. Effort means money. Shamans need paycheques, military payrolls. This includes remote viewers and all manner of people who have mental powers that can be brought to bear on earthly concerns. If the shaman is good, they can contact the devas who actually do the big work, as is true of the State Oracle of Tibet. The necessity is to channel through to the great devas who can get great things done. It helps if the shaman does not act alone. During World War II both the Germans and the English employed shamans to battle each other. The English 'witches' tried to deflect the bombers off course during the Nazi raids. During the 21st century, our new age movement will result in shamanism making it into mainstream society. The day will come (perhaps it already has) when CIA Remote Viewers will rub shoulders with military shaman personnel.

> Rule #1: Never underestimate the power of the devas. The more faith
> you have in the devas, the more you will connect with devas of
> greater power.

Visiting Prisoners

In my work at the Chinese temple they would send me out to visit Buddhist prisoners in various penitentiaries in the Abbotsford area near Vancouver. This is a better way of going to prison than what I did in Thailand. The Buddhist Chaplin, Anila Anne McNeil took me as a visitor. When we arrive at Matsqui Institution we can't take our wallets in with us — no money, so we lock them in the car. No Buddhist books or practice materials can be taken in unless they have been preapproved. No spontaneous generosity! The main gate electronically opens as the guards let us in thorough the double barbed wire fences. They check the register to be sure that I am an invited guest. Anila nurses me through the inevitable confusions we face. Sometimes they have a lock out, or a shut down, so visits are cancelled without notice. If the prisoners have internal strife and fighting, everything shuts down.

Sometimes the prisoners refuse to see the Chaplin. Once I brought many posters of the Buddha that were donated by the Buddha Educational Foundation in Taiwan. The posters are held, then given out later. At this time the prisoners were behaving badly so the prison Chaplin refused to give the posters to them right away. Since the prisoners don't have power they responded by boycotting the visit of Anila. That's the only power that they have — saying no. This occurred at a time when I brought out a Chinese nun, Venerable Wai Fan, from the temple where I worked. Fortunately we went to another nearby prison and the Chinese prisoners there came out and were delighted to see her. "I never thought a nun would ever come out to see us!" one of the inmates exclaimed.

There was a murderer who became a Buddhist in prison and was practicing for nine years. He wanted to see a Theravadin Buddhist since he hoped to become a monk in a Theravadin country like Thailand or Sri Lanka. Anila was a Tibetan Buddhist, so she called me because I had been a monk in Thailand. I went to the prison to see him. We walked through several long corridors outside in the rain. Entering the chapel I found a multi religion oasis with many pews. The prisoner I came to see, Donald, lead me upstairs into a small loft with windows looking down on the main Chapel. Inside there was an alter set up for the Sikh and Muslim religions. It was Donald's turn so he had the Buddhist shrine nicely arrange with candles, incense and a poster of the sitting Buddha. We sat on cushions before the shrine and I taught him the Vipassana meditation technique I had learned as a monk, as he wanted Theravadin meditation, so that's what we did. Sitting quietly, I had one of my better meditations. There was some feeling about transforming the energy of the place that gave me a calm kind of pulsation or inner glow. The sounds nearby, and the whole atmosphere made me feel as if we were meditating inside of the Bob Dylan song, *Visions of Johana*:

> Ain't it just like the night to play tricks when you're trying to be so quiet
> We sit here stranded, though we're all doing our best to deny it
> Lights flicker from the opposite loft
> In this room the heat pipes just cough
> The country music station plays soft
> But there's nothing, really nothing to turn off
> (Dylan, 1966; *Blonde on Blonde*)

I listened to Donald going on about his problems in the penitentiary. And, we talked dharma. I listened to him teach the dharma. Isn't this what students want? Our personal connection was good but I knew I couldn't just chat and be a nice guy. In his situation I needed to cut through some neurosis. I could see that to some extent he may have been using Buddhism to gain some control within the prison, but I can understand why he would feel that way. We were discussing the karma of his murderous deed and Donald said apologetically "Another way of looking at the karma of the person that I killed is that it was their karma too." I couldn't let that go so I raised my right hand with a polite interruption and said "Well aside from what their karma was, it was your intentional action to do what you did, so as far as your karma is concerned, that was intentional. You did that, so it's pretty heavy karma." He looked down, then to the side, indicating that he had heard me, then he carried on from there. I did have heart for him and I looked forward to enjoying being with him and listening to his prison world. I liked this guy. I have never met a killer that I didn't like. The results of my efforts seemed positive.

Anila and I would go to the penitentiaries with Vietnamese Master Hoa and he experienced obstacles in working with the Vietnamese Buddhist prisoners. Some would listen and be with him, others would be less respectful and not pay much attention. Prisoners have all day to meditate it seems but it's difficult in that environment to have a settled enough space to develop the practice. Prisons are not Buddhist monasteries.

Racism

The next thing on my dharma calendar came up when the administrator of a Chinese temple asked me to give a talk on rebirth to the Buddhist Community of the University of B.C. After having lunch, he and a few others drove me out and we had a pleasant time. On the way back as he was driving he felt apologetic that the audience was smaller than usual. "Well, I'm just a Canadian," I said, cutting to the core. "I can understand people preferring to see an Asian teacher, than some white guy."

There is a prejudice in any culture against their own culture. Paul McCartney called this the foreigner's syndrome, explaining the Beatles success in America. This racism within Western Buddhism is so commonplace that people don't even realize that it's racism. There is general racial discrimination in the West against any Buddhist teacher with white skin. There are fully qualified Westerners who have graduated from the Tibetan style three year reatreat training but positions are, too often, given to Tibetan monks who don't speak English. They sit hobbled in Western Buddhist centres while Western Lamas of equivalent or better qualifications (who are native English speaking) end up on their own. In many cases, even though these senior Buddhist students are more than qualified enough, anything they accomplish to teach others they have done all by themselves. This process is wrong. It is not good and it looks real bad on Tibetan Buddhism altogether. This indicates that head office doesn't care that much about Buddhism. Head office cares about the Tibetan people. At least we do have qualified people around who can carry the torch with a firm grip. Conversely, Nepalese hucksters have turned a good buck by going to Taiwan and passing themselves off as visiting Tibetan Buddhist Lamas. It's all true.

White Buddhist teachers in the West may take refuge in the teachings and the example of Martin Luther King Jr. In comparison to his civil rights struggle, there is no burden upon us at all. This racism was noticeable at Karme-Chöling Buddhist Centre in Vermont. John Rockwell Jr. is an insightful Buddhist scholar and he was then their co-director, but he is an American. He was kept busy with administrative work, taking care of complaints between the residents, while Tibetan teachers, some of them obscure and with less impressive credentials, would come and teach through translators. Hopefully, within the next century and a half this racism will be eracism. Probably the 8th century Tibetans felt the same misguided attraction to Indian teachers. In Vancouver, in 1998, a couple of Tibetans gave a talk through interpreters about their experiences in a Chinese prison camp. A multitude of people streamed in for their dramatic talk and slide show because stuff like that is very sexy, but not much dharma was shared.

In *Awakening the Buddha Within*, Lama Surya Das emphasised that it's probably a mistake for a Westerner to seek out a great Eastern guru at the beginning stages of their path. It would be better to find a teacher more like yourself from your own culture who is better suited to relate the teachings to you, he said. A highly advanced eastern guru might give teachings beyond your capacity. One advanced Tibetan guru who has moved to Vancouver is the Venerable Dzogchen Pönlop Rinpoche. I became a Buddhist by taking my refuge vows with him in 1991 and I have since come to appreciate his very warm, humorous and light manner, combined with wisdom and insight.

Ruth, one of my students at the VSB invited me to give a talk to a Jewish ladies group and before I arrived they also invited Pönlop Rinpoche because he lived in the same building where the meeting was being held. We arranged a joint talk and I introduced Rinpoche to the 25 women present. It was an honour for me to be speaking with Pönlop Rinpoche, the guru who gave me my refuge vows seven years before. Pönlop asked me to lead them through the insight meditation period and I felt like it was a test. Afterwards one woman commented on how her thoughts would keep coming without stopping. Rinpoche said "That's a good sign," and then he explained how meditation can be like a waterfall. At first the thoughts may come like a waterfall, but later the thoughts become like a clear silent river. He made several wonderful comparisons that I had never heard before. I thought of a still pool of water, and then the image of a deep vast lake came to mind.

After our talk Rinpoche invited me up to his apartment in the building. Sitting before his shrine of the Karmapas and gazing at his splendid view over English Bay in Vancouver, I told him what I had been doing and I gave him a copy of my book. He said that it was good that I wrote it and he asked me to help out with the study group for his students in Vancouver, so over that summer I gave several talks to the Vancouver branch of his organization of Nalandabodhi study groups, while he was on tour in Texas and at Gampo Abbey in Nova Scotia. I asked him about the future direction of his work and one thing he said was that he is working to preserve Tibetan texts that are in danger of being lost. He does much computer work and his organization inputs Tibetan characters directly into their computers to preserve these texts.

Pönlop Rinpoche was interested in Pia's shamanic talents so he invited us to his home for a visit. Pia gave him a psychic reading and also told him a lot from his palm. As we passed the shrine on his mantelpiece I explained to Pia who the monks were in the photos, as she is not into Tibetan Buddhism. It was a rainy day but we had a wonderful view over False Creek towards our own apartment building directly across the Burrard Street bridge. The bridge seemed symbolic to us.

Rinpoche told us about the early days of my guru, Chögyam Trungpa, living in a Toronto Zen centre, before Trungpa got a visa to go to Vermont in 1970. This was fascinating for me! Pönlop first met Trungpa and the Vajra Regent when he accompanied the Karmapa (head of the whole lineage) on his last trip to America in 1980 when Pönlop was only fourteen and a half years old. He said that Trungpa Rinpoche showed them around his home at Kalapa court. They were taken to each room of the house. He met the Regent several times, the last time being 1987 at Karme-Chöling in Vermont, at the time of Trungpa's funeral. Pönlop was very impressed with the Regent's eloquence and he felt that the Regent had a good heart with pure intention.

I suggested that Pönlop should write more dharma books, and that he would come across well in dharma videos. He showed us his sacred photo collection of his three visits to Tibet and of his time spent with his teachers and colleagues. Each photo was like a Tibetan Buddhist postcard or shrine image. Pia asked all kinds of innocent questions, not knowing much about their tradition of Buddhism.

Pönlop told us the story of how the Karmapa recognized him as a "tulku," as the rebirth of the previous Pönlop Rinpoche who passed away in 1962. The Karmapa asked his father if his wife was expecting a baby. His wife said no, and later the Karmapa predicted that they would conceive the next Pönlop Rinpoche. Soon after, his mother became pregnant, so the Karmapa recognized him even before he was conceived! Vancouver is so fortunate to have one such as Pönlop Rinpoche living here as his primary residence. Chögyam Trungpa planted the Kagyu lineage in the West and Pönlop Rinpoche is watering those Kagyu lotus flowers. Although I am an outrageously proud Theravadin Buddhist, I do yearn for the success of the teachings of Trungpa and Pönlop Rinpoches.

The Future is More Important Than the Past

Looking to the future I want to help put the spotlight on what a committee of the BSSG believes are the most beneficial teachings and teachers because people do not know what is good dharma and what is unskilful dharma. They don't, you know. People have no idea at all about what is good medicine and what is Pepsi Cola, and it's getting worse with all of the spiritual materialism exploding around us. People are impressed with things that "look good," but they are impatient with teachings that require them to work, or think for themselves — such as the Buddhist religion.

I wrote to many publishers and authors to get permission to copy their work in this book. Bhikkhu Bodhi at the Buddhist Publication Society (B.P.S.) in Kandy, Sri Lanka, surprised me by giving me permission to reprint with credit, sections from any of their publications! There are few people in the West, carrying the torch for Theravadin Buddhism in particular. Also, in response to my letter, Brian Tracy, the world class #1 speaker on human potential also surprised me by responding with the letter below:

Dear Brian,

I remember you well. I am delighted to see how far you have travelled on your path toward spiritual realization and enlightenment. You have come a long way and you get the full credit for your success.

With regards to quoting me, please feel free to use any of my materials in any way that you possibly can, in any medium, with or without attribution. As you know from studying Buddhism, which I have done over the years, there is nothing new under the sun. Everything has been thought of and said by someone, somewhere at sometime.

I wish you the very best of continued success in everything you do. I hope that all of your ventures bear fruit and enable you to help other people. Good luck!

Kind regards,
Brian Tracy

With Brian Tracy's blessings, my mind began to expand into the possibility of synthesizing his popular secular teachings with the B.P.S., and other teachers, plus fresh, new inspirations. Now I'm interested in collaborating with other writers, Buddhist and non Buddhist and inviting them to contribute to the remainder of this trilogy, as well as being guest speakers in my courses, as I am full up.

These have been some of my experiences treading the path of dharma. Sometimes my path has been a bit overgrown and I have gotten lost, needing a compass and a survival kit but the adventure continues!

Chapter 23

National and Personal Karma
The Virtue of Hiroshima

W as it a truly virtuous deed to blast Japan with an atomic bomb? Opinions may differ on this sensitive historical incident but a deeper under standing of the Buddhist teachings on personal and national karma shed light on the virtues of Hiroshima. About 900 years ago a book was written in which the relationship between national and individual karma was revealed. This was *The Jewel Ornament of Liberation* by S. Gampopa in Tibet; one of the fathers of Tibetan Buddhism. Today, for an excellent contemporary example we can use something from World War II.

The Americans didn't want to bomb Hiroshima. History records that they had another target in mind, but it was cloudy. They then gave up and followed their orders to waste the precious weapon by dumping it, undetonated, at sea. This is because they were under orders not to drop the bomb without establishing visual contact with the target. Suddenly there was a break in the clouds and just enough opportunity left, to blast a lesser target. And so, Hiroshima blasted onto the pages of history.

The decision by Harry Truman to launch the first atomic weapon attack upon planet Earth, has nothing to do with Buddhism. This is a secular argument. Was it right or was it wrong? Opinions differ. Perhaps we never will know if it was the right decision. Oppenheimer clearly recommended to the new President that the bomb should be detonated over the ocean next to Tokyo so that lives could be preserved while the terror of the bomb demonstration would still cause the Japanese to surrender.

So, was it right to kill 100,000 people in just the first atomic attack against Earth? Some people say no, because of the tremendous suffering experienced. Some people say yes because it was a war and the Japanese were bad people doing bad things on purpose — to innocent people. Considering the 35 million Chinese they killed, many routinely tortured to death, the Japanese had very bad national karma.

Karma can be defined as intentional actions. The results of deeds in the past can be seen happening every day. Trying to figure out why things happen is impossible because of the complexity of the karmic process. The Buddha said that trying to figure out karma makes you crazy. Chögyam Trungpa Rinpoche said "there is national karma, which continues beyond individual karma. The death of George Washington did not stop Americans from operating in their own way — which is national karma." Likewise, there is individual karma that is attributed to an extension of national karma, which means that an individual can get off the hook. In particular situations that people find themselves in, such as being in the Enola Gay airplane, with unquestioned orders to drop an atomic bomb on the Japanese, or faced with huts full of suspicious people in the Vietnam war, the environment where their intentional actions result in more exquisitely painful karma is, in these situations, an intentional national karma that will rebound upon their country mainly and, upon themselves to a much lesser degree, or not at all. The good news is that you can sleep like a baby with total peace of mind, after mowing down huts with dozens of completely innocent civilians. Suppose that it was you who did this killing job decades ago in Vietnam. You were just doing your assigned job just like the guys that had to do kitchen duty that morning. Some cheerfulness should be extended to those many people now drinking in a bar somewhere pondering their hellish fate for what they did during times of war. If only they knew... they could find peace, right now in this very life.

Visualize that it was you who was about to drop the first of two atomic bombs on Japan. As you deliberately carry out the action of blowing up the city of people below, the virtues or the demerits of that action are almost entirely attributed to the national karma of the situation. The karmic weight of your actions which will come back to you and affect you personally, does not add up to very much; not even 1%. Not even President Harry Truman, who gave the order, can claim the merit for this accomplishment. This credit must be shared with millions of people exerting war effort and the hundreds of people who worked at Los Alamos, New Mexico who struggled for three years to develop such a weapon.

Because of the realities of war the first atomic attack was good and the bomb was detonated in a good, wholesome and uplifting way. Even as melting flesh dripped from children's arms as they began a slow painful death due to radiation poisoning, shaking their wretched fists at the sky, the Americans flew through the sunlight blameless. Imagine that each crew member was in a quiet reverie humming to themselves while their health grew vibrant after their soft landing and imagine that they aged happily, ever after. Is there justification for this in the teachings of the Buddha? The 27-year-old pilot who delivered the atomic bomb to Hiroshima was asked, two decades later, if his feelings had changed about his terrible deed. He stepped up proudly with his chin in the interviewer's face and he said, "I'd do it again in a minute."

Going one better, nuclear weapons have done more to preserve world peace than any other single thing in the past 50 years (but there are too many of them). It would be frightening to live in a world without nuclear weapons. Conventional wars would rip countries and ethnic groups into shreds. This world is not made of Mahatma Gandhis. You cannot expect human beings to remain civilized. You must have a container of law and order around them to help them move their minds upwards. War generally brings out the worst in people — never the best, always the worst. There is military high ground but higher still is the deva high ground of beings living in the god realm. The devas can see human affairs but we can't see them. Higher still is the emptiness of outer space and the emptiness of emptiness. Enlightened mind.

Another benefit of blowing away Hiroshima is one of the most important words in the English language: container. Today we look back in each present moment with vivid images in our mind of recalling the memories of Hiroshima. This provides us with the unending and immeasurable benefit of the reminder principle. Because we have graphic eye and ear and physical recordings of this terrible destruction, we are provided with a little bit of encouragement to keep our containers in life tight and clean so that we can avoid having to spill out blood like this again in such a horrible way.

If Oppenheimer got his way we would have less of this endless benefit today. So, perhaps President Truman did the right thing. We can't change history because it will never be possible to travel back in time (contrary to Star Trek mythology) so we should make the most out of what actually did happen. You are mentally healthy to the degree that you look for the good in each situation. You are not living on the dot to the degree that you look for what is wrong in each situation.

The virtues of the atomic attack against Hiroshima can be seen in the national karma of the war situation in 1945. There is evidence that there was no virtue in blowing up Nagasaki three days later. It is possible that a communication breakdown caused the Japanese to feel that the Emperor would not be guaranteed safety. Without this misunderstanding, the Japanese may have quickly surrendered, sparing the lives of 80,000 people in that city. Now that's war agony. Real suffering. Real useless suffering.

Chapter 24

Buddhist and Taoist Military Strategy

Whatever hen people think of Buddhism or Taoism, military strategy is the opposite of some concept perhaps of a monk in robes sitting in meditation. But the maintenance and use of a military and police force for the defense of society is in accordance with the Buddhist and Taoist teachings. The greatest military genius of all time was the Taoist master Sun Tzu who lived around 100 AD in China. His teachings are being studied today by corporate power brokers. This wisdom is contained in the popular translation of the book which is called *The Art of War*. The Taoist path is in accordance with Buddhism. Buddhism embraces Taoism and Taoist military strategy. In the Chinese tradition they incorporate Buddhism, Taoism and Confucism as three precious gems to guide a person's life. The three are one the Chinese say, in the sense that Confucism teaches wise proverbs to guide you in relating to your family and others. Taoism has the greatest insights into governing and insights into the nature of leadership, group dynamics and process. Buddhism dwells more on unravelling the self and it is a spiritual path that takes you all the way to the ultimate of the direct experience of reality. All three of these Chinese traditions are non theistic and complimentary.

In ancient Sri Lankan Buddhist times, about 2000 years ago, the military beliefs of the Buddhist kings and their subjects were that they needed to maintain a strong army to protect the container of the dharma and of society in their land.

They were subject to invasion and attack by non Buddhist countries and tribes. As Buddhists, it was clearly their belief that they possessed the highest spiritual teachings and path in the world. Therefore, it was their duty to protect future generations from losing the precious triple gem of the Buddha, the dharma and the sangha. They did whatever they had to do to defend their country and they have survived to the present day, albeit tenuously. They killed a lot of people doing that. There is no problem or contradiction here with Buddhist teachings. Although the first precept is 'do not kill', the precepts are affirmations of our intentions; they are not vows. The precepts are not iron clad rules which are inflexible. Buddhism is a path of sanity. If you were a Buddhist police officer with a gun in your hand and you saw a man shooting people with an automatic weapon, one after the other, the sane thing for you to do would be to shoot him dead, and you would not be transgressing the Buddhist religion of compassion. Not only would that be compassion for the lives of the many people you saved but it would also be compassion for the killer. By killing someone like that, in this example, you prevent them from committing the heinous crime of killing even more people. So, you would do him a big favour. Later on, his spirit might even thank you for having killed him and for having prevented him from committing even more bad karma.

In ancient Sri Lankan times, they felt that the sane Buddhist thing to do was to use their strong well trained military forces to fight off attack. They were right. They were strong. The mistake of Tibet's weakness was that they allowed their military strength to wane. From 1950 to 1959 Tibet as the Tibetans knew it was pretty much wiped out by the communist Chinese. Of course, the Chinese were a much bigger force than small Tibet, but in the 1800's Tibet had a fearsome military strength and the Chinese at that time were scared to death of the Tibetans. The mistake of Tibet's weakness which led to the destruction of one of the greatest homelands of a Buddhist tradition occurred in the 19th century when the Regents were in power at a time in between Dalai Lamas. After discovering the incarnation of the next Dalai Lama, the tradition is that appointed Regents govern the country until the boy Dalai Lama grows up and is able to rule by himself. During one of these periods the Regents were concerned about the great military power that the warlords had. These were men with land, money, servants and soldiers. The Regents asked them to disband their armies and 'go back to the farm' and give power and control back to the Regents. The landlords and warlords agreed, out of respect to their religious leaders, and then Tibet's army reduced in size. This is what led to the weakness of the Tibetan military and the increase in Tibet's vulnerability. This was Tibet's big mistake. They did not have the common sense to build up a decent sized army and follow the example of the ancient Sri Lankan Buddhist governments.

When the U.N. was formed in 1945, *before* the communist overthrow of

China in 1949, Tibet was warmly invited to join the U.N. but for some reason they chose not to, and they paid dearly for that backward looking decision. In the 1920's the Thirteenth Dalai Lama allegedly made foreboding predictions that the Chinese would invade and crush the practice of Buddhism in Tibet. His people, who wanted to maintain the status quo rather than adapt to modern politics, allegedly ignored his warnings. Tibetan history, from Padmasambhava in 760 A.D. on down, is full of exaggerations about how great their gurus are so perhaps these claims are not true. The communist crush of the Tibetan people fulfilled the first of the two stages in the prophecy of Padmasambhava. In the 8th century A.D., Padmasambhava was an enlightened Indian Buddhist master who brought Buddhism up from India into Tibet. The Tibetan people regard him as a 2nd Buddha. Padmasambhava's incredible prophecy was:

> "When the iron bird flies, and horses travel on wheels,
> the people of Tibet will be spread across the world like ants,
> and the dharma will come to the land of the red faced people."

The Taoist military Master Sun Tzu said that the war heroes who win battles and kill thousands are venerated as the greatest of warriors (like Stormin' Norman from the Gulf War, or William Wallace of "Brave Heart" fame). But the greatest of warriors, Master Sun Tzu says, are the ones who are not regarded as being very good. They do what comes easy and they don't get people killed. They take what is easy. They attack where it is undefended. They avoid a head on confrontation with an enemy army. They tire their enemy out by attacking in the north. When the enemy moves forces to the north, they attack in the south, and so on. The skilful way to win is to array your forces so impressively that you magnetise your enemy into wanting to join you. Instead of killing everybody, you win them over, encompass them and invite them into your more worthy rulership.

A real war hero is one who brings home victory over war. A real live continuous war hero is all victorious beyond war itself. He transcends over the mountaintop and sees and reclines where there was never even any concept of there being such thing as an "enemy." The concept does not even register. In nirvana there is nothing to fear not even fear itself. What's that? This is a place awake beyond the sleep of ego. An enlightened military campaign is awake, beyond confusion.

The Buddha outlined military policy in his discourse on the Seven Practices of No – Regression. This is in the Digha Nikaya (long discourse no. 16). Vassakara came to see the Buddha. He was the foreign minister of the country of Magadha and King Ajatasattu sent him to inform the Buddha of his intentions to send his army to conquer Vajji, a country that lied north of the Ganges River. Before launching his attack, the king wanted to know what the Buddha thought of his plans. The Buddha thought that both Vassakara and King Ajatasattu were schemers. The King's father, King Bimbisara was a close friend and devoted supporter of the Buddha for over 30 years until he was starved to death in his own palace by his wicked son, Ajatasattu. This was just so that Ajatasattu could take over and become the fearless leader. Ajatasattu changed his mind and called off invading Vajji after his foreign minister returned from his meeting with the Buddha. When Vassakara was meeting with Buddha, Ananda was fanning him and Buddha asked Ananda about the moral excellence of the kingdom of Vajji. With every question Ananda would confirm the virtues of the Vajji kingdom. The Buddha asked about their practices of gathering together for discussion, cooperation and unity, how they respect laws, follow worthy leaders, refrain from rape and violent crime, protect ancestral shrines, and respect teachers who have attained the Way of Awakening.

After Ananda confirmed the virtues of Vajji, the Buddha said "As the people of Vajji continue to observe these seven practices, the Tathagata believes that it would be impossible for Magadha to defeat Vajji." The king realized that if his army had weaker moral fibre then they could not invade their neighbour, no matter how big his own army was. What matters is the moral virtue of the people. Good can not be conquered by evil because nothing that is real can be threatened. Nothing unreal exists (*Course In Miracles,* 1975). The wicked king knew this instinctively, and so he backed off at the Buddha's words. In the Buddha's time, military strategists invested a lot of importance upon the moral qualities of their adversary. According to the thinking of the day, if a kingdom was full of immoral corrupt people, then that would be justification to invade them and take over under your more morally superior kingdom's rule. Therefore we should take over Burma. In conclusion, my interpretation of the Buddhist teachings is that it is OK to sustain and use a military force for the defense of the people. It is alright to make and use weapons for this purpose. Buddhism is the middle way. It would be an extremist view, even a theistic view to deny the use of force for defense. Even closer to home, the manufacture and sale of guns to the police force is not a problem either. Buddhist military strategy means a sane approach to life. Sanity means protecting the container of society. Protection means the legal use of force against the illegal use of force.

Take Out the Military Government in Burma

"When people will beg the United Nations to kill them but they won't be able to die."

Burma is described as the most Buddhist country in the world. Burma is a 90% Theravadin Buddhist country. Consider how your own suffering would unfold if your country was taken over by a dictatorship for one year. Sit in meditation for two minutes and then begin a contemplation on this ilk of bad government. Contemplate your city, your leisure time, your income. Sit and do an analytical meditation with your eyes closed, on all of the manifold ways your family could suffer from one change in government as bad as that. Government matters. Never take your freedom for granted as long as people in power have egos. Vote. One person can make a horrifying difference (see: Joseph Stalin). Extend some sympathy to the right wing anti-communist fear of past decades, by practicing the give and take contemplation. Breathe in the black tar of McCarthyism and breathe out the white light of strength. Breathe in the black tar of communist and authoritarian ideology and breathe out confidence and self reliance to them. As you contemplate your country being lost to tyrants, allowing your heart and breath to go faster, if they do, multiply your suffering by all the years since the 1962 coup d'etat in Burma. Beyond doubt, it absolutely transcends your ability to even imagine 1% of the suffering of the Burmese people. Try to abstractly multiply all of this suffering by 40,000,000 people! That's dukkha.

In accordance with Gotama Buddha's military policy to overcome the moral degradation of a government, it would be courageous if the political powers that be had the compassion for the Burmese citizens and the bravery to fight this massive military invasion of the inner, outer and secret territories of freedom. Cross the Rubicon. Naturally people shy away from such a contemplation but what would you do if you experienced violence within the family? The answer is never easy is it? Toppling the Burmese government means that people die in the process. Gotama Buddha's idea of compassion is: *flexibility — not rules.* Rehabilitate people when you can rehabilitate people. Kill people when you cannot avoid killing people. This is the Buddha's way. There's an ancient story about a bandit who threatened to kill a dozen Buddhist monks who were travelling across the countryside. In response, the head monk stepped up and asked the bandit if he could put aside his vows as a monk so that the bandit would incur less negative karma upon himself by killing an ordinary man rather than a monk — a Buddhist teacher. The bandit appreciated the monk's thoughtfulness and agreed, so the monk took a moment to put aside his vows. Suddenly he lunged at the bandit and killed him!

Not only is that compassion for the dozen monks, but it is compassion for the bandit as well because the monk prevented the bandit from incurring incredible bad karma upon himself because an action not taken cannot produce negative karma. Therefore, it is O.K. for people with a good intention to kill people in Burma in an effort to liberate the country. No bad karma there.

How can you just turn the page when 40,000,000 people in a Theravadin Buddhist country are suffering while your own country's government spends little thought on Burma, and much more concentration on trivial matters. Thought minus action equals zero. The goal of compassion, the goal of education — is beneficial purposeful action. It is a sincerely kind aspiration in life to earn good karma by using force to stop those in Burma who are harming millions. World War I and II were composed of sincerely kind deeds committed by millions of sweet hearted people. Consider the virtues of Hiroshima.

Burma is like a wicked stepfather that beats his wife and stepchildren. The family has no money, no place to go, and everyone in the community knows all about it. People talk to the stepfather, the source of the problem; they console the mother and the children, but they only talk. They don't kick the stepfather out of the house.

The Impossible Dream

To dream the impossible dream. Dream this dream... dream this illusion. See your illusions, others' illusions... Many people take actions, many different actions. Few people are at the top of the pyramid of decisive power — the vertical mosaic. Big business and big government power means big opportunity for big benefit for big numbers of big and little people which earns big merit for future rebirths. This illusion is just one fictional fantasy. No one knows as of this printing how the Burmese military government will finally resign...

The Fictional Story

Once upon a future time, the above village co-ordinates a U.N. sponsored American and allied military exercise along the west coast of Thailand, while they wait for other aircraft carriers to arrive from the Indian ocean. Inside Burma the people are rising up and from outside Burma they are being encouraged to do so over a planned build up period of several months. A surprise strike at Burmese military forces could be launched first with cruise missiles from anywhere. Anyone care for a submarine perhaps? "Timing is everything," the Buddha taught. Bewildered by the cruise missile strike combined with an undisclosed conventional strike, each calculated escalation will bring the Burmese captors closer to their knees. Aung San Suu Kyi, although the popular people's choice, is regarded as extraneous protoplasm, just as are the other civilian casualties. Richard Nixon stated that President Jimmy Carter's mistake in Iran in 1979 is that he should have regarded the American Embassy hostages as prisoners of war rather than placing the highest priority on the safety of the hostages. That just paralysed the American response and it also harms others by encouraging terrorism in the future. Each day that the Burmese military government exists is a comfort and an inspiration to future autocrats everywhere.

Regarding Aung San Suu Kyi as extraneous protoplasm is wise because in this way we are not held captive. If you were in her shoes, you would agree. She cares far more for her people and country than she does for her mere life. What can we do, but do our best and work to keep down the numbers of the dead? Ideally the Burmese should rise up and throw out the military junta themselves but they are such an easy going sweet people that they haven't done so. This kind of problem was echoed regarding Vietnam when President Kennedy told Walter Cronkite "We're not going to fight their war for them." Normally foreign governments won't spend the money or the lives to do such work. Such compassion cannot be expected in world politics. This dream remains a dream. It would have been better to kill 20,000 innocent, sweet, calm, Burmese civilians and 100,000 soldiers in an invasion a long long time ago, back in 1965, than to do it now. Logically, this is so, because more than a million people have died from lack of medical advancement and from inept government since 1962, not to mention persecution. A great many of those one million people would be alive today if the U.N. was kind and decent enough to sacrifice those 120,000 people back in 1965. You can't even imagine how much other suffering would have been avoided with a free economy (but created too of course). The suffering of 40,000,000 people multiplied by decades is beyond imagination.

Now is the winter of our discontent!

End of fictional story.

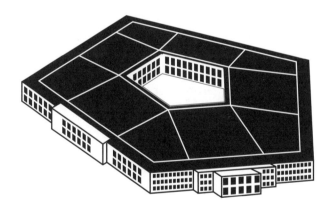

The Pentagon

The Tao Te Ching teaches that the master rarely uses force, and then only with the utmost restraint. Restraint is the cause of inheriting even more powers. Pacify enrich magnetise and destroy. This is an ancient policy. The shortest distance between two points is a straight line. We must ultimately bring our concerns to the ultimate place on earth. That one place is: the Pentagon. Even the most gifted artist has great difficulty drawing a straight line. Jesus says that the Kingdom of heaven is within. Instead of the short line that he recommends humanity spins circles through samsara to create the Pentagon. The United Nations walks too softly and the Pentagon carries a big stick. Visible heavy hand. The devaloka is an invisible heavy hand. I believe that the devaloka caused the helicopter crash thwarting the rescue of the American hostages in Iran in 1980. This one incident gave the presidency from Jimmy Carter to Ronald Reagan. That crash and the eight deaths of the crew were like a dead leaf that falls from a tree. It's easy to see the leaf fall from the tree. The devaloka is the wind that caused the leaf to fall off at that particular present moment. What you can't see is the air around the leaf as the leaf buffets and descends to the ground.

Although terrified by President Reagan's Star Wars aspirations, even some of the most severe critics of this President, later openly confessed that his right wing hard line resulted in a free Russia. The devas could see further ahead than the Democrats. That's prajna. A policy of appeasement results in more of what you appease — an aggressive country, panhandlers on the street or a nagging husband. The Soviet Union didn't have the money to keep up with the American military, and it collapsed.

Consider Vietnam. Fail in the direction of success. Double your failure rate in order to reach success. Let go of Vietnam. Mistakes are not a justification to stop moving forward. It takes courage to forge ahead after you were totally wrong and after you were totally at fault and after your country killed two million people but this is the only moral thing to do. Proceed with life. The only question is: How shall we proceed with life? *This is our question. This is our only question.*

In Your Face

General Patton was right when he made his clear recommendations to the new and unprepared President Truman in 1945. Considering the future of communism this visionary leader wisely advised that the allied armies continue heading east and push the communists right back into the Soviet Union. The army was already there, they were well equipped, supplied, fed and everybody loved them. If that decision had been made, the suffering of millions in Eastern Europe from 1945 to today would never have existed. It is mistaken to believe that the past had to be the way it was just because the sequence of events that happened in the past never changes. This perception falsely creates exaggerated ideas of solidity about the past leading to false views that past events somehow were meant to be that way in some solid sense, because of the law of karma. That is false. Just as today you have infinite options about what to do, history has always been this way. We can always wake up, we don't have to hurt each other habitually.

We should have gone to war in Bosnia. It is regretful that we didn't go to war there in the 1990's. We were haunted and paralysed from Vietnam and we were too self absorbed with our own affairs so we had too little compassion to fight for the victimized civilians. If the mayor of a city goes crazy and forces ethnic cleansing on the east side of town, the state and federal government will do something about that. This indicates the unfulfilled ideal of the UN. Wisdom in the future, sagacity in community life, will mean that our most compassionate leaders of the free world will be hawkish military right wing conservatives. They will all share together a deep personal pain: pseudo Muslim expansionism. Their allies will be the true Muslims helping to undermine pseudo Muslim terrorists.

Several times the Buddha threatened to split people's heads open into seven pieces if they would not cop to the truth. One dishonest brahmin backed down when he saw Sakkha brandishing a lightning bolt aimed at the brahmin's head! This is historically true and on each occasion the Buddha did not have to preside upon Sakkha to actually have the person's head split open into seven pieces. The UN could aspire to act like Sakkha if it was reformed to reflect a fair balance of power (instead of a 1945 balance of power) and if it had the support of its member countries. When lightning hits the earth in a storm the reason for this is solely because of causes and conditions. A strong United Nations, a just United Nations could be a cause and a condition which brings a focus upon the countries lowest on the morality list. Defining morality and proper conduct for governments has already been ratified by the UN.

The just must always have courage, never complacency. You can relax in your courage like a tiger, meek in the jungle. You're on top, so you relax into your world view and you relax into your view over your world — but you're never complacent! Like the virtuous Sakkha living for an entire age, you keep order. Heaven's first law is order and Earth's first law is order as well. There will be order. Gentleness, peace, kindness and having wise people in power means that there will always be wars to fight, history proves that beyond a reasonable doubt. The good wards off the bad. The good puts down the civil insurrection of evil. There is no room for doormats in a dharmic world. There will never ever be a lasting peace, because the nature of ego proves that, beyond a reasonable doubt. Once 50,000 subjects of the Sakya kingdom were killed in an invasion. The Buddha was just leaning against a tree and someone asked him how he felt about the near extinction of his people. The Buddha replied "I feel a bit sad today because 50,000 of my clansmen have been killed," but the Buddha understood the natural fruition of their past karmas so he easily glided through this patch with equanimity.

As long as egos possess weapons, we must go to war. We must keep vigil, always. We must establish a gentle world order. If not, we will perish confusingly into disorder. Because the future is more important than the past, do not stay cozy at home and turn away from the pain of foreign countries. "The hottest places in hell are reserved for those, who, in a moral crisis, chose neutrality," Dante said. If we protect other populations now, they may protect us in future lives. In fact, the karmic laws of cause and effect assure us of this. Dr. Martin Luther King Jr. said "An injustice anywhere is a threat to justice everywhere." This is a helpful lesson even though technically Dr. King was incorrect because the laws of karma teach that an injustice will rebound upon the initiator anyway because the universe is absolutely just. Therefore an injustice will not threaten justice everywhere. Reality is a complex weave which includes past injustices coming to ripen upon people who behave very justly right now. The vital point to appreciate here is the five precepts. Regardless of the imperceptible past we must still encourage ourselves and others to do what is right now and be sane decent people no matter how complex our past karmas are. Just keep doing good!

Relationships are so fickle and change so much in samsara. If we're on top today it behoves us to take full advantage of our powers to benefit others as much as we can before we go through our tough time, maybe in future lives, and we need the help of these same people to bail us out. This is truly protecting your future interests because the law of karma doesn't lie, it never lets you down. "People are no damned good," some of the dismayed say but the law of karma is always there to support you forever and ever. Lifetimes cover a very long period of time but still the clock is ticking. Go. A sense of urgency is necessary in the Buddhist application of right effort. We must succeed. Failure means spinning out of control until World War III engulfs us all in mass global fear. The time is now. The time has come. *We must succeed.* Press the button.

Dharma wheel on Jokhang rooftop

Chapter 25

All Universes Mythology

At the end of an eon the universes burn up together and collapse. At this time, the Buddha described in the abhidharma, beings burn off their negative karma as mere particles in intense heat. This constitutes the most exquisite suffering of hell fire, because this is the end of an eon when the universe degenerates. It is units of consciousness that holds particles and gravity together, Buddha taught. At fantastic speed, he said, these units of consciousness "revolve" once every three billionths of a lightning flash! At the end of an eon, life is so degenerate that even gravity falls apart. Between universe periods, or cosmic cycles, beings reside in the "World of Radiance." After beings have burned off all of their bad karma, the particles start to group together and form larger beings again. This heralds in the next cosmic cycle...

There is a big bang from which all universes blow out.

All sounds can be found within the great range of the chant
for all universes, which is "Aum"

All universes mythology sub-part one

The nature of the other universes is a mystery. There are devas present in the other universes.

um...

aum um... aum

um

Universe Mythology

Universe mythology sub-part one

This universe

...Thisness suchness...

The great deva Brahma descends from the World of Radiance and is the first being born into this cosmic cycle. Brahma is an asexual non gender deva in the Fine Material sphere, who mistakenly believes that 'he' is god.

This universe sub-part 20,000,000

The island universe, Milky Way galaxy

A long time ago in an island universe far far this way...
The Fine Material sphere asexual deva Jehovah is born into this galaxy and is later acknowledged to be the god of the Bible.

Our galaxy sub-part 100,000,000,000

Buddha said there are 100 thousand million world spheres in this island universe.

World system, the Sun, sub-part three

The deva Jehovah believes that it created planet Earth

Home

Global Mythology
Part one – The Big Bang mythology

The purpose of this creation is to illustrate the fantastic precision of the Buddha's description of the astronomy and cosmology of our universe. This attempts to be consistent with astronomy, mystery, science and Buddhism. The Buddha actually gave teachings revealing the Big Bang, which may shock, stun and amaze you. The Buddha even taught the process, over vast periods of cosmic time, of the formation of galaxies, which he called "island universes." Only from his direct realization could he tell us about island universes. With the naked eye anyone could have guessed the existence of world spheres as described by the Buddha. But no one could possibly have guessed the existence of galaxies. Shocked, stunned, and amazed!?

Astronomers may yet find a way to confirm what the Buddha taught. This gives them something to live for, a meaning for their existence. Astronomers and quantum physicists can try to figure out what happened, and why, like a car accident. But, this extraneous information is not necessary to overcome suffering because right now you can take the dharma and run with it all the way to nirvana. The Buddha once held some leaves in his hand and pointed out that all the other leaves in the forest represented useless information. To you, your personal mythology is the one vital leaf of existence that gives meaning and purpose to your life.

Beyond the big bang, there exists a beginningless and endless series of cosmic cycles. More than 15 billion years ago, six days after the big bang, came day seven. On that day the surface of the big bang was at rest. It was devoid of form, and without life, a spherical glow of plasma growing outwards. Then, something further happens resulting in the complex but discernible pattern that we today call the universe. Somewhere in there is the mythological solution to whatever is ticking inside of you. Something in there needs to get straightened out! "Any mythology that has to be explained to the brain, isn't working," said Joseph Campbell, the mythology scholar. Without a belief system, you bounce around in the elements like a billiard ball. With a mythology you erase anxieties and guilt. You are comforted by being at one with something that is bigger and something that is giving of a true benefit. Carl Jung said, "I made it the task of tasks in my life to find a mythology by which to live."

Buddhism provides a ready made package of mythology and a cosmology of the entire universe, seen and unseen. This includes how you fit into the universe and how you can get out of it, to an ultimate reality beyond suffering. Nirvana, or the dharmakaya, is what lies beyond the six realms of samsaric existence. The dharmakaya is also inside of this sphere of samsara, penetrating this conventional reality where all beings live. You could visualize this panoramic scene as an eclipsed sun. Inside of the bright corona, instead of having a black sphere, visualize it as a bright sun like sphere. Bright in and bright out. Totally upbeat.

The Buddha's belief system, if you want to call it that, is that Buddhism provides more than the "myth to reality." It is a path which will deliver you back to the promised land of ultimate reality. The promised land has nothing to do with real estate, just as the virgin birth has nothing to do with a biological problem. The virgin birth means being born or reborn into a spiritual life that reconnects you with primordial wisdom, bodhicitta — your Buddha-nature. The promised land is the dharmakaya.

The Buddha started off by telling people the very worst news of all, and that was his enlightenment. Life is suffering (dukkha), unsatisfactoriness, transitoriness, insubstantiality. The cause of suffering is desire. The third of these truths is the myth, that there is such as thing as the end of suffering, nirvana, reality, ultimate reality, enlightenment, peace. The last truth is that this myth of freedom can be a reality if you apply effort and know how to work at it. That is the path which leads you to the direct experience of the all universes mythology. You then know that the mythology is in fact the reality.

Emerald Buddha, Temple area, Bangkok, Thailand

Chapter 26

Supernormal Powers

Twenty-nine out of thirty-two portions of her being, her consciousness, were buried under the ground trapped inside of a voodoo doll. This Vancouver woman and her stricken sister are daughters of my wife's client. The ineffectual doctors say that the victims are schizophrenic. My wife Pia Ruhe is a Thai Shaman. She has an in born power and gift that West coast new age psychics could die for. To harness her natural power Pia Ruhe was trained for three years by Cambodian Master Sang, using more than Buddhist chants and Buddhist techniques. Pia is trained with shamanic chants and practices from Burma and Cambodia so she can protect people from deadly black magic, which is common in that part of the world. "You will have a very hard life if you do this," Master Sang told the 16 year old Nualanong Pia Viturut. "Teach me then!" Pia insisted. She didn't give his warning nearly enough consideration and now it's too late for her to stop. She must help people when they come to her.

The identities of her clients are not revealed. What happened was that an enemy living in Canada sought to utterly vanquish their family. So, killing them is not very desirable because then they might go on to a better rebirth. Utterly vanquished in this case means that the wicked person responsible hired witch doctors in Bruni to condemn the victims with the heaviest black magic that they could do, which resulted in snuff consciousness. One has to think long and deeply to conceptualize a more powerful method of inflicting harm on human beings. Nuclear weapons will just bump you out of your present form into another form, such as a deva in heaven, or you could take rebirth as a human being on this or another planet. Being killed in a limited nuclear exchange is no big deal. You'll just be reborn. But you can't fully move on to a rebirth, if black magic gets you and you're stuck in undeserved hell, as in this horrific case. With my own eyes I saw snuff consciousness manifested as a living human ghost. The victims' consciousness was 90% glued to a voodoo doll with many pins sticking in the doll's head, buried in the ground. Look at the wrong person sideways, and this could happen to you for more than the remainder of this lifetime, if your karma makes you susceptible to this.

Not everyone is vulnerable to black magic voodoo. For those who are hit death does not free the hold of the dark side of the higher realms. The best way to release this innocent Vancouver lady and her sister from this hell, was to find the voodoo dolls and pull out the pins in their head and then completely burn them up. Pia had a vision of where the dolls were but she selected her son Kachon Boonchuvit to do the job. Kachon is an even more highly gifted shamanic master of the higher realms and he is a known healer. Kachon flew to Bruni, psychically located the voodoo dolls, pulled out the pins and burned them up. One sister then became coherent. The other was partially healed, but later they both went in and out of relapses. This is the most serious case of black magic Pia has worked on in Canada.

At the time of our first meeting, the victim was only 10% in her own body. Since 1985, her body has also been occupied by a few different ghosts who relate with her body the way you relate with a revolving door. The evil shamans in Bruni consciously used their unspeakable powers to deliberately insert those ghosts into the lady's body. This is about the worst karma anyone could initiate — far worse than putting a bullet through someone's heart. There is no logical motive for such a heinous crime, which remains above the law as long as there are no International Deva Laws or Dimension Laws (which include the ghost and the god realm). The idea of such laws does not seem so strange in countries where the blight of black magic is well known. Black magicians will pay for their evil deeds just as surely as people who harm others by physical means, with weapons. The law of karma treats everyone the same, like the law of gravity.

It is understandable why sorcerers would curse people with black magic. It's the same reason why lawyers will accept $2000 per hour to push and lie for a guilty client. The reason is the ego's shortsightedness caused by short term gain. Bad people are fully aware of the long term disastrous consequences of their deeds, but they still do what is wrong, extremely wrong. Isn't this so very simple to understand? Yes, of course. The Buddha said that beings have the urge towards self annihilation.

The Beatles

When I was a teenager I began an unceasing love affair with the Beatles. I learned everything about them. I developed a theory about the death of the Beatles' manager which I still cling to from time to time. At the age of 32, Brian Epstein died in the summer of 1967 just at the very moment when the Beatles were learning a new way of life from the Maharishi Mahesh Yogi. I believed that the Maharishi, who popularized Transcendental Meditation (TM) may have decided that it was necessary to change the course of human history. There was probably no bigger influence on the social scene in 1967 than the Beatles. Sociologists say that the Beatles were the greatest social movement of our age. In 1967 they had just come out and publicly declared their use of hard drugs. In my youth I felt the ultimate conviction that the Maharishi decided to influence the Beatles to encourage others to take a more constructive route with their minds by practising meditation instead of dropping acid. I didn't feel sure whether the Maharishi was an agent for a higher power consciously or unconsciously, but I totally believed that there was a deliberateness to the death of Brian Epstein because he died at the very minute that the Maharishi had all four Beatles sat down for instruction.

John Lennon later said that he knew for sure that the Beatles were finished when Brian died. That was the end of the Beatles right there and then, and John knew it. The rest of the Beatles probably felt the same way but Paul tried to hold things together by taking on a leadership role. It was only a matter of time before forces would drive them apart. My theory, as an infatuated 17 year old fan of the Beatles, and TM, was that the Maharishi decided to initiate snuff consciousness against Brian Epstein out of his compassion for the world. I visualized the unspeakable dimensions of the guru's mind pounding waves down upon Brian Epstein. Epstein took some drugs that day and it seems that that is why he died, but the real reason was to change the Beatles influence on the world. The Sergeant Pepper's album had recently been released and it was their most influential album in history. Individuals of higher consciousness, I believed, sometimes had to make decisions about who lives and who dies just as governments choose to send people to die in battle. Brian Epstein had to be sacrificed to keep the Beatles alive but change their influence upon the world. Tremendous theory, but I don't expect any law firms to give me job offers.

Another fantastic theory about the Beatles is that President Kennedy's assassination caused the Beatles phenomenon. The explanation is that the karmic flow moved from one person and his administration to another person and their administration. Kennedy got the world marching forward with tremendous karmic force inspiring over one billion people. His death could not stop that momentum. Johnson ruined the New Frontier because he hated the Kennedy's, so the devas chose John Lennon, and Paul McCartney to carry the torch of love and inspiration forward to the world. Yes, the Beatles wrote She Loves You, and a few good songs while Kennedy was still alive, but they flowered big time immediately after his death. 77 days after Dallas, the Beatles landed at JFK in New York, and the rest is history. The world needed to be cheered up after JFK and the Beatles did exactly that. The devas quite probably channelled down songs to John and Paul. Paul couldn't write songs like that after the Beatles split up. Days before his death, John Lennon said of the Beatles, "We never wrote our best songs. They were delivered to us."

This theory may be totally bogus but the mythologist Joseph Campbell said that it is good to live with a sense of the mystery of life and a sense of the immense forces in the world. It is good to think of things on a deep level because it gets you straightened out inside, he said. Live your whole life feeling and believing in vast cosmological powers. It's a thrilling experience and you can live your life that way regardless of what the 'truth' is.

Higher Realm Music from 1966 to the Summer of Love

The Bob Dylan of 1966 was one of the greatest examples of someone tuned into a source of inspiration higher than himself. Even god himself — John Lennon was so infatuated with Bob Dylan that he wore the same kind of cap that Dylan did. Bob's voice became a vehicle of the higher realms and his mind received songs during the 1966 recording of the *Blonde on Blonde* album. The Buddha made many references to what he called the "deva ear." Buddha taught us that the deva ear is the opening up of the ability to hear heavenly sounds or earthly sounds at a great distance. Bob Dylan had something of this deva ear quality as he wrote timeless songs within minutes, one after the other, while Robbie Robertson and The Band played cards. The higher realm emanations just flowed through him effortlessly. Brian Wilson's *Pet Sounds* album with the Beach Boys was the same thing and it considerably influenced the creation of *Sergeant Pepper's Lonely Hearts Club Band* by the Beatles. Brian Wilson visualized a halo around his head when he was in the recording studio all through the creation of *Pet Sounds*.

Bob Dylan's songs were not particularly uplifting or better than 100's of other songs, so how can we recognize them as higher realm connections? The play of the god realm includes the most ordinary arts and music of the human realm. There's nothing in the human realm of arts and music that the god realm beings can't get their deva hands on. The important distinction about Bob Dylan in 1966 is the speed with which he wrote his socially significant songs. This indicates higher realm interest and assistance. There is no reason to assume that the higher realms are much better than human beings, at least at the lower levels of the 28 classes of celestial beings listed in the commentaries. They just like music and they pass it along to us through people, like Bob who have opened their deva ear, at least to some extent.

Bob said that the *Blonde on Blonde* album represents the closest sound to the mercurial sound that he heard in his head. Play of the higher realms. In the mid-1980s Bob Dylan referred to those songs from 1966 and he said "I can't write songs like that anymore. I can't. I just can't write songs like that anymore." This is because he has lost the deva connection he once had. It is so ephemeral a thing it seems. On July 29, 1966 Dylan's motorcycle struck a rock and he broke his neck on his farm in upstate New York. That was pretty much the end of his deva ear, right there. His next album in 1968, *John Wesley Harding* was completely different and nowhere near as hip as *Blonde on Blonde*. Of course, Bob has since and still does write great music. But what we have here is an incremental increase in the covering of cloudiness on his once clearer deva ear connection to the inspiring sounds of the higher realms, such as Tushita heaven.

Mozart was also an example of a man with the deva ear connection. He claimed that he just heard the music in his ear. He wrote down some of the most beautiful melodies in the world as though he was taking dictation! Was *Andante from Piano Concerto No. 21* from the Tushita heaven of sensual pleasures or from the more orderly Tavatimsa heaven?

The False Threetles

George Harrison was right on the dot, when he said "The Beatles exist apart from my self," in a rare interview conducted by fax. "I am not really 'Beatle George.' 'Beatle George' is like a suit or shirt that I once wore on occasion and until the end of my life people may see that shirt and mistake it for me." What he's saying is that like John Lennon, George Harrison the Beatle is long dead and gone too. So, the good news is that John Lennon's death does not prevent us from having a Beatles reunion. We couldn't have it anyway! All four of the Beatles haven't been Beatles for a long time because the energy that was fundamental to what they were, a deva connection perhaps, died away. That happened long ago, perhaps in April of 1970. This illustrates the Buddha's teachings on anatta, non self, impermanence and dependent origination. The mind of a person now is not the same mind they had during Beatlemania. The mind a person has now arises and ceases and arises and ceases in every moment. The causes and conditions that spawned the Beatles right after John Kennedy's death were better for creating Beatles music than the causes and conditions of today. The Beatles were, because that was. Now the Beatles aren't, because this isn't. That's dependent origination. This is because that is; this isn't because that isn't.

If you were a totally dedicated and gifted Bob Dylan or Beatles fan, you could know "them" better than they know themselves. In interviews John Lennon commonly couldn't remember in which year the Beatles did what, but millions of his fans could recite the precise sequence of events of their entire careers. Even while John Lennon was alive, other people knew the Beatle John better than he knew his past self! This is no exaggeration, so if you want to get info on some famous person, it doesn't make much difference whether they are dead or alive. Go to the library. Mick Jagger started writing his autobiography but he quit because he said, "There are large portions of my life which I cannot remember."

You Do Take It With You!

When you die you take your good karma with you and your money stays behind. Or does it? Evidence indicates that unhappy or happy relatives take your money so that you can't take it with you. However, money is a form of power and energy. A person has as much money as he does because of his karma. Since karma is something that you do take with you into your next life, you do in fact take the equivalent of your money with you, if you earned it in accordance with right livelihood. Because of your karma, that money or something similar to it may come your way during your next worldly rebirth. It could take the form of the wealth of the family that you are born into. So, enjoy spending in your retirement, but don't squander it needlessly.

President Bill Clinton

It was wrong to try to impeach Bill Clinton because he had an affair. That was absolutely and totally a bad thing. That was absolutely and totally a bad thing, without equivocation. Chögyam Trungpa Rinpoche did it right. Trungpa had a wife and seven female consorts. He was a family man with five children and his wife 'Lady Diana' was accepted as the queen within the sangha. Trungpa gave his consorts public titles and they were honoured within the sangha. He was a chackravartin, a dharma king. That's how Bill Clinton should have played it but society would not allow him to. As a real king with real political and worldly power, like President Kennedy, Clinton should be free to have sex with whoever consents to it. That is truth. That is justice. That is the American way. That is reality. The American public is stuck because they have a morality based upon an ancient 'conspiracy' of monogamy. In Buddhist countries, people accept the role of a leader and they do not block the flow of energy when the principal one has consorts. This is acceptable. Those who want to oust Clinton are wrong. French President Mitterand has a consort and people accept that. Europeans are more sexually mature than Americans. Bill Clinton should be spared the insensitivity of the media machine and American adolescent sexuality because this weakens the fabric of government and it weakens honesty and sincerity in government, not the other way around. It is reckless to destabilize the American government because of one man's private life. The needs of the country and globe outweigh the need to blame a few.

The Value of Human Life

Titanic makes you think. Was it right that the women and children got on the life boats while the majority of young men died? No. Young people of the age twenty to twenty-five are the most valuable to society. Suppose a twenty year old's life was worth one dollar in proportion to a sixty year old woman, who's life is worth thirty-eight cents. A two month old baby is worth seventy cents. Forty-five year old men and women, at the height of their careers and family responsibilities to their own children are worth eighty-four cents. Because people are reborn, this totally affects the decision about who gets into the lifeboat and who dies. If we only have one life, then there would be more emphasis on saving younger lives. If a baby loses her one life, that's real bad. If the baby is reborn to the same parents seventeen months later, then her death isn't so bad. But if her father died in the sea while her widowed mother eked out a living, that's bad too. No rebirth in that family.

Meditation practice:

Contemplate the value of human life for 20 minutes
with your eyes closed while visualizing the sink scene
in the Titanic *movie.*

There is much less collateral damage to society if you toss a baby into the cold Atlantic, than a twenty year old. Babies can be replaced, at less cost. Twenty year old's embody over $100,000 dollars invested over many years of emotional love and bonding to others in the community. Their lives are more important than the lives of babies, and especially that of old men and women. The President or Prime Minister of a country is the captain of a ship so, in the days to come, they must be prepared to make these calculated decisions the first day on the job, or they are not fit for the job. This essay can save lives.

Snuff Consciousness

This essay won't kill lives but snuff consciousness is horrible, a horrible thing to consider. In the sutras, the Buddha described the asanna-satta devas as 'unconscious beings,' that are a class of heavenly beings in the fine-material sphere. "There are, O monks, heavenly beings known as the unconscious ones. As soon, however as in those beings consciousness arises, those beings will vanish from that world. Now, O monks, it may happen that one of those beings after vanishing from that world, may reappear in this world..." Those devas could be unconscious beings for many many years before awakening—not a pleasant thought.

In other sutras the Buddha describes cosmic battles going on in the upstairs between the titans of the jealous god realm, and the peaceful devas. The Buddha described that devas can kill each other in their existence, so that dead devas must be forced to move on to another rebirth. How is it that titans destroy each other, and other devas? It is mind to mind combat. Is this combat carried out by the practice of snuff consciousness? Is it possible for beings, human beings with highly attained powers of concentration, to focus the gravity of their minds upon one person in an effort to snuff them out? Is it possible to not only snuff out their lives, but to actually snuff out their consciousness? This question staggers the imagination because premeditated murders could be done above the law. There are no laws to stop or convict such people. Is it possible for some person who is still bound by the power cravings of ego, to deliver their enemies into the state of the unconscious asanna-satta devas? (Boys and girls are asked not to do this at home.) One thing is for certain. All of the powers of the devas in the higher realms are within the reach of human concentration. Buddhism explains that the basis for what is called black magic is the development of higher powers of concentration without the intention of benefitting others. Even with evil intention people can use Buddhist practices and meditation to build up their mind for a destructive purpose. It is wise to be aware of this and discourage it in yourself and others. Never forget the law of higher consciousness, 'Love everyone unconditionally — including yourself.' Because of the inescapable law of karma, deeds committed against others using black magic will rebound upon you just as surely as if the police caught you poisoning someone to death. Even if the law doesn't catch your crime, the law of karma will always catch your crime, without fail. Therefore, for anyone with intelligence, there is no motive at all to engage in black magic.

In the *Dhammapada* the Buddha said (Byrom, 1976; 35):

As dust thrown against the wind,
Mischief is blown back in the face
Of the fool who wrongs the pure and harmless.

Nowhere!
Not in the sky,
Nor in the midst of the sea,
Nor deep in the mountains,
Can you hide from your own mischief.

Not in the sky,
Nor in the midst of the ocean,
Nor deep in the mountains,
Nowhere
Can you hide from your own death.

Wilfully you have fed
Your own mischief.
Soon it will crush you
As the diamond crushes stone.

By your own folly
You will be brought as low
As your worst enemy wishes.
So the creeper chokes the tree.

But virtue also is yours,
And purity.
You are the source
Of all purity and impurity.

The higher powers described in Buddhist scripture which some people demonstrate today, are based on powerful practices that are self secret. It's not a matter of getting some secret technique that you can successfully apply. Self secret means that even if someone told you how, you would not understand it, or you would not be able to do it. You must first build up your concentration of mind and then apply your mind to your task. The four noble truths could be called self secret. You go to your first ever introductory talk on Buddhist meditation and the teacher teaches you the four noble truths. It may make no impression on you, but those are the most powerful teachings of the Buddha. Self secret.

The mystical powers associated with higher human states are within reach for those who have attained to one of the appropriate samadhi absorptions. There are eight levels of these states of one pointed concentration and the Buddha described each and every one of them again and again and again in countless sutras. When I was a monk in Chiangmai, Thailand at Wat Ram Poeng, I coached people through month long meditation retreats where about 25% of them attained to the first or second samadhi absorption. So, these are not exceptionally rare gifts, as many of these Westerners had no background in meditation, or Buddhism for that matter. The method by which magical powers are developed was taught by the Buddha. He said that a person enters and abides in one of the samadhi absorptions. Then when they come out of that samadhi they advert their mind to whatever magical power they choose to invoke in that situation. So, the samadhi is used to build up the concentration level of the mind first. Then, you go from there. As of this printing the most famous person alive today, who has demonstrated adverting the powers of samadhi concentration, is Sai Baba from southern India. I am convinced beyond doubt of his authentic virtue, and his power to materialize objects. I am not qualified to say at which level of sainthood he has attained from a Buddhist view (and he does not claim to be a Buddhist) but I am confident that his benefits to others and his compassion are a blessing for the world, without stain.

Examples of using the samadhi concentration for supernormal powers are categorized in the *Visuddhi Magga*. This translates as *The Path of Purification.* Even the loftiest teachings of Tibetan Buddhism can be found in the wording of this commentary, which greatly illuminates the voluminous original canonical scriptures of Theravadin Buddhism. Chapter XII deals with the Description of Direct-Knowledge—The Supernormal Powers. Here Buddhaghosa writes:

The Benefits of Concentration

It is said with reference to the mundane kinds of Direct-knowledge that this development of concentration 'provides... the benefit of the kinds of direct-knowledge.' Now, in order to perfect those kinds of direct-knowledge the task must be undertaken by a meditator who has reached the fourth jhana in the earth kasina, and so on. And in doing this, not only will this development of concentration have provided benefits in this way, it will also have become more advanced; and when he thus possesses concentration so developed as to have both provided benefits and become more advanced, he will then more easily perfect the development of understanding. So meanwhile we shall deal with the explanation of the kinds of direct-knowledge now (Nanamoli, 1956; 409).

By way of explanation of these terms, in Nyanatiloka's *Buddhist Dictionary,* the term mundane means all those states of consciousness and mental factors — arising in the worldling, as well as in the Noble One — which are not associated with the supermundane paths and fruitions. Direct-knowledge means knowing from direct experience, rather than through study. Jhana is another word for samadhi. Kasina is the name for a purely external device to produce and develop concentration of mind and attain the 4 samadhi absorptions. It consists in concentrating one's full and undivided attention on one visible object as prepatory image, e.g. a coloured spot or disc, or a piece of earth, or a pond at some distance, etc., until at last one perceives, even with the eyes closed, a mental reflex, the acquired image. Now, while continuing to direct one's attention to this image, there may arise the spotless and immovable counter-image and together with it the neighbourhood — concentration will have been reached. (This is the point just before getting sucked into a samadhi, like a black hole, where you then have a blackout and all five senses shut down, accompanied by joy and rapture.) While persevering in the concentration on an object, one finally will reach a state of mind where all sense-activity is suspended, where there is no more seeing and hearing, no more perception of bodily impression and feeling, i.e. the state of the first mental absorption, samadhi.

The 10 kasinas mentioned in the sutras are: earth-kasina, water, fire, wind, blue, yellow, red, white, space, and consciousness. The Buddha described the kasina-spheres, "someone sees the earth kasina, above, below, on all sides, undivided, unbounded."

Curiously, Buddhaghosa wrote his commentary to better explain the Buddha's teachings. Now, we have to explain the meaning of the terms in Buddhaghosa's commentary. Carrying on with Buddhaghosa's comments on concentration above, he continues (Nanamoli, 1956; 409):

The Five Kinds of Direct Knowledge

In order to show the benefits of developing concentration to clansmen whose concentration has reached the fourth jhana, and in order to teach progressively refined dharma, five kinds of mundane direct-knowledge have been described by the Blessed One. They are (1) the kinds of Supernormal Power, described in the way beginning 'When his concentrated mind is thus purified, bright, unblemished, rid of defilement, and has become malleable, wieldy, steady, and attained to imperturbability, he directs, he inclines, his mind to the kinds of supernormal power. He wields the various kinds of supernormal power. (1) Having been one, he becomes many..., (2) the knowledge of the Divine Ear Element, (3) the knowledge of penetration of Minds, (4) the knowledge of Recollection of Past Life, and (5) the knowledge of the Passing Away and Reappearance of Beings.

The Kinds of Supernormal Powers

If a meditator wants to begin performing the transformation by supernormal power described as 'Having been one, he becomes many,' etc., he must achieve the eight attainments in each of the eight kasinas ending with the white kasina. He must also have complete control of his mind.

The *Path of Purification* commentary goes on to describe each of the supernormal powers, such as, flying through the air cross legged, flying through a mountain as if through air, jumping into and out of the earth as if in water, walking though walls, dematerialization, and more. The Buddha said that some arahants are dry arahants, meaning that not all fully enlightened ones have all of these magical powers.

In the sutras the Buddha won a debate about the laws of karma with a Jain disciple. The Buddha made the point that the intention of the mind is more fundamental and more important than the actions of the body. As written in the 'Future Dharma' chapter, the Jain religion held the opposite view. Buddha asked the householder if it was true that some ascetics and brahmins had the power in their mind to destroy an entire city like Vesali. The gentleman agreed and commented that some ascetics and brahmins had the power to destroy two cities of Vesali, five, ten, even fifty cities of Vesali! This is the Buddhist scriptural basis for the postulation that such fantastic human powers of mind could today snuff out life— entire cities of people anywhere in the world, and maybe even functioning consciousness itself. Ancient Indian literature chronicles nuclear style annihilation of cities. Alien beings from outer space were not necessary to explain that. People in those days were more spiritually advanced than humanity is today, so it is even easier to accept the possibility that such horrid powers were unleashed in the past upon innocent civilians. Fortunately, good Buddhists don't do such impolite things, but others could. What is the cause of earthquakes? The Buddha said that there are eight causes of earthquakes, and one of them is the averting of the mind after a samadhi absorption, as described above.

The Royal Naga Story

The disciple that had the greatest magical powers was the Buddha's left hand man, his number two chief disciple, Maha Moggallana. Moggallana's fantastic and noble life story provides many examples of powers at the highest levels. At one time, it seems, the Buddha surveyed the ten-thousand-fold world element in the early morning. Then the Royal Naga called Nandopananda came within the range of his knowledge. A naga is a deva serpent, a particular kind of good or bad higher realm being depicted as a dragon.

The Blessed One considered him thus (Nanamoli, 1956; 436):

'This Royal Naga has come into the range of my knowledge. Has he the potentiality for development?' Then he saw that he had wrong view and no confidence in the Three Jewels. He considered thus 'Who is there that can cure him of his wrong views?' He saw that the Elder Maha-Moggallana could. Then when the night had turned to dawn, after he had seen to the needs of the body, he addressed the venerable Ananda: Ananda, tell five hundred Bhikkhus that the Perfect One is going on a visit to the Gods.' (This meant that the Buddha was going for one of his frequent business trips upstairs into the god realm where devas live.)

It was on that day that they had got a banqueting place ready for

Nandopananda. He was sitting on a divine couch with a divine white parasol held aloft, surrounded by the three kinds of dancers and a retinue of Nagas, and serving the various kinds of food and drink served up in divine vessels. Then the Blessed One so acted that the Royal Naga saw him as he proceeded directly above his canopy in the direction of the divine world of the Thirty-three (Tavatimsa Heaven, the second heaven in the sensuous sphere, with thirty-three principle devas, ruled over by Sakkha), accompanied by the five hundred bhikkhus.

Then this evil view arose in Nandopananda the Royal Naga: 'There go these bald-headed monks in and out of the realm of the thirty-three directly over my realm. I will not have them scattering the dirt off their feet on our heads.' He got up, and went to the foot of Sineru (or Meru, a mythical mountain at the centre of Earth's surface). Changing his form, he surrounded it seven times with his coils. Then he spread his hood over the realm of the Thirty-three and made everything there invisible.

The venerable Ratthapala said to the Blessed One 'Venerable sir, standing in this place formerly I used to see Sineru and the Ramparts (embankments surrounding a fort) of Sineru, and the thirty-three, and the Vejayanta Palace, and the flag over the Vejayanta Palace. Venerable sir, what is the cause, what is the reason, why I now see neither Sineru nor...(the sutras tend to repeat the whole thing all over again) the flag over the Vejayanta Palace?'—'This Royal Naga called Nandopananda is angry with us, Ratthapala. He has surrounded Sineru seven times with his coils, and he stands there covering us with his raised hood, making it dark.'—'I will tame him, venerable sir.'

But the Blessed One would not allow it. Then the venerable Bhaddiya and the venerable Rahula (the Buddha's son) and all the bhikkhus in turn offered to do so, but the Blessed One would not allow it. Last of all the venerable Maha-Moggallana said 'I will tame him, venerable sir.' The Blessed One allowed it, saying 'Tame him, Moggallana.' The Elder abandoned that form and assumed the form of a huge Royal Naga, and he surrounded Nandopananda fourteen times with his coils and raised his hood above the other's hood, and he squeezed him against Sineru. The Royal Naga produced smoke. The Elder said 'There is smoke not only in your body but also in mine,' and he produced smoke. The Royal Naga's smoke did not distress the Elder, but the Elder's smoke distressed the Royal Naga. Then the Royal Naga produced flames. The Elder said 'There is fire not only in your body but also in mine,' and he produced flames. The Royal Naga's fire did not distress the Elder but the Elder's fire distressed the Royal Naga.

The Royal Naga thought 'He has squeezed me against Sineru, and he has produced both smoke and flames.' Then he asked 'Sir, who are you?'—'I am Moggallana, Nanda.'—'Venerable sir, resume your proper bhikkhu's state.' The Elder abandoned that form, and he went into his right ear and came out from his left ear. Likewise he went into his left ear and came out from his right ear. Likewise he went into his right nostril and came out from his left nostril; then he went into his left nostril and came out from his right nostril. Then the Royal Naga opened his mouth. The Elder went inside it, and he walked up and down, east and west inside his belly.

The Blessed One said 'Moggallana, Moggallana, beware; this is a mighty Naga.' The Elder said 'Venerable sir, the four roads to power have been developed by me, repeatedly practised, made the vehicle, made the basis, established, consolidated and properly undertaken. I can tame not only Nandopananda, venerable sir, but a hundred, a thousand, a hundred thousand Royal Nagas like Nandopananda.'

The Royal Naga thought 'When he went in, in the first place I did not see him. But now he comes out and I shall catch him between my fangs and chew him up.' Then he said 'Venerable sir, come out. Do not keep troubling me by walking up and down inside my belly.' The Elder came out and stood outside. The Royal Naga recognized him, and blew a blast from his nose. The Elder attained the fourth jhana, and the blast failed to move even a single hair on his body. The other bhikkhus would, it seems, have been able to perform all the miracles up to now, but at this point they could not have attained at so rapid a response, which is why the Blessed One would not allow them to tame the Royal Naga.

The Royal Naga thought 'I have been unable to move even a single hair on this monk's body with the blast from my nose. He is a mighty monk.' The Elder abandoned that form, and having assumed the form of a Supanna, he pursued the Royal Naga, demonstrating the Supanna's blast. The Royal Naga abandoned that form, and having assumed the form of a young brahman, he said 'Venerable sir, I go for refuge to you,' and he paid homage at the Elder's feet. The Elder said 'The Master has come, Nanda; come, let us go to him.' So having tamed the Royal Naga and deprived him of his poison, he went with him to the Blessed One's presence. The Royal Naga paid homage to the Blessed One and said 'Venerable sir, I go for refuge to you.' The Blessed One said 'May you be happy, Royal Naga.' Later the Buddha was met by Anathapindika, his billionaire benefactor. Buddha said to him 'There was a battle between Moggallana and Nandopananda.'—'Who won, venerable sir? Who was defeated?'—'Moggallana won; Nanda was defeated,' the Buddha explained.

So it was with reference to this enlarged form created during the taming of Nandopananda that it was said 'When he makes his body big, does it not then become big, as in the case of the Elder Maha-Moggallana?' Although this was said the monks observed 'He enlarges only what is not clung to supported by what is clung to.' And only this is correct here. What this means is that although the clung-to and unclung-to occur mixed up together, it is the unclung-to that is enlarged.

In conclusion, using such supranormal powers is not an ego trip, and displaying this power is not an ego trip. It should be taken that it is the consciousness-born matter that is enlarged by the influence of the supernormal power.

A Supanna is a good deva with a golden bird-like/dragon appearance. In Thailand the front end of Royal Barges are carved and painted gold in the form of Supannas. This indicates the high level of respect afforded Supannas.

Afterword
Outer Peace

"Our greatest challenge is still the world that lies beyond the cold war," John F. Kennedy envisioned. "But the first great obstacle is still our relations with the Soviet Union and Communist China." Today is history. Like the out breath, the cold war is dissolving into space. Now we are moving past the point where Kennedy led us. We're poised beyond the obstacles that blocked this great leader. And, we're waiting for our greatest challenge. To know what that star in the sky is, go into the silence and find an answer. Go back to chapter eleven and ask yourself those eight questions again, then choose your major definite purpose in life.

Peace within our mind is not the absence of aggression. It's the presence of mindfulness. Mindfulness is gentleness. What is the greatest thing that we could ever hope for? Peace on Earth? Today, our greatest challenge is still building a world of compassion. But the first great obstacle is still our own ignorance and aggression. Compassionate people can only be destroyed from the inside, not the outside. Our greatest threat is still our ignorance.

Creating a compassionate society will not come to pass in the next 1000 days, nor in the next 10,000 days of our efforts. But let the manifestation of enlightened society begin to thrive. All peoples wherever they may be, hold a vision of an enlightened world, like a Kingdom of Shambhala. However people feel it or choose to express it, the true aspiration for a good and gentle world yearns deep in our being. Let us begin with sitting meditation. You are invited to infuse your energy into the Buddhist Spectrum or develop and teach your own sangha. You have the blessings of the devas.

World peace begins on your meditation cushion. The unraveling of world ignorance is your personal preoccupation. That's what meditation practice is all about and that's what all of our political struggles are all about. All great people, wherever they have been, have looked into their hearts. A heart purified from meditation is the greatest kind of heart to go outwards and refresh the world with compassion. The heart and the head meet on the cushion and then they go beyond the cushion and delight in freedom.

Keep up your inner work and keep up your outer work. Heed the exhortation of the Buddha's last words as he lay on his right side "All composite things are by their nature impermanent. Strive on with diligence to enlightenment. These are the last words of the Tathagata."

Stainless Tutor Vajra Regent

Stainless guru Osel Tendzin
When your voice cracks across my Sony Walkman
I cannot separate it from my mind
And your shrine cannot be separated from my heart

Humbled with gratitude to visit you indestructible tutor
On the second floor of Karme-Chöling I enter your suite
Inside Practice and Study your hundreds of tapes are as terma
Oh stainless guru Osel Tendzin
Where shall I place my devotion for you Vajra Regent?

As the Vidyadhara's mind mixed with the western hemisphere
He mixed with you
I hear the Vidyadhara in your voice
My mind is inseparable from the yidam of your noble voice Vajra Regent

The wakeful presence of your step is now standing in the bardo
Or have you returned to fulfil your vow to beings?
How shall I find you stainless guru Osel Tendzin?
Of course... in the tape library
Speak to me
Speak to me quickly with compassion

Your voice will ring out for endless kalpas
We will destroy the forces of darkness upon this earth
I long to serve with you under his command
The 25th Rigden King of Shambhala
The Dorje Dradul Chögyam Trungpa Rinpoche

Karme-Chöling, Vermont. July, 1992

Bibliography and Recommended Reading

Books

Joyful Path of Good Fortune, the Complete Buddhist Path to Enlightenment, Geshe Kelsang Gyatso, Tharpa Publications - Perhaps the best exposition of the stages of the Tibetan Buddhist path. Ideal for a long term course. Easy to understand and put into practice with illuminating analogies. "It tells you what to do!"

Old Path White Clouds - Walking in the Footsteps of the Buddha, Thich Nhat Hanh, Parallax Press - The #1 best book on the Buddha's life story with pithy dharma teachings included. Simply written and very absorbing, like a movie script.

What The Buddha Taught , Dr. Walpola Rahula, Gove-Weidenfeld - Concise explanation of the major aspects of Buddhist teaching. Many excellent quotes from the Buddha. One of the very best introductions to Buddhism. A classic.

How to Win Friends and Influence People, by Dale Carnegie, 1937. The breakthrough book on human relations skills.

Shambhala: The Sacred Path of the Warrior, Chögyam Trungpa, Shambhala Publications—A secular path of meditation, and creating enlightened society written in plain English without Buddhist technical language.

The Meditation Handbook, Geshe Kelsang Gyatso, Tharpa Publications. Clear and potent contemplation instructions.

Buddhism Explained, Bhikkhu Khantipalo, printed in Bangkok, Thailand, or in Taiwan by The Corporate Body of the Buddha Educational Foundation. Readable, stimulating and provocative.

Myth of Freedom, Chögyam Trungpa, Shambhala Publications. Explores the meaning of freedom.

Bibliography

The Great Path of Awakening, Jamgon Kongtrul, 19th century Tibet. Translated by Ken McLeod, Shambhala Publications - The actual practice instructions on bodhicitta, "awakened heart" - the core of spiritual development in Mahayana Buddhism.

Transforming Problems Into Happiness, Lama Zopa Rinpoche, Wisdom Publications
A Policy of Kindness, the Dalai Lama, Snow Lion Publications
Cutting Through Spiritual Materialism, Chögyam Trungpa, Shambhala Publications

A Path With Heart, Jack Kornfield, Bantam Books

Dhammapada, The Sayings of the Buddha, Thomas Byrom's translation, Shambhala Pocket Classic. A most revered collection of poetic sayings and spiritual teachings by the Buddha. "The Buddha's greatest hits."

The Miracle of Mindfulness - A Manual on Meditation, Thich Nhat Hanh, Beacon Press, Boston

Zen Mind, Beginner's Mind, Shunryu Suzuki, Weatherhill

A Short History of Buddhism, Edward Conze, Mandala Books, England

Pali, the Early Beginnings, Buddhist Publication Society, Kandy, Sri Lanka

The Art of War, by Sun Tzu, Taoism. 100 A.D. China - for management and interpersonal strategy

Brahmanism Buddhism and Hinduism, Lal Mani Joshi, B.P.S., Kandy, Sri Lanka

The Bodhicaryavatara, A Guide to the Bodhisattva's Way of Life, Shantideva

Paritta Pali and Protective Suttas, (deva invocation chants) Sayadaw U Silananda, Aggamahapandita, Dhammananda Vihara, 68 Woodrow Street, Daly City, California 94014, U.S.A. (free book)

After reading a few introductory books on Buddhism, go straight to the Buddha's mouth by reading this Theravadin commentary and the sutras:

Visuddhi Magga - The Path of Purification, by Buddhaghosa, 412 A.D. The greatest commentary ever written on the original authentic Theravadin Buddhist scriptures. Indexing of vital information on all Buddhist topics, referencing relevant quotes from the Buddha. In depth and technical.

The Majjhima-nikaya - The Middle Length Discourses of the Buddha, exciting recent translation (1995) by Bhikkhu Nanamoli and Bhikkhu Bodhi, Wisdom Publications, for the Pali Text Society. 152 discourses, approx. 10 pages each, covering all aspects of the dharma. 1400 pages.

The Digha-nikaya - <u>The Long Discourses of the Buddha</u>, Wisdom Publications, for the Pali Text Society. 34 long discourses, approx. 30 pages each, with many stories, historic information, and all aspects of the dharma.

Audio Tapes

The Vajra Regent Osel Tendzin:
"Space, Time & Energy" - 1983, Karme-Chöling, Vermont, 3 talks.
"Mind and Meditation" - 1978, 3 talks
"Discipline" - 1988, Halifax, 3 talks
and, dharma tapes by Chögyam Trungpa Rinpoche, and the Dorje Loppön Lödro Dorje
Tapes can be purchased from:
Kalapa Recordings, 1084 Tower Road, Halifax, NS, B3H 2Y5
Shambhala International headquarters. Kalapa Tel: (902) 421-3214
Fax: (902) 423-2750 Web: www.shambhala.org/recordings Catalogues available.

"The Phoenix Seminar," by Brian Tracy, and other audio tapes:
Brian Tracy International, 462 Stevens Avenue, Suite 202, Solana Beach,
CA 92075 Tel: 1-800-542-4252 Fax: (619) 481-2445 Web: www.briantracy.com

Web Site

The Buddhist Spectrum Study Group updated web site: http://home.istar.ca/~bar/
email: bar@istar.ca

Glossary

abhidharma Third basket of scriptures, a technical and very detailed analysis of the mind and the universe.

alaya The base consciousness below the unconscious mind, the source of all creative thought.

arahant A fully enlightened person.

ascetic One who leads a very austere and self-denying life, a yogi, Prince Siddhartha before his discovery of the middle way.

asura A jealous god realm deva, titan, demon.

bardo Interval, the state between death and rebirth.

bhavana Mental development or culture, meditation. lit. "calling into existence, producing."

bhumi The ten stages of enlightenment on the bodhisattva path in Mahayana Buddhist philosophy.

Blessing The transformation of our mind from the inspiration of our spiritual guide or devas.

bodhi Awake, awakenment, enlightenment. From verbal root *budhi,* to awaken, to understand.

bodhicitta Awakened heart, seed of awakening, Buddha-nature, basic goodness.

bodhisatta "Enlightenment Being," is a being destined to Buddhahood, a future Buddha. In the Theravadin Pali Canon, this designation is given only to Prince Siddhartha before his enlightenment and to his former existences (Nyanatiloka, 1980; 41).

bodhisattva Mahayana term for a person who has generated spontaneous bodhicitta but has yet to become a Buddha.

Brahma The greatest deva in the cosmos, the Hindu god; also meaning "the highest."

Brahma Vihara Four "divine abodes," the contemplations on loving kindness, compassion, altruistic joy, equanimity.

Brahmin The highest caste in Indian society, the religious leaders.

Buddha Awakened man, Siddhartha Gotama.

Buddha-nature See bodhicitta, unrealized enlightened mind, the essential nature of all sentient beings (Tai Situpa, 1996; 170).

dana Generosity, giving, offering, particularly to the Buddhist sangha.

deva Heavenly beings in the god realm, angels, spirit guides.

dharma The Buddhist teachings, natural law, the way things are.

dukkha The first noble truth of suffering, impermanence, insubstantiality, etc.

ego Self, belief in the existence of a self.

emptiness Empty of the nature of a separate independent self.

enlightenment The ultimate goal of the Buddhist religion, the final extinction of the ego and the cessation of suffering, nirvana, a state of mind impossible to define.

Hinayana A derogatory term for Theravadin Buddhism, coined by the Mahayanists, meaning lesser vehicle, crummy or lousy vehicle.

jhana Absorption or samadhi state.

kalpa An age, varying in length, approximately an ice age, subdivided into four sections.

karma Volitional actions, or intentional actions, not the results of karma.

kasina An external meditation object used to develop concentration.

kleshas Habitual patterns, "spinning wheel of fire." passion, aggression and ignorance, etc. Defilements.

loka "World," the whole universe.

lokapala The deva/s associated with a particular geographic location.

Mahayana The northern school of Buddhism, "great vehicle" or "great wheel." The corporate name change of the Mahasanghika school initiated three or four centuries after the Buddha. An illegitimate tradition renounced by Theravadins as a heresy.

Mahayanasutras A mixture of authentic and false discourses of the Buddha, which comprise the most sacrosanct and fundamental Mahayana scriptures.

mantra "That which the mind leans against," or "mind protection." A word or phrase repeated by oneself.

merit Good karma created by virtuous actions.

mindfulness Keeping your mind on what you are doing while you are doing it, not straying from the present.

nirvana Enlightenment.

paramitas Perfections.

prajna Insight, discriminating awareness, wisdom.

preta Ghosts.

realms The six realms of existence where all beings live: human, god, jealous god, animal, hungry ghost, hell.

rebirth Reunion, relinking, of the five skandhas, which arises at the moment of conception with the forming of new life in the mother's womb.

refuge vow Committing oneself to the Buddha, dharma and sangha as your spiritual guide.

Sakkha "King of the gods," principal deva and lord over Tavatimsa heaven, second heaven in the sensous sphere.

samadhi A meditative state of one pointed absorption where all five senses shut down.

samsara The world of suffering, continuous struggle, "round of rebirth," lit. "perpetual wandering."

sangha Buddhist community of four or more persons.

sentient being A being of limited awareness.

Shakyamuni Buddha A Mahayana term for Gotama Buddha, "sage of the Shakya kingdom."

sila Morality, discipline.

skandha Five parts of the self: form, feeling, perception, mental formations, consciousness.

sutra "From the mouth of the Buddha," the discourses of the Buddha.

tantra sutra false Vajrayana sutras attributed to the Buddha.

tathagata "Perfect One," "thus gone," an epithet of the Buddha referring to himself.

Theravadin "Doctrine of the elders" the southern school of Buddhism, closest to the original teachings of the Buddha.

tripitaka "Three baskets" of the canonical Theravadin Buddhist scriptures: sutras, vinaya and abhidharma.

tulku The recognized rebirth of an advanced Buddhist master, in the Tibetan tradition only.

umdze Group meditation time keeper or leader.

Vajrayana "Diamond-like or indestructible vehicle" or wheel. "Tibetan," or tantric Buddhism.

vinaya The second basket of original scriptures in the tripitaka, the rules for monks and nuns.

vipassana Insight, wisdom, that is the decisive liberating factor in Buddhism, the intuitive light flashing forth and exposing the truth of impermanency, the suffering and the impersonal and unsubstantial nature of all corporeal and mental phenomena of existence (Nyanatiloka, 1980; 230).

windhorse Riding a wind of energy and delight.

yana A wheel or vehicle of the Buddhist teachings, Hinayana or Theravadayana, Mahayana and Vajrayana. A term invented by the Mahayanists.

Meaning of Buddhist symbols

 swastika - or Chinese "Maan" is an ancient Hindu symbol adopted by the Buddhists for 2000 years which has several meanings including "ultimate power," and "the sun," often seen in statues on the Buddha's chest.

 wheel - with eight spokes is the Buddha's eightfold path to enlightenment. Theravadin Buddhist symbol, as well as the most universal symbol of the entire Buddhist religion.

 knot of eternity - Mahayana symbol for endless meditation.

 lotus flower - symbol chosen by the Buddha to represent enlightened mind.

 dorje - "thunderbolt" in Tibetan, is an instrument that zaps through the kleshas of passion, aggression and ignorance like a Star Trek phaser; symbol of the Vajrayana.

shell - symbolizes hearing the traditional oral transmission of the dharma.

three jewels - the Buddha, the dharma and the sangha.

Bronze Buddha, built in 1252 A.D. , Kamakura, Japan

Order Form

Look forward to Parts II and III of the exciting "Freeing the Buddha" trilogy.

Freeing the Buddha Part II
The New Frontier
The Next Chapter

Freeing the Buddha Part III
Complete Enlightenment
The Final Chapter

And then... *Mindfulness*
a new beginning

Telephone for information on orders:
Call (604) 733-8477 or Cell (604) 720-8477

Postal Orders:
Payable to: Buddhist Spectrum Study Group
#217 - 1450 Chestnut Street, Vancouver, B.C. V6J 3K3 Canada

- ❏ Please send me _____ copy/ies of *Freeing the Buddha* for $26.95 each (tax included).

- ❏ Please add my name to your mailing and telephone list so that I may receive more information on upcoming classes and meditation retreats.

- ❏ I want to subscribe to The Spectrum, the quarterly newsletter of the Buddhist Spectrum Study Group, for $10 a year.

Name:_____ Telephone:_____

Address:_____

City:_____ Province/State:_____

Country:_____ Postal/Zip Code:_____

Email:_____

Shipping in Canada: Parcel Post: $3.00. Free shipping for extra copies.

Payment: ❏ Cheque ❏ Money order